THE CHURCH AND I

FRANK SHEED

THE CHURCH AND I

1974

DOUBLEDAY & COMPANY, INC.

GARDEN CITY, NEW YORK

Excerpt from "Trees," copyright 1914 by Joyce Kilmer. Used by permission of Jerry Vogel Music Company, Inc.

Excerpts from *Sonnets and Verse* by Hilaire Belloc. Used by permission of A. D. Peters and Company.

Excerpt from "Absolute and Abitofhell" from *Essays in Satire* by Ronald Knox. Used by permission of A. P. Watt & Son.

Excerpts from *The Collected Poems of G. K. Chesterton.* Used by permission of Dodd, Mead & Company and Methuen & Co., Ltd.

Library of Congress Cataloging in Publication Data

Sheed, Francis Joseph, 1897–
    The church and I.

1. Sheed, Francis Joseph, 1897–   2. Catholic
Church—Doctrinal and controversial works—Catholic
author. I. Title.
BX4705.S587A33   282'.092'4 [B]
ISBN 0-385-08440-4
Library of Congress Catalog Card Number 73-83670

CONTENTS

Part Two
REFLECTION ON EXPERIENCE

We're all in the same boat
and we're all seasick.

G. K. Chesterton

PART ONE

THE CHURCH AS I HAVE EXPERIENCED IT

This book is not about Dogma or Morals. It is about my experience of the Church. To that extent, but only to that extent, it is autobiographical. I have tried to confine myself to incidents which have some bearing on my growth in knowledge of the Church. Some things are here which gave me so much pleasure in the telling that I did not scrutinize too closely their right to be included. I could always tell myself that they might help readers to get the feel of the Church.

CHAPTER 1

I MEET THE CHURCH

I was born into religious conflict, Scotch Presbyterians and Irish Catholics warring over my small self, in Sydney, New South Wales.

Of my four grandparents, the one whose name I bear, Frank Sheed, was born in Aberdeen. He had been baptized in the Episcopal Church there, his parents had been married by the Dean: but he was a Presbyterian by the time I arrived: I doubt if he knew the difference or cared. My other three grandparents were from County Limerick, Catholics naturally. But one of them, my father's mother, Margaret Casey, left the Church when my father was five and became a Presbyterian. So that religiously my grandparents divided two and two. Unhappily the two Catholics had died when my mother was a child and take no part in my story. The other two do.

As far back as my memory goes, I was aware that my young brother and I were being fought over. My mother, Mary Maloney, took our Catholicism for granted. But my grandparents, and still more their daughters, were of the type who dream of the Pope and wake up in a cold sweat screaming, "Rome!" When I was four I was staying a few days with my father's eldest sister. She had lost something or other and I advised her to ask St. Anthony to find it. She said, "You'd better ask him yourself. I don't know him." She was not pleased. She told my father and he was not pleased either. (I have had a devotion to St. Anthony ever since, I feel he owes me something.) Thinking as they did, our Sheed relations very properly saw it as their duty to save us from our mother's religion. The odd thing is that they all liked her, and she them. I liked them all, especially my grandmother.

She was a Casey from Shanagolden, County Limerick. After the Famine, the family had scattered, the girls going to Australia, the boys to America (one of these became a millionaire—I have never been able to trace his descendants). One of the girls (my great-aunt) joined the Sisters of Mercy, became Provincial in Sydney, and founded a girls' college, a hospital and (with the aid of her rich brother in America) a foundling home—all these institutions are still

flourishing seventy years later. Eight years ago my wife had an operation in the hospital.

My grandmother had been a very practicing Catholic. My father
remembered her taking him to St. Mary's Cathedral for a visit to the
Blessed Sacrament when he was five or thereabouts. She never talked
religion to me, and I long assumed that she had left the Church under pressure from her Presbyterian husband, who was not only a
Freemason but a member of the Orange Lodge. Late in life I learned
that the reason was quite different. The family lived near a convent.
A nun escaped! The first house she came to was theirs. She told the
usual story of maltreatment, and it shook my grandmother's faith:
from time to time nuns have told me stories that would have shaken
mine—if I had not had a better Catholic formation than my grandmother was likely to have had: she was only ten or eleven when the
Famine came to torture Ireland. Instructed or not, she turned from
a pious Catholic into a pious Presbyterian, and never lost her bitter-
ness against the Church. Later her nun sister often tried to reason
with her but got nowhere. After one attempt she summed up the
situation to a young nun who, as an old nun, told me what she had
said: "The leaders of our Church don't know the harm they do."

So far I have said nothing of my father's attitude to all this. While
his sisters were avid churchgoers, he dropped religion early. By my
time, he had been won to Marxism by some very able outdoor speakers in the Sydney Domain, and used his great gift for invective on
priests and parsons alike as "black-coated confidence men." He mon-
ologued on Marx continuously. It was from him that I heard for the
first time that religion was the opium of the people. I remember his
scrawling across two pages of a physics book I had left lying open:
"Ignorance is the mother of devotion." He once wrote on one of my
history books: "History is the playground of liars." If either phrase
was a quotation, I do not know where he got it. About the first there
was a touch of comedy, for he wrote it across an account of the gal-
vanometer—and Galvani was a Franciscan Tertiary.

One might think that as between Presbyterians and Catholics he
would have been neutral, since he regarded all religions as fossil
survivals. And so for the first eight years he was. When he decided to
intervene, he struck surprisingly.

I was baptized in Sydney when I was a week old. In my first few
years I went to Mass and paid visits to various churches with my

mother. I learned my prayers—Our Father, Hail Mary, Gloria, Confiteor, a prayer to my Angel Guardian. I cannot remember when I did not say the three prayers beginning "Jesus, Mary and Joseph" which end: "May I breathe forth my soul in your blessed company." I say them still. And I was conscious of the friendship of St. Francis of Assisi (in honor of whom, *not* of my grandfather, I was named) and of St. Joseph. My mother had prayed hard that I should be born on St. Joseph's feast day, March 19. In a sense I was, though she did not realize it. I emerged early in the morning of March 20—it was still March 19 in Palestine!

So far, I was a typical little Irish Catholic child—a Catholic born round the turn of the century in Sydney might as well have been in Ireland. All my mother's friends were either Irish-born or first generation out of Ireland. On my father's side there was one Catholic, one of his mother's sisters; eccentric, as I remember, and no help at all in our special problem. She said the Rosary every day and never went to Mass at all. I gather she thought it would be an insult to the Blessed Mother to think Mass necessary if one said the Rosary.

Whether my father would have allowed me to make my first confession and Communion I do not know. But when I was six (and my brother four) his work took him out of Sydney, and for a couple of years the three of us lived with my mother's very Catholic sister. In effect we and her children were (and always remained) brothers and sisters: and we practiced our religion in all freedom. Those were the happiest years of my childhood. I see them still in a haze of gold.

One incident of that period, mildly relevant to my story, stays in my head. One of my father's sisters came to visit us. A priest from the parish happened to look in while she was there. She ignored his hand and flounced out of the house practically in the middle of a sentence.

Other children of my age were already in school. But my father had a theory, for which I have always been grateful to him, that no one should go to school, or even learn to read, before the age of eight. What with the surf at Coogee and the bush between Randwick and Long Bay, I filled my days blissfully. At eight my mother sent me to the parish school run by the Sacred Heart nuns—headed by a frightening woman, Sister Brendan, very quick with a cane. I never attracted her notice, for I had only two weeks there—all the Catholic schooling I have ever had. For my father ordered me to be sent to the public school at Coogee.

But I still got Mass, and made my first confession and Communion under the instruction of the Sacred Heart Fathers, a French missionary order (now quite notably Australian). I was only eight, in those days young for Communion, but the priests realized that my father might at any time be having us back, and who knew what line he might take? As it was, I barely made it. Two months after my first Communion, we were back with him, living within a walk of my grandparents' house. We learned soon enough what line he would take.

The weekend began agreeably. On the Saturday my grandmother, once Catholic now Presbyterian, arrived, bringing new suits for my brother and me. On the Sunday morning my father told us to put them on and took us to the Methodist Church in the next block. There, three times every Sunday, we went for the next six years—Christian Endeavor at nine-thirty, the main Service at eleven, Sunday School in the afternoon. The occasional questioner who tells me I believe as I do because I had been brainwashed in my childhood hasn't a notion of the variety of washings—Methodism three times every Sunday, Marxism at breakfast and dinner every day, confession to Father Rohan in his study on one Saturday morning in the month, daily Mass and Communion during the two weeks of my father's annual vacation.

My clearest memory of that first ghastly Sunday is of my mother's heartbroken crying, with eight-year-old me assuring her that she didn't need to worry about us. Nor, as it happened, did she. My brother, who died when he was sixteen, loved the Faith. My own love for it has never waned. My mother lived on to be eighty-five, growing spiritually to the end.

I wonder what the Methodists made of the two little mavericks wished on them. For mavericks we made ourselves from the beginning.

We never joined in the prayers, never sang a line of a hymn. Our bodies were there, that was all. Every year I won a prize for attendance, which my father remarked should have been awarded to him. At the beginning I misbehaved, not only small-boyishly but small-Catholic-boyishly. My one concession to the decencies was that I never really misbehaved when a visiting minister was in charge. Apart from that, I blush to think of my behavior, especially to one of the most perfect Christians I have met, Blanche West, who presided over Christian Endeavor. My only excuse is that I was a little Catholic who didn't want to be there.

I remember a time when three or four other boys and I made a small fire behind the church and burned a mass of newspapers we had collected. The others saw the superintendent coming and fled over the fence. I was left to face him. "What are you burning?" he demanded. "Bibles, sir," said I. For an instant he was back with Wycliffe and the bible-burning Church. I left him poking among the ashes to make sure it wasn't true. It was the grossest impertinence on my part, but I had found that I could get away with murder. They would not expel me, I felt certain. But this unnatural tolerance was their only reaction to the strangeness of the situation. They knew about it of course. In Balmain East we were a small community, everybody knowing everybody. They knew about my Catholic mother and my Presbyterian grandparents. But they did not lift the smallest proselytizing finger. In my six years I never heard a word against the Catholic Church.

It is not really true, of course, that only my body was there. Taking no part in praying and singing, I heard every word sung and thousands of words said. To this day I know more of the hymns I never sang than lots of Methodists, and I sing them now as I did not then. Few Catholic boys were getting as much Scripture as I got—partly by listening to the readings, partly by dipping about in the Bible during sermons.

The result was a growing affection for Methodists, and a devotion to John Wesley. Thirty years later we were to publish a superb work in his praise, *John Wesley in the History of Protestantism* by the Franciscan Father Piette: putting it through the press, I found myself remembering warmly and nostalgically those distant Sundays.

On alternate Saturday afternoons my brother and I visited my father's parents and their two unmarried daughters. It was a very anti-Catholic house. My grandfather, as I have said, was a member of the Orange Lodge, and the dining table was dominated by a colorful William of Orange on an extremely prancing steed—he had just defeated the Irish Catholics at the Battle of the Boyne.

We met proselytizing there, but of a special kind. Not a word was ever spoken. But in our play room there was always spread anti-Catholic writings of a virulence hard to credit. It was from them I learned about the Church as a bible-burner. I remember a couple of periodicals, especially the *Christian Herald,* and a couple of authors named Hocking. The harlot seated on the Seven Hills had never been more scarlet.

I was on the edge of my teens when my grandparents played their ace, a book called *The Awful Disclosures of Maria Monk*. Published in 1835, it purported to be the story of a nun who had escaped from a convent in Montreal. It gave lush descriptions of the murders committed and the immoralities practiced by priests and mother superiors. Actually it was established—by Protestant witnesses—that at the period in which she placed her story she was a prostitute in Montreal, and had transferred to the convent incidents which belonged to the brothel. She died in prison, where she was serving a sentence for picking pockets. The book was a best seller in the No Popery world: for close on a century it ranked with Foxe's *Book of Martyrs* as a bedside book. My grandparents evidently thought it just right for me.

I read everything they laid out for me with the liveliest interest and didn't believe a word of it. I put it all down to bigotry: behind that word my faith was invulnerable: it covered everything. It covered, for instance, Charles Kingsley's *Westward Ho!*, which I won as a prize for an essay on Cruelty to Animals in a competition open to all the public school children of Sydney. I enjoyed the excitement of the story and dismissed its anti-Catholicism as the sort of bigotry to which I was already hardened. I did not then know that Kingsley's description of the Catholic Spaniards as monsters of cruelty concerned a time when Topcliffe was racking Catholics in the Tower of London and Englishmen filled the boots of Dermot O'Hurley, Archbishop of Cashel, with molten pitch so that he could not walk to the gallows—they had to carry him. Soon after, a Catholic uncle gave me Robert Hugh Benson's *Come Rack, Come Rope*. I cannot remember how early I came to realize that cruelty was pretty evenly divided, and that the lesson for mankind lay in there being men on both sides who were prepared to suffer and die for what they were convinced was God's will.

Meanwhile our faith was untroubled. As I have said, my brother and I went once a month to confession to the parish priest, Father Rohan. On my father's annual holiday we were daily communicants. I had a fair general knowledge of Catholic doctrine, based on the Apostles' Creed, a great devotion to Mass and Communion, a habit of making visits to the Blessed Sacrament, a great confidence in my guardian angel though neither in the Catholic Church nor in the

Methodist was I reminded that Jesus had spoken of the angels of the little ones—"who see the face of my heavenly father continually."

I remember indeed being sorry for Methodists because they didn't seem to have any angels or saints, and almost never mentioned Our Lady—with her and my guardian angel and St. Joseph and St. Francis and St. Anthony I felt I could at any time discuss my own small troubles and pleasures. What Henri Ghéon calls "the come-and-go between this world and the next" was certainly real to me. It still is. I read any number of pamphlets. One was on St. Gerard Majella, a Redemptorist lay brother who worked some astounding miracles. These impressed me so much that when I came to be confirmed by Archbishop Kelly I chose Gerard as my Confirmation name. It was long afterwards that I learned he was the Patron of Pregnant Women. I have met a lot of Gerards since, and wonder if they know.

At my primary school—Gladstone Park, Balmain—I had two years under the headmaster John Walker (you're quite right, we called him Johnnie). He said we were too young to read Shakespeare, but he loved poetry, and introduced us especially to Byron and Tennyson. I did not realize at the time the oddity of some of his pedagogy. We had to learn *The Lady of Shalott* by heart, each boy would stand up and recite one line. Any boy who did not know his line was brought out and caned. Then the next boy took over. Tennyson would have been surprised at the alternation of his own lovely words and the bruising of schoolboy flesh. But when we came to

> Lancelot mused a little space;
> He said, "She has a lovely face;
> God in his mercy lend her grace, . . ."

the headmaster's eyes were filled with tears.

I really don't know why I mention this. My memory being excellent, I did not get any bruising, and anyhow it has nothing to do with my religion. Another incident I have slightly more excuse for relating. We were doing Tennyson's *Home They Brought Her Warrior Dead*. At the lines,

> Rose a nurse of ninety years,
> Set his child upon her knee,

Johnnie pointed to the first three words as an example of putting the verb before the noun. I asked, "Couldn't Rose have been the nurse's name?" He said, "But she was ninety years old." I said, "Perhaps she was christened as a baby, sir." His hand started towards the cane, then he decided (wrongly) that I was not being cheeky. It was a close thing.

As it happened, I knew what he meant to say—that Tennyson, being the sort of poet he was, would not have given the name Rose to so old a woman. But he didn't say it. I cannot remember an earlier lesson on the value of saying exactly what you mean. It has stayed with me. No rule could be more valuable in theology.

One other incident of that period. At least once a year up to that time we would be asked to name our favorite book. Every hand would go up, we all knew the expected answer, and the boy the teacher pointed to gave it—the Bible. Johnnie duly asked the question. The boy gave the ritual answer. Johnnie caned him for telling a lie. For a publisher no rule could be sounder—if you commit yourself to a book you haven't read, you'll get a caning.

When I was close to thirteen I moved on to the Sydney High School. The headmaster was a Methodist. There was the same absence of No Popery as in the Methodist church which I had, under my father's eye, been so regularly attending (round this time I stopped, with no comment from my father). In fact, religion of any kind was not much in the atmosphere of the school. The three best-liked teachers were Catholics, but I learned about this long after; the school's first senior prefect was a Catholic, but this too I learned only afterwards: we became friends for life.

The only matter on which I felt the Church to be attacked was the Sale of Indulgences by the Dominican Tetzel which detonated the Reformation. I asked Father Rohan about it on one of my monthly visits to the presbytery for confession. His answer satisfied me. I wish I could remember what it was! Anyhow I applied to the accusation that the Church had sold indulgences the phrase my father had written in one of my history books—"History is the playground of liars."

In my last year at school one of the masters, a man given to moralizing, told us that any boy worth his salt intellectually would have religious doubts in his later teens and that his faith would emerge all the stronger for them. I remember wondering briefly if I was intellectually inferior, because I had never had one. Catholics to whom I have told the story assure me that if I had gone to a Catholic school I'd have had plenty.

CHAPTER 2

A CATHOLIC IN AUSTRALIA

I

Which brings me to the Catholic Church in Australia, in which I spent my first twenty-three years. The Methodist Church as I knew it was so very English (with a dash of Scotch—which reminds me that every Methodist I met was a teetotaller). The Catholic Church was so very international. The Marist Fathers, one of whom baptized me, were French. I was instructed for confession and Communion by a Sacred Heart father—an Alsatian, I think.

Mention of the Marists reminds me of a story about one of them. A most charitable man, he was asked for money by a beggar. He said that he had come out without any money at all. The beggar urged him to search his pockets. The priest said there was no point; he had had nothing all the previous day, had meant to replenish, but forgot. The beggar said, "Say a prayer to Our Lady, Father, and try again." The priest said the prayer, and found a pound in a trouser pocket. He gave it to the beggar, returned home and told his brethren of the miracle. One of them said, "You were wearing my trousers." A silly story, but I never hear report of a miracle without thinking of it. Curious, the things that stick in a boy's memory.

To return to the question of nationality: the first and second archbishops of Sydney were English Benedictine monks from Downside Abbey. Under the first, that very great man Polding, St. Mary's was made a Benedictine cathedral with a chapter of monks, and the presbytery was made a Benedictine priory. The dream of an English Benedictine church in Australia had from the first a kind of eerie improbability about it: for the overwhelming majority of priests and people were Irish. The dream did not last long. The second Archbishop, Roger Bede Vaughan, dissolved the Benedictine chapter, and some of the monks became secular priests. He himself reigned only four years, dying on a visit to England. The new Archbishop, Patrick Moran, would not pay the cost of bringing his body back to Sydney for burial in the cathedral. The Irish were in full possession.

In my time, whenever a see fell vacant, a priest was brought from Ireland to fill the vacancy. What the Australian priests thought about this succession of Irishmen by Irishmen I had no way of knowing. But I never heard it questioned. It seemed to us in the nature of things. The King's representatives—the Governor General of the Commonwealth and the governors of the six states—were invariably Englishmen. Well, then—

I have forgotten when the first born-Australian became a bishop. Long after my time, certainly. Probably about the time the first Australian-born became Governor of New South Wales.

The Irish bishops became fully Australian, or at least Australianized. Cardinal Moran urged the foundation of the Australian Commonwealth, of an Australian citizen army and an Australian navy. Archbishop Mannix of Melbourne was to lead the fight against conscription of Australians for World War I.

By the non-Catholic world their Australia First line was taken to be a mere pretense, a continuation of Ireland's conflict with the Old Enemy: it was Sinn Fein applied to Australia, simply as a stick to beat England. Catholics did not see it so, not clearly anyhow. There was a division in our own selves. For myself, I thought of myself as Irish-Australian with the emotional accent on the Irish. It was on my first visit to Ireland at the age of twenty-five, at last meeting the Irish-Irish, that I realized my full Australianness.

But in my beginnings I regarded myself as an Irish-Australian. It was largely emotional, but the emotion was deeply felt—St. Patrick and Brian Boru, Elizabeth and Cromwell, Robert Emmet and Daniel O'Connell and John McCormack, Moore's *Irish Melodies*, the Famine and the Mountains of Mourne which ran down to the sea: with a dash of Ned Kelly. Actually I knew almost nothing of Irish history: I could not, for instance, have mentioned anything that happened in the decisive century and a half between the Confederation of Kilkenny and the '98. Of Gaelic literature I had not read a line, while England's literature was my paradisal garden.

It was on my first visit to Dublin in 1922 that I became dehyphenated. The process had begun in England a year or so earlier. Out of Australia for the first time, I found myself so homesick that I could hardly bear to read an Australian book, so passionately was I longing for Australia. But Dublin settled the matter.

I had at last met the Irish-Irish, delighted in them but knew that they were different, knew myself for an Australian. I was reminded of all this when I heard Father Vincent McNabb, an Irishman who had joined the English province of the Dominicans, say: "Ireland is my mother, but England is my wife. And I am one of those who think that his wife has things she could teach his mother."

In the light of my new awareness I did a lot of remembering. One incident came especially to mind. There was not a trace of sectarian feeling at the Sydney High School, we were not interested in one another's religion. But there was one brilliant boy moving up the school with me of whose religion we were all aware because his parents were in the Salvation Army and appeared at school functions in uniform. I remember one difference of opinion I had with him, not religious exactly. In 1910 King Edward died, the school was purple-draped, the boys wore purple ribbons or other signs of the national mourning. I wore no sign, and when accused by my friend of want of feeling, said that one death was like another and the King's death caused me no more grief than any of the thousands of deaths that happen every day.

He became a minister, and rose to be chairman of the Methodist Conference of Australia. I am sure he has forgotten the incident. It has remained vividly in my mind. At the moment I was only aware that my answer had avoided the issue: my real reason for wearing no sign of mourning was that I held Edward to be King of England, imposed on Ireland only by force: I felt he was no king of mine.

Forty years later an incident occurred which brought the whole episode vividly back to me. I was speaker at a dinner in America. The chairman, introducing me, expressed surprise that I, with my Irish background, should owe allegiance to the Queen of England. The audience was horrified—no audiences in the world equal the American in courtesy to a visitor. In my speech I matched the chairman's surprise with my own—that he, a lawyer, should make so elementary a mistake. By the Constitution of the Commonwealth, the Queen was Queen of Australia, as of Canada and New Zealand. Her relation with the English was not my affair. It was as Queen of Australia that she had my allegiance, as herself that she had my affection.

But those forty years had indeed seen changes, not only in me. Archbishop Mannix had led the fight against conscription in World War I. Yet England's Foreign Minister, I was told by Arthur Calwell, a leading Australian politician, was to express a wish in Rome that Mannix might be Australia's second cardinal. He wasn't, as it happened (the Hat went to a born-Australian). But in

World War II he was Senior Chaplain to the Australian Forces. And Archbishop Duhig, that other born-Irishman, had accepted a knight-hood from the Queen.

In between, I had a different kind of reminder of King Edward's death. Just fourteen years after it, I was in Toronto. There I was re-ceived by Archbishop McNeil, who told me—a complete stranger—on authority which seemed to me pretty definite, that the King had been received into the Catholic Church on his deathbed. The Arch-bishop even gave me the details—the priest who received him was Father Foster of the Catholic church alongside Buckingham Palace, and the Archbishops of Canterbury and York were kept waiting in another room meanwhile. It set me wondering whether my attitude to the King's death would have been different had I known him for a Catholic.

And that raised the whole question of Church and State, religious society and civil society. Just as the mixture of religious influences—Catholic, Methodist, Presbyterian—forced me to use my mind on religion, so the mixture of national influences kept me thinking about nationality.

Society is not just a piece of machinery to make life livable, still less a necessary evil to be got along with somehow. It is a positive good. In it powers come into action, powers to serve and be served, a rich profusion of them up to full co-operation in a developed social order. There will always be tension between the individual person-ality and the social order, but it will be less if individual and society each realizes the value to itself of the fullest development of the other. And it is becoming clearer that there are depths of develop-ment still to be reached by each, and problems arising as each de-velops.

The tension is worse, can be unbearable, for any who are left out of the main stream of the life of their society, Negroes in America, for instance. As I wrote in *Society and Sanity* (pp. 169–70):

> It may be by exclusion, not by refusal, that men are outside the fullness of Society. The Catholics in England, between the Reforma-tion and Catholic Emancipation, were thus excluded, permitted barely to live upon the fringe of society: they suffered in a noble cause, but they did suffer, not only materially but psychologically and spiritually, the contribution to human and political life that they had it in them to make not made, the strength that flows from recognition and fellowship not flowing for them. That England lost

more by excluding them than the Catholics by being excluded does not make their loss less real. They were forced to seek in the Church the compensation for what Society denied them. And indeed, by the accident of history, this remains a tendency of English-speaking Catholics everywhere. In Ireland, even more than in England—and in the new worlds growing from both, America, for instance, and Australia—they were too long excluded from full recognition as members of Society and full participation in its life; they existed on sufferance, and functioned socially hardly at all. Disowned by their natural Society, they were driven more and more to think of, and live in, the Church as their only *patria*; and the habit lingers.

It is not a good habit. The Church is a more perfect society, meeting deeper needs more richly, more of a community, uniting its members more intimately, than any purely human organization. But life in the supernatural society was never meant as a *substitute* for life in the natural society. It was never meant as a substitute, and is not in fact a substitute. The Church is a society of too special a sort, its structure and functions created by God, not developed by its members, not made by them in the first place nor alterable by them; its members do not make the same *sort* of contribution to the supernatural society as to the natural, do not exercise their powers in it or exert their influence upon it in the same way; they belong to it, but they do not feel that it is their property as civil society is; it is not theirs to re-make if they will—a citizen could take action against a bad king, for instance, that a Catholic could not take against a bad pope; and though their profoundest needs are met in it, there are all sorts of other needs, profound too and related to the full development of their manhood, which it was not created to meet. The Church is no more a substitute for civil Society than for the family.

I have said that the Catholic habit of making the Church a patria lingers. The non-Catholic habit of seeing us as not belonging lingers too. In England, Catholic Emancipation was voted in 1829. But instinctive distrust of us did not die. At lunch in London's Café Royal, Australia's High Commissioner Beasley told me of an incident which happened in the mid-forties. Conversing with Prime Minister Chiffley of Australia, King George VI remarked that America's Secretary of State, James F. Byrnes, was a Catholic and therefore "would be against us." The King had been badly briefed—for Byrnes was not a Catholic, but Chiffley was. Byrnes had been brought up Catholic but had become a Baptist.

II

The Australian Church of my boyhood and young manhood was a very good sample of the pre-Conciliar Church—very good as a sample, very good in itself. Looking back, one can see the defects which made inevitable the chaos in which Catholic life now everywhere is. But the explosion was still in the future, and meanwhile the Church was a pleasant, peaceful place to be in.

Framing the whole picture was the relation between priests and people. That our bishops invariably came from Ireland hardly troubled most of us: we were used to our provincial status. After all, in Cardinal Moran and Archbishop Mannix we were convinced Ireland had given us two churchmen greater than any it had kept for itself. Irishmen are usually not disposed to grant this, but I have observed that the names of two to match them do not come readily to their lips.

That the Church was authoritarian hardly troubled us either: we accepted our lay status. I remember the shock when a Catholic, Judge Heydon, entered into public conflict with Archbishop Mannix on conscription in World War I. My own first reaction was a kind of horror, almost as if the judge had been guilty of sacrilege, challenging the Lord's anointed. But I quickly saw the point. The Archbishop had stated that, in opposing conscription, he was merely exercising his rights as a citizen: but civil argument can be a bloody business, and a citizen who gets into civil argument must take what he gets.

Up till then we had lived in unbroken peace with our clergy. We liked them and admired them. In the hour of need we felt we could always be sure of them. The priests who served the bush, the back country, we admired particularly. Some of them said Mass three times on Sunday at places from twenty to thirty miles apart. There were no motor cars, only horses or bicycles. And the priests could not eat or drink till the last Mass was over. Most of them died under fifty. It did not occur to us that anything could be done about it. Fasting Communion belonged to the nature of things. It was not till I reached Europe that I heard anyone say that we owed its lethal strictness to the cardinals in Rome, who could say their one Mass in their own rooms and did not eat breakfast anyway.

The respect we had for the priests did not mean any dewy-eyed idealization. We could smile at their foibles. There was a story about a baby who swallowed a coin, and its mother sent for the parish priest because he would get the last penny out of anyone—it must have been told about lots of them. Again we delighted in the parable of the Good Samaritan as told to his congregation by one very individual parish priest who was in frequent conflict with the Chancery. He told how the man fell among thieves, who robbed him and left him for dead: along came a cardinal, who passed by on the other side, then a vicar general, who didn't give the man so much as a look: at last came a simple parish priest, who looked after the victim properly. I believe his own cardinal smiled when the story reached him the following morning.

It all added up to a mingling of reverence and affection which was wholly healthy. I think the combination in our priests of celibacy and masculinity was the secret of it. I never heard anyone suggest that celibacy ought to be optional. We could not imagine a married priesthood in those days. Nor for long afterwards. I remember an experience of my own on the Hyde Park platform of the Catholic Evidence Guild: I had mentioned that not only in the Eastern Orthodox Church (which did not accept the Pope's supremacy) but also in the Eastern Churches in communion with Rome there were married priests: for some of the Catholics in the crowd it was as if I had denied the Trinity: half a dozen reported me to Cardinal Bourne. When he told them it was true, I fancy some of them wondered if he too had lost the Faith.

Thinking back on the accepted celibacy of those days and today's movement towards a married clergy, I am reminded of an incident which happened a good many years ago—forty maybe, my memory is uncertain. A man in England whose wife was dead, and his children grown up, became a priest. He and another priest were giving a mission in Ireland. In his opening sermon he told the story of his own life. Then both priests went into the boxes to hear confessions. Everybody lined up outside the other priest's box. The first priest went across and invited some of the people to come to him. The answer he got was, "We'd rather have a virgin, Father."

The Australian Church in the first twenty years of the century was a very compact body, few lapses, few conversions. We just did not think of Protestants as convertible. We lived our own separate, satisfied life without giving much thought to them—except when one of their more excitable ministers attacked the Church. For there was a solid and articulate No Popery element in Sydney and Melbourne, and we reveled in the replies of our two champions—Dr. O'Reilly in Sydney and Archbishop Mannix in Melbourne.

Mannix was a very tall man. His opposite number, Dr. Head, the Anglican Archbishop of Melbourne, was short. After one of their interchanges in the newspapers, a Catholic racehorse owner asked Archbishop Mannix's permission to name a two-year-old after him. The Archbishop refused—he would not like to open his paper one morning and read that Mannix had been beaten by a short head.

Even for an Irishman he was notably unsentimental. He once remarked of the Trappist Abbot of Roscrea, "He meets all situations with kindliness." I said, "What do you meet them with?" "With acerbity," he answered. A group of priests were discussing the possibility that Cardinal Spellman might be made Pope. One of them wondered what name he would take. "Bolonius the First," said the Archbishop.

Acerbity was not the whole of him. When the son of a local Episcopal minister became a Catholic and wanted to study for the priesthood, the Archbishop wrote to his father offering to send the young man to another diocese if his being a Catholic priest in Melbourne would be an embarrassment to his father. And considering how fiercely he had fought the Prime Minister, William Morris Hughes, over conscription in World War I, it is pleasant to think of their reconciliation when Hughes was dying.

Dr. O'Reilly was a Vincentian, Rector of St. John's, the Catholic college in the University of Sydney. He was a first-rate classical scholar, with a pleasant command of English, admirably equipped for his role as head of a college. But he could not resist making a point: which meant that he made enemies. The rank-and-file of us rejoiced in him, but I doubt if our leaders did, lay or clerical. Some of Sydney's richest Catholics he described as having nothing of the Faith save Mass and the sacraments, "in respect of which they are not gluttonous."

When he wrote in the Sydney *Morning Herald* that a starving man was entitled to take food, and that this would not be stealing because in extreme necessity all things belong in common, there was a great clamor of protesting voices; I cannot remember any Catholic authority writing to say that this was standard Catholic teaching.

Certainly the Church made no impact on the life of Sydney University—it must have been getting on for a hundred years old before it got its first practicing Catholic professor. It did not make very much impact either on the life of society as a whole. And this was not by chance. There was real withdrawal. An older bishop advised a younger bishop on his relations with Government House—be courteous but distant. I know this because the younger bishop told me. And a governor told me that when he invited an archbishop to dinner, the archbishop did not come but sent one of his priests!

As I have said, *Ecclesia est patria nostra* was the rule. The State was our residence, we lived there. But the Church was our homeland. And about the Church we had the siege mentality.

When Wilfrid Ward first spoke of the Church's being in a state of siege he had no notion that I would be his son-in-law. I had not left Australia when he died. I had not been long in England when the idea of being his son-in-law entered my head. But all that lay in the future—including my hearing about the state of siege and the siege mentality resultant. It fitted precisely the Church I had known in Australia and, I fancy, the Church just about everywhere.

As Wilfrid Ward saw it, after the century of actual warfare following the Reformation, the Church saw herself under siege and adapted her life to the siege condition. In a siege the one virtue is discipline, and the one consideration is the defense of the walls. The ordinary life of the city must get along as best it can. So the great defensive doctrines—the Visible Church and its marks, Supremacy, Infallibility, apologetics generally—had the first call on the Church's energy. At all costs the walls must stand. The real life of the Church based on Trinity, Incarnation, Redemption, the life to come, could not receive the degree of attention which would have been normal. The one essential was that the great doctrines should be stated correctly and not denied. So St. Peter Canisius produced the first Catholic catechism—in reply to Luther's. In this, as in so much else, the enemy called the tune. There was no development of the doctrines of Heaven and Hell because they were not attacked, but endless writing on Purgatory, which was.

Because the nature of Protestantism caused the Catholic defense to concentrate on the Visible Church, the vitalizing doctrine of the Church as Christ's Mystical Body went into eclipse. The First Vatican Council decided not to use the phrase because some Jansenists had used it! And in the *Catholic Encyclopedia* published as late as 1911 it got half a column—and even then under the heading "Mystical Body of the Church." It was the Dominican Père Clérissac who brought it back to the ordinary Catholic; and it was Robert Hugh Benson, convert son of an Archbishop of Canterbury, whose *Christ in the Church* gave the doctrine to the English-speaking world.

Thinking on Mass and the sacraments had suffered from concentrating too closely on the Protestant attack. Because the Protestants asserted that the Mass could not be a sacrifice, as no victim was slain, Catholic theologians bent over backwards to find some sort of slaying at our altars. But at least the practice of Mass and Eucharist had been magnificently maintained. Pius X's ruling on Early Communion and Frequent Communion meant that we were the most sacrament-fed generation in the Church's history. If only we had been as well fed doctrinally! To that Pius X's contribution is less distinguished.

In 1902 came a notable religious hoax—it fooled a future Pope. It was a book on the Gospels and the Church by a French theologian, Loisy. It began disarmingly: "It has not been my purpose to write a defense of Catholicism and traditional dogma." It had not indeed. The book was a root-and-branch denial of both. A generation earlier that brilliant English unbeliever Samuel Butler had done something of the same sort. His book *The Fair Haven* was a murderous attack on belief in Christ's Resurrection in the form of a defense of it.

Both books were at first taken at face value. An Evangelical periodical praised *The Fair Haven* not in one review but two. *L'Évangile et l'Église* gave great satisfaction, "apart from a few obscure passages," to Cardinal Sarto, who was to be Pius X. Eight years later he struck back at the author with a decree of excommunication. For with Loisy's book the Modernist Movement had surfaced. Three years before the excommunication Pius issued the encyclical *Pascendi*, in which the movement was summarized and condemned. Reading it now, we are startled at the violence of the papal language —"sacrilegious audacity," "a thousand noxious devices," "puffed up like bladders with the spirit of vanity." Was the Pope relieving his feelings at having been hoaxed?

In fact, of course, this sort of language had become habitual in Roman condemnations. At the moment the habit seems to have been dropped. Compare Pius XI's *Casti Connubii* with Paul VI's *Humanae Vitae*. Both are against contraception. But whereas the first carries invective to a high peak—"God detests this crime with unspeakable loathing"—the second has no invective at all—contraception "is in contradiction with the will of the Author of life." I cannot remember meeting the words "heretic," "anathema," "excommunicate," in any of the documents of Vatican II.

A tempest was certainly blowing up. The Loisy ideas were spreading in France and Italy, and Rome was alarmed. But it is hard to know the numbers involved. In England there was a flurry of excitement, especially round the names of the Jesuit Father Tyrrell and Baron von Hügel. A few priests left the Church. Rome has seldom countered any rebellion more rapidly and vigorously.

A little before *Pascendi* came the decree *Lamentabili*, listing sixty-five Modernist teachings for condemnation. Then an oath against Modernism was drawn up which all priests were called upon to sign. The English newspapers gave it all plenty of space. The ordinary layman, unaccustomed to papal documents, was in unhappy confusion: we are told of one lady who thought the sixty-five condemned propositions were being offered by Rome as true doctrine and almost sprained her faith trying to accept them!

Anyhow, whether because of the vigorous papal action or the outbreak of World War I, the tempest died away. The Church had two generations of internal peace and considerable intellectual development.

How far the Church in Australia was affected by the Modernist crisis I do not know. Certainly none of it reached my ears. In England, we are told, priests signed the Anti-Modernist Oath with anguish—the choice was "perjury or ruin," as one of them phrased it. I can only say that I never heard it referred to. I seem to remember the name of Father Tyrrell as a troubler of Christian peace, but then we had a priest of our own—a geologist—who had left the Church and was used as a warning against intellectual pride. Baron von Hügel's name never reached my ears till I came to England in 1920 and met his sister-in-law's goddaughter (I married her later).

There may have been a seething within the clergy, but if so it remained within. The rest of us were peacefully unaware. That indeed was our normal relation to the rest of the Catholic world: we were very Roman—Leo XIII's face being on the walls of so many Catholic homes, to be followed by Pius X's—but we did not know much about what went on in the Vatican. The one extra-Australian Catholic fact known to all of us was the conversion of Newman in the previous century. But I never heard a whisper of Newman's difficulties in the founding of a Catholic University in Dublin. If we had heard of

Cardinal Cullen, who came close to breaking Newman's heart, it was only as the uncle of our own Cardinal Moran.

III

But my provincialism was to be shattered. I was sixteen, in my last year at Sydney High School. The English master handed me two books, by authors unknown to me, with the remark, "These will suit you." They did indeed. One was Hilaire Belloc's *Danton*, the other G. K. Chesterton's *Heretics*. I had just discovered P. G. Wodehouse for myself. The three of them consumed a vast amount of my reading time from then on.

I can't trace that Wodehouse made any difference to my "me." There is no measuring the difference the other two made. Later I was to come to know both of them and publish books by them. For the moment I shall write of the difference they had already begun to make to the Catholic outlook of the English-speaking world. I have spoken of the state of siege into which the Catholic body let itself enter after the Reformation. For lots of us, Belloc and Chesterton meant an end to the three-century-old siege mentality.

In the second half of the nineteenth century the outside world had grown into a kind of automatic contempt for the Catholic intellect. Carlyle had spoken of Cardinal Newman as having the brain of a moderate-sized rabbit, Arnold Bennett despised Chesterton's "inferior intellectual equipment": Dean Inge called Chesterton "an obese mountebank." A little later I was speaking on the Incarnation at an outdoor meeting of the Catholic Evidence Guild in North London: a man in the crowd said, "Either you're paid to say these things or you're mentally defective": and a moment after he continued, "And I can't imagine anybody paying you."

For an outsider, I say, it had become axiomatic that Catholics couldn't think. It was part of the siege mentality that too many Catholics believed this themselves. Not all, of course. William George Ward had sought debate with John Stuart Mill: even Mill's followers were not confident that Ward had lost. His son Wilfrid had the same audience among the educated as Christopher Dawson was later to have—Chesterton was to say Wilfrid Ward was the man who made the Church intelligible to the educated English. But of the mass of Catholics I think it was true. They were proud of being Catholics, but there was an unstated feeling that while we had the Faith, the others had the arguments!

There had been the Darwin evolution business. The Church had come out of it, not exactly damaged perhaps, but with not much credit, they felt. And now there were the new discoveries in Comparative Religion, there was Scripture Criticism putting all under question. One way or another, Catholics felt it better to stay within the walls. That within a couple of generations the Professor of Comparative Religion at Oxford would be a convert to the Church and his opposite number at Chicago University a very orthodox Rumanian Orthodox, no one could foresee.

Certainly things did not look that way at the turn of the century. The gigantic intellects imagined as prowling around our walls seemed so very formidable. It was safer inside. If any of them attacked the Church—which fewer and fewer at the highest level did—then they had to be answered. But for the rest it was better to live our own lives, attract as little attention as possible. We felt there was an agreement, which all gentlemen would observe, that if we kept quiet they would ignore us! Belloc, born in the Church, and Chesterton, not yet a Catholic, but as good as, ignored the agreement and were not ignored.

They were out in the open, they said whatever they felt like, and they not only got away with it but found their Catholicness taken seriously. They were both considerable writers, and I shall discuss them as such when I come to talk of our publishing. For the moment I am considering what they did to change the atmosphere, simply by their willingness to be themselves. They were not the only ones, but they were the most colorful. And for this particular function color was essential. If one is going to change things by being oneself, one must be a rather notable self. You and I could go on being ourselves forever without attracting a passing glance.

The result was that we had two Catholics who could not be overlooked. Nobody wanted to overlook Chesterton—one might miss something amusing. His book *The Napoleon of Notting Hill*, for instance, opens with the words, "The human race, to which so many of my readers belong . . ." Naturally one went on reading. There was his remark on the Women's Liberation movement as it was then: "Ten thousand young women stood up and said 'We will not be dictated to.' Then they went out and became stenographers."

The two jests don't prove anything—they were just a flourish of heels. Was he wise to do so much of it? He himself noted in his *Autobiography*: "People cannot believe that anything decorated by an incidental joke can be sensible." Anyhow he felt like jesting, he jested, and people read him.

There was no flourish of heels in Belloc, his Latin gravity forbade it. He could be immensely entertaining. There were the children's books—*The Bad Child's Book of Beasts, More Beasts for Worse Children, Cautionary Tales*. Remember his lines on doctors—

> They murmured as they took their fees
> "There is no cure for this disease."

And there is his account of the llama:

> The llama is a woolly kind of fleecy hairy goat
> With an indolent expression and an undulating throat
> Like an unsuccessful literary man.

Ogden Nash did a llama too. You might compare their llamas.

Writing for grown-ups Belloc could be amusing, but often enough you could feel the cold steel in his jesting:

> I'm tired of love, I'm still more tired of rhyme
> But money gives me pleasure all the time.

He wasn't only jesting—he could write a book on economics, but handled his own finances with no great competence.

There was the Christmas card he sent out with two lines of his own verse on it:

> May all my enemies go to hell
> Noel, Noel, Noel, Noel.

He wasn't jesting here either. He had a great power of anger, in controversy especially. A man with so much bite in his Christmas greetings—imagine his bite when he was angry. No one enjoyed controversy with Belloc. I am not saying that biting belongs in religious discussion. But so many teeth had sunk into our quivering flanks so often, that it was a pleasure to see other flanks bloodied for a change.

It was Bernard Shaw who created the monster he called the Chesterbelloc. The monster was not wholly mythical, yet the two men were very different. Both were unmistakably "characters"—they had not what we now call charisma, exactly, but something more ebullient, lighthearted even. But to apply to them a contrast originally applied to the men of England's oldest universities, Belloc went about as if he owned the earth, Chesterton as if he didn't care who owned it. In fact they both knew who did own it.

We shall look further at the double change they worked—in getting the outside world to listen to Catholics, in getting Catholics willing to talk. These first two books turned my mental world upside down. What these men did to sixteen-year-old me was only one example of what they did to the whole world of my youth. I shall talk of this first, before coming to me.

Back in the thirteenth century, King Louis IX had offered two simple rules for discussion with a heretic: "If you are a learned cleric, reason with him. If you are a plain man-at-arms, thrust your sword into his belly as far as it will go." Some of us may have longed for those dear dead days: but the swords not being in our hands, silence was the obvious alternative. Belloc and Chesterton ended all this, not only by what they had to say but far more by the total devil-may-careness with which they said it, the sheer high spirits with which they took on anybody and everybody. Later Catholics criticize Chesterton's immoderate fooling and Belloc's aggressiveness, without realizing the battle they fought and won against a world which thought Catholics not worth listening to, and against unnerved Catholics who did not try to speak to it. They were indeed immoderate, but battles are not won by moderation—as Chesterton said: "You can't be moderate with a battle axe."

Each had his own way of being himself, which means that they had their different ways of forcing men to listen. I shall tell a story of each, well known to men of my generation, not perhaps to our juniors.

(1) Belloc was kneeling at Mass in Westminster Cathedral. A sacristan whispered to him, "Excuse me, sir, we stand here."

Belloc: "Go to hell."

Sacristan: "I'm sorry, sir, I didn't know you were a Catholic."

(2) Chesterton was a vast man physically—over twenty stone, say three hundred pounds. During the war a patriotic lady accused him of cowardice.

Patriotic lady: "Why aren't you out at the Front?"

Chesterton: "Madame, if you will go round to the side, you'll see that I am."

The stories are typical—Belloc rude to the polite stranger, Chesterton polite to the rude stranger, each quite unlike anyone else. Given that the world's eye had no habit of seeing Catholics, its ear no habit of hearing them, the need of the moment was for Catholics who could not be overlooked, whose voice had to be heard. In these two the need was met in measure pressed down and (sometimes) overflowing.

So there was I, immersed in, enthralled by, Belloc's *Danton* and Chesterton's *Heretics*. I still remember the start Belloc's second paragraph gave me: "What was the French Revolution? It was essentially a reversion to the normal." I wondered what he could possibly mean. I had read Dickens's *A Tale of Two Cities*. Normal? Belloc went on to explain—the Revolution was "a sudden and violent return to those conditions which are the necessary bases of health in any political community." The guillotine, which had wholly dominated my own picture, is relegated to the margin with the adjectives "sudden and violent." The substance of the Revolution was far different.

I was only sixteen. I had not read much history. I have read plenty since. I still feel something of what I felt then, that there never was a historian who could have written of the French Revolution as a reversion to normal. He was his own kind of historian, he had his own mastery of language. (Long afterwards we published a surprising view of the normal, by another Frenchman, Jean Charlot—"When Church dignitaries are thrown into jail it appears to me to be a return to normalcy.")

Heretics gave me not one shock (of the electric sort, you understand) but a score. I jot down a few sentences which, as I read them again, take me back sixty years.

"A young man may keep himself from vice by thinking of disease. He may keep himself from it by continually thinking of the Virgin Mary. There may be a question about which method is the more reasonable or even about which is the more effective. But surely there can be no question about which is the more wholesome."

"A permanent possibility of selfishness arises from the mere fact of having a self." (Not sufficiently realized in discussion of original sin, not realized at all by Marx and the Utopians.)

"Charity"—in judging others—"is a reverent agnosticism towards the complexity of the soul."

On the idea—stated explicitly by Auguste Comte but growing everywhere—of the scientist as a kind of secular priest whose trained mind could be trusted for sure guidance in the life of society generally, *Heretics* has two remarks which enchanted me then and still seem to me wholly realistic.

"That same suppression of sympathies, that same suppression of intuition or guesswork, which make a man preternaturally clever in dealing with the stomach of a spider will make him preternaturally stupid in dealing with the heart of a man."

"Science cannot analyse any man's wish for a pork chop and say how much of it is hunger, how much custom, how much nervous fancy, and how much a haunting love of the beautiful." He should not have put in that last phrase, of course; it convinced the ordinary reader that he was fooling. But once he thought of it he had to say it: it practically said itself. I reveled in it.

Two comments Chesterton made, on statements one was hearing all the time, have held my mind from that day to this. I know I bored my high school friends with them.

(1) "Neither in religion nor morality lies the hope of our race, but in education." Chesterton's comment: "This, clearly expressed, means that we cannot decide what is good, but let us give it to our children."

(2) There were those who urged a simplification of life with the slogan "Plain living and high thinking." I had been rather taken with it myself. Said Chesterton: "They would be improved by high living and plain thinking." I have never forgotten the phrase. As it happens, I have no constitutional habit of high living. I try to thank Chesterton by making up by plainness in thinking what my living lacks in height.

IV

When in 1910 I stood outside the *Worker* office in Sydney till the early hours, cheering the figures which showed that New South Wales was to have its first Labour Government, I hadn't a notion of one particular difference it was going to make to me. It opened Sydney University to the poor.

Approaching seventeen, I was able to enter the university as one of a couple of hundred holders of bursaries or exhibitions. At our first Commencement, the students welcomed us by singing:

> Come along, undergrads,
> And grab a bursary,
> All the Lizzies and the Lils
> And the nuts of Surry Hills
> Are going to be dubbed M.B.

Surry Hills was a slum, a place of poverty and violence. If you feel moved to sing this snatch of sociology, which I still occasionally do *con brio*, the tune is that of the chorus of Pollywolly doodle.

None of this last-ditchery affected daily life at the university: no one could tell by looking at a student whether the state or his parents had paid his fees.

Religiously, those university years were as free of anti-popery as my time at the Sydney High School. I never heard a word against the Church or her teachings. Had I been reading History or Philosophy, it might have been different. But with a vague feeling, the result probably of reading Belloc and Chesterton, that I might grow into a specialist on the Middle Ages, I concentrated on Latin, Early and Middle French, Early and Middle English. None of this called for any utterance on doctrine by the professors. Two of them had been Catholics, one of them was to return to the Faith; but at the time there was nothing to show that either retained the faintest interest in religion.

In a way it was disappointing. Filled to the brim with the strong wine of Belloc and Chesterton, feeling like the two of them rolled into one, I was ready for controversy, but no one offered me any. On my generation of Catholics these two produced a kind of Walter Mitty swagger, a parody of their splendid swashbuckling. "Il me faut des géants"—we were looking for giants to fight, we did not even get windmills.

Yes, it was disappointing that no one of intellectual quality was interested enough in the Church to offer us battle. And very fortunate. We would have been cut to pieces, for we would have been fighting with wooden swords. "An ingrained habit of the defensive," Belloc had told us, "is a prime condition of defeat." A condition even more prime is ardent ignorance. Knowing no Church history, we would have found ourselves defending the indefensible, denying the undeniable. Knowing no theology, we would have been valiantly asserting the meaningless.

That at least would have been my condition. Ardent Catholic I was, a daily communicant. I loved the Church then as I always have. But I did not then know what the Church *is*. I was loyal to the Pope, but I did not know what his infallibility means. I had not even heard of the 1870 definition.

Similarly, while proud that the Church had all the truths, I was not curious to know the truths I was so proud she had. I had a strong devotion to Father, Son, Holy Spirit individually. But I never asked myself why the Third Person should be called Holy Spirit, given that Father and Son were each holy and each spirit! The fact of mystery did not bother me: not being a complete fool, I realized that we could not know God as well as he knows himself. But why didn't I wonder what it was that he was telling us about himself?

I never opened a theological or spiritual book and never felt the slightest desire to. I hadn't a single doubt—I didn't know enough! Given the course my religious thinking has taken since, I cannot make any sense of my late teens and early twenties.

Just before the visit to England which was to change all this, a friend gave me the *Imitation of Christ*, the richest spiritual fare that had come my way. I read it and read it. It seemed to me that it contained everything, the Christian warrior's whole equipment. I wondered why Thomas à Kempis had not been canonized. I mentioned this to a priest, who told me that when his coffin was opened it was discovered that he had moved. So that he must have been buried alive! He could not be canonized because it was not known in what disposition he had died—an explanation which at the time I found wholly satisfying. Later I was to hear it said that à Kempis was only the writer in the literal sense, that he had written it out by hand; the author was the head of his community Gerard Groote. I don't know which of them had turned over in his coffin. And I imagine that one head of the University College in Belfast could not have told me: to a suggestion that a Chair of Scholastic Philosophy should be founded in the college he is said to have said: "While we all admire Thomas Aquinas's *Imitation of Christ*, he seems to have believed in the Inquisition."

What I never guessed was that a simple phrase in the book, which I took in my stride as so obviously true as to be hardly worth saying, would one day have me rejoicing that the man who wrote it was not canonized. It was to the effect that it was better to please the Trinity than to be able to discuss the Trinity. It was one of those half-truths which (Chesterton again) are like half-bricks, they carry further. I wonder how much harm that single statement has done. I shall come back to it. I shall indeed.

In the century's late teens, which were my early twenties, I was fervently Catholic but had no interest whatever in theology. Nor did

I know any priests socially, so to speak. It was an odd interlude which
brought my first personal contact with clerics.

The World War then ending had kept in Australia a number of
Jesuit novices who would normally have already gone on to studies in
Europe. I was asked to give them some lessons in English literature.
One task I set them was to "compare and contrast" (or some such
jargon) Ben Jonson's

> Drink to me only with thine eyes,
> And I will pledge with mine.
> Or leave a kiss but in the cup,
> And I'll not look for wine.
> The thirst that from the soul doth rise
> Doth ask a drink divine;
> But might I of Jove's nectar sup,
> I would not change for thine.

and Robert Burns's

> O, my Love's like a red, red rose
> That's newly sprung in June:
> O, my Love's like the melody
> That's sweetly played in tune.

One of them startled me by finding Burns's poem artificial in comparison with the naturalness of Ben Jonson's. I remember thinking
that this must be a result of his celibate vocation. But in the event,
he never went through to ordination. When I next met him he was
married. I have since known two of the group as Provincials, but I
retain no other memory of the classes. Nor, I imagine, do they.

But the Father Superior, George Byrne, S.J., gave me articles to read
on two early Christian writers—Tertullian and Origen. Both were
a new experience to me, though I had not enough theology to get
much out of them. I liked Origen's idea that at the end of the world
the damned would attain salvation: it made me feel a bit safer myself: but only a bit; I have always been—unrealistically?—optimistic
about my place in the next world. The fear of hell never bothered
me, then or since. I have always had a better reason than that for
trying to do God's will and for repenting when I have failed to.

Tertullian's "It is certain because it is impossible" set me thinking
more. I had already met it as "I believe because it is impossible," or
"I believe because it is absurd," and had taken it in my stride. I was
still young when I came to the conclusion that all epigrams get the

neatness which is their main point by leaving out some piece of the truth: an epigram is not a legal document. In the new form—"*certum est*"—I gave more attention to it. But it carried me no further than the view I had already formed about mystery, namely that a God my mind could fully comprehend would have to be small enough to fit into my mind, no God therefore.

I smile when I remember my one contact with spiritualism. I was coaching a boy in Latin for matriculation, the text being the third book of Horace's Odes. The last weekend before the exam I was spending at his house, using every moment. On the Sunday night a visitor suggested we try table-turning. We sat around the table, thumbs touching fingers. The table began to heave. The visitor asked the "presence" to answer questions with knocks on the table. Some pointless questions were asked, and pointless answers rapped out. Bored, I asked, "Please knock on the ceiling," and the knocks came on the ceiling. I asked "Please knock on the piano keys," and so it happened. Having thus discovered that I could get what I wanted, I decided to get some use out of it. I asked which Odes of Horace would be set in the examination, and sat there willing that the raps would count up to the numbers of the two most difficult Odes. They did. My pupil really studied those two Odes. He did not get them of course. At no point did it occur to me that there was another intelligence in action, only that the human mind has powers over matter which have not been developed. It was not my line of interest. I never tried again.

In these years I was teaching at the Sydney Grammar School and studying for a degree at the Sydney University Law School. I had every intention of being called to the bar. No other future occurred to me. I felt no enthusiasm about it, no sense of being summoned to a life work. Simply it seemed the obvious profession, I being naturally talkative, and having none of the talents needed by doctors or engineers. Years later I was talking on the Catholic Evidence Guild platform in Hyde Park: a friend was in the crowd: a man alongside her remarked, "He's bright all right, but he isn't educated." She asked him to elaborate. "Well, you can see he hasn't been to a university." She said, "I happen to know that he has a university degree." "Must have been in engineering," he said. She told me the story and I felt I could read the man's mind—he had understood every word I said, therefore I couldn't be a university man.

Law at Sydney was a four-year course. At the end of my second year I decided to take a year off and go to Europe. I had only the vaguest reasons for going, in fact I can no longer remember what they were. I had an idea that I might do some more work on Latin in Germany, or even on Gaelic in Ireland.

Fortunately the ship I was on went by way of Africa and took ten weeks to make the journey. It was the longest break I had ever had from study. For years I had lived with the next examination ahead of me. Now, with a chance to think, I saw that I was not meant for the academic life, whether as teacher or pure scholar.

When the ship arrived in England I saw my future clearly. I would enjoy my year in Europe, I would go back to Sydney and practice law. I could not have been wronger.

CHAPTER 3

FIRST VISIT TO ENGLAND

The ten-week voyage had been uneventful religiously. There were seven or eight Redemptorist novices on board and we said the Rosary together every night. The Captain was a Catholic. They invited him to join but he said he didn't like the Rosary. I wondered what sort of a Catholic he could be.

Our arrival was—religiously—spectacular. For it was the fifth of November, and all the way from Tilbury to London we passed bonfires, with the Pope being burned in effigy, celebrating Guy Fawkes's failure three centuries earlier to blow up the Houses of Parliament. I was reminded of a quatrain in the Rejection Column of my school paper:

> On the Fifth of November, not in Lent,
> Englishmen did foully conspire,
> To blow up the Houses of Parli-a-ment
> With gun-pow-dire.

Later Hilaire Belloc told me that the Gunpowder Plot had been arranged by the King's Minister, Robert Cecil, to discredit the Catholics. I said, "How do you know?" He said, "Historical intuition." I have never learned if that is the sole foundation. But at least one would not put it beyond Robert Cecil: his father had spies among the monsignori in the Vatican: priests were hanged, drawn and quartered whose time of arrival in England he knew in advance.

On my first English Fifth, all I knew of the Elizabethan persecution of Catholics was gained from Robert Hugh Benson's *Come Rack, Come Rope*. What Queen Mary did to Protestants I had read about, as I have recorded, but I did not believe it. It was all part of my Catholic un-instruction—I had no means of knowing how close I was to its end.

I

Though nobody at the time saw it, Cardinal Moran of Sydney changed the course of my life one morning when I was around seven years old. He was visiting Rome: he looked in at Propaganda where a successor to Cardinal Vaughan, Archbishop of Westminster, was being chosen. The three names before them were of two Benedictines, Bishop Hedley and Abbot Gasquet, and Bishop Bourne of Southwark. I hasten to say that I was not there, what follows came to me from one who was. Apparently the choice lay between the two Benedictines. Cardinal Moran told of his grim experience of succeeding two Benedictine Archbishops in Sydney, a matter I have already mentioned. So Propaganda chose Bishop Bourne for Westminster, and he was made a Cardinal.

Cardinal Bourne let Vernon Redwood, a visitor from New Zealand who knew even less than I did about the Faith, found the Catholic Evidence Guild in his name and set up a platform in Hyde Park for the Faith's defense. It was probably the only incautious thing that cautious Cardinal ever did in his life. It was one of his successors who was known to his clergy as "the Safe Period." It might well have been he.

Coming out of St. Patrick's Soho on my second Sunday in London I was sold a ticket to a concert. Fate taking over? Having nothing else to do on the night I went to the concert. It was to raise money for a society I had never heard of, the Catholic Evidence Guild. With no thought of joining them I went to one of their training classes. It was conducted by Jack Jonas, who ranks with the Methodist minister Donald Soper and one other as the best outdoor speakers I have ever heard. The subject was the Marks of the Church, a phrase unknown to me though I knew of the words One, Holy, Catholic and Apostolic from the Nicene Creed. Having given his lecture on how to handle the Marks outdoors, he called on us to answer the questions hecklers had asked him. I volunteered, and he cut me to pieces. It was a superb demonstration, to me wholly convincing, of my ignorance of the Faith.

It was a shattering experience. I did not mind being taken apart thus publicly. What bothered me was the realization of my intellectual barrenness. Obviously I could not leave it at that. I came back for more. I attended the classes, I became a speaker. The year abroad I had planned became four. Since the Guild speakers were not paid, I got a job. My very Catholic mother came from Australia to join me in London.

In those four years I read practically nothing that had not a bearing on the Faith. I lived, breathed, ate, slept, theology. Yes, slept it. I once had a high temperature. When my Catholic secretary came to wake me one morning I told her that I had just been seeing quite clearly how man's freedom could be reconciled with God's eternal foreknowledge, and I must tell her at once. She insisted that I take my medicine first. By the time I had taken it, I had fogotten the answer to that towering question. Pity.

All that I have done in the fifty-three years since bears the mark of the Catholic Evidence Guild: some of it would be incomprehensible without the refashioning my whole self underwent in it.

At my first Guild class my ignorance of the Faith was stripped bare for me to see. In the next months I was to have four others firsts—my first outdoor effort, my first lost crowd, my first retreat, my first defeat by a heckler. All very educational.

After a couple of months of attending classes and reading furiously, I appeared before two priests, who heard a lecture by me on confession, heckled me hard, and gave me permission to speak and answer questions about it outdoors. I was told to speak at Highbury Corner the following Sunday night. There were to be two other junior speakers and an experienced speaker was to be in charge. I went to Highbury praying that rain might wash out the meeting. (I learned later that the Guild speaker might hope for rain but it was not good form actually to pray for it!) My prayer was not exactly answered. There was fog, which prevented the other two juniors from arriving: so that the senior and I had to run the whole three-hour meeting: I having the stronger voice did two hours.

My voice showed me Australian, so that there were questions about Archbishop Mannix of Melbourne. The troubles were on in Ireland and the British Government had sent a destroyer to take him off the ship on which he was on his way there. "The greatest British naval victory since Jutland," said the Archbishop, poker-faced. At the end of my two hours I felt that street speaking was right up my street.

I was soon cut down to size. It was at Finsbury Park. The senior speaker, a woman, had a vast crowd. She came down. I got up. In five minutes I had lost them all. She got me down, got up herself, and won the crowd back. I touched a low point in misery. I was able to balance things up later by marrying her: but the wound still throbs faintly. My wife dislikes my telling this story on the ground that she too has lost her share of crowds. I myself have lost a number since, but I don't remember a single one of them in detail, just an effect of human backs moving away from me. That first one is stamped on my memory. To say it made a speaker of me would be an exaggeration. But the speaker who has never lost a crowd remains a novice.

On Good Friday some other speakers and I went on retreat, my first. It was given by Father Ketterer, a Jesuit, at Campion House, Osterley. Naturally he talked on the Passion. I had never before seen anyone talk with his whole body as this Jesuit did. He fairly agonized. It was not to be my kind of speaking, but in him it was effective. Late on the Sunday afternoon the retreat ended. The small group of us were so fired with zeal that we went up to Highbury Corner, borrowed a fruit box from a stall nearby, and ran a meeting.

I met my first Christadelphian. As I understand their doctrine, they teach that everyone, good and bad, dies and stays dead till the end of the world: then the good rise to eternal happiness, the dead continue dead. He challenged me to prove that, apart from Christ, there had as yet been any life after death. I fell apart.

I could not even remember Dives and Lazarus. When in meeting later Christadelphians, I did quote them, I was met with the answer, "That was only a parable"—which was not much of an answer but the crowd thought it was! That night anyhow, I didn't remember even them. Still less did I remember Our Lord's saying on Calvary to the repentant thief, "I say unto thee, this day thou shalt be with me in Paradise." I was out on my feet. Years later I did quote this verse at an Australian street corner and was told: "You've put the comma in the wrong place. Christ said, 'I say unto thee this day, thou *shalt* be with me in Paradise'—at the end of the world of course," the questioner concluded triumphantly.

I told my sad story at the next Guild class and was referred to the fifth chapter of II Corinthians, where Paul notes how he would rather die sooner in order to be with Christ sooner—"We would rather be away from the body and at home with the Lord" (5:8).

Some time after, I learned how in the fourteenth century Pope John XXII had preached something very close to the Christadelphian doctrine (at least as regards the dead) in sermons in his church at Avignon: and had apologized for his error after instruction from a Cistercian who later, as Benedict XII, stated Paul's doctrine with all clarity.

On the Hyde Park platform one Sunday I was discussing the Incarnation with a heckler. I was fairly new to the doctrine myself, and the heckler and I were soon out of our only slightly different depths. There was a cleric in the crowd, not looking happy. When I got down I spoke to him.

"Are you a priest?"

"Yes."

"A Catholic priest?"

"Yes."

"A Roman Catholic priest?"

"Yes."

"Didn't I make a mess of it?"

"Yes."

As it happened, he was very Roman indeed. He was Cardinal Merry del Val, Papal Secretary of State, and a leader in the war against Modernism of which I have already spoken. By this time the war seemed to be over: it might be truer to say that Modernism had been driven underground in the century's teens, to explode in the sixties. With the ripe wisdom of hindsight, I feel that if the victory had been less crushing then, with more mind given to examining the questions raised, there might have been less of an explosion now.

The Cardinal fortunately had listened to other speakers besides me. He told Cardinal Bourne of his satisfaction with the work. In due course we were given by Rome the canonical status of catechists, with an indulgence granted each time we spoke outdoors. I remember how pleased we were about the indulgence. Who, apart from me, cares about indulgences now?

Coming to London with no Catholic schooling and a minimum of doctrine, I was for the first time living in a Catholic atmosphere, and I found it entrancing. The men and women of the Guild were intoxicated with the Church's doctrines. But if they were rigidly orthodox there was nothing else rigid about them. I have never since been in contact with a group so little cut to pattern. There was the General Secretary, for example, James Byrne. A heckler called him a liar. "You're another," he answered, "now let's get back to something serious." To prove that Catholics put the Virgin Mary above her Son, a heckler quoted praises of her by St. Alphonsus Liguori; Byrne answered, "Hot air, my dear fellow. Have you ever heard an Italian organ grinder making love?" I heard him say to a heckler who had been quoting a rash statement of Father Bernard Vaughan's, "There's nothing in the Code of Canon Law against ordaining fools." I remember his warning one of our priest chaplains against another of them—"If you go on listening to him you'll become as big a bloody fool as he is." "That's no way to talk," said the priest. "It's the way I talk," said our General Secretary. With a habit of daily Communion and the profoundest reverence for the priesthood, he treated each priest on his merits (he once explained to me that his brother was a priest, so he had no tendency to idealize!). None of the other Guild leaders talked like that: but I think there was an advantage for us in occasionally seeing the distinction in the Church between the man and the office applied here and now, so to speak.

For the making of that distinction occupied most of our time on the outdoor platform. Our lectures usually took round fifteen minutes, in the rest of the hour the crowd questioned us. Upon the papacy and Church history generally we had week after week, year after year, as unsparing a viva voce examination as has been known in the world—every charge ever brought against a Pope was leered at us, sneered at us. And from the beginning we were bound to the strictest honesty—there must be no bluffing or sidestepping. If we did not know the facts we must say so. We must find them out and tell them to the questioner at the next meeting.

So that, under the crowd's compulsion, we grew ever more clear-eyed about the distressingly human side of the Church, while remaining wholly determined to teach what the Church taught. You might think that this would be an impossible balance to maintain. In fact it was not. It was one of those dilemmas which solved itself in the doing.

We talked theology with one another all the time—at the meal we ate together before the class, on our way to and from the outdoor meetings (some of us spoke at four or five meetings a week). A powerful theological influence was one of the speakers who earned her daily bread scrubbing floors. Louisa Cozens had as gifted a theological mind as I have met. She had only a primary school education but had read and thought and lived theology. From her I first heard Boethius's definition of "person"—"a complete individual substance of a rational nature." In a Cockney accent but with an utterly lucid choice of words she told me what it meant. In 1928, after Maisie Ward and I were married, she came to our apartment after her day's scrubbing (having no quiet place of her own), and without reference books wrote A Handbook of Heresies, which is still in print. More than anyone she helped me to see the value of precision. The last conversation I had with her was on the problem of how the infinite simplicity of the divine mind could know individuals.

II

When, eighteen years ago, I fell off a platform in Hyde Park and was carried unconscious into hospital, the doctor said, "A street corner speaker is he? They're all crackpots." The Guild speakers, most of them anyhow, were not. Their sole eccentricity was that they could not sleep quietly while millions were starved of food Christ meant them to have. They were an unusual combination of dead-seriousness and total lightheartedness. They took the Faith seriously but not themselves. They sang about the work they were doing in songs that would have left some of our hearers wondering. Three especially are a reminder of the kind of people we were.

In all three my wife's brother Herbert had a main hand. He was a learned liturgiologist, Latin and Eastern. He handled English with notable neatness. He once said that he would have liked to be abbot in a lax monastery—the liturgy done perfectly, *and* the cooking. The first of our three songs was wholly his. It was about a Father O'Sullivan, parish priest of Sittingbourne, who advertised for money in the Catholic weeklies:

> You never will miss any trifle that's sent
> To Father O'Sullivan, Sittingbourne, Kent.
> What is given to his cause to the Lord it is lent,
> And the Lord will repay you ten thousand per cent.
>
> Ri-tooral-i-ooral-i-ooral-i-ay
> There's no need to worry the Lord will repay
> And it's clearly laid down by the Council of Trent
> That the rate of repayment's ten thousand per cent.

Ten thousand per cent is, of course, what the scriptural "hundredfold" works out at arithmetically.

With a Methodist friend, Herbert wrote, to the tune of "My Little Grey Home in the West," a sort of ode to the devil. It opened:

> Oh, Beelzebub's calling for thee
> His horns at the gate I can see
> His eyes are a-flashing
> His tail is a-lashing
> His face is a picture of glee.
> If you hurry up you will be
> Just in time for his afternoon tea,

> Hurry up, hurry up, for Beelzebub's calling
> Beelzebub's calling for thee.

It ended:

> Yes, Beelzebub's calling for thee
> He delights in a fixed liturgy
> So no hanky-panky with Moody and Sankey
> For they're on his Index you see.
> And vain repetition will be
> Exacted in large quantity
> Do you hear that dull moaning?
> 'Tis Satan intoning
> A welcome in plainsong for thee.

I wonder who now remembers the revivalists Moody and Sankey? And who remembers Our Lord's calling "vain repetition" heathen, a text thrown up at us all the time as against the Rosary? Anyhow the Index is not forgotten.

In 1923 there was an inter-faith meeting at Lausanne with the idea of a re-union of the Churches, based on what they all hold in common. Herbert and his brother Leo wrote to the tune of "God Our Help in Ages Past" their idea of what that was:

> The Pope who is infallible
> And seldom goes far wrong
> Has always taught that time is short
> Eternity is long.
>
> And in the East the Patriarchs
> Are singing this same song
> That time's comparatively short,
> Eternity quite long.
>
> And Lambeth thinks there is a sense
> In which 'tis not too strong
> To say that time to us seems short
> Eternity seems long.
>
> But some there are who tremble lest
> The march of modern thought
> May some day prove that time is long
> Eternity is short.

Bishop Darbyshire of the Scottish Episcopal Church introduced us to a stanza written—by Dean Swift, I have been told—against Calvinists, and singable to the same tune:

> We are the sweet selected few
> The rest of you are damned
> There's room enough in hell for you
> We can't have heaven crammed.

We cheerfully added it.

In fact we could do with a little cheering. Meetings could be splendid, but they were not all splendid. Talking outdoors in all weathers can be dreary, talking to a handful of people does little for one's morale. To a Catholic questioner who told me that we did the work because it gave us a sense of power, I said that the Guildsman's nightmare was of talking through all eternity on the windiest street corner in hell to three devils and a dog.

Small audiences and bad weather were not the worst of it. Our own performance could leave us miserable—answers muddled, Scripture misquoted, tempers lost, crowds antagonized. Coming back from a meeting one of the girl speakers said (in response to my request for a criticism), "You have an ugly face and an ugly voice and very bad manners. I don't know why anybody listens to you." The occasional letter to the Catholic papers asking if we were not doing the Church more harm than good we could have taken in our stride, if the same question was not bothering our individual selves.

We really did care, especially about the lost tempers. My wife began one meeting by telling a heckler she was sorry she had been rude to him the previous week. The heckler said, "You'll have to confess that to your priest." Maisie said, "I already have."

It has always been our rule to begin every meeting by saying the Our Father and Hail Mary, and end with the Creed. One of our songs ran:

> With a Pater and Ave and Gloria too
> We offer these prayers that some good we may do
> But if by our teaching our crowds we mislead
> At least we are orthodox saying the Creed.

It was pleasant fooling. But about the work we weren't fooling. We constantly compared our experiences, analyzed our failures, made rules for ourselves. Talking to audiences who could walk away and leave us talking to nobody at all, we learned the art of communication the hard way.

III

The outdoor speaker needs questioners if he is to gain and hold a crowd. We had them. At almost every meeting in those days we could count on members of certain violent No Popery groups, of whose existence the ordinary Protestant knew nothing, to heckle us about the bloodstained history of the Church and the sexual misconduct of popes and priests and nuns. It all took me back to my early boyhood when my Presbyterian grandparents introduced me to the fires of Smithfield, the Inquisition, and the Awful Disclosures of Maria Monk.

A whole parade of these men passes before my mind's eye. One of them was a man with burning eyes who seemed to loathe us. One night he failed to appear—the previous week at a meeting of his own he held up and ridiculed what he said was a consecrated host; Catholics in his crowd advanced on him menacingly, he ran, they caught him and threw him bodily over the park railings. He came back to heckle us only after a while.

A comrade of his, quieter in manner, concentrated on sex in the confessional. A number of junior speakers joined in a novena, praying that they might be free of him. They did not specify how. Before the nine days were over, he was arrested. He got two years for bigamy.

We who knew all these men were enchanted by an account in their magazine of one of them arriving at a Catholic outdoor meeting and "finding Brother X standing firm for the Lord." Their way of standing firm could be so very odd.

One of them used to stand in front of my platform facing the crowd and telling them of abominable crimes for which I had been imprisoned. Once he told me that he had been challenged by an atheist on the existence of God: he asked me to instruct him in some of the arguments he had heard me use: over a pot of tea I did my best. When I arrived for my next meeting he told me that he had won the debate. Five minutes later he was telling my crowd of my unspeakable past.

Another would tell the crowd that our young women speakers had solicited him the night before in Piccadilly. When this one died a young woman speaker said the De Profundis on the Hyde Park platform for his soul's repose.

There were any number more of them. They were paid for their performances, very poorly, as we learned. And we got the impression that some at least of them thought (wrongly of course) that we were paid as they were, had no more belief than they in what we were saying, and had, like them, to put on a colorful act to keep our jobs.

They were not an ideal context for the delivery of Christ's message. But there was no avoiding them. We learned to handle them, keep them in proportion so to speak, and use their questions as a basis for the instruction of the crowd. But we occasionally ran into an interjector who could spoil the meeting. There was an old man in Hornsey—over eighty—a bellowing voice, non-stop. I tried everything—outshouting him, threatening, appealing. Desperate, I tried cajoling. I said, "It's dangerous for an old man like you to be out on a cold night like this. You should be sitting at home by the fire, meditating on your latter end." "I'd like to put my boot to yours," he said. The crowd could not take me seriously after that.

One of our Dominicans was on the Hyde Park platform, discussing the commonest sins, helping his listeners to examine their own consciences. He came to "sinful thoughts." He said, "I won't go into detail. You have all had thoughts of lust, for instance, you know how trying they can be." A voice from the crowd: "Ow! I've got one now."

At every religious meeting outdoors there is a religious lunatic. He is usually on the platform. By training and testing we of the Evidence Guild saved ourselves from that. But we had them in the crowd. There was a man who believed he was the "whosoever" so frequently referred to in Scripture: he would repeat texts containing the word, after each text smiting his chest and saying, "That's me." There was a woman who spent the whole meeting praying for me—aloud! It was very distracting because I couldn't help listening with half an ear to find out what she was saying to God about me.

The professional hecklers were paid to raise trouble. But there were plenty of enthusiastic amateurs. I remember one at Newcastle upon Tyne. He was convinced that he was saved—beyond the possibility of loss. "I couldn't go to hell if I tried." That was fifty years ago, I hope he hadn't tried too hard. But he was a pain in the neck. He had a loud voice and seemed to be consumed with rage at all who were not as sure as he of eternal life. As I think back the "saved" as we met them outdoors were a gloomy lot. I can't remember a happy face among them.

One of them floats back into my head as I write. He heckled me at Southall. (Southall was the place where children were paid a penny each to be a nuisance. They earned their pennies. One of their habits was to pull out my shoe laces while I was speaking. Once they tied the laces to the uprights of the platform: I knew what they were doing, but to stop them I'd have had to interrupt my lecture.) At the end of the meeting my saved man walked back to the station alongside me, breathing abuse and threats. "Next week I'll bring my son to thrash you. I'd do it myself if I wasn't a Christian." That's what Salvation had done to him.

The questioners who were out for fun were a relief and could sometimes be made into an asset, keeping the crowd and ourselves happy. There was the man in the Sydney Domain who said to me, "*Your* brain is what you sit on." There was the woman who told a very young speaker that he still had the marks of the cradle on his backside. There was the man at Hampstead Heath who said to me, one night when I had a bad cough, "Excuse me, sir. I think there's something wrong with your throat. If I were you I'd get it cut." After forty years I have not been able to think up a snappy retort. Then there was an amiable old atheist who rebuked a woman who kept interrupting my wife: "Cease twittering, wench. The damsel *shall* speak." Courtly, don't you think?

The samples I have chosen have stuck in my memory from thousands of meetings. Not all crowds were difficult. American crowds in particular are notably courteous: I have never been called a liar on an American street corner. But the Catholic speaker who goes "out into the highways and by-ways" must be prepared for humanity in the rough. As one of our ablest speakers, Cecily Hastings, said: "We are the ones who work the stony ground." If anyone finds the idea repulsive, he can always stay indoors—the world that needs Christ so urgently will not be there to trouble him.

The man in Hyde Park who asked if there were lavatories in heaven was no profound theological thinker: he could not face the thought of eternity without a wall to write on, or he was just being funny. The speaker answered, "There will only be lavatories in heaven if there is waste matter to eliminate, as to which I have no information." I would doubt if an Ecumenical Council could have improved on that.

I was talking to a colored crowd on Chicago's South Side. A very tall Negro arrived, listened to me for a moment, then said, "Why do men love women more than women love men?" I told him that there seemed to be no statistics but I thought it possible that women loved men more and men loved sex more. His face lit up, and he went on his way, not thinking of religion.

Over the years the Guild helped a number of people to join the Church, but conversions were not our immediate concern. Most of our listeners were too far away from any active belief in God. When we did hear of converts from our meetings we were delighted of course. From one lunch hour meeting on Tower Hill, a few yards from the spot where Thomas More was beheaded, two hecklers joined the Church and went on to become Cistercians.

One other story of conversions pleases me by the way it falls into a pattern. It concerns two atheist hecklers—one in London, one in the Midlands. Atheist Number I became a Catholic, became a Guild speaker. When his daughter was nine she was found to be suffering from a kidney disease. Our ex-atheist prayed that she might be spared the pain, that he might have it instead. She died without much pain. Then it was found that he had the disease. I used to visit him in St. Thomas's Hospital. He suffered greatly, and died thanking God that his daughter had not suffered. Atheist Number II became a Catholic, a Guild speaker, a priest; he said a Requiem Mass for Atheist Number I.

P.S. A small grievance. A few years ago a TV comedian told the story of a Quaker gentleman and an atheist. The atheist ended a long catalogue of what was wrong with the universe by saying, "I could make a better universe than your God made." The Quaker gentleman replied, "I won't ask you to make a universe. But would you make a rabbit, just to establish confidence?" In fact I was the speaker, and told the story often enough before it reached television. It happened at a street corner near Liverpool. The atheist's name was Murphy. He did not make the rabbit.

CHAPTER 4

AN ECCENTRIC SCHOOL OF THEOLOGY

I am writing so much about the street corner crowds to whom I tried to teach the Faith, because they played so large a part in my Catholic intellectual formation. My university years in Arts and Law gave me one kind of formation, the writers I met in over forty years' publishing gave me another. But the crowds forced a general intellectual and specifically theological development not to be had elsewhere. One had to examine every doctrine—not only to answer the questioners, but to relate Christ's revelation to their appallingly various natures, in order that they might discover unrealized needs in themselves and find those needs met in Christ. Very early we learned that we could not meet their depths with our shallows.

One trouble was that a union of minds in depth was not easy, because of the hecklers, who were out either to make life impossible for us or simply to have fun. We could not invite the serious among our listeners to come apart into a quiet place with us. We had to take the crowd as we found it. That was our context and we learned to work in it. After all they had not invited us, we had invited them. And if our guests found us boring, that was their privilege. We had no right of complaint.

I

In our first days on the Catholic outdoor platform we had not a notion of the intellectual labor we were letting ourselves in for. As against the Reformation Protestant we felt we had only to prove that Scripture was not the sole rule of faith. As against the materialist we would prove the Existence of God, the Immortality of the Soul, the Credibility of the Gospels, plus of course the Divinity of Christ.

On all these topics there were well-tried "proofs," we had only to make sure we understood these, then go out and use them victoriously. We were the first body of Catholics who tested out the sword of apologetics in actual operation—not on paper, not on the convinced, but on the people whose doubts they had been devised to answer.

Very early we made the discovery that, valid as the arguments might be, they made precious little impression on the man in the street—that abstract figure who was so living a reality to us. There were a handful of concerned opponents who would fight them with considerable ingenuity. But on the ordinary listener they made no impression at all, because he did not attach enough meaning to God, or the soul, or the Gospels, or even Christ, to care whether the proofs were valid or not. How in any event could he weigh our reasons for believing till he knew what it was that we believed? If our conflict with the hecklers entertained him, he would stay and listen to it; but he himself remained untouched behind an indifferent "So what?" To contend with that we had to go ever deeper into the reality of God, and the soul, and the Gospels, and Christ. The outdoor crowd turned into a school of theology.

An eccentric school, I admit, but then we had our own share of eccentricity. It had none of the calm or the ordered procedures of a seminary. But it had an immeasurable, very unseminarian, vitality, with more than a touch of that wrestling with wild beasts at Ephesus which St. Paul tells of. Our listeners were their natural selves, only more so; they forced us to be ourselves, our worst selves too often.

And of course our examiners were different. In a seminary the examinations are conducted by men who already know the answers. On the street corner we offer our answers to men who do not. The seminarian's object is to show that he knows them, the outdoor speaker's is to get other men to change their lives. I doubt if marking seminarians' papers has ever led a professor to change his life. I tested all that my father said about Marxism by applying it to the people I knew. I came to do something similar with the Church's teaching, almost automatically thinking out how I could make this or that truth clearer to this or that audience.

Whatever we accomplished by our teaching, we ourselves certainly learned as we never could have learned elsewhere.

One way or another we learned the first rule of Ecumenism, that we must not attack other religions, but must find out what they meant to those who held them and lived by them. That rule grew easily into a habit. But its practical corollary that we must never try to score off, or raise a laugh at, a questioner—while easy to accept as a principle—could sometimes be hard to live up to. Yet it is the sheerest common sense. To make a questioner look foolish is to push him further away from the Faith, thus cutting right across our whole reason for being on the platform. One occasion I remember on which the rule was broken but the speaker was not censured. He was speaking on Confession. A rather ghastly woman in the crowd called out, "Your priests send young men from the confessional to make love to me." The speaker said, "I didn't know they gave such severe penances nowadays." We didn't find it in our hearts to censure him.

It was the obscene questioners who tested most fiercely our understanding of the rule of courtesy. One of our regular hecklers was especially foul-mouthed. One time the topic under discussion was Evolution. He said, "I am convinced I am descended from a beast." The speaker answered, "I don't know about you, but your son is." He should not have said it, of course; but the scurrilous, the blasphemous could get under our skin. When a man had spoken obscenely of Our Lady or the Eucharist, every instinct was for raging back at him. But we were on the platform to offer the Faith as help and healing. By his very foulness he showed how urgently in need of healing he was. It might seem hopeless, but our duty was to help.

I think the strangest objection I ever heard was made at a meeting in Walham Green (London, if you don't know). A man said, "Christ on the cross was unnecessarily melodramatic. He made too much fuss." I doubt if anyone had ever said or thought that of Calvary. The speaker, stunned by the objection's strangeness, said, "If ever you come to be crucified, I hope you will set us all an example of quiet good taste."

An occasional test of our charity was the Catholic who had had a few drinks, and who insisted on helping. It seems that three martinis will turn the most lukewarm Catholic into a crusader (or at least they used to—crusading is out of fashion). The non-Catholic drunk was easier on the whole. I remember one such at a meeting in Times Square, New York. He was a big man and he wanted a fight. He said to the speaker on the platform, "How much of a man are you?" The speaker said, "I fulfill the definition." The other stared at him for ten minutes, then went away muttering.

Talking of Times Square. A man said to me, "What's the use of giving us all this religious hogwash? Why don't you give us something to eat? *I'm hungry.*" He was well dressed and looked well fed. I offered him a dollar and told him of a hamburger stand fifty yards away. He would not take the dollar—he was only making a debating point. So, I suppose, was I.

Talking of "debating points" reminds me how common is the habit of dismissing an argument one cannot answer as "a mere debating point." I met a nice variant of this forty years ago at a meeting of a secularist society in Newark, New Jersey. Three or four times a rather persistent heckler, unable to counter some statement of mine, said "That's merely verbal." It is all part of the feeling that provided one says something, anything, the argument is not lost. Once I was discussing Our Lord's Ascension:

Objector: If he'd gone up into the sky in Australia, he'd have been upside down.

I: I can correct you on that. I have been up in the sky in Australia, and I was not upside down.

Objector: Ah, but you were in an airplane.

The truth is that the hecklers were a kind of mirror in which occasionally we might catch a glimpse of ourselves. They were bigoted and prejudiced—what about us? Their one desire was to win the argument at all costs—so too often was ours. In the order of practicality nothing was more useful in our outdoor life than being forced to consider bigotry and prejudice, in our hecklers, in ourselves. Bigotry does not mean believing that people who differ from you are wrong, it means assuming that they are either knaves or fools. To think them so is an immediate convenience, since it saves us the trouble of analyzing either their views or our own. "Christians are right, pagans are wrong," says the Song of Roland. If we have to answer the other people and find that we can't, then our bigotry grows more intense. It can turn to hatred: and one can reach the lowest point of all—measuring our loyalty to our own cause by our hatred of theirs.

Once we have faced bigotry in ourselves we can do something about it. Prejudice is harder to cope with. It is so instant, so easy, that we do not catch ourselves at it. Outdoors we saw enough of it, directed against ourselves, to begin to understand it. But I was suddenly shown its very essence by a story told at a Catholic Truth Conference. I remember the place of this Damascus vision, it was Birmingham. I remember the year, it was 1922. And I remember who told the story, it was a new convert from Ireland, Shane Leslie. He told of two old Catholic ladies in Dublin, passing by a lawn on which an elderly cleric was throwing a ball to a dog. Said one lady, "That's the Archbishop of Dublin." Said the other—"Ah, the dear old gentle man, simple and innocent as a child, playing with his little dog."

Said the first lady, "It's the Protestant Archbishop, you know."

Said the second, "Ah, the silly old fool, wasting his time with a pup."

I wonder if Shane Leslie knew he had given me a vision, did he even see the vision himself? Oddly enough in the fifty years of our acquaintance I never asked him. But vision it was.

Prejudice means weighing our side and the other side in different scales. The other side kills a lot of people, and it's a bloody massacre. Our side does exactly the same, and it's a regrettable necessity. Our side is accused of evil action and we demand the most rigorous proof: the other side is accused, and we accept the accusation out of hand, it's just the kind of thing those people would do!

Yes, it was a vision. Do I exaggerate in being reminded of Paul on the Damascus road? I'm afraid I do. What I saw is not to be compared with what Paul heard. But then I am not to be compared with Paul: the proportion between the experience and the man who had it may not be so very different in the two instances! Prejudice—in us—reduces the effectiveness of the Mystical Body, which is what Paul was being told about. Was Paul himself wholly free of it—not the sting in the flesh, but a sting in the mind? In any event it is a barrier to understanding between Catholics and Protestants.

It conditions not only our judgment but our memory. We remember what *they* did to us—the martyrs Queen Elizabeth hung, drew and quartered at Tyburn, for instance. They remember what *we* did to them, the martyrs Queen Mary burned at Smithfield. They remind us that we burned Cranmer. We remind them that Cranmer was one of the judges who sent Thomas More to his beheading: and for good measure we throw in the Anabaptist, Joan Bocher, whom Cranmer burned. And we all feel so reasonable—if we haven't seen the vision.

And with all the noise and confusion and mockery and lost tempers of the outdoors, we learned to get true dialogue. Probably the most learned man to speak on our Hyde Park platform was Abbot Cuthbert Butler, author of a vast work on the First Vatican Council. In his seventies he retired as Abbot of Downside, moved to London, came to speak for us. At first the crowd could not understand what he was saying. By the end of a year he had become a model of lucidity. If he had met the outdoor crowd earlier in life, what a towering writer he might have been.

II

What has half a century of speaking under the open sky done for my understanding of the Church? It forced me to study the Church as teacher and as ruler. Teacher first. We taught that we normally get the Church's teaching from our bishops; a given bishop or group of bishops might teach error: but anything clearly taught by the whole body of bishops we could accept as certainly true: it did not exhaust the subject, but further development could go on from there. For example, the definition by the Council of Ephesus that there was but one Person in Christ needed to be followed twenty years later by Chalcedon's definition that there were two Natures. As a sort of final resort, there was the Bishop of Rome. On the rare occasions—say on average one per century—on which the Pope had defined some part of Christ's revelation for the universal Church there would be no error in the definition. So we taught, anticipating the teaching of Vatican II on the Collegiality of Bishops. Very early we made the point about "definition": there might be a wide freedom of discussion and speculation in the Church: but a solemn definition by Council and Pope was infallible.

But, said the crowd, this meant two infallible voices: if the Pope taught one doctrine and the Episcopate taught a contradictory doctrine, whom should we believe? Our answer was that infallibility resulted not from any special ability in either Pope or hierarchy, but from the guardianship of the Holy Spirit over both. There could be no contradiction, because the same Holy Spirit which guarded the Pope against teaching us error likewise guarded the universal hierarchy. Were we, fifty years ago, anticipating Vatican III?

The crowd raised a further difficulty: if the Pope was infallible all by himself, why go to the trouble and expense of a General Council to guard him against teaching error? Today's reader may smile to think how we floundered about this, until we came upon the illustration used by the Jesuit Father Rickaby. It seems he would put to his students the question—If the Pope were infallible in algebra, how many marks would he get in an algebra exam? They all said 100, whereupon Father Rickaby gave them 0. He explains: For the rest of men there are three possibilities—we can give the right answer, the wrong answer or no answer. Infallibility means that the Pope cannot (in the appropriate circumstances) give the wrong answer— the Holy Spirit will not let him. That leaves him with two possibilities as against our three—he can give the right answer, or no answer. What decides? Whether he knows: infallibility does not in itself mean inspiration. The Holy Spirit might in a given case enlighten the Pope's mind, but that is not what infallibility is about. In the general way what a Pope does not know he must find out, like anyone else.

We and the crowd had much jesting about a Pope who might want to give an erroneous definition, but couldn't because the Holy Spirit wouldn't let him! Among ourselves we applied W. S. Gilbert's lines about the Lord High Executioner—"He always tries to utter lies, but every time he fails"—to papal infallibility.

At any rate we had no doubt that only the Holy Spirit could guarantee infallibility. Our questioners, and the reading of Church history they forced us to do, left no possibility of unawareness of the human defects of popes—like Benedict IX and John XII, who knew less theology than we ourselves. But whatever the condition of popes and bishops the solemn definition—the interpretation of Christ's revelation given to the whole Church—contained no error. This was no mere technicality: a solemn definition meant that the Church was prepared to commit herself and her Founder to her interpretation of his teaching. The definitions, I say, were not meant to be the last word. Given that they involve the infinite they could not be. But they are light-bearing, making them our own, we are in the light and can grow with light. Mastering, organizing, living fully in the territory already won is at best preparation for bringing new areas within the light. But definition or no definition there was the daily running of the Church—commandings and forbiddings by Pope or hierarchy for which no infallibility was claimed.

Revelation is not a labor-saving device. It gives men truth which without revelation they could not have. But its application to concrete situations as they arise is left for the Church to use its own mind upon: the men in charge praying for God's guidance; their prayers answered according to their sincerity—sincerity including the effort of their own thinking to understand both the situation and revelation's light upon it. Papal decisions could be made after profound examination, or they might be little more than routine. Not only that, they might be made with no special reference to Christ's revelation, solely on a best judgment of the situation. The burning of heretics, for instance, in the sad centuries when it happened, seemed to the popes who established the Inquisition the obvious way to save the heretic from damaging the souls of Christian men. They did not say Christ had explicitly revealed it as right, or that it flowed from anything he *had* revealed. There was no question of a definition, of course. It seemed to them such obvious common sense, God help them.

All this we were teaching fifty years ago. It might have made a trained theologian squirm. But it was not so very far from Vatican II's statement that civilization has its own law of growth, that God had not revealed what scientists and psychologists and archeologists and anthropologists were to discover about his universe: and that the application of what God had entrusted to the Church will change as the human situation comes to be better understood.

We grew in our understanding of the Church as ruler too. Laws, decisions, are needed for the running of the Church. We obey them, because all societies need laws: if men obeyed only the laws they thought good and wise, the result would be chaos, and chaos serves nobody. Only if conscience forbids are we justified in refusing obedience. In that also we were anticipating Vatican II—not that we needed Vatican II: it was what the Church had already taught us.

We knew, for instance, about that ghastly period in the fourth century when such a vast number of bishops, in terror of the Emperor Constantius, joined in an Arian condemnation of Athanasius. We know how, in terror of Henry VIII, all but one of the bishops of England signed a declaration that the King was head of the Church, in spiritual matters.

Our hecklers licked their lips as they taunted us with the Theophylact family, which appointed popes for the first sixty years of the tenth century. They paid special attention to Theophylact's daughter Marozia. She may have been the mistress of one Pope (though one must allow for the necessity, under which chroniclers are, of being interesting and Liutprand was very much the German Emperor's man). She appointed three popes, including her younger son. Her elder son Alberic defeated her in war and appointed four others— not bad as popes then went; but his son, Marozia's grandson, aged sixteen, became Pope as John XII—there surely never was a worse.

Yet within the Theophylact period, the monastery of Cluny,

which was to be so strong a civilizing and spiritualizing influence, was founded and grew mightily. And it was from the hands of John XII that St. Dunstan, one of the greatest and holiest of all Canterbury's Archbishops, received the pallium. The document accompanying it could hardly have been written by the not very literate Pope: it is a reminder that the Curia managed to carry on under the least pleasing popes, very much as the old human civil service kept the Empire somehow functioning under a chaos of emperors.

As to individual bishops, we were not allowed to forget the Bishop of Mainz whose financial deal over indulgences with Fuggers, the international bankers, had sparked Luther's revolt; or the boy of eight who had been made Patriarch of Lisbon because his family needed the money. And always of course there was the Inquisition.

III

Upon the human failings of popes and bishops, as I hope I have shown, we of the Guild were the best-instructed body of laymen in the Church's history. And none of this dimmed either our loyalty to our own bishop, or our certainty that from papacy and hierarchy the Holy Spirit would see to it that we got true doctrine and true sacraments. Unworthy pastors were the Holy Spirit's problem, not ours. It took us a while to grow into this knowledge. At the beginning we had a general notion that there had been some morally eccentric popes (but they had never defined anything!). We had not a notion of the tidal wave of papal and hierarchical ill-doing that was to break over us.

I smile when I think of our beginning, when we plunged to the defense of Christ's vicars with as little actual knowledge of papal history as our objectors had. I don't think I ever used the apologetical cliché of the time—there were only six bad popes out of 260, and that the Apostles had a far worse average, one traitor in twelve. The number six was arrived at by ignoring all the Commandments save one —the Sixth as it chanced—and assuming that only six popes had ever sinned against that one. There are of course other sins and worse sins: some of them can be in the depth of the soul, where only God can see them. We learned soon enough that one cannot list good popes and bad popes in two columns, gratified that the bad column is so much the shorter.

Before long we were telling our crowds that at the beginning of every Mass the Pope says like the rest of us that he has sinned exceedingly, in thought, word and deed through his most grievous fault. This may strike us as truer of some popes than others. But, looking simply at what history records, while we may feel that the popes present a magnificent totality, they have their souls to save. I am devoted to the papacy—without it there would be hundreds of debates and no adjudicator for any of them. I hope that if the test came I should die rather than deny it, as St. Thomas More and St. John Fisher did—though in their boyhood they had lived under Alexander VI and they went to their deaths under Clement VII. I admire all the popes I have lived under, but there have been some whom no one could admire. For them and for us, Christ is the point.

We used to give a splendid talk on the glory of the papacy: and we gave it hoping no one in the crowd would remind us of one of the handful of popes we and they had heard of as having had trouble with the Sixth Commandment. The mere raising of the question (however well we might deal with it) would smudge the idyllic picture we had painted.

Invariably someone did raise it. A questioner would say, for instance, that Pope Alexander VI had four children. At first, our speakers usually reacted in one of two ways. The diffident ones would say, "Oh no, only three were ever proved"; the truculent would say, "What if he had? Henry VIII had six wives" (the odds clearly in our favor six to four). It took us a while to realize that we were missing the point totally.

We were there to introduce people to Christ's Church. We were not prettying the Church for its photograph. Still less were we like lawyers with a shady client, trying to keep his worst crimes from the jury's knowledge. We had to show them the Church Christ founded exactly as it was and is. If they were scandalized by what they saw, they must take it up with Christ, who founded it, or with the Holy Spirit, who vivifies it.

The plan adopted by me and others was to *begin* our talks on the papacy with some "bad" popes. And I don't mean only ones who were sexually corrupt, like John XII, but worldly popes, cruel popes, frightened popes, like Clement V and Innocent X—one behaving badly, one madly, before the threats from French monarchs. Our aim was to show why we, knowing the worst—knowing indeed a worse worst than they themselves knew—still knew ourselves in union with Christ. However ill he might be served by his representative at any given time, we could still find in his Church, as nowhere else, life and truth and the possibility of union with him to the limit of our willingness.

The principal fact of life I did not know when I began is that one must never talk for victory—to show oneself right and the other man wrong. An immediate reason is that, if you talk for victory, sooner or later you will cheat. All polemic, religious or other, is stained with cheating. You may not actually lie, but you will be tempted to shade such facts as might seem to weaken your case, soft-pedal them, divert the discussion away from them. This sort of cheating or near-cheating goes with talking for victory. Whereas, if your sole aim is to show what you hold, and what are its effects upon life as it is lived, there is no temptation to cheat; there is quite literally nothing to cheat about. You open your mind, you ask your hearers for their comments. You are not trying for a decision. The questions under discussion are too serious for that sort of quick settlement, their roots lie too deep in the person.

In every man there is an unpinpointable element which makes the vital decisions, he himself hardly knows how and why: it accounts for what Chesterton has called "the mood of mystery, the nameless convictions, the certainties that have no origin and the hopes that have no end." The speaker cannot aim at this, he cannot pinpoint it even in himself; and what cannot be pinpointed cannot be aimed at: you may of course, by chance it would seem, touch a vital nerve. But what you hope is to have the other man's mind slowly react to the realities the Christian lives in and by. The way of it is the presentation of the truth. If we can show any truth clearly, it will do its own work in the mind. It is not the intellect which makes the decision, but it is the best way through to that in men which does.

The best way indeed, yet how poor a best we feel it. Any speaker, putting any piece of divine revelation into words, is conscious that he cannot convey his own best reason for holding it, which is what it means to him as he lives it, however imperfectly. Belloc has spoken for every one of us—"If I could have drawn a picture of that Face which commands us, written a score of that music which we hear, or presented a map of that country which we see, I should have done better." So should we all.

But since we cannot we must make do with words, which does not only mean choosing them well and saying them clearly. Teaching science or mathematics, even history or literature, the main thing is to be lucid. But for ideas which could call upon a man to change his life, lucidity is not enough. The self of the teacher has to make contact in depth with the self of the hearer. To say that the speaker must give himself with the truth adhering may sound pretentious, especially if you have the standard picture of the soap-box orator. But it is the minimum. The speaker and his message reach the hearer together. If the hearer finds the speaker repellent, the message hasn't a hope—it arrives discolored by, smelling of, the one who uttered it.

It may seem to be carrying pretentiousness to the point of fantasy when I say that what the speaker is aiming at is a union of minds between himself and his listeners as a result of which a truth living in one mind becomes a truth living in another. The analogy with bodily union is precise—and it goes with the analogy that both unions demand a concentration on the other party. The speaker who is listening spellbound to himself is not affecting a union of minds: in the bodily order there is a name for what he is doing, masturbation. In plain words each sort of union demands love. The speaker is genuinely making love to his audience. I have found the experience of making love to a different indoor audience every night in a long lecture tour, pretty draining. At the end of many a tour I have felt that I don't want to see another audience as long as I live.

Anyhow, whether or not the speaker is communing he must at least communicate; which means that he must labor at his utterance. If a speaker on religion does not spend a good part of his time making sure his hearers know what he is saying when he says "God," he wastes the whole of it. A closely related word that is little more than a familiar noise is "spirit." A questioner once asked me what it meant. I answered, "A spirit has no shape, no size, no dimensions, no color, does not occupy space." His comment, admirably just, was, "That's the best description of nothing I ever heard."

Somehow one must get one's listeners to see that the truth one is uttering actually matters, makes a difference that matters. But this means finding what *they* think matters. Time is wasted talking on the forgiveness of sins to people for whom sin is a dead word—with only actions that damage others seen as wrong, the notion of sins against God quite meaningless. There is no gain in talking about an infallible teaching authority till you know whether you and your hearers attach the same importance to certitude in religion. Before entering on a discussion of the Virgin Birth find out whether your hearers think there is any value whatever, spiritual or other, in virginity; if they regard the word as only a religious label for anemia, you had better spend some time on that before discussing whether Christ had a human father.

Dialogue is only superficially a to-and-fro of question and answer. It means two people looking at the same reality and comparing what they see. If on some matter—animal suffering perhaps—we see no light, there must be no pretense. Sharing our vision includes sharing our darkness.

Thus described the Outdoor Dialogue may sound too good to be true. So it is. I have described an ideal tried for, and once in a blue moon attained.

I have said we get them interested in God by bringing to the surface needs in themselves that only God can meet. This is only a beginning. A man thus brought into contact with God can come to want God not as healer or provider, but as himself. Religion has come alive in him. With this I am at the high point of what the platform has taught me: there is no stopping short of the Trinity. If we do, we are withholding the God of Jesus Christ. And there is no topic, not even the Inquisition, on which we can be more certain of holding a crowd. This is our secret: we shout it from the housetops, but we are not believed. I have never heard a sermon on the Trinity in my own Church. The books which tell one how to teach religion to the modern man vary in value (some of them would make a cat laugh, an experienced outdoor cat); but not the best of them mention the Trinity. Nor is there much indication of the modern man's ability to respond to mystery—in the sense that we cannot know God as well as he knows himself. All this means hard thinking for ourselves.

Upon what interests a crowd we of the outdoors cannot be wrong —because of our hearers' inalienable right to go away. When I began, I assumed that the Trinity would be beyond the minds of all but the highly educated. I was wrong. There is a real difference between highbrows and lowbrows, but intelligence has nothing to do with it. There are stupid highbrows, intelligent lowbrows—intelligence is pretty evenly distributed over the brows. Anything you can teach a highbrow you can teach a lowbrow, provided you can learn to say it in words the lowbrow understands.

Finding the words. Words are the problem for every teacher of religion, from God down to the street corner speaker. It is not only that it is impossible to utter a sentence which cannot be interpreted in more ways than one. More profoundly, it is the simple fact that words cannot contain the infinite (and if they could, finite minds could not extract it). Yet words are indispensable. The right words are light-giving. They are life-giving, provided the "unpinpointable something" responds. And over that the speaker has no control at all, and even the listener not very much.

I have mentioned occasions on which the response surprised the speaker. I end with the one which has surprised me most, namely the fascination the doctrine of the Trinity—not flat-footed figures of speech but the doctrine—has for the man in the street. With all diffidence I advance my own explanation. We have all had the experience of recognizing a photograph of ourself that we had never seen before. I think the response to the Trinity is rather like that, but in reverse—not the original recognizing the image, but the image stirring towards the original. For in God's image we are made.

CHAPTER 5

"AND REMEMBER THE INQUISITION"

I was speaking one evening in Baltimore—Hollins Market, I think. I had one persistent heckler. He made four or five accusations against the Church which it was easy to show had no substance. Discouraged, he turned to leave. At the edge of the crowd he swung round, raised his hat with old-world courtesy, said, "Good evening, sir, and remember the Inquisition," then went swiftly off convinced that with all my cleverness I could not get out of that one.

Crowds have changed greatly in the fifty years I have known them, questions once burning have burned themselves out. But two objections survive all changes of mental and spiritual fashions. One is the fact of suffering as an argument against belief in God. The other is the Inquisition, as a proof that the Catholic Church is a danger to human freedom. The Inquisition is the albatross forever hanging round the Church's neck.

People who do not know a single fact about the Inquisition take utterly for granted that it is of the Church's very nature to persecute when she can. Without the pressure from the crowds—without the questions we got at every meeting everywhere—we wouldn't have studied the Inquisition. If we hadn't, we should have been left with a gap in our own understanding of the Church. Heretic-burning was a question we had to face not only as speakers for the Church *but as members of it ourselves.*

I

I once heard the great English Dominican Father Bede Jarrett answer the question, "How can you defend the Inquisition?" by saying, "I would not dream of defending the Inquisition." One understands the feeling which produced the answer, but it won't do to leave it there. We cannot throw our ancestors in the Faith overboard quite like that. The Inquisition procedure may make our stomach heave. But the stomach is not what we judge with. We must find out why our fellow-Catholics of that distant day, members with ourselves of a Church we believe Christ founded, did what they did.

Having done no reading on the subject since my boyhood in my grandparents' very Protestant house, I still assumed that the stories of heretic-burning were a pack of lies. Some Protestants, I knew, had been burned by Catholics, but I comforted myself with the thought (which I saw no need to document) that Protestants did worse things to us. But all this was quite extravagantly beside the point. What others did is a matter for their conscience; our concern is with what we did. Beating one's own breast can be of great spiritual value, beating other people's is of none. So we settled down to look more searchingly at our own history—we have such a long space of time and such a vast area of the world for things to happen in; and wrongdoing catches the mind and clings in the memory more than virtue. When Dean Inge, the Anglican Dean of St. Paul's, called the Church "a bloody and treacherous corporation" he had quite a lot to go on.

The first effect upon me was sheer horror, I had not realized that things were so bad; when I got the facts into some sort of order the effect upon non-Catholics was disappointment, they had thought we were worse! My first concern was with the universally held idea that persecution is of the Church's essence.

In fact the Church has never claimed the right to inflict the death penalty. We have the great codification, made by Gratian in the twelfth century, of all the Church's laws up to that point; and since then we have actual records of every law the Church has made. Individual theologians have made this claim for the Church, but she has never made it for herself. So I told our crowds. They retorted that this only proves that the Church is hypocritical as well as cruel—she got others to do the killing for her. With that we were at the very center of the question. I had read everything I could lay my hands on.

At various points in history we find Catholic rulers slaying heretics —and occasionally Catholic mobs lynching them. The Church's attitude towards the action of the rulers varied with the centuries from disapproval through tacit approval to full-scale co-operation. But I think we can say that all the incidents which have branded the Church as a persecutor in the public mind are to be found in roughly one quarter of her existence. In the first twelve hundred years there were happenings we hate to read about, yet not sufficient in number or continuousness to fill the whole mind as it studies the Church. We wish they were not there, but they do not establish a character for the Church. The centuries in which the main charges against her are contained are the thirteenth through the seventeenth; and even in those centuries the level did not stay at one height throughout. There was the Mediaeval Inquisition, which had its main activity in the hundred years or so from 1230 onwards, there was the Spanish Inquisition, very much in operation in the hundred years or so from 1480. There was a good deal of sixteenth-century activity in Italy. And the Inquisitions did not tell the whole story, there were slayings in which they were not involved: England did not recognize the jurisdiction of the Mediaeval Inquisition, so that the Lollards like the Smithfield martyrs were burned under English law.

We might guess that the outburst of heretic-slaying in those centuries may have had something to do with the special circumstances of the times and the special nature of the heresies, rather than being read as symptoms of an ineradicable craving in the Church to persecute all who differ. And there was in fact something rather special about the heresies—we shall misread the Mediaeval Inquisition totally if we picture the Catharist of the thirteenth century as though he were twin brother to our own Methodist or Baptist friends.

When people talk about the Inquisition, they nearly always mean the Spanish Inquisition. But the Mediaeval Inquisition, established by Gregory IX two and a half centuries earlier, really involves the Church as the terrible court set up by the Spanish monarchs does not. The earlier Inquisition actually was the Church's own affair. There is no understanding the whole matter of heretic-burning without studying it. And the key to the study is the heresy called Catharism. The machinery set up to handle Catharists was later used against others, like the Waldensians, but it is a fair bet that it would not have come into existence but for the panic Catharism aroused.

The heresy was a close relation of Manicheeism, founded by the Persian Manes in the second century and best known to Christians because for so long it held the great Augustine. In the tenth century we find it flourishing in Bulgaria. From Bulgaria it moved to the South of France, where in 1022 King Robert sentenced thirteen people to death for professing it. Its adherents were called by half a dozen names, but principally Bulgars (which gives us one of our more vulgar words), Cathari, from the Greek word meaning pure ones, and Albigensians, from the town of Albi in the South of France, which they held.

There were sects among them; but fundamentally Catharism was based upon the principle of two powers in conflict, Light, which held the spiritual world, and Darkness, which held the world of matter. The supreme sin was to bring children into the world, since it meant drawing spirits down into the darkness of matter. All sexual activity, therefore, was sinful. We might wonder how a religion which thus made celibacy a rule of life could have spread as rapidly as this one did. The answer lies in the two levels of membership: there were the *perfecti*, who accepted the full rule, initiated by a kind of sacrament called the *consolamentum*; and there were the *audientes*, who accepted the ideal, but did not bind themselves to practice it—they might indulge themselves sexually with a good deal of freedom, this being understood as a weakness of the flesh: their plan was to receive the *consolamentum* on their deathbed and die as *perfecti*. The one really grave sin for such people was marriage, because this appeared to treat the sexual act as though it were legitimate.

One of our difficulties in understanding Catharism is that while it has left some statements of its fundamental doctrine and its liturgy, it has left no statement of how its members lived it. We learn of it only from those who hated it. And Catholics have reason to know how untrustworthy is any statement about a religion by those who do not know it. We have one piece of evidence, namely handbooks published by Inquisitors for the interrogation of Catharists. Unless the questions really did apply to Catharist practice, they would have been of no use for their grisly purpose. What is quite certain, anyhow, is that what I have outlined is what Catholics *thought* Catharists believed. Knowing that this is how they saw it puts us in a better position to understand the way they reacted to it. The truth seems to be that while many were attracted to it, those who were not saw it as a nightmare. If we are horrified at the ferocity with which they fought it, we must remember that nightmare.

It was not a matter of the Church's using secular rulers as her instruments in the warfare. The rulers were fighting it long before the Church. We have noted that the first Catharists were burned in Europe in 1022. The Inquisition was not established until 1231. In between every ruler who had to deal with them tried to destroy them —as indeed the pagan ruler Bahram (Omar Khayyám's "great hunter") had slain their founder Manes. In the two-hundred-year gap that we are now considering, we find mobs lynching them and rulers (often enough hostile to the papacy) making death the penalty for the practice of their religion. Among these we find Henry II of England, who had St. Thomas à Becket murdered and spent a good part of his reign fighting the Pope. Even more notably we find the Emperor Frederick II, who led armies in battle against the Pope, and was only dubiously a Christian himself. Such men saw Catharism not as a danger to religion, but as threatening the very basis of society —very much as England was to see the widow-burning of the Hindoos and America was to see the polygamy of the Mormons.

There was a horrible crusade against the Catharists just after 1200. In the twenties of that century the Pope's greatest enemy, the Emperor Frederick II passed a law making burning the penalty for heresy, and explaining in the preamble to the law that he did so in defense of the state. Why, with such a flood of repressive action unloosed against Catharism, did the Church have to intervene after so long an interval? Why in 1231 did Gregory IX establish the Inquisition? It seems probable that it was to check the Emperor, Frederick II, whom he saw as always acting to widen his own power. Gregory did not deny the state's right to protect itself: these heretics were a threat to life itself, and the state was entitled to put them to death: but, as to whether people were in fact heretics, that was for the Church to decide, not the state.

So he set up his Courts of Inquiry—that is what Inquisition means. If a man was accused of heresy, two ecclesiastical judges would examine him; if they found he was a heretic, and if he refused to change his mind, they would hand him over to "the secular arm"—the state: the law would then take its course. The Inquisitors were usually Dominicans, as being trained theologians, occasionally Franciscans.

Stated like this, the idea seems not unreasonable. But there was more to it. To start with, the Inquisition did not restrict itself to examining people accused by the state. The Inquisitors took the initiative. They would come to a town and call upon the citizens to denounce heretics known to them. Later we find popes urging the states on to greater rigor under threat of excommunication. And it was an appalling chance that two of the first Inquisitors—Conrad of Marburg in Germany and Robert le Bougre, a convert from Catharism, in France—were ferocious men, Robert indeed a homicidal maniac. In one day he had 180 heretics burned, all of them examined within a week! Conrad was assassinated, Robert ended in a lunatic asylum. The Mediaeval Inquisition never again reached such peaks of horror.

As courts went, this one was conducted with reasonable care to get at the truth—informants who made false accusations, for instance, were liable to the same penalties as heretics. But twenty years after the Inquisition was founded another Pope, Innocent IV, introduced torture into the procedure.

I was invited to lecture to the Dominican novices at Hawkesyard Priory in England on the feast of St. Peter of Verona, an early Inquisitor murdered by a Catharist. I had mentioned that Peter had not tortured any heretics, torture not being part of the procedure. A novice asked how long after his death was torture introduced. An older friar in the front row boomed out, "Centuries." I said, "Months."

It was all to be very "legal," as Innocent stated it, not lasting more than a certain length of time, not causing mutilation; in general it was to be applied only when guilt was certain. It would be as foolish to get one's idea of the Inquisition from Poe as of Hell from Dante. The famous circular saw swinging ever closer to the victim lying bound beneath it is pure Grand Guignol: the Inquisitors would have thought it unprofessional! And a genuinely holy Inquisitor like St. Peter Arbués would have been horrified at the cat-and-mouse torturing of which he is accused in a famous story by Villiers de l'Isle-Adam. All the same the whole business is sickening, and we reflect with relief on what Pope Nicholas I had said four hundred years earlier—that the "use of torture is against all laws, human and divine."

This particular Inquisition was in normal operation from 1231 to about 1340. It continued to exist, and there were periods of activity afterwards: the English used it to have Joan of Arc sentenced as a heretic. How many heretics did it hand over to death? There is no way of knowing. But we have figures of individual courts for particular periods. Thus at Toulouse, a strong center of heresy, in the fifteen years from 1308 to 1323, out of over 900 tried and over 700 found guilty, forty-two were burned. The figures are unpleasant enough. But it was no bloodbath.

II

As I have said, Catharism seemed a nightmare to the men of that day. But Catharism is long dead, and for us the nightmare quality does not exist. We read of it with curiosity but no horror, for to us it carries no threat. What remains is the historical fact of the Church's part in its repression and destruction. Which raises the question how her action is to be reconciled with the love of Christ.

As we read what happened, we are startled to find that Gregory IX, who founded the Inquisition in 1231, loved St. Francis of Assisi and established the Franciscan order. We may be even more startled to find the Inquisition approved by saints—like St. Thomas Aquinas— who had more love in their little finger than you and I in our whole body. To have maltreated heretics through hate they would have known to be sinful. They were driven by love—love not only of God, whom they saw the heretic as insulting, but of the souls they saw brought to mortal peril by the spread of heresy. Such men would themselves have suffered torture and death for love of souls: it was no passage from love to hate that made them feel that men should suffer no less who were putting souls on the way to hell. Men who scourged their own bodies—as all the Inquisitors did, as all members of religious orders were bound to do by their Rule—might not be as delicate as we about scourging other people's.

There were brutes among the Inquisitors, but the men behind it were not brutal. We shall not grasp the meaning of the Inquisition if we see it as defect of love. It was defect of vision—a defect shared by all the Protestant Reformers. We note this not for their blame or the Church's defense, but for our own understanding of the whole thing.

They assumed that the heretic was an evil man in bad faith—for we note that the Inquisition was concerned only with the baptized, with those who had had the Faith and rejected it; it had no jurisdiction over Jews or infidels. Psychology had centuries of development still to make before it could be realized that the heretic might truly love God, that the guilt of his rejection of the Church could be diminished by all sorts of personal factors. There was ill-instruction, for instance, many a Catholic-turned-Catharist had never had a pennyworth of instruction in Catholic doctrine; and only a very well-instructed Faith could be sure of standing up against the contrast between the luxurious lives of many a Catholic ecclesiastic and the austerity of the *perfecti* among the Catharists.

And it was not only the danger to souls from heresy in general that moved popes first to approve, then to take a leading part in, the repression of Catharism. With their teaching that it was a deadly sin to bring children into the world, the Catharists were threatening the human race with destruction. That the race should react is natural, that it should react ferociously is not surprising.

I have used the word nightmare more than once. And it is precise. In addition to this certain horror in Catharist teaching, there were rumors of horror, less certain perhaps but not improbable, and certainly believed. Since homosexuality was the surest way of keeping children unborn, it was assumed that the Catharists practiced it; Bulgar has actually come to mean bugger. Earthly life being evil it was assumed that the Catharists thought suicide a virtue. Above all, there was the *endura*. The rank-and-file Catharist received the *consolamentum*, binding himself to total celibacy, only on his deathbed. But supposing it proved not to be his deathbed? If he recovered, he might easily fail to stay celibate. The *endura* meant that once he had received the *consolamentum* no food was allowed to reach him. He died perfect. And the rumor spread that the *endura* killed more Catharists than the Inquisition.

That the state should try to stamp out Catharism with any degree of rigor is comprehensible: that the Church should co-operate is comprehensible too. But the use of torture sticks in our throats. It was normal in the civil courts of the time. In the ecclesiastical courts it was supposed to be used only when the man's guilt was certain— it was thought to be spiritually good for him to confess. The psychology behind this is primitive to a degree—as if saying what one's torturer wants, in order to stop the agony, could be of any spiritual value at all. To me the Inquisition is more of a nightmare than Catharism ever was to Innocent IV.

We seem to be facing a lag in civilization, with the ecclesiastics taking for granted what their age took for granted, in spite of the strong attack on torture made four hundred years earlier by Pope Nicholas I. As Vatican II pointed out, civilization is not the Church's special business. She could not make Einstein's discoveries, or those of hundreds of others, but her rulers have to apply Christ's revelation to a world changed by Einstein and those other hundreds. We can no more blame mediaeval Catholics for not knowing modern psychology than for not knowing modern physics.

People who have forgotten all the reasons their grandparents may have had for disliking the Church, still have a feeling that if the Catholic Church ever got power again, she would certainly burn all who disagreed with her. Glance at that If. It looks highly unlikely that it will be realized in any measurable future. Are practicing Catholics a majority in any large country anywhere? Spain perhaps. Not that Catholic majorities mean that the Church is in control. Throughout what we call the Catholic centuries, kings fought popes: and today the Spanish Government has demanded and received a larger say in the appointment of Catholic bishops than any other in the world.

Would the Church ever want the Inquisition restored? Foreseeing the future is a difficult business. Even before the Council's Declaration on Religious Liberty it seemed unthinkable that the slaying of heretics would ever be urged by the Church in any conceivable future. But then the thirteenth-century Inquisition would have seemed unthinkable to—say—St. Martin of Tours, who in the fourth century raged against the beheading of the heretic Priscillian, or to Pope Nicholas I, who in the ninth century declared that the use of torture was against all laws human and divine. All the same it remains unthinkable that the mediaeval repression of heretics should return. Burning, of course, belonged to that age: it was not simply thought up against heretics, it was the normal punishment for public crimes, crimes against the structure of society: we need not anticipate its return. But will any sort of religious persecution return? And will the Church be involved?

There are two special reasons why the Church would not again want the state to use violence in the interests of religion. One of them is in the practical order; the slaying of heretics has done more harm to religion than the heretics, left alive, could possibly have done. The minds of the generations that followed have found it revolting, and see the Church as hateful because of it. Catharism was indeed destroyed in the South of France by the end of the fourteenth century, but the Faith is not very much alive there. The Protestants Queen Mary burned at Smithfield did more to "establish" the Church of England than all Queen Elizabeth's legislation. It has never been good for the Church to have the world think it sees on heretics the suffering face of Christ.

But the other reason goes far deeper. The realization has grown that men can be in error about religion yet love God passionately all the same. It is hard for us to think ourselves back into the mind of our ancestors—Catholic and Protestant alike—to whom a heretic was, could only be, a bad man. On both sides they compared heresy with forgery—each debased the currency: the penalty for a forger was a particularly cruel death: the penalty a heretic deserved, they argued, could hardly be less. But there was one enormous difference—the forger was acting solely for his own gain, and knew that he was defrauding the state, but the heretic was convinced that he was serving God and the souls of men.

It is a whole advance in civilization. At any given time the rulers of the Church will apply the teaching of Christ to the world *as they see it*; with advances in anthropology, psychology and science, as Vatican II reminds us, with the sheer experience of living, they come to see the world differently—better and more deeply—and the application of the teaching changes accordingly. That is my strongest reason for saying that the return of mediaeval repression is unthinkable—even if it were physically possible.

I have gone into some detail about the Inquisition, partly because it has stood as a deep and continuous accusation against the Church, partly to show how seriously we of the street corner took our duty to the audience. Above all, I had to get my own mind, my own faith, clear about it. Until recently one found a minority of Catholics who defended the Inquisition and regarded our exploration of it as disloyalty. Neither they nor we knew that at Christmas 1958, John XXIII would describe other Christian bodies as "bearing the name of Christ on their forehead," thus writing finis to the whole grim business. Nor did we know that Vatican II would make a Declaration of John's finis.

CHAPTER 6

I LOSE MY AWE OF BISHOPS

I had left Sydney halfway through my law course, meaning to spend a year in Europe: after which, a citizen of the world, I should come back to Sydney, do the last two years of my course, and take my chance as a barrister. For that plan I had saved enough to pay my way for a year. But once I decided to stay on in England and speak for the Catholic Evidence Guild, I had to find a job. Neither the speakers nor the officials of the Guild are paid anything at all.

I

I became Organizing Secretary of the Catholic Truth Society, founded some forty years before, by James Britten, to publish pamphlets on Catholic teaching and Catholic practice. In my time, and ever since, one could find their pamphlets offered for sale at the back of churches throughout the British Isles.

The Society was about to begin a Forward Movement—to raise the number of annual subscribers from 15,000 to 30,000—under the direction of an American, William Reid-Lewis. He was quite definitely a character. We were told that he had barely been restrained from shooting a man who was showing too great an interest in his wife. For all I know, the story may have been an invention—his own or someone else's. Anyhow one always had a feeling of a gun on his hip. I remember his telling me that he was planning to establish a fund for buying penny catechisms for Dominicans, and one of my earliest duties was to go to Brighton and persuade a parish priest not to delate to Rome a Dominican who had preached in his pulpit that there was no reason why Christ should not have married.

In no time at all, Reid-Lewis was quarreling with the Society's founder, James Britten. As I have related, I had been born into religious strife—my Presbyterian grandparents, my Marxist father, my Catholic mother. But I was to discover that this was as nothing compared with the ferocity of infighting among Catholics. As it happened, I had already been blooded in the Catholic Evidence Guild. Its founder had also founded the Fellowship of Freedom and Reform, financed by the brewers to fight against Prohibition. We felt that he saw the two societies too much as one thing. Those of us who didn't—headed by the secretary—were trying to persuade him to restrict his activities to the other society. There was a great deal of sound and fury.

One night I was lecturing to the training class on the Incarnation. The secretary was in the Chair, just behind me. The founder strode in, and began a whispered argument with the secretary. The argument grew hotter. I heard this pleasing bit of dialogue:

Secretary: You're a bloody liar.

Founder: You dare to call me that, *me*, a daily communicant!

Secretary: They're the worst.

I continued to talk on the Incarnation.

In the Catholic Truth Society battle, my immediate superior was Reid-Lewis. I had no contact with James Britten. I should have liked to tell him that when my mother was a small girl, she had been in the choir he conducted at the Catholic church in Brentford. But that would have been consorting with the enemy. Cardinal Bourne ended the uproar by asking them both to resign, and appointing Stephen Harding in their place. He had been assistant to my wife's father, Wilfrid Ward, when he edited the *Dublin Review*. I worked most happily under him.

But a continuing trial to me—and I think to him—was the Episcopal Chairman, the half-Spanish Bishop Emanuel Bidwell. He was my first Ecclesiastical Bureaucrat, and a master of the art of stopping anything happening. He had a bald, egg-shaped head. A friend of ours said she never saw him without wanting to take a teaspoon and crack it. There were times when I would have liked to crack it myself, and not with a teaspoon. I remember the mild pleasure we got from hearing a female relative say to him, at a Catholic gathering, "Come along, Manuelito." It seemed to reduce him to size. But that made no difference at Committee Meetings of the Catholic Truth Society. At those he was full-size.

Though he never did me personally any harm, it was clear he didn't think much of me. But there was nothing he could do about me, as subscriptions were rolling in. When I was leaving London to return to Australia and finish my law course, I asked him for a testimonial. I did not expect to need one as a barrister, but I thought it would be fun to see what he would say. Fun it was. "Mr. Sheed

worked for the Catholic Truth Society for four years and gave satisfaction." I wonder how good a job that would have got me.

As organizing secretary I was supposed to double the number of
annual subscribers to the Catholic Truth Society. In the past
members had been won by an occasional sermon in church. My first
plan was to send special preachers and have an appeal made at every
Mass in every church of a given town—saturation preaching—followed by a meeting in the town hall on the Sunday night. Soon I
added an outdoor meeting on the Saturday night, addressed by me
(and often by Maisie Ward, who did voluntary work for the Society
as its Librarian) along with as many of the visiting preachers as I
could entice onto the platform.

I cannot remember if it was at this time or later that I got Archbishop McIntyre to agree to speak in the old Birmingham Bull Ring.
I was to get up for ten minutes, gather the crowd, and promise them
the Archbishop. At the end of an hour he had not appeared. The
crowd was threatening to lynch me. I learned afterwards that he had
put on his episcopal robes, but some of the older clergy kept urging
that to speak outdoors would be undignified for an archbishop. He
robed and unrobed a couple of times. At last he came, gave a
splendid sermon, and led a vast crowd back to the cathedral for
Benediction. (The only other bishop with whom I ever spoke outdoors was Bishop Wright, in a park at Pittsburgh. I learned that here
too some of the clergy were troubled. One of them urged him at least
not to wear his episcopal purple. He said, "I am a bishop. I will not
speak in disguise.")

Catholic societies being what they are, there were those who mur-
mured that I was using the Truth Society to enlarge the Evidence
Guild. Enlarged it certainly was. Within a couple of years there were
Guilds all over the country.

The Catholic Truth Society had two branches—in Manchester
and Liverpool—and with the flood of new members, they felt increasingly that some of the funds should be given to them to use in
their own areas. The Society's Episcopal Chairman, Bishop Bidwell,
of whom I have already spoken, held them off masterfully. He saw
to it that the business of the branches came late on the agenda, and
he spun out earlier items, so that they had to leave to catch the last
train home before their business was reached. Incredibly, they put

up with it. Bishops were given such a degree of deference then: it was a different world.

But with Scotland, London overreached itself. There had been some talk about giving the CTS of Scotland branch status. The London officials thought that there was complete agreement, and sent me to finalize arrangements. When I got there the heather was on fire. Before I could open my mouth the Glasgow Committee set about tearing me apart: I represented England, chains and slavery. Scottish Nationalism had a field day—Flodden was avenged and Bonnie Prince Charlie. They all but sang "Scots wha hae wi' Wallace bled." As an Australian, my withers unwrung, I found it fascinating. I wouldn't have missed it.

There was one Englishman on the committee, Professor Philimore, who held the Chair of Latin at Glasgow University, or Greek perhaps, I don't remember. He was a new convert, a close friend of Belloc and Chesterton. Chesterton tells how he completed the third from last stanza of *The Ancient Mariner*. It begins, you remember,

> He prayeth best who loveth best
> All things both great and small.

Philimore altered this to

> All things however small

and added

> The streptococcus is the test
> I hate him worst of all.

Another story I heard of him on that visit. As at Sydney University, students were accustomed, by shuffling or stamping their feet, to remind lecturers when the hour was up. There was an occasion on which they thus reminded Philimore. He answered, "I'm sorry, gentlemen, I still have some pearls to cast."

As I have said, he was a member of the committee that tore me apart. He took no part in the rending. He entertained me lavishly after it. Through him I met Dr. Flood, whose habit it was to enter the Glasgow pubs towards the end of the evening, carrying a large stick, and persuade his parishioners to leave. I had often heard of the Father O'Flynn type of priest—

> Helping the lazy ones
> On with a stick

but Dr. Flood was the only one I ever met. To me he was wholly urbane.

I returned to London to report the failure of my mission: the Scottish CTS would remain independent. Bishop Bidwell, I think, thought it was all my fault: they should have sent someone else. Ah well!

II

The nearest I had ever come to a bishop in my Australian boyhood was seeing Cardinal Moran lay a foundation stone at Leura, in the Blue Mountains. Apart from that all I knew about bishops I had learned from Canon Sheehan's novels of Irish life. From them I got the general impression that bishops were lordly beings, unapproachable, formidable. It was later I heard the answer to the question, How many bishops are there in Ireland?—"There are no bishops in Ireland. There are sixteen popes." On my first visit to Dublin I met Archbishop Walsh, rather shy, very gentle. I was told that he regarded Eamon de Valera as a murderer, refused to speak to him or see him, dealt with him through secretaries when he had to. True? Half true? I don't know.

Through the Truth Society and the Evidence Guild I came to know a dozen English bishops in their own houses. They had neither the lordliness nor the corruption of the bishops served up to us by our street corner objectors. With a couple of exceptions they were disappointingly like anybody else. Certainly I never met a cardinal like Cesare Borgia or even Richelieu.

My first cardinal was Bourne of Westminster. I met him, so to speak, before I did. At Highbury Corner a heckler accused him of living extravagantly in the midst of poverty—he had a suitcase which cost the then equivalent of a thousand dollars. I said, "How do you know?" "I made it," said the heckler. Long afterwards I was startled by the contrast between the Cadillac which met my wife and me at an Indian airport and the squalor of the slums through which we drove. I learned that the Cadillac was a present to the diocese from Cardinal Spellman.

My guess is that the expensive suitcase was a present too. I came to see a lot of Cardinal Bourne, and nothing could have been more moderate than his living style. He was a man rather cold in manner. One could not imagine him telling a funny story or laughing at one.

But there was warmth in him somewhere. During the Modernist uproar twenty years earlier he had insisted, against all pressure from
heresy hunters in Rome, that there was no Modernism among his
clergy. When his successor in Southwark forbade Maud Petre the
sacraments for her support of the Jesuit Father Tyrrell, she had only
to cross the Thames and receive Communion in Westminster.

I had nothing but kindness from him. He gave me two rules,
"Don't ask my advice. Just tell me what you're doing. I'll stop you
if I think it necessary." He never did. Another time he put it even
more concisely: "I never start anything. But I never stop anything."
When I was a publisher his censor demanded a vast number of
changes in one of our books. I complained to Cardinal Bourne. He
said, "I won't alter the censor's decision. But I won't mind a bit if
you appeal to Rome." I said, "To whom should I direct the appeal?"
He said, "I have no idea." We got along splendidly.

Bishop Dunn of Nottingham had inherited a troubled diocese.
Into the compassionate ears of one of his predecessors, priests in
trouble with their own bishops had poured the stories of their wrongs
to such effect that the diocese became known by a title from the
Litany of Our Lady, "Refuge of Sinners." When this particular
bishop visited Rome, the Pope suggested that he might resign.

Bishop: But why, Your Holiness?

Pope: Because of your age.

Bishop: But I am younger than Your Holiness.

Pope: Ah, but I have kept my faculties.

Bishop Dunn, with whom I stayed many times, was as cool and
unemotional a man as I have met—perhaps because his mother had
become a nun when he was a child. He told me that towards the end
of the war, when there was an acute paper shortage, he had managed
somehow to secure a number of toilet rolls and had given one to each
of the cathedral clergy as a Christmas present. Someone asked him
if he had had each roll monogrammed.

In Newcastle upon Tyne I found a good friend in Bishop Thor-
man. He told me of the first visit he paid after his appointment, to
an old priest friend. As he left the friend said, "Well, good-by Joe,
and remember you've heard the truth for the last time." I cannot
resist repeating a story of his predecessor, Bishop Wilkinson, told
me by the Dominican Father Hugh Pope. Father Hugh was giving
a retreat to the seminarians at Ushaw. The Bishop had invited the
local Anglican vicar to meet him at dinner. In a booming voice the

vicar told of his curate, who insisted on going to confession to him: "And he only has one sin. I'll tell you what it is." The enchanted seminarians laid down their knives and forks: Bishop Wilkinson tried to hush him, but the vicar boomed on, "His only sin is that he doubts my power to absolve him. And as I doubt it myself, I find it very difficult."

I have come across plenty of episcopal oddness since—about which bishop was not on speaking terms with which, for instance; or whose influence got which diocese for whom. I do not go into detail, because such things are merely evidence that the hierarchy is composed of human beings, people like ourselves, a fact which will emerge throughout this book. But one story floats into my head which it amuses me to tell about two bishops whom I happened to know. Bishop Browne of Galway, a magisterial man, issued an order that the priests of his diocese should not smoke in public. One day driving across a bridge he saw a cleric, a stranger, smoking. He stopped the car and sent his secretary to tell him he mustn't. The answer was, "The Archbishop of Baltimore presents his compliments to the Bishop of Galway and will smoke where he likes." The Archbishop of Baltimore was even more magisterial, as his clergy knew. Yet he once told me of his pleasure in Bruce Marshall's highly irreverent novel *Father Malachy's Miracle.*

I am putting in all these bits and pieces to indicate how early I lost my awe of bishops. It has made communication easier. But it has carried a danger with it. When bishops take a man for granted they will pay him the compliment of speaking freely in his presence: one learns soon enough what things are told in confidence, not meant for publication. But I learned something else. In the give and take of clerical conversation as of all conversation, men express opinions, spur-of-the-moment things, or things said to see what the others will make of them. I know two bishops, one of them a cardinal, who would make odd statements simply to start an argument. Solemnly to quote such things against them would show that one has not understood the nature of civilized discourse.

III

On the Feast of the Assumption, in 1924, I asked Maisie Ward to marry me. I returned to Sydney to finish my law course and begin real life, after four years of doing what I wanted in the Catholic Truth Society and the Catholic Evidence Guild.

I have never had a busier eighteen months. I persuaded the Dean of the Law School to let me do the last two years in one: which involved my attending a double set of lectures. To support myself I taught at St. Aloysius College two hours every morning, and twice a week I taught Workers' Educational Association lectures at night.

But the street corner work was in my blood. I got my old parish priest, Father Rohan of Balmain, to approach Archbishop Kelly to ask permission for me to open an Evidence Guild platform in the Sydney Domain. The Archbishop must have got it wrong, for when I went to see him I found him pleading with me to speak in the Domain. I consented. So every Sunday afternoon I spoke there: and I opened a Saturday night meeting at Newtown Bridge. I conducted a training class for speakers one night a week, taught theology every Sunday morning at Santa Sabina, a Dominican secondary school for girls at Strathfield. I remember someone asking me how I managed to do so many things at once. I answered, "By doing everything less well than it should be done."

After my class at Strathfield, I went most Sundays for lunch with Archbishop Sheehan, who lived nearby. He had been appointed Coadjutor with right of succession to Archbishop Kelly, who didn't want him. I never got to know Archbishop Kelly, but of his vanity there seems to be small doubt: what other archbishop ever had a statue of himself erected in front of his cathedral while still alive? It became an obsession with him to make sure his people realized that though there was an apostolic delegate in Sydney and a coadjutor, he, Michael Kelly, was their Archbishop. According to the stories, he did all he could to make Archbishop Sheehan's life difficult as apparently Cardinal Moran had made his when he had held a similar position; and as, also apparently, Archbishop Mannix was to make the life of the coadjutor Rome wished on him.

No word of this did I ever hear from Archbishop Sheehan—I know he resigned and went back to Ireland soon after. He was a Gaelic scholar—he told me he had never preached a sermon in English till he came to Sydney, where he was given few opportunities to preach at all. He was known in the English-speaking world for his textbook on Apologetics, a subject on which I had not yet thought out my own position. All I knew was that in giving the proofs of God's existence to outdoor crowds I had never lost an argument with an atheist, and never convinced anyone that there is a God.

I had proposed marriage to Maisie Ward before leaving England. Soon after I arrived in Australia she accepted me by telegram. I looked forward to my law degree a year later, then marriage and the Bar. But as the months went by, I found myself comparing and contrasting the work of a lawyer with the work of teaching the Faith in the street. In the street one was meeting people with problems which went to the very depth of man's being, and helping them to a fuller life in Christ. Compared with that, fighting people's legal battles in court seemed trivial. In themselves such battles are not trivial, of course, only in comparison with what I had experienced.

I saw no issue, because Guild speaking was unpaid, and I wanted to get married. Maisie's mother thought up the solution. She was not happy at the thought of losing her daughter to the ends of the earth. She had herself done Evidence Guild speaking wearing her widow's black and she knew the reality of the work. I remember two remarks made to her by hecklers. One man, accusing her of shuffling, of not meeting his objections, said: "You are old, madam. When you have one foot in the grave, it's dangerous to shuffle." The other remark was briefer: "Widders are wicked."

She had been a successful novelist. *Punch* had done some jesting about the two novel-writing Mrs. Wards, Mrs. Wilfrid and Mrs. Humphrey. She knew a lot about publishers, she suggested to Maisie that publishing was my vocation. Maisie wrote to ask me what I thought of the idea. I jumped at it. The only thing I knew about publishing was that it was not Law. It needed no other virtue.

I remember my law finals: sixteen three-hour papers in two scorching hot weeks. The last was on a Friday. On the Saturday I staggered on to the ship for England. At Marseilles I received a telegram that I had passed. And that was the end of my legal career.

IV

It was the end, too, of an epoch in my life. The Sheed who returned to England, with marriage and publishing ahead, was a very different Catholic from the man who had landed at Tilbury in 1920 and seen the Guy Fawkes bonfires all the way to London. I shall try to summarize what had happened to me theologically. After that, I shall show how I, and most Catholics, so innocently saw the Church and its prospects, not foreseeing the explosion thirty years in the future. Today's twilight Catholic has no notion of the blissful Catholic summer of the twenties.

But first, my movement into theology. I can date its beginning, a Tuesday evening in the spring of 1921. Maisie Ward gave us newcomers a class on the Supernatural Life. Quite literally, I had never heard the two words uttered together, supernatural had meant ghosts, life I had enjoyed without reflection. I have lived in their awareness ever since. I already knew that Christ had said, "Unless a man be born again of water and the Holy Spirit he *cannot* enter the Kingdom of God." I had not grasped that he was saying that merely by birth into the life of the human race we are *unfit for salvation:* we must have a second birth, a birth into the life of Jesus himself. By re-birth men's souls are indwelt by Father, Son and Holy Spirit as his was. Thus indwelt, we have our natural life lifted into new powers of action—Faith, Hope and Charity and the rest—and these powers make possible the seeing of God face to face which is the life of heaven. I found this new vision of reality intoxicating as I first heard it. It is intoxicating still. I seem to remember, incorrectly perhaps, walking home on air from the lecture.

The Guild's Director of Studies, Dr. Arendzen, introduced us with a beautiful lucidity to the distinction of person and nature which does so much to clarify the doctrines of Trinity and Incarnation. From him I first heard a lecture on the Trinity. Though I found its mathematical precision a delight, the reality of it did not at once come alive in me. I saw it as the summit of theological thinking, not yet as the foundation.

But a group of lectures on Père de la Taille's theory of the Mass meant another great stride forward. I had been devoted to the Mass as long as I could remember, but had very much seen it—in the phrase of Maisie Ward's brother Herbert—simply as machinery for producing Communion. I had been doing a lot of reading about the Mass as sacrifice and could make no meaning of it. Especially I had been puzzled by its identification with Calvary. Book after book had tried with incredible ingenuity to get some kind of death of Christ into the Mass while leaving him alive!

Years later we were to publish De la Taille's three volumes, and we ran into the controversy he had raised about Calvary as not a complete sacrifice save in union with the Last Supper. But for the moment I was enthralled by the distinction he drew between the slaying of the victim (the immolation) and the offering (the oblation). In the Temple sacrifices the slaying might be done by the Temple servants, but only the priest could do the offering. So on Calvary—the soldiers did the slaying, but the sacrifice was offered by Christ. I did not yet see the full richness of this in relation to Christ's continuing priesthood. But at least I saw that, whatever other identity there might be between Mass and Calvary, at least Mass *is* Calvary as Christ now offers it to his Father.

To a third reality I was introduced in this fruitful four years—the Church as Christ's Mystical Body. St. Paul's Epistles are full of it; right up to the sixteenth century it was central in Catholic teaching. But with the Reformation it went into eclipse. The attack on the Visible Church forced a Catholic concentration on the Church's structure: Mystical Body sounded too close to the inward Church of Protestantism. Eclipse, I have called it: outer darkness would be closer. Incredibly, the bishops of the First Vatican Council in 1870 decided not to use the phrase because it had been used by some Jansenists. In the first edition of the *Catholic Encyclopedia*, it gets a half column (as the Mystical Body of the Church!). About the same time the French Dominican Père Clérissac had written a small book on it. Robert Hugh Benson had developed this into a brilliant book, *Christ in the Church*. The doctrine is now wholly back in possession.

To us of the Evidence Guild it was a godsend. With the aid of our questioners, we were already more aware of the human side of the Church than any group of Catholic laymen had ever been. Now we had the other side.

v

From the twenties on into the sixties, euphoria reigned among Catholics. We were happy in the Church and confident in its future. Converts were pouring in—up to thirteen thousand in one notable year in England, over thirty thousand a year in the United States. And they were not only a nameless mass. Father Ronald Knox had joined the Church three years before I came to England, G. K. Chesterton two years after. Every few weeks one seemed to hear of somebody. The Converts' Aid Society was formed for the support of ministers who had become Catholics, especially the married ones who could not go on to the priesthood. Any writer not actively hostile might, we felt, be on the point of joining the Church. The normal urbanity of C. S. Lewis showed the strain of being asked (not by me!) why he didn't. A group were wondering whether the American-born T. S. Eliot might not take the plunge. On this occasion Jacques Maritain made one of his rare jokes. "No," he said, "Eliot exhausted his capacity for conversion when he became an Englishman."

It is true there were Catholic priests leaving the Church but we were convinced that they were few, and we reminded ourselves of Cardinal Manning's dictum that, if a priest left, the reason was either Punch or Judy, alcohol or women. We heard of some priests becoming Anglican ministers, but we throve on stories of how ill they got on with their new bishops (just as Anglicans told each other stories of the unhappiness of their men in the Catholic Church!). We liked to quote an Anglican bishop (none of us knew who he was) who was supposed to have said that the Pope threw his weeds into their garden. It really was an untroubled Catholic life for most of us.

We contrasted it with the disturbed life of the Church of England, wondering how long that troubled institution could last. There was Bishop Barnes of Birmingham, appointed by the Labor Prime Minister Ramsay MacDonald. Nominally a Modernist, he seemed to us to have no religion at all. One of my Catholic friends amused himself by inviting him to write an article, "Why I am not a Buddhist." I remember an article Bishop Barnes did write dismissing sacraments as magic. One day he found himself sheltering from the rain with the Catholic parish priest of the church nearby. They chatted agreeably. The Bishop asked the other who he was, "Oh, I'm the local magician," said Father Askew.

Catholics made much mock of the High Anglicans. Stories abounded of their efforts to imitate Rome. One I remember was about a vicar who had heard that in our Church there were "reserved cases," sins that the priest could not forgive, they were "reserved" to the bishop or even the Pope. So he applied this to one of his own penitents, telling him he would have to refer the matter to the bishop. The penitent returned a week later as directed, knocked on the vicarage door. The door was opened by the vicar's wife—"Oh," she said, "you're the reserved case."

In the twenties, I think, a letter appeared in the Anglican weekly, the *Church Times*. The writer said that a celibate clergy could flourish in the Church of England only with the co-operation of the women. She urged the formation of a new order—the Dames of the Order would be those who had refused a priest in marriage, the Members would undertake to refuse if a priest proposed. It struck us as comical, the celibacy of our own clergy seemed to us as rocklike as Gibraltar.

I have picked two out of a number of stories, to show the state of mind. We were particularly incensed at talk of Anglican reunion with Rome, convinced that foreigners simply did not know the Church of England as we did. There were the Conversations at Malines between Cardinal Mercier, hero of the Belgian resistance in the war, and a group of Anglicans headed by Lord Halifax. There was the Belgian Benedictine Lambert Beauduin, who, we heard, allowed Anglican ministers to say Mass at his monastery at Amay. We preferred the story of a very tall English monk who recognized an Anglican cleric saying Mass in the Grotto at Lourdes and threw him bodily off the altar. I remember how pleased we were when Rome ordered Amay to confine its reunion efforts to the Eastern Orthodox Church.

I was preparing this chapter for the press when I learned of a life just published of Dom Beauduin by Sonya Quitslund. He had been a leader of the Belgian underground in World War I. But I imagine it is not that which causes the Roman archives on him to remain closed, but his work for Reunion. He saw it not as submission of the other Churches to, or their absorption by, Rome but as "a free and voluntary union, with each keeping its own traditions, ethos and jurisdiction" (I quote from the New York *Times* review).

As I say, we took an unholy joy in the troubles of the Church of England. We felt that we were riding high, wide and handsome, with no notion of what awaited our own Church in the seventies. We heard of High Anglicans discussing their bishops as a sort of Mafia, enemies holding the places of power. That we should live to see our bishops picketed by their own seminarians was unthinkable.

When a group of clergymen visited Spain during the Civil War and reported how freely religion was practiced in the Communist-controlled areas, I remember a poem:

> They came, they saw, they marked what they were told
> By friendly hosts, who showed them what was shown;
> And then returned, uplifted and consoled,
> By churches even emptier than their own.

At that time we were building churches all over the place and filling them as fast as we built them. Our pride was asking for a fall, and it was quite a fall when it came. He laughs longest who laughs last, of course. I don't know when the last laugh will be. Certainly it is a long time since we Catholics had much to laugh over.

None of this mockery was uttered on our outdoor platforms. We were coming to an immense respect for Protestantism as we met it in so many of our listeners. But it only slowly dawned on us that their churches were bringing Christ Our Lord to people who, for whatever reason, were too deeply suspicious of our Church to accept anything from us, even Christ.

CHAPTER 7

THE CATHOLIC INTELLECTUAL REVIVAL

I

In the spring of 1926, with my legal career ended before it had begun, I returned to England. Years later the Guild for the first and only time prosecuted a heckler—he was so uproarious that we either had to prosecute him or close our meetings. When I was in the witness box his lawyer said to me sarcastically: "So you came all the way from Australia to convert England." I said, "Not at all. I came to marry Maisie Ward." Which is what I did, on April 27.

We were married from her brother's house on the Isle of Wight, by Bishop Cotter of Portsmouth. He was a fervent Irish republican, had spoken out strongly on behalf of Terence MacSwiney (the Mayor of Cork who had died in prison after a hunger strike), and had written a pastoral so anti-English that some of his English clergy would not read it. The problem at the wedding was to keep him from meeting Maisie's uncles and aunts. They were staunch Unionists—convinced that MacSwiney's death was suicide. From long before, Maisie had been the only member of her family to take Ireland's side.

Later in that same year Sheed & Ward began its curious life. As the firm was first planned, the "Ward" had been Maisie's brother Leo. He had tried his vocation with the Jesuits, had broken down, was now mended and ready to begin life again. But with renewed health came a renewal of his determination to be a priest. Cardinal Bourne accepted him for the secular priesthood. I leap forward a few years to his final examination. He was intensely nervous, and was convinced (rightly) that under the pressure of examination he would go to pieces. "Let me give you a rehearsal," said Dr. Griffin, the Archbishop of Birmingham's secretary. In a long walk, Dr. Griffin asked him the toughest questions he was likely to get. He answered them well. At the end of the walk Dr. Griffin said: "That was your exam. You passed." Leo went on to the priesthood, Dr. Griffin to the cardinalate. With Leo gone, Maisie became the other half of the new publishing house.

From the moment he heard of our venture, Hilaire Belloc wanted to be in on it. We had several meetings, but it soon became clear that he did not mean to put money into it, that he could not give us his books (already contracted for), that he would not have time to look for authors or read manuscripts. But he maintained the liveliest interest in us, and did in fact give us our first book.

H. G. Wells had just published his *Outline of History*, which was sufficiently anti-Catholic and anti-Christian to infuriate Belloc. He wrote a series of articles in the *Universe*, attacking Wells's book, and arranged that we should publish these as A *Companion to H. G. Wells' Outline of History*. But while it was still in the press Wells produced a pamphlet "Mr. Belloc Objects." Belloc insisted on our publishing a reply, "Mr. Belloc Still Objects." So Sheed & Ward was born in religious strife—as I have already related that I myself was. But religious strife was not to be our line.

Actually Belloc and Wells were made for each other—as opponents. To Maisie Wells once remarked that his arguments with Chesterton never affected their friendship, but that controversy with Belloc was always a quarrel. He told her that once, having seen Belloc in profile against a window, he said to him, "Are you a quarter Jew or one eighth?" He said Belloc answered, "One eighth." Considering Belloc's reputation as a Jew-baiter, the incident seems odd.

The difference between Chesterton and Belloc as controversialists was noticed by themselves. Chesterton once remarked that there was a "sundering quality" about Hilaire's interventions. Belloc thought that Chesterton's kindliness diminished his value as a champion of the Faith. J. B. Morton said in his splendid *Memoir of Belloc* that when Belloc entered a room, he changed the room. I know exactly what he meant. The personality was so very marked—anyone seeing him for the first time anywhere would wonder instinctively who he was. I never knew a man less overlookable. And in a general way he looked like trouble! Like everyone else I knew the lines:

> England to me who never have malingered,
> Nor spoken falsely nor your flattery used,
> Nor even in my rightful garden lingered,
>   What have you not refused?

And like everyone else I assumed that by his "rightful garden" he meant France, where he had done his military service and whose citizenship he gave up for England's.

I said something of the sort to him and he corrected me. By "rightful garden" he meant poetry. He gave it up for prose, "because one
fights with prose." As I have said, Belloc's fighting quality rendered
the Catholic body great service in the early years of the century—
forcing the outside world to listen, nerving Catholics to stand up and
declare themselves. But by the time Sheed & Ward began publishing,
its necessity—and so its effectiveness—was lessened. The Catholic
Intellectual Revival was in full flow.

Writing of Thomas à Becket, Belloc surely wrote his own apologia:
"I will believe that those who appear before the throne of God after
heavy battles in the right cause yet clouded with too much opinion
will have it easily forgiven them, especially if they have been defeated
in the battles of the Lord."

II

All through the twenty years between the two World Wars we
talked happily of the Catholic Intellectual Revival. By 1926, when
Sheed & Ward began publishing, the Revival and our happiness in
it were both at the flood. I first lectured on it in 1933 at Denver in
Colorado. For the next dozen years, I must have given scores of talks
on it, and other scores of lecturers were doing the same.

From the beginning I was fascinated by the word revival. From
what swoon were we all so delighted the Catholic intellect had re-
vived? It must have been deep: our delight at our revival was at once
an admission of the swoon and a measure of its depth. Certainly only
the occasional Catholic voice had talked of the swoon while it was
on. My wife's grandfather, William George Ward, while remaining a
layman (married at that!) had become a seminary professor. It is
worth remembering that Rome suddenly made him a Doctor of Philosophy. He wrote:

> The whole philosophical fabric which occupies our colleges is rotten
> from the floor to the roof. No one who has not been mixed up prac-
> tically in a seminary would imagine to what an extent it intellectually
> debauches the students' minds.

It was his son Wilfrid who spoke of the state of siege in which the
Church had accepted to live for the best part of three centuries—
its whole energy given to defense of the city walls, not to development of the very life of the City of God. There was tremendous mis-

sionary activity among primitive peoples, a solid sacramental piety in
the civilized world; but the thinking mind was not at work upon the
revealed realities Christ had entrusted to the Church. In that dark
time Newman was a blazing light, but his effect was not at once felt.
Reading his essay on the Participation of the Laity, Pius XI wept—
not tears of joy. There was the cardinal in Rome who complained,
"Newman miscet et confundit omnia"—he muddles and confuses
everything. Theology had all been so neat and teachable. I remember
meeting in 1922 a parish priest who had won a gold medal in Rome:
he was perfectly frank about it—all done by memory, he said. (He had
a way with words, this one. He told his congregation that he doubted
if there was enough grace in the whole parish to save the soul of a
newly baptized baby.) From the seminaries down to the catechism in
the primary school, the one aim seemed to be a doctrinal teaching
which could be memorized.

Theology had become not so much the study of God as of established theologians. With his mind searching into the meaning of
the dogmas, Newman was making them harder to package for accurate repetition. With his interest in the light shed upon them by the
heretics, he was challenging the textbooks which dismissed the great
challengers with some such phrase as "Zwingliani, Sociniani, Luther-
ani et generatim novatores decimisexti saeculi"—a lot of sixteenth-
century troublers of the peace.

In the last days of the siege mentality at the end of the nineteenth
century and the beginning of the twentieth, occurred the Modernist
revolt of the Abbé Loisy, Father Tyrrell and a score of others. It was
crushed: but it was not answered: the Modernists too were dismissed
as troublers of the peace: their questions remained—to explode sixty
years after. If only the questions had been discussed fully and freely
then, the explosion of the seventies might not have occurred. Authority naturally likes disorders tidied up: but in this instance they were
only swept under the rug. Wilfrid Ward was a leader of those who
urged at once the rights of the thinking mind and the duty of respect
for authority. Like all men who see both sides he got precious little
thanks from either side.

Up to the death of Pius X, the repression was still on; theologians,
philosophers, bishops even were being "delated" to Rome; fourteen
books a year were being put on the Index Expurgatorius. Under Benedict XV the number sank to three a year. His decision for freedom
may have been helped by the discovery, on his first morning at the

papal desk, of a list of names "delated" for disciplining by Pius: his own name was on the list. If, as I have been told, it was one of his auxiliary bishops who had delated him, their first meeting must have been interesting.

By the time we began publishing, all this seemed to have been forgotten. Freedom was in the Catholic air: I don't mean that the magisterium had abdicated, or that the relation between it and the theologians had suddenly become improbably ideal: I don't see how it ever can be. But the strain was relaxed. Theologians did not feel that they were working under the lash, as Newman had phrased it. I remember saying in my exuberance that if you wanted a book put on the Index you'd have to bribe a cardinal. In forty years of publishing we had no books "indexed," and were asked to withdraw only four (two of them temporarily).

There was, of course, Rome's condemnation of the extremely rightwing, insanely nationalist, Action française, with a French cardinal "unhatted" because of it; but the question at issue was hardly theological, and there was general acceptance of the rightness of Rome's action.

In the explosion which accompanied and followed Vatican II there grew up a contempt for the pre-Conciliar Church which might have had some application to the time before Benedict XV, but had none to the twenties and onwards. In those years the intellectual activity was enormous. Without it Vatican II would have been impossible.

III

The twenties of this century saw writers converted to the Faith in England in numbers which could not be matched in any previous century and have not been matched in the half century since. In the past, England's writers—I mean writers on the nation's reading lists —were not much given to conversion. The only one that leaps to mind before Newman is Dryden, two centuries before. Three others did join the Church—Ben Jonson, Gibbon and Boswell—but their conversions apparently did not take!

In the century's teens we had Robert Hugh Benson, son of an Archbishop of Canterbury, Ronald Knox, C. C. Martindale, and as far as the reading public was concerned, we should count Gerard Manley Hopkins, for though his conversion went back into the previous century his poetry was not published till 1915. All four became priests.

The pace quickened incredibly in the twenties—with the philosophers Christopher Dawson and E. I. Watkin, the poets Alfred Noyes, and Roy Campbell (though he did not make the actual plunge until the thirties), the biographer D. B. Wyndham Lewis, the satirist J. B. Morton, the writer-of-all-trades Chesterton, the artist-writers Eric Gill and David Jones, novelists Compton Mackenzie, Philip Gibbs, Maurice Baring, Arnold Lunn, Sheila Kaye-Smith, Bruce Marshall, Graham Greene and Evelyn Waugh. This in-flight of novelists is peculiarly interesting. The novel as we know it was a post-Catholic invention. Catholics had not much tended to become novelists, novelists were suddenly becoming Catholics. And it was not only in England. In Europe there were François Mauriac, Léon Bloy (who helped in the conversion of Jacques Maritain and his wife), Péguy, Henri Ghéon, Giovanni Papini, Gertrud von Le Fort, Sigrid Undset.

Notice one strangeness. Almost all the Catholics who entered the nation's reading lists were either converts or (in Europe) reverts, people who had been born inside the Church but had for a time lost touch. The one born Catholic was Hilaire Belloc. Does this silence of the born Catholics give you pause? Pause is what it gives me. For it is fantastic. I remember writing twenty years ago, "Converts, one imagines, can be hardly ten per cent of the Catholic body: that eighty per cent of the first-rate writers should come from this ten per cent seems to argue either a monstrous articulateness in the converts or a monstrous inarticulateness in the born Catholics. I do not guarantee my percentages, but the disproportion is beyond question."

By the time I wrote that, I had arrived at my own theory. It is as likely to be right as any other I have heard, as I have not heard any other. And it is easy to state. It is simply this—that *converts have studied the Faith as grown-ups.*

The ordinary Catholic is baptized in infancy and educated at a Catholic school. He studies the dogmas of the Faith at school—more or less well, according to the skill of the teacher and his own inclination. The chances are that he never gives a consecutive half-hour to them again. He maintains contact with the worshiping Church when he leaves school, but he loses contact with the teaching Church. There are sermons—but more on morals than on doctrine, and some of those on doctrine would only refresh his memory on what he learned in the sixth grade. In the very best circumstances, sermons cannot carry him on beyond the point of understanding he reached in school—which may or may not have been a high point but would, in any event, have one limiting condition—the degree of his maturity: the boy at school or college has most of life's most developing experiences still well ahead of him, so that there is much in the Faith he simply cannot appreciate yet.

With school behind him, the Catholic is the subject of two processes—his knowledge of life as it comes to him in the experiences of every day is growing all the time: his knowledge of life as the dogmas of the Church teach it to be is growing less, as his schooldays recede further into the misty past. His mind leaves its heritage unpossessed and lives on its poverty—voluntary poverty with a vengeance, but of the sort that impoverishes: one is hardly likely to see meagerly and pray richly. The result is that he is looking at life with two eyes that do not focus—a strong eye which sees life as it comes at him (which is pretty much the way people around him see it), a weak eye which sees life, or half-sees it, in the light of the Church's dogmas. The result of having two eyes that do not focus is that one cannot look intently at anything—the thing begins to wobble and blur. Most of us avoid the annoyance of this by not looking too intently—we live by routine and do not question life or ourselves very closely. But the man who takes this easy way cannot be a writer of any quality: the artist—writer or other—is a man of searching gaze: if he does not look intently at life, he cannot create.

The convert, if he happens to have the writing gift, thus becomes a writer almost as a matter of course: he studies the dogmas as an adult, for he *is* an adult, and he studies them with the intensity proper to the decision he is about to make.

IV

I have learned a lot about the Church from the converts I have known. And I have known plenty—all the writers who came flooding in during the twenties, and hundreds of others comparatively or totally unknown. Each stirs in me the same question—if I had not been a Catholic from the start, would I have found my way in?

The Holy Spirit is always in action of course. But the Holy Spirit does not do violence to mind or will: he offers each man enough, but the decision remains with each. Would I have been likelier to resist the light and strength he offers all men, or to accept? I don't feel that

I know the answer. The converts I have known don't help me to clarify, so different are they not only from me but from one another. Their friends are full of theories. I remember being told that homosexuals join the Church because the smell of incense excites them: today's liturgy does not give them much incense! Anyhow that was said by the kind of man who told me that I myself taught religion on street corners because it gratified my libido. Freud has a lot to answer for.

Of this sort of explaining or explaining away Hilaire Belloc writes in his Introduction to Chesterton's account of his own conversion:

> When you have predicated of one what emotion or what reasoning process brought him into the fold, and you attempt to apply your predicate to another, you will find a misfit. The cynic enters and so does the sentimentalist; the fool enters and so does the wise man; the perpetual questioner and the doubter and the man too easily accepting immediate authority.

For myself I have never found two converts alike. There was the Jesuit Father Martindale, for instance, in whom response to the forms and colors of the world was as keen as in that earlier Jesuit Gerard Manley Hopkins: against those two, balance Graham Greene, whose writings are more spattered with excreta—things the body gets rid of as of no use to it—than the writings of any other writer of his quality. When I was younger I used to have a wager with myself when I got a new book by Greene—could I open at excreta? I often won it. I opened Lawless Roads, for instance, at his telling the color of his seasickness. He really seemed to revel in the body's ignominies.

For another contrast consider Maurice Baring—in love with melody, learning the violin almost before he could walk, as a small child leaning out of the window "the better to absorb the whole perfection of a lark's song." Now think of Ronald Knox, who could not carry a tune sufficiently to sing High Mass. Once he and I were walking to the railway station in Durham. We passed a brass band. He remarked, "Of course good music is better than bad music. But the best music is inferior to silence."

And no contrast between converts could be more startling than between the Frenchmen Léon Bloy and Jacques Maritain. Bloy was Bohemian plus, with his own kind of sanity, verging on the insane; Maritain was the quintessence of sanity, living up to the mental quality of the Aquinas he knew so well. He lived a long married life with his wife, Raissa, and on her death became a lay brother in the community of Little Brothers of Jesus. Bloy had a tendency to bring home helpless women in order that he might care for them spiritually, and then found himself unable to resist them. Yet not only did both become full Catholics, but Bloy converted Maritain. Which of them had the greater influence on the Catholic Revival? Bloy, I think. His novel *La Femme Pauvre*, which we published as *The Woman Who Was Poor*, has affected Catholic novels since, partly because of the sheer violence as of boiling lava. It is close at times to insanity, as in his other novel *Le Désespéré*, yet you cannot blame a volcano for hurling lava off its racked chest.

Closer to Bloy than to Maritain was a convert I heard about from Father Healy, one of our examining chaplains. This one had picked up a Catholic prostitute on a Saturday evening and spent the night with her. At seven-thirty next morning she made her apologies for leaving him, she wanted not to be late for the eight o'clock Mass. He was so startled that he simply had to find out what the Church had which could make that girl feel that she must not miss her Sunday Mass. Father Healy instructed him and received him into the Church. (One remembers that in the Middle Ages there were towns in which the municipal brothels were closed on holidays of obligation, the Church's major feast days.)

The intellectual and the un-intellectual enter the Church. As Mauriac says in *God and Mammon*—"Intellectuals join in the name of reason, reasons of the heart come later." Intellect does not seem to have played a major part in the conversion Father Healy told of. Consider what Christopher Dawson said of his own in the *Catholic Times* of London close on fifty years ago: "I realized that the Incarnation, the Sacraments, the external order of the Church and the internal work of sanctifying grace, were all parts of one organic unity, a living tree whose roots are in the Divine nature, and whose fruit is the perfection of the saints."

I have mentioned the advantage that converts have over the rest of us—namely that they study the Faith as adults. Yet something depends on the priests who instruct them. The instruction given to intellectuals, for instance, can be rather sketchy, based on the assumption that such learned men probably know it all already. I know one very able writer who had been in the Church over a year before he learned that Sunday Mass was supposed to be of obligation. Reading Graham Greene, I get the impression that his idea of

God stops at the God-Man dying on the Cross and that divine love reaching its infinite level in the Trinity is not living in his mind. I do not know for certain who instructed him. If it is the priest I think, then the Trinity would not have been omitted. It may be something in Greene himself, responding especially to Christ crucified. He has done more to make the general reader conscious of sin than any novelist. Yet I think he would have seen sin better for seeing the whole God.

In *The Heart of the Matter* there is Scobie, a believing and practicing Catholic, who has just committed adultery but receives the Eucharist because his wife, who is watching him like a hawk, will know of his guilt if he doesn't. I was in the Chair at a lecture Evelyn Waugh gave in the Waldorf Astoria—on Converts, as it happened. At question time he was asked, "Is Scobie in hell?" He answered, "Yes," and sat down. Evidently both he and Greene took Scobie's damnation for granted! So did the Catholic audience in Chicago for whom I reviewed the book. I certainly did not—not even twenty years before the explosion: Scobie's weakness was the kind that Purgatory exists to cope with! It may be that novel writers have responses special to their occupation—as Waugh himself could make a biographical portrait of Ronald Knox, showing his relations with men and women in full color, but hardly showing his priesthood at all. And when Mauriac writes directly on Christ, he sees the sternness more clearly than the love.

The oddest convert I met wasn't, so to speak. He was a Hindu who had come to the conclusion that he could prove the doctrine of the Trinity. He took his proof to Rome expecting a hero's welcome. He was told that the Trinity cannot be proved, it is sheer mystery to be known only by revelation: while he thought it could be proved, the Church would not baptize him. He told me all this in London. He was aching for baptism but could not deny his "proof." He did get himself baptized—by a bishop of another communion who had said publicly that the arithmetical aspect of the deity was no concern of his. But when I last met him he still wanted to be a Catholic.

I could go on and on about the variety of converts. Perhaps some day I will. For the moment I look at one kind of convert mentioned by Belloc—"The man who comes in out of contempt for the insufficiency or the evil by which he has been surrounded." Is that a good reason?

Father Martindale (C.C.M. to thousands) told my wife and me

of a curious incident close on fifty years earlier. He was a guest in a
friend's house: Father Ronald Knox, still an Anglican, arrived in a
state of agitation and insisted on speaking with him. C.C.M. pointed
out that the dinner bell had rung, and suggested that he come back
later that night. He did. He begged C.C.M. to receive him into the
Church. He poured out a stream of complaints about the impossibility of the Church of England. C.C.M. pointed out that while all
this might be a reason for leaving his own Church, he would need
more positive reasons for joining ours. Ronald Knox did join ours
three years later! Was C.C.M. right or Belloc?

Men do give reasons for their joining the Church which seem to
others inadequate—naturally, since the main reason, the impulse of
the Holy Spirit, is beyond their own gaze. Certain ecclesiastics of an
older fashion said Newman had entered the Church for the wrong
reasons: he told them it was too late: he was already in. And most
converts have Newman's experience—life in the Church is more convincing than any of their reasons for joining it.

Newman thought he had given his reasons in the *Apologia*. But
one mystery he does not discuss there—how *could* he have joined
the Church of Pius IX? Was that even a problem that needed solving
for him? Cardinal Suenens told me that Pope John had told him
that he would have liked to canonize—by his own act, avoiding the
long process of canonization—Cardinal Newman and Pius IX. If
Pope John saw in each a holiness deeper than their differences, perhaps Newman did too. Perhaps the convert is wisest who gives no
reasons: a few years ago that very considerable poet Siegfried Sassoon answered some reporters who had come to ask him why he had
joined the Church—"It's my own affair." But in his poem *Lenten
Illuminations* (*Selected Poems*, Faber, 1968) he did tell something
of it to those who care to know:

This, then, brought our new making. Much emotional stress—
Call it conversion; but the word can't cover such good.
It was like being in love with ambient blessedness—
In love with life transformed—life breathed afresh, though yet half
                                                                understood.

There have been many byways for the frustrate brain,
All leading to illusions lost and shrines forsaken . . .
One road before us now—one guidance for our gain—
One morning light—whatever the world's weather—
Wherein wide-eyed to waken.

One sees why he did not try to tell the reporters that.

Notice one phrase in it—"emotional stress." Arnold Lunn tells of the sheer anguish in which he woke on the morning of his reception. Chesterton speaks for many converts when he says, "I had no doubts or difficulties just before. I had only fears, fears of something that had the finality and simplicity of suicide."

There is a kind of wry pleasure in thinking of the converts who came pouring into the Church in the twenties now that the flood has thinned, and the outgoing stream is moving towards flood level. Why did the bright promise of the twenties, thirties and even forties, fade away into the sadness of the seventies? Writing as a Catholic publisher I remember singing, to a tune of my own, Wordsworth's lines—

> Blest was it in that age to be alive
> But to be young was very heaven!

It was a rather tuneless tune, and I can't recall it, so long it is since there would have been any point in singing it. I am in no mood to sing it now. I wonder if I ever shall again?

What went wrong? Were the Intellectual Revival and the Literary Revival only sunset flashes?

If I had to think back I would say that both Revivals depended too much on the Intellectual, and the Intellectual was too much confined to intellectuals, leaving the main body of Catholics very much as they were.

The Literary Revival indeed was rather an outflow of the Intellectual Revival than a literary phenomenon in its own right. There was an immense new life in philosophy and theology, in history and biography and sociology: but of the arts only in that which is closest to the word-using intellect, the novel. In poetry there was some renewal, but neither in poetry nor in drama, painting, sculpture, music, architecture, was there anything comparable.

The absence of a Catholic Poetic Revival is all the more remarkable because the most influential voice in English poetry in the twenties and until the emergence of T. S. Eliot was that of the Catholic Gerard Manley Hopkins. I pause upon Hopkins. Long ago I knew an old man, Professor Howley of University College, Galway. As a young man he had been a pupil of Father Hopkins at University College, Dublin, and he told me a story that sticks in my head. At one class Hopkins paused in what he was reading, stayed silent for a long moment, then said, "I have never seen a naked woman. I wish I had." He resumed his reading to the stunned class.

To return to the revival, poetry was being written by Catholics but not in quantity, and most of it by men formed as poets before the discovery of Hopkins. Belloc as I have related gave up poetry for prose—"because you fight with prose." I never heard Chesterton refer to Hopkins. The best-known poet-convert was Alfred Noyes, and he simply could not abide Hopkins or refrain from mocking him. "Happy is the temperament," he wrote in *The Opalescent Parrot,* "that can meet the biliousness of its contemporaries with a smile." Happy indeed but not his. He had been the last of what one may call the Tennyson line: I think his influence might have been considerable if only he could have refrained from attacking the "new line" of poets even more vigorously than he attacked Hopkins. My guess is that when his battles are forgotten, he might have a revival of his own. But that is prophecy—safe therefore, since it will be tested when I am no longer here.

v

In the eighteen-nineties St. Thomas had been drawn, or dragged, out of the mist which for too long had shrouded him, by Pope Leo XIII. And at the highest level the effect was notable. But, at the level next-to-highest, his philosophy was already being turned into a theology, not to be examined by reason but swallowed as dogma.

Even at the highest level there was a hint of this. I remember being at a lecture given by Jacques Maritain. A questioner was so exalted by the lecture that he asked, "Why doesn't the Church make Thomism binding on Catholics?" Maritain smiled and said sweetly, "She trusts our intelligence." (I remember a small incident at the end—the [English] chairman congratulated Maritain on his French.)

The Catholic jungle was full of man-eating Thomists (a phrase invented I think by Algar Thorold, editor of the *Dublin Review*). I made a point of asking each one I met, What is the next step? What are the questions un-met by Aquinas that the Thomists are about to work on? They invariably seemed puzzled. And in a book by a learned Spanish Thomist I came upon the astounding statement that he was not going to discuss a particular problem because Aquinas had not written on it!

In our excitement over the Intellectual Renewal of the twenties, I was one of those who realized that with all its brilliance it hardly touched the great body of Catholics. I realized it because it had been my function in the Catholic Evidence Guild to meet the incoming members and find out how much they knew about the Faith which they wanted to teach to others, by which they were trying to live, and for which they hoped they would have the courage to die. The finding out was a gloomy experience.

They came at all ages, some fresh from school, some twenty or thirty or forty years after. With the rarest exceptions they were barely literate doctrinally. Catholic schools had a good record in public examinations, but most of them were defective in the one area which was their special reason for existence. I got the impression that doctrine was left to teachers who would not have been allowed to teach any other subject of which they were so ignorant. A regular defense of the catechism used to be that though the children might not understand the formulas, they would come back to them in later life. In discussion with those who entered the Guild long after their school days, I had some marvelous examples of what came back to them! I have told how in my first Guild class my own ignorance was mercilessly exposed: but I thought in my innocence that this was because I had not been to a Catholic school!

Once in a while I had pleasant surprises. In Bolton, that remarkable priest Father Leighton took me into a class of children aged eleven to thirteen in his parochial school—and said: "Question them." I said, "What about?" "The Faith," he said. This was my dialogue with a girl of thirteen:

I: Does the Pope go to confession?
She: Yes.
I: How can the superior receive absolution from his inferior?
She: The priest in the confessional represents Christ and is not inferior to anybody.

As the years went by, the gloom began to lighten, but how slowly! Right up to the explosion of the sixties, and helping to produce it, one still found in too many schools the same repetition of catechism formulas, with no effort made to get inside them and show what effect they might have on life as we have to live it. I remember comparing learning the catechism with eating walnuts without cracking the shells. This swallowing of doctrines unenjoyed was the normal practice at all levels, right up to the teachers. I once had to give a three-day course in doctrine to all the nuns of a particular province of a particular order in a particular country. I explained that heckling—calling on the group to deal with the questions unbelievers ask—was part of my teaching method. I was told that I must heckle only the senior nuns, that sort of treatment might be bad for the faith of the younger. The result was a shambles. After half an hour I had to stop the questioning. The old ladies had spent dedicated lives teaching doctrines on which their minds had never stirred. And it was not only that one group. I could make a horror comic of things taught in our schools.

That the doctrines did not manage to get through alive did not in those days seem to anyone but us a matter of great concern. Theology was for theologians. No, one got nowhere by complaining of the ill-teaching of doctrine. I tried it for forty years or so, but nowhere was where I got, even with bishops. I remember one in particular. I had poured out my heart to him about the shameful teaching of doctrine in his schools. He listened with all politeness. When I had finished, he said, "Yes, indeed." I felt I could read his mind: theology had never done *him* any good: it was just an obsession of mine, very creditable in a layman. It was only when some of us began to see and to say that Christ himself, taught as an item in the syllabus, was growing ever less real to teachers and pupils alike that we did at last cause discomfort! But not enough, not soon enough, not yet.

It was not as if sermons at Mass were likely to supply for the failure of schools to make either the truths or Our Lord real. We of the street corner had the advantage of knowing when our audiences were bored —they walked away and left us talking to no one. The preacher in Church has to function without this priceless advantage. I don't see how anyone learns to hold an audience without it.

I have heard good sermons. But from too many I came away wondering that a teaching Church should give so little thought to teaching its teachers to teach.

CHAPTER 8

FIVE WRITERS AND A SIXTH

I

The foundation of Sheed & Ward was not one of the major religious happenings of 1926. That year, if my memory is right, saw John of the Cross made a Doctor of the Church and Thérèse de Lisieux canonized (her career and mine had touched once before—in 1897 I entered this life, she entered the next).

I have talked of the Catholic euphoria of the twenties and thirties. No one could have been more "euphorious" than my wife and I. We had had a splendid honeymoon in Venice. We returned to an England in which writers kept joining the Church. We were now sure of first-rate books to publish. We did not for a while realize how small was the Catholic reading public for books just above the middle of the brow. That we had to learn, painfully. A glimpse of the financial anguish of the next ten years would have jolted our euphoria to a dead stop.

But we were not granted one. Anyhow, our pains were our personal problem and did not trouble the general Catholic sense of well-being. We had a couple of lecture tours in America, which led in 1933 to the founding of our New York house. There we found the same atmosphere of quiet confidence—the Church was growing, how long could the other religions last? Certainly in England there was all through the twenties and thirties a lightness in the heart of which today's Catholic can have no conception. And ours was the first Catholic publishing house to be in the thick of the fun. The great house of Burns and Oates did not radiate good cheer. One of their catalogues at the time listed hair shirts and scourges, moderately priced, for the ascetical-minded. Of ourselves Ronald Knox wrote:

> Sheed and Ward
> Offer sacrifice to the Lord
> Not of the blood of bulls and goats
> But of Burns and Oates.

David Jones wanted some of our books and gave us in payment a woodcut of a stag. It was a handsome brute and became our colophon. We made so much use of it that people were asking us what it signified. We didn't like to say that it signified nothing but David Jones's desire to read our books. Then we discovered what St. Bernard wrote about Jacob's son Naphtali—the name means literally a "stag set free": "Its leaps and bounds well typify the ecstasies of the speculative mind; it is able to thread its way through the densest thickets of forests, as such a mind penetrates obscurities of meaning." So that's what our colophon meant.

Chesterton and Belloc writing from the beginning of the century and Ronald Knox from its teens had done more than their share in bringing mirth into the Faith. But soon there were any number of others. The ordinary reader could hardly help seeing Catholics as a pretty cheerful lot. If he read the London *Times* he found the "light leader" written by Douglas Woodruff—rather notable in that period for being a born Catholic. If he read the *Daily Express*, he turned first to Beachcomber's satirical column. Beachcomber was J. B. Morton, who had joined the Church after leaving Harrow—humor must have come pretty easily to him, since his father had made the English version of *The Merry Widow*.

I shall pause for a moment on these two. Woodruff I met back in Sydney while I was finishing my law course. He and Christopher Hollis (a new convert from Eton) had come by way of the States and New Zealand with a debating team from the Oxford Union. A New Zealand paper summarized their devastating odyssey in the phrase "The Oxford men were stronger in wit, the local men in statistics." They certainly revolutionized debate in Australia. It was very early in our acquaintance that I got a taste of Woodruff's quality. After quoting Wordsworth's "Heaven lies about us in our infancy," he added his own comment, "Later we lie about ourselves." I had read things like that, but I had not often heard one actually said.

Johnny Morton had been a friend of Maisie's priest brother, Leo. His *Daily Express* column can be howlingly funny; it can be sheerly idiotic—"From the lighted tavern we stepped out on to the dark moor, we called it Othello." He can do things to proverbs—"The worst of being a hog is that you never know when some fool will try to make a silk purse out of your wife's ear." But his power lies in the cold, clear eye with which he looks on the follies of the world and the cold, clear English into which he casts them. If you want the House of Commons in one sentence, he gives it to you: "The Minister declined to add anything to the answer he had refused to give to a different question the previous week." I remember two of his "definitions": "*Statistics*, a branch of rhetoric; *Logic*, an unfair means sometimes used to win an argument." I have never had a chance to forget them, since not a week goes by without my coming upon something said or written to remind me of their ghastly relevance.

I have been told that the owner of the paper, Lord Beaverbrook, could see no point whatever in the column, but kept it because his friends seemed to read it, and anyhow every test of reader interest showed it at the top. Beaverbrook had so great a loathing for Belloc and Chesterton that, according to a friend of mine who saw it, there was a notice posted on the office wall of the *Daily Express* to the effect that neither name must ever appear in the paper. Early on, we published *By the Way*, a selection from Beachcomber's columns. Half a century later he is still writing. It is impossible to calculate what he has done for the general sanity, to say nothing of my own.

I have forgotten in what year Arnold Lunn and I had our debate at Hunter College on whether converts or born Catholics were of more value to the Church. Someone wanted to raise money to help the missions: Arnold and I donated our services: people bought tickets at a large price: the missions got the profits. It was decided that it would be more graceful that he as a convert should state the case for the born Catholics, I as a born Catholic, for the converts.

I dwelt especially on what converts had done for the Catholic Intellectual Revival—they had provided 80 per cent of the notable writing. When Lunn's turn came, he found it hard to think of anything at all to be said for born Catholics, and gave as witty a talk as I have ever heard even from him on the oddities of Protestants! But he seized on my statement about the converts writing the books and set against it the fact that in the modern world practically all the canonized saints had been born of Catholic parents. I answered that canonization is a process for declaring that Italians are in heaven: there are no converts in Italy, so . . .

It was fun at the moment: but of course it was a sheer debating point, which in a serious discussion I would not have dreamed of making. The question whether saints are more valuable to the Church than writers cannot be settled like that. All the same, the Gemma Galganis and Maria Gorettis would not have kept Sheed & Ward in business. It was the converts who filled our seasonal lists.

I have already said that I am not writing an autobiography. Nor am

I writing a history of Sheed & Ward. My concern with that curious firm lies in the part publishing played in my maturing as a Catholic. The books we published had their influence on vast numbers of Catholics: but on no one more than on me. I see myself very much as one of Sheed & Ward's public.

II

As I think back over our beginnings, five of our writers—Belloc, and the four converts, Chesterton, C. C. Martindale, Ronald Knox, Christopher Dawson—spring to my mind as having done most for my re-shaping. Yet I must make a further distinction. The men themselves had more effect on me than their writings. A religion must of course be studied in the statement it makes about itself: but for reality it must be studied in the living piece. And these were five very living pieces. On the key question, What makes Catholics tick? most Catholics tell us little; so dim is their tick that they hardly hear it themselves. There was no dimness in these five. I never knew men more concerned with the Faith or more articulate about it. As their publisher I was on the receiving end of their articulateness. There will be those among my readers who know nothing of them. For my present purpose that does not matter. They might have been anybody. I am trying to show what they did for my understanding of the Church, and could do for my readers'.

Of Belloc I have already written a good deal. Here I simply glance at the question, What did the Faith mean to him? As I have noted more than once, Belloc was that rarity—a Catholic writer of the top rank who had been born and schooled in the Church. He tells us that there was a moment in his young manhood when his faith wavered, but it was a brief wavering. In his prime he could write:

> This is the Faith that I have held and hold
> And this is that in which I mean to die—

(if you are interested in the English language, observe that those two lines are made up of monosyllables). As a Catholic he did not pick and choose, he took his religion as a whole. There was doctrine, for instance:

> The moral is, it is indeed,
> You cannot monkey with the Creed.

He might have phrased it more elegantly, but I defy anyone to make the point more clearly.

He had a chapel in his house with the Blessed Sacrament reserved. If there was to be Mass next morning, his mind was filled with the expectation of it overnight—though at Mass itself he was not a model of recollection: he moved about in his chair, muttered, could not take the Mass quietly. There were moods indeed in which he could not take anything quietly—he wanted what he wanted when he wanted it.

When a side chapel was being opened to Chesterton's memory in the church at Beaconsfield, there was a great crowd down from London. One could hardly breathe for the press of people standing. Suddenly there was a commotion in the back of the church. It was Belloc demanding to go to confession. He thrust his way through. As he passed me I heard him say, "It's not essential, but it's urgent." He went into the sacristy, told the altar boys to clear out, and made his confession there and then to the priest already vested for the altar.

Belloc said of himself, "I have no piety, that is I have no attachment to the Church's practices, except sometimes Low Mass and always Benediction. But I have tremendous attachment to the Church." It was as the Body that the Church held Belloc. He once told me that he would regard controversy with other Catholics as "against the discipline of the Body."

I remember Christopher Hollis, when he and I were young, referring to Belloc as "the Latin thing." In his *Companion to Wells' Outline of History* Belloc spoke of the Roman Empire as "the unity of the European world as it was prepared by Divine Providence for the advent of the Catholic Church, the noble antique soil on which was planted, as alone worthy of it, that institution whereby alone Man can be put in tune, or a right civilization preserved." (Chesterton put this last idea in his own way, comparing the Church to the Ark—"If we fall out of the Faith we fall into the fashion.")

About Chesterton and Belloc the general public felt as John Byrom felt about Handel and Bononcini—

> The difference I can scarcely see
> 'Twixt Tweedledum and Tweedledee.

Apart from the high tenor voice which Monsignor O'Connor remarks they shared with Charlemagne, they were very different men, working in quite different fields. Belloc was saying—among a hundred other things of course—that English history was written wrong whenever it touched the Church, Chesterton that the Faith fits the nature of man as a key fits the lock that the Locksmith made it for. Chesterton was essentially a philosopher, Belloc essentially a historian—not of the academic sort but of the artistic, the Macaulay sort. It is a minor evidence of the Church's Catholicity that it could have brought two such different men so close. They both loved the Church —equally indeed but each in his own way.

The Roman order was inbuilt in Belloc—in his speech, in his prose and his poetry, in his politics, in his very appearance. As an old man he grew a large and shapeless beard. I accused him of defacing a public monument: the splendid order of his features had vanished into something vaguely Old-Testament-prophetlike, revenge on him perhaps for describing the Old Testament as "Oriental folklore."

Mass and the sacraments were a nourishment he could not imagine life without. But mentally it was in the Body that he lived. After reading his *Bad Child's Book of Beasts* and *More Beasts for Worse Children* I asked why he did not write a *Bad Catholic's Book of Popes* and *More Popes for Worse Catholics*. The notion amused him mildly. But he would not have written books of the sort. As a historian he could write objectively of unattractive popes. But to have made a comic book of them he would indeed have seen as "against the discipline of the Body."

The great dogmas did not draw him to closer study. I am sure his spirit, wherever it is (I think I know), will forgive me for saying that I had occasionally to suggest theological corrections when preparing his books for press. When he read my own *Map of Life*, he wrote to me with a kind of excitement the book could not have stirred in one who had much habit of reading theology. Yet he had been at the Oratory School when Newman was still head of the Oratory Community. Newman of course was not running the school in Belloc's time, but he still "coached" the annual Latin play. "He knew his Plautus," said Belloc—not much of a tribute to a master of English prose with whom Belloc himself has been compared.

In saying nothing of Belloc as a writer of English, I do real violence to myself. As a poet I rate him with my earliest love, Horace. He does the shop-soiled themes of wine and roses as Horace might have done them if he had believed in the Incarnation and Our Lady.

Chesterton gave no such instant sense of order. The famous telegram he sent to his wife—"Am in Market Harborough where ought

I to be"—could not have been sent by Belloc, who always knew, with total precision, where and when he was. But he could not have written anything of the order of Chesterton's book on Thomas Aquinas. For the order of the thinking mind, the order at the center of being which is a magnet to the metaphysician, was a deeper craving in Chesterton. As my friend Monsignor Lee of Los Angeles phrased it, "His mind wheels in wider circles." He could write of his own conversion: "I know that Catholicism is too large for me, and I have not yet explored its beautiful and terrible truths."

It had to be too large for him, or it would not have been for him at all. A faith that could fit compactly into his head would have had to be smaller than he: he would have none of it. Into the truths, beautiful and terrible, he had in fact seen deeper than most even before he joined the Church, and his explorings never ceased. They were his own country. He saw them when he saw anything, to an astounding extent lived in the totality, moved freely about the totality, might alight anywhere in it. It is in a Father Brown story that we come suddenly upon Our Lady—"the silver sword of pure pain that once pierced the very heart of purity." From the created order his mind could swing in an instant to the Absolute. "This vast variety in the highest thing is the meaning of the fierce patriotism, the fierce nationalism of the great European civilization. It is also incidentally the meaning of the Trinity."

I am certain he did not recognize how extraordinary he was. In *The Common Man* we find this: "Will made the world. Will wounded the world. The same divine Will gave to the world for the second time its chance. The same human will can for the last time make its choice." If I'd given birth to that, I'd have taken to my bed for a couple of months. He went right on with his essay and probably thought no more about it. His greatest things did not stay in his head: considering the sheer volume of his writing, it is notable how rarely he repeats himself.

But if Chesterton was in love with light, he saw mystery—the darkness which for the finite eye must always ring light—as an essential element in seeing. And all this he helped me to see. Not that I ever fooled myself that I could remake my mind in his image. His anguished realization of what he was receiving in Communion could not be mine, whether the anguish lay in his awareness of Christ's worth or his own un-worth.

What fascinated me was not only his awareness of that in

mystery which he could not see but his passion for clarity in the utterance of what he did see. We sometimes say of a man that he loves
to hear himself speak: in fact the conceited man is not hearing himself: he is hearing Cicero or Demosthenes or whatever orator he feels
himself to be. But, vain or not, most of us do not hear what we are
actually saying, being quite happy to know in a general way what we
mean. In this matter Chesterton could teach almost everybody. He
heard each word as he said it. Over the radio, on one occasion, he had
just said that something or other was dull as ditchwater. In the next
moment he said, "But is ditchwater dull? My friends with micro-
scopes tell me that it teems with quiet fun." We take it as praise of a
man to say that he "knows his own mind." "You might as well praise
him," said Chesterton, "for blowing his own nose."

His acceptance of mystery and striving for clarity were each an outflow of his love for light. One effect of this was the kind of joy
in speaking of Our Lady that he shared with Belloc. In their shared
devotion to Mary of Nazareth, the Mother of God, we see most
clearly what the Faith meant to them. Chesterton was not given to
invective, but he described the turning from her of many Christians
as "The little hiss that only comes from hell." Belloc, given to anger
and a master of invective, reached a peak in both when she was attacked. A Low Church Anglican bishop had ordered a High Church
rector to remove some statues—especially "a female figure with a
child." The cold insult to Child and Mother stirred Belloc to write a
ballade. In the first three stanzas he wrote what he felt about the
bishop, using those words as a refrain. But by the poem's end he had
forgotten the bishop. His mind moved forward to his own death:

> Prince Jesus in mine agony
> Permit me, broken and defiled,
> Through blurred and glazing eyes to see
> A female figure with a child.

The first book Chesterton published with us was *The Queen of
Seven Swords*, poems about her. Father Martindale wrote of one of
the poems—*The Return of Eve*, I think—"Francis Thompson is here
outpassed." Chesterton was wholly without vanity. A friend of mine
asked him which he thought his most important book. He answered,
"I don't think any of my books important." And he was putting on
no act. I never heard him refer to a review that praised him—save
this one of Father Martindale's. He repeated the words to me, then

said, "He wouldn't have said that if he hadn't meant it, would he?" Had the poems not been about Our Lady he would not have been thus tremulous.

As I think back I cannot remember a Catholic writer of the time who had not a special love for her. After his conversion Siegfried Sassoon wrote,

Is it not well that now you call yourself her child—
You and this rosary, at which—twelve months ago—you might have
shrugged and smiled?

Nothing in the explosion Catholics are now living through would have seemed so far beyond the understanding of all these men as the turning from her. A Catholic reviewer, reviewing a book of mine in a Catholic paper, found it a proof of my bravery that I should show my devotion to Christ's mother so naturally. Long ago I knew an old man who, when he was a young man, said to the girl he was to marry, "I feel bound in conscience to tell you that I cannot accept the Virgin Birth." Both felt the vast seriousness of the issue. Fewer people would feel it now.

Of the five writers at Sheed & Ward's beginnings who helped towards my maturing as a Catholic by what their membership of the Church meant to themselves, there remain C. C. Martindale, Ronald Knox and Christopher Dawson. I shall write of them in the order, not of their importance for me, but of my meeting them.

III

Father Martindale I met for the first time on the platform of a meeting I had arranged in Plymouth to win members for the Catholic Truth Society (of which, as you will excusably have forgotten, I was organizing secretary). He enchanted me by quoting lengthily from *Ginger Mick*, a poem by C. J. Dennis about a very rough and tough Australian soldier. The enchantment lay in the contrast between the exuberantly Australian accent in which Ginger Mick would have said the words and the precise, rather dry, Oxford accent in which Father Martindale quoted them. I could have listened all night.

I learned only later that this contrast marked the great turning point in his life. He had become a Catholic at Harrow, still in his teens. On leaving school he joined the Jesuits, who sent him to Oxford. There he performed with rather notable brilliance. He was on the way to a career of pure scholarship. The War brought a number of wounded Australian soldiers to Oxford. He spent every spare moment with them. The contact was decisive. He saw that his special vocation lay not with scholars but with plain people. He was not a wit in the Chesterton or Ronald Knox sense but he could use the quick phrase. To a sure-of-himself young man who said he had committed every sin, C.C.M. said, "Suicide?" More typical of him was what he said to Leo Ward, "Please regard me as a suitable object for the blowing off of steam at."

Whenever he traveled anywhere by ship he said Mass for the crew in the engine room in the very early hours. Many other priests may have done this, I have heard only of one, Maisie's brother Leo. His accent never changed: it was a mark of the sureness of his vocation that this never came between him and them. Throughout his life he retained his devotion to Australians. At our meeting he was probably getting as much pleasure out of my accent as I out of his. That may have been why he replied to my letter of gratitude with a postcard saying he expected to get into heaven hanging on to my braces (neither of us then knew that Americans would have called my braces suspenders). As it happens, I still have my braces. He has gone ahead of me.

He gave us as a wedding present the rights of his book *Christ Is King*. Over the whole space of our life together he was closer to us, I think, than any other priest. When he was very old, the Society sent him to be superior of their house for aged Jesuits at Petworth in Sussex: he told us that he arrived barely in time to give the Last Sacraments to the previous superior. He and we sometimes lunched together at the Swan in Fittleworth near by. He was one man who could converse brilliantly with no lapse into uncharity.

My concern here is with what the Church meant to him, and so what his vision of the Church did for mine. The essence of it lay in a clear awareness of the distinction between Christ, who energizes in his members, and the members in the variousness of their response to Christ's energizing. The clarity of his awareness of the contrast did not affect the totality of his submission to the commands either of the Church or his order.

What submission meant to him we could for the most part only conjecture. Occasionally, but rarely, something came through. As a young Jesuit, he told me, he had been asked to express an opinion on the desirability of a Catholic University in England. He had been unenthusiastic about it, and had spoken of the great possibilities for Catholic students in the universities already there. This, he said, had been circulated among American Jesuits as an attack on Catholic universities in America, and an order had gone forth that he must not be allowed to visit the States. He never did.

Towards the end of his life he told me of an occasion long before when he had received a rebuke from Jesuit headquarters in Rome for something he had in fact not done: the rebuke was accompanied by a command that he must not defend himself. He made no comment on the incident, dropped the subject immediately.

We had already published Père de Lubac's *Splendour of the Church*, with its chapter on the spiritual value of unjust rebuke from superiors, and the moral he drew that one must not only obey but be in love with obedience. Father Martindale told me that he and De Lubac had been students together fifty years before. I did not feel that he shared the other's view on that particular sort of injustice —my guess is that he felt it not as injustice but as a kind of lunacy. But he did profoundly believe in the positive nature of obedience.

What I learned from his actual teaching, particularly on Grace and the Supernatural Life, it would be difficult to un-thread from what I have learned from a score of others. But one evening stands out quite clearly. The Catholic Evidence Guild was having its annual meeting. Father Martindale spoke on the impossibility of intelligently handling anything at all—one's own self included—without knowing the purpose for which it existed. Obvious as this is, it was a revelation to me. It has been structural to all my own thinking on the Faith ever since.

On one point I admired but was not tempted to imitate him. He made it a rule never to refuse to do anything he was asked if it could be physically fitted into the time. It meant that most nights he slept three hours. P.S. I have just been told of a prostitute who sent for Father Martindale when she was dying, because when she had accosted him on the street he had refused her so kindly.

IV

Mary of Holyrood may smile indeed,
Knowing what grim historic shade it mocks,
To see wit, laughter and the Popish creed
    Cluster and sparkle in the name of Knox.

That was G. K. Chesterton's comment on one of history's more pleasant ironies—that the first priest ever to enlist laughter on the side of the Faith should have borne the name of the grimmest enemy the Church ever had. The second Knox was by half the Catholics of England referred to, and by a host of friends addressed, as Ronnie. I doubt if even his own wife would have dared to call the first Knox Johnnie.

The fun began while Knox (Ronald) was still an Anglican clergyman, highest of the High Church. There was *Absolute and a Bit of Hell*, his poem in the manner of Dryden's *Absalom and Achitophel*. It had these pleasing lines about the progress of Scripture criticism:

> First Adam fell, then Noah's ark was drowned,
> And Samson was in close confinement bound,
> For Daniel's blood the critic lions roared,
> And trembling hands threw Jonah overboard.

One remembers the nursery rhyme, "Matthew, Mark, Luke and John, bless the bed that I lie on," and Chesterton's comment:

> Tell me do Matthew, Mark and Luke and John
> Bless beds that Higher Critics lie upon,
> Or if while the Fourth Gospel is re-read,
> Synoptists sleep on a three cornered bed?

One sees why, when he had made up his mind to join the Church, Chesterton went to be instructed in the Faith by Ronald Knox, who had found his way into the Church nine years earlier. The actual reception was performed by Monsignor O'Connor of Bradford, the original source from which grew the towering, legendary figure of Father Brown. It tickled Chesterton to be received into the Church by one of his own characters.

For sheer speed Ronald Knox could outwit even Chesterton. Lutyens, the architect of the monstrous Imperial Palace (or whatever he thought he was building) at Delhi, had a habit, on being introduced, of saying something entirely meaningless. It amused him to note the other person's surprise. Introduced to Knox he said, "Did you know that if you chop vegetables, the temperature rises?" Ronnie answered, "Yes. And if you cut acquaintances there's a coolness." That seems to me the speed of light.

But not only those who were being smiled at, even many who appreciated the wit as wit, felt that it raised a doubt of his seriousness.

Before and after he joined the Church—at Oxford as a student, at Oxford as chaplain to the Catholic students—his jests were quoted, especially the limerick

> There was a young man who said God
> Must find it exceedingly odd
> That the juniper tree
> Continues to be
> When there's no one about in the quad.

Jests whose origins were forgotten were quoted as "Ronnie's latest" —he suggested that I might publish a book of these *pseudephigrapha.* One of these, invariably quoted as his, ran

> Dear Sir, it is not at all odd.
> I am always about in the quad
> And the juniper tree
> Continues to be
> Since observed by
> > Yours faithfully,
> > God.

Actually this one annoyed him—he said that it was no more than a re-wording of his own limerick. I hadn't the heart to disagree with him.

Had there been nothing but the wit, he might have been remembered only as bracketed with the most entertaining of all Anglican clergymen, Sydney Smith. You remember "the Smith of Smith's" definition of the joy of heaven—"Eating foie gras to the sound of trumpets." (Hardly what Bunyan meant when he spoke of the death of Mr. Valiant-for-Truth—"The trumpets were sounding for him on the other side.") Even thus bracketed, Knox's wit would have been worth while. To have wit "clustering and sparkling" in a Catholic was good for morale, mine certainly.

But no one quotes Sydney Smith for his learning. Ronald Knox was quite monstrously learned. As a boy at school he published a book of verse in English, Greek and Latin. Scholars tell me that they could not always be sure that one of his imitations of Horace was not by Horace. And he accomplished the feat—unparalleled in the modern world with its vast multiplication of textual criticism—of translating the whole Bible single-handed. In nine years. St. Jerome took twenty!

Nor does anyone quote Sydney Smith for his religious values. Ronald Knox was deeply and continuously religious. Fun was fun, but only God mattered. As a boy of seventeen, still at Eton, he had bound himself by a vow of celibacy. As a young clergyman he made a resolve never to preach on any topic without bringing in Our Lady. One who knew him only from Evelyn Waugh's book about him would hardly have guessed that "priesthood was his natural air."

Yet, though an intense intimacy with spiritual realities was always his, for a long time his spiritual writing was almost wholly intellectual. I remember writing, "That time seems to have ended. There is a meditation on Our Lady in A *Retreat for Priests* which promises writing of great spiritual depth still to come. After all he is only sixty-eight."

At sixty-nine Ronald Knox died. To me who had been publishing him for thirty years—he had more books on our list than any other author—and discussing every book with him during the writing, it seemed like the end of an era, almost of a world. Seemed, I say. It was. Pope John was waiting in the wings, and Vatican II, and the Great Explosion.

If I did not explode with the rest, Ronald Knox was a large part of the cause. If I had to put in a phrase what in him affected me most, it was the combination of total devotion with total realism. If there is to be a Christian swing-back to reality, his retreat books—two for priests, two for laymen—could help enormously. One goes into retreat in order to meet two strangers, God and oneself. In his books one meets them both.

I met myself in them because he knew the human race. He was wholly charitable, but no one ever fooled him. Some years after the war a priest wrote to me: he and a girl had been fire-watching during the blitz: he married her, they had two sons: Ronald Knox was paying the boys' school fees: would I help with the rent? I mentioned this to R.A.K. at lunch. He made two comments: "He writes a good letter, doesn't he?" And, "I pay the fees direct to the school, of course." Wholly charitable, not to be fooled.

It was with the same realism that he looked at the Church. He loved it, even to the point of harshness with Anglicans, something I never felt in Chesterton or Father Martindale or Christopher Dawson—perhaps he was provoked as they were not. For years he preached on the feast of Corpus Christi at Corpus Christi Church—diagonally across Maiden Lane from Sheed & Ward. He dined afterwards with the parish priest and a group of his priest friends (plus an occasional layman). You couldn't know him long without realizing that priests were the company in which he was most wholly at home. One night he told them (I quote from memory): "Anglican friends occasionally ask me if I don't find the Roman Catholic clergy not quite gentlemen. This is my answer: My father was the Low Church bishop of Manchester. When I was a very High Church Anglican I used to spend a month every summer with him. Every High Church in his diocese wanted me to preach. I told them all that in my father's diocese I could not preach what he would regard as heresy. As a Catholic priest I continued my annual visit to my father. While he lived no Catholic church within his area ever invited me to preach. Which were the gentlemen?"

Certainly he was under no more illusions about the Church he had joined than about the Church he had left. The reason he gave for not having visited Rome as a Catholic has become a classic—"If you are a bad sailor, stay away from the engine room."

But however well or ill its officials may behave, it is the Church of God. And God was all in all to him. No one ever took more literally Christ's statement that you cannot serve God and Mammon. I remember my excitement as his publisher when Life magazine wanted to do a feature article on him, with masses of photographs. He refused to receive the photographer, so the article never appeared. I made no attempt to argue with him, one never did. His decisions came from the depths of his character; one might like them or dislike them but there was nothing one could do about them. It would have been wholly useless to remind him of the increase in sales and therefore royalties such publicity would bring.

Money left him unmoved. He gave the royalties of one book to a convent. He refused to touch the royalties on his translation of the Bible—nine years' vast labor. He directed that all should be paid to the Archbishop of Westminster for good works. I imagine, though I can't be absolutely sure I heard him say it, that he could not bring himself to make money out of the Word of God. We published the American edition. One day he asked me at lunch how much it had earned in royalties. I told him that up to that point we had paid the authorities at Westminster $40,000. "You know," he remarked amiably, "they have never thanked me." He obviously felt that all was as it should be.

He had prepared a neat Latin inscription for his tombstone,

> Domine, si potes et tu,
> Salva et me.
>
> Lord, if even you can,
> Save even me.

He told me if it wasn't used, I could have it. It wasn't.

v

There was once a university graduate who thought Socrates was a Roman, not only thought it, but said it. Caught by surprise, I was rude enough to look surprised. She explained that her subject was Sociology, not Classics. Thus it emerged that she did at any rate know that the Classics have to do with Romans and Greeks. But apart from this chance gleam of general knowledge, this one flaw in the otherwise unflawed integrity of her specialization, she was an excellent symbol of that dividing of the mind into separate departments which has for long ruined education and looks like ruining civilization.

I described this incident to Christopher Dawson. It depressed him. But then my Classics-dismissing sociologist would have been scandalized by Dawson. Sociology is about Society and Dawson said that the society which does not know its own past is like a man suffering from amnesia. If we don't know what made our ancestors tick, we don't properly understand our own ticking. His sociology was rooted in history, his history was rooted in theology: in him there was a continuous, enriching interflow among all three. I once heard Father Vincent McNabb say that the worst part of philosophy is the history of philosophy, the best part of history is the philosophy of history. Dawson was a philosopher of history, but he saw that a philosophy was not enough. Unless we know what history's goal is, our philosophizing about it must be only a guess: and its goal can be known only by God's revelation. Like St. Augustine, Dawson was a theologian of history. They both knew the beginning of the human race and its goal.

Which does not mean that he was a theologian with a smattering of history. His key principle was that the dynamic element in every society is religion, and that as religion fades a society weakens. All this he established as a historian relying on the facts of history, not as a theologian quoting the word of God. So the remedy for our present confusions lies principally in a spiritual awakening, and only after that in a change of social-economic mechanisms. But though these mechanisms come second, Dawson sees that the mind must work upon them. The social order must not be abandoned as not worth repair. The world was entrusted to man by God and we shall not serve God by neglecting it. Unless a Christian sees both sides of the problem he will only add one more muddling finger to a pie already over-fingered.

All this way of thinking was new to me. As I have shown earlier I had more or less accepted the old tag *ecclesia est patria nostra*—if one had the Church one needed no other community. It is my principal debt to Dawson that he made me see on how serious a misunderstanding of the Church this was based.

I won't say he knew everything, but there was nothing you could count on his not knowing. He lunched with us when I was reading Hegel for my book *Communism and Man:* I remarked that I thought a book could be written on the way the Church both attracted and repelled some of Hegel's predecessors like Fichte and Schelling: he thought aloud on the topic for a couple of hours, quoting at length. Talking of Freud's id and ego and super-ego he went on to develop a structure of a super-id whose possibility Freud had overlooked! In *The Ordeal of Gilbert Pinfold*, Evelyn Waugh writes of a man who heard voices and such, and gives us to understand that the experiences were his own. Dawson made three comments: (1) that Dante Gabriel Rossetti had had exactly similar experiences; (2) that there was the same apparent physical cause in both instances, whiskey and chloral; (3) that the first book Waugh had written was on Rossetti.

He knew the Scriptures as few non-specialists know them. And though I do not suppose he had read the whole of Migne's monster books, the Greek Patrology and the Latin, I never mentioned any of the Church Fathers on whom he could not speak with knowledge. I have told elsewhere of the solitary fact of Church History known to me and not to him: I had remarked that Hormisdas was the only Pope whose son became Pope: he seemed surprised, asked was I sure, checked and found that it was so: he asked me how I had happened to know: I said, "You told me." That slip apart, his memory was close to infallible—I imagine because each new thing learned found its place in a mental structure he has spent his whole life building. Edward Watkin reminded me of how Dawson could pick up a new book, skim over its surface, and find just what he wanted—rather as a diviner's rod finds water.

But he set me a problem about himself which I never managed to solve. He lived more wholly in the mind than anyone I ever met. I remember a visit I paid him after a long absence in America. He met me in the doorway and asked me if I had noticed how strange were the similarities between the religions of the Hairy Ainu and the Northern Siberian nomads, similarities all the stranger because they were ethnologically quite distinct. I admitted that this had escaped my notice.

At the end of December 1940 the first fire blitz on London had destroyed our offices, I doubt if a sheet of paper survived. A few days later I went to see him. He said he was sorry about Sheed & Ward, and went on immediately to express his concern about some newspaper article. I was so much bothered by the problem of continuing to exist that I no longer remember what the article was about; I should be surprised to hear that anybody else cared two straws about it.

But he could be as detached from his own troubles as from mine. I once visited him when he was quite seriously ill: he plunged at once into the difference between English and American puritanism, and his conversation could have been published as it came from his mouth.

The problem was how, living so completely in the mind, his views on how the world was going could have any relation to reality. But they had. He usually lived well off the map (to visit him in Devon I had to take three trains); he saw very few people (when he was teaching in Harvard's School of Divinity, he rarely attended faculty meetings); but he could take you under the skin of what was happening in Turkey today, or what would happen in Wisconsin (or wherever) tomorrow. As I have confessed, I never solved the problem.

VI

These five men I knew personally and closely. The sixth had been long dead—we published a volume to celebrate the sixteenth centenary of his death. Yet I felt his influence to be as personal, as close, as theirs.

Nothing could have been more casual than my meeting with St. Augustine. The meeting took place in America, when I was editing a Catholic Tutorial Masterpieces series. The absence of a Catholic reading public was our continuing problem. As a businessman the Catholic publisher is a parasite on the reading habits of the public— if they read well, he eats well. Like all intelligent parasites we studied the plant to which we had attached ourselves and found it depressingly weedy. In the previous century Coleridge, in his *Biographia Litteraria*, had stated one human dilemma—we are naturally lazy and hate having anything to do: but we are easily bored and cannot bear having nothing to do. So we are forever inventing things to do which are equal to nothing. Coleridge notes among such no-things, reading the advertisements in railway waiting rooms, and spitting over a bridge. Everybody can make his own list—playing cards, smoking, watching television—all ways of escaping the intolerable boredom of our own company.

Since universal education taught everyone to read, most of the reading done in our world comes high on that dreary list. Certainly it comes higher than it should on mine. We all do some of it, but this kill-time reading is very enfeebling, if it is the only kind of reading we do, if we never turn to reading for its true purpose, which is to feed our mind on minds richer than our own. That enfeeblement we found in Catholic reading: it was too undernourished to nourish us.

I wrote desperately about it under the heading "The Return of the Giants" in our house organ *This Publishing Business:*

Men who in music and poetry will have none but the masters are in their spiritual reading satisfied with writers of the standard of Ella Wheeler Wilcox—at this standard a great deal of spirituality is written: reading some of it is like chewing a mouthful of fur.

This double standard is not the incredible disharmony it might seem, for even the least excellent Catholic writing does contain the word of God, and two grains of the word of God, cluttered up with ever so many mediocre words and images provided by the human writer, can storm the mind more powerfully than "Hamlet" or the Fifth Symphony. All the same, there is a certain penuriousness in reading only the lesser moderns; and fortunately in our own days we are seeing the return of the Giants. St. Thomas was the herald of their return. Eyes clarified by him peered into the mist from which he had so lately been dragged, almost violently, by Leo XIII; behind him loomed vague and shadowy the figures of St. John of the Cross and St. Augustine, and over them the mightier figure of St. Paul, and over all, the Gospels. The mist still shrouds a hundred other figures, but these are the giants. These a Catholic owes it to his own maturity to know.

When I wrote this I knew only bits and pieces about St. Augustine myself. I knew some of the great phrases, that is all—"Give me chastity, but not yet," and, "The idling of grown men which they call business." Upon the Church which I was learning to understand, I knew two other phrases of his—"But for the Church I should not believe the Gospels"; and the one usually quoted as "Rome has spoken, the cause is finished." My meeting with him, as I have said, came through the Masterpiece-a-Month series. The plan was to publish each month a notable Catholic book with a Tutorial Introduction showing how it might be studied by groups in four weekly meetings. For the month of June (1941, I think) we had promised the *Confessions of St. Augustine*, which I had never read. I had planned to use the translation by Dr. Pusey, Newman's friend. At the beginning of January I took it from its shelf, meaning to write the Tutorial Introduction.

At the end of half an hour I knew it could not be used. It must surely be the least readable translation ever made of a masterpiece. For some reason Pusey, a contemporary of Dickens, translated the book into seventeenth-century English, a cacophony of "didsts" and "shouldsts." But it had been promised for June, and the year's tutorial plan needed it at that point. So I decided that the only thing to do was translate it myself. Given the time books take to print, it had to go to the printer in six weeks. And I was already committed to a lecture tour. I dictated part of the translation straight to the typewriter in the office, part on the tour. I would give my lecture, catch a night train and arrive in the early morning at the place of the next night's lecture. I would then dictate a few more pages to young women with typewriters. I never told them what the book was, they thought it was about me. The book came out in paper in June. Fortunately I had another two months to revise the translation for the cloth edition (finding only one appalling mis-translation).

By the time I had finished, I felt I would recognize Augustine if I met him in the street. I was wrong about this. I learnt later that he was a little thin man, which is not what the book felt like the product of! I am not writing about the book, or even about the author, save for the part he played in my own effort to get under the skin of the Faith.

The book really is timeless. There is nothing in it to date it—save a reference to the Emperor Valentinian, and even then we are not told which one! It is the most extraordinary combination—at once the most personal book ever written and the least personal. The author does not even mention his own name, gives no detail of the overworked and exciting life he was living when he was writing it. His concern is with God and the human soul, and there is no point of time to which these two realities and the relation of one to the other are not relevant. At the God end, so to speak, there has been no greater theologian; at the man end, he is practically the creator of psychology. He is unique for the combination in him of the passion of the flesh and the passion of the mind, both at white heat.

He knew the arguments developed by the Greeks for God's existence, and was not impressed by them. They might remove obstacles in the way of seeing God, but the seeing was the point and there was a surer way, the living of his revelation. The seen reality is a surer proof than any argument. Professor Ross Hoffman has phrased it perfectly: "The Faith is a reality to be recognized, not a thesis to be established." It would be for Aquinas, eight centuries later, to bring the Greek arguments to full life in this profounder light. Myself I had met Aquinas first. I came to Augustine from him. It may be the best way.

How much of this I realized at the time, I can no longer remember. But what to my present purpose I drew from Augustine very early was his conviction of the power of the human intellect. The mystic has his own way of ecstasy in direct contact with God, not as Infinite Meaning certainly but as Infinite Energy. Was that experience Augustine's? In the utterance of the ecstasy of his experience of God he equals any mystic: "What do I love when I love God? Light, melody, fragrance, food, embrace." So he says in the tenth book of the *Confessions*. I can but record my own conviction that it was not mystical contact that brought him to this, but the richest use of the mind in its striving for the apprehension of the truths of revelation. And that is a stimulation to a non-mystic like me. I can say, as Ronald Knox once did, that I have never had what is usually called a religious experience, an actual awareness of this other dimension of reality, the very feel of divine contact. I had been led to use my mind on the Mystics, partly by Edward Watkin, to whom my indebtedness in every intellectual area is wholly beyond measure, partly by Étienne Gilson's *Philosophy of St. Bonaventure* of which I translated half, partly by a study I made of Dionysius the Areopagite for my book *God and the Human Mind*. But I was always the little boy pressing his nose against the windowpane. The discovery of how deep Augustine could penetrate by sheer use of the grace-aided intellect was reassuring.

Most of the *Confessions* might have been written by a monk in his cell or by a philosopher in his ivory tower, so little of the world's clamors pierce through to them. In the concrete fact no bishop was ever busier. The Donatists had set up a bishop of their own in every see of Africa and Augustine was preaching and debating and writing against them, as against Manichees and Pelagians, almost getting himself assassinated. None of this is in the book. Nor does it give a hint that the Roman world was close to collapse—barbarians taking over Illyria and Spain and Africa. In 410 Alaric and his Visigothic regiments sacked Rome itself—and Augustine wrote his greatest book, *The City of God*, as a reply to the pagans who attributed this to the anger of the old gods against Christianity. He died while the Vandals were besieging his city in 430, two years before Patrick landed for the conversion of the Irish.

Christopher Dawson wrote, in *St. Augustine and His Age*, "To the materialist nothing could be more futile than the spectacle of Augustine busying himself with the reunion of the African Church while civilization was falling about his ears. It would seem like the activity of an ant which works on while its nest is being destroyed. But St. Augustine saw things otherwise. To him the ruin of civilization and the destruction of Europe were not very important things. He looked beyond the aimless and bloody chaos of history to the world of eternal realities."

Thus concentrating on the eternal, he affected history as no other man ever has. To quote Dawson again, "He was to a far greater degree than any emperor or barbarian warlord, a maker of history and a builder of the bridge which was to lead from the old world to the new." All the men who had to bring Europe through the six or seven dark centuries fed upon him. At the end of the sixth century Pope Gregory the Great was reading and rereading the *Confessions*. At the end of the eighth, Charlemagne was using *The City of God* as a kind of Bible. To that appalling period he taught that while spirit was primary, the body had its own sacredness—and these truths were life-preserving.

How Luther and Calvin used—or as I think, mis-used him—hardly needs saying. In our own day we find Albert Camus writing an essay "Hellenism and Christianity, Plotinus and St. Augustine"; as I am told, he planned his own return to the Church in the image of Augustine's—if only he had not been killed in a motor smash.

And we find Bertrand Russell, who couldn't stand Augustine, saying that his analysis of the meaning of time—with its contrast between the *"nunc fluens,"* the "flowing now," of time and the abiding now of eternity—was as far as philosophy could go along that line. Certainly it has conditioned all my own understanding of the Church and her teaching, and I have seen crowds held attentive by it in New York's Times Square.

CHAPTER 9

I WRITE A BOOK MYSELF

Up to the age of fifteen I had assumed that I would be a writer, indeed that I would be a poet—though I had not written a line of poetry then (or since). I can remember the very classroom in which the notion died in me. Ludicrously, I found myself realizing that I would never write as well as Shakespeare, so what was the point?

Once I was in publishing, working with writers, I might have been expected to feel a stirring of the old idea, but I didn't. I did some translating, beginning with Henri Ghéon's *Secret of the Curé d'Ars*, only because we had no spare money to pay translators. Publishing does not give one any strong feel of the romance of authorship. One of our authors told me that writing a book was as painful as giving birth to a baby. I mentioned this to another of our authors and he sniffed scornfully—writing to him was more like getting rid of constipation.

It was with no sense of a vocation reborn that I wrote and published my first book. In fact if I had not already solved the new writer's first problem—how to get a publisher—I would almost certainly not have written it.

I

I smile when I think how near I came to dedicating *Nullity of Marriage* to my wife. I remember one of the earliest comments on the book. Alice Curtayne's *St. Catherine of Siena* had been a standard-bearer in the New Hagiography as Karl Adam's *Spirit of Catholicism* in the New Apologetic. She asked me if I hadn't reduced marriage to very bare bones indeed. I suppose I had. I tried to do something about the flesh and blood reality of marriage in *Society and Sanity*—including my reflections on Chesterton's definition of marriage as a "duel to the death which no man of honor can decline." Anyhow even Helen of Troy had a skeleton: she couldn't have started the Trojan War if she hadn't. And there are forms of sickness which mean that the skeleton has to be looked at. From that kind of sickness modern marriage has long been suffering.

It was the street corner crowds who forced me to write the book. The Marlborough nullity case (he was a Duke) and the Marconi nullity case (everyone had heard of him as the inventor of wireless) put even the Inquisition into partial eclipse. They convinced just about everyone—Catholics included—that nullity decrees were simply a fictional name for divorce, enabling rich Catholics to buy their way out of marriages that hadn't worked. Literally for years our crowds kept up the attack—throwing in for good measure Napoleon's ridding himself of Josephine, who had not given him a son, in order that he might marry Marie Louise of Austria.

The crowd pressure meant that we had to make clear, first to ourselves, then to them, the distinction between divorce (a decision that an existent marriage is ended) and nullity (a judgment that the marriage never existed, that what looked like a marriage wasn't one). The mere statement of this roused in our listeners the kind of passions which had led rebellious mediaeval peasants to make "Hang the lawyers" their slogan. When we told them that this was not only the law of the Church but the Civil Law of England, they still held that it was a distinction without a difference. We found that we had to discuss marriage itself, a discussion not at all to the taste of our listeners, who thought it more fun to talk about dissolute dukes and money-mad clerics.

But we persisted, to our own clarifying at least. We were bored at having to bother with it. And the two nullity cases did at last fade out of people's memory, taking Napoleon and Josephine with them. But the study they had forced on us was to be valuable in the collapse of marriage itself which became clear to everyone during World War II. Clear? It was then that a daily communicant I knew—I had stood as godfather at her baby's baptism—divorced her soldier husband and married another man outside the Church. I am told her husband had thought it couldn't happen. So had I.

The first clarification we made was that the standard phrase "marriage is a contract" was disastrous. There is no such thing—so the crowd reminded us—as a contract that cannot be ended by the consent of both parties: if marriage is a contract, then it can be ended in the same way. But as the Church sees it, the contract—the agreement of the man and the girl to take each other as husband and wife —is only the beginning: marriage is the relationship which results from the contract. By the contract they have stated their will to be husband and wife: God makes them husband and wife. This is the sense of the phrase "marriages are made in heaven." It does not mean, as those who quote it cynically seem to think, that *matches* are made in heaven, that God thrusts that girl into that man's arms. They are free not to marry each other or anyone. It is up to them. But if they do utter their desire to be husband and wife, God takes them at their word and makes them so.

They make the agreement to marry, God makes the marriage. They are husband and wife by their own consent, but by his act they are now related to each other in a relationship directly made by him. "They are no longer two, but are one flesh," says Christ. Because their oneness is God-made, man cannot alter it. "What God has joined together," Christ continues, "man cannot put asunder."

Whereas divorce claims to terminate the relationship, nullity says there was no contract and therefore no relationship to terminate. To quote myself: "In any civilised society that allows marriage, there may or may not be a law of divorce; but in every such society there is a law of nullity—a law governing the conditions under which the marriage contract is valid. And this must be so unless either by some odd chance the contract of marriage is the one sort of contract about whose validity no question could ever possibly arise; or else marriage itself is so strange a relationship that any sort of contract—good bad or indifferent—or even the appearance of a contract, will suffice to bring it into being."

As we stated all this, it was perfectly logical, but no one was happy. I can remember Catholic friends either listening patiently as I expounded but still feeling that it was all pretty fishy, or else only seeming to listen but ending the conversation with, "After all, marriage is marriage, isn't it?" Fundamentally, people felt, marriage is a matter of feeling: romance couldn't live with all this (1) (2) (3) (4) stuff. And indeed it was hard to make clear to people with no legal training.

It was this last realization which decided me to write my small book *Nullity of Marriage*, comparing the English Law of Nullity with the Roman. I had taken my Law Degree in Sydney only six years before, and the English Law of Nullity was still fresh in my mind. I compared it with the Roman, giving cases which had been decided under each code. In 1959 I brought out a new edition, adding a comparison with the Matrimonial Law of New York State. In large part the principles are the same in all three codes, since they are the application to marriage of the general principles of Contract. The chief differences arise from the simple fact that the Church *is* the Church—a religion, and not the religion of England or the United States—above all from the Church's teaching that marriage of the baptized is a sacrament.

I have said that I was driven to write the book by the uproar, filling the newspapers and redoubled in our outdoor crowds, about the Marlborough (want of consent) and Marconi (not an agreement to marry for life) cases. The excitement about these somehow stirred up excitement about the decree granted Napoleon and Josephine—a curiosity all by itself. I shall say a word of all three.

The Marlborough Case

Consuela Vanderbilt, aged seventeen, was secretly engaged to a man with whom she was in love. Her mother, determined that she should marry the Duke of Marlborough, invited him to her home. He proposed to Consuela, who did not accept him; but her mother had the engagement announced in the papers. Her daughter pleaded, there were violent scenes, the mother threatening suicide. On the wedding day a guard was placed at Consuela's bedroom door. This was in 1895. The marriage was unhappy from the beginning. Two children were born. In 1905 the couple ceased to live together. In 1920 they were divorced and each remarried. The Roman Rota held that Consuela was quite incapable of standing up to her mother. The mother herself testified, "I forced my daughter to marry the Duke. . . . When I gave an order no one argued. Therefore I did not ask her I commanded her to marry the Duke . . . I considered that I was justified in over-riding her opposition as simply the folly of an inexperienced girl." The marriage lasted as long as it did, the Rota explained, because Consuela did not know about Nullity.

It was reported in the papers—I don't know how truly—that the American Episcopal bishop who had officiated at the wedding of the Duke and Consuela felt that the nullity decree was an insult to himself. If he did, he showed that he had not understood the Church's doctrine. It is not the officiating minister who makes the marriage: it is made by the man and woman. The minister is only a witness required by Church and State. If a priest is too far away to be available, the man and woman may marry each other in the presence of witnesses—or, on a desert island, for instance, with no witnesses at all. The Marlborough Case would equally have resulted in a nullity decree, even if the Pope himself had been the celebrant.

The Marconi Case

In 1905 Guglielmo Marconi married Beatrice O'Brien, a Protestant, on the condition that he would not oppose her seeking a divorce if the marriage did not work out happily. They lived together till 1918. Then they separated and later Marconi divorced her for adultery. In 1924 he petitioned for Nullity. Evidence of the condition was given by both parties, by her brother and sister, by a friend of his. The Court held that such a condition was not the taking of each other as husband and wife for life, which is what marriage is.

Napoleon and Josephine

If a Catholic does not follow the required form, the Church says the union is null, because of clandestinity. To the lay ear the word seems oddly chosen. A Catholic film star, let us say, marries in a registry office. The street is blocked with sightseers, newspapers from all over the world send their reporters, the newsreel cameras are there that the world's screens may show it. In due course the actor applies for and gets a decree of nullity from the Church, on the grounds of Clandestinity—which means secrecy, hiddenness. But the ceremony had not been witnessed by the one witness required by the Church, a Catholic priest: it was hidden from the face of the Church. England and most of the States are rather more rigorous than the Church in refusing to accept marriages where the due form has not been observed—lawyers even use the same word, Clandestinity.

Napoleon's first marriage to Josephine Beauharnais, in 1796, was indeed "clandestine," for it was by a civil ceremony and both were Catholics. All the excitement arose about the second, which took place because the Pope, brought from Rome to crown Napoleon as Emperor, refused to do so unless the defective marriage was put right. It took place without witnesses, in Napoleon's private rooms, late at night. When Napoleon wanted to marry Marie Louise of Austria, he petitioned for nullity on two grounds: (1) his consent to marry Josephine was not free (the Pope wouldn't crown him unless he did); (2) Clandestinity (absence of the two witnesses required by Church law). The petition was granted, not by Rome, which was not asked, but by two ecclesiastical courts in Paris, which would have found it difficult to refuse the Emperor anything. Local hierarchies indeed have always found it a problem to refuse strong monarchs. In France, especially after Leo X's agreement with Francis I to have all bishops appointed by the kings, they did not try very hard. That may have been one reason for an oddity I came across in somebody's Memoirs (I have forgotten whose). When the King had to go to Mass publicly, it would cause scandal if he was refused Communion: yet he was coming to the altar from bed with his mistress. Some bright person thought of the incredible solution—the King was given an unconsecrated host. There is something to be said for a non-established Church.

I have lingered on all this matter of nullity because it was—apart from the time Cardinal Merry del Val was in my crowd at Hyde Park! —my first chance to study the Roman Curia in action. Whether or not the Cardinal was impressed by my performance on the platform, I was vastly impressed by the performance of the Rota, the Court of Appeal, in marriage cases. In the scores of cases I studied, a closely thought-out body of law, rooted in Christian teaching on marriage, was applied with rigorous logic to an incredible variety of situations —I had had no notion of the ways in which human incalculability could complicate the simple act of getting married.

And I was able to check the accusation that the Church used the law of nullity for the advantage of the rich. The expenses of a case in the Rota vary widely, according to the extent of the inquiries that have to be made—usually totaling between $100 and $500, which as any civil court lawyer would agree is derisorily small. If the parties are too poor to pay even these expenses, then no charge at all is made. I got the exact figures for eight individual years—1927-30, 1952-54, 1956. Out of 608 applicants paying their own expenses 526 were successful, just 43 per cent. Out of 458 who could not pay, 215 were successful, just over 47 per cent.

II

No book of mine has ever brought me such a mass of letters. Its publication in 1932 had two immediate results, and scores of others spread over the years.

The first was a reaction from that towering Anglican scholar Bishop Gore. I had already met him at the house of Maisie's mother. He wrote and complained that I had made no reference to the nullity law of the Church of England. I answered that my book was about the law of my own Church, English Civil Law being introduced only for comparison. I added that I had not realized that in this matter there was a separate Anglican law and practice apart from the general law of England, and I should be very glad of information about it. I think I must have satisfied him, at least as to my good will, for he did not answer my answer.

But later came an incident which would have interested him. An Anglican vicar wrote to me that he had read my book and would like me to give him an opinion. A woman in his parish who had divorced her husband and remarried wished to receive Communion. He knew the common practice about it in his Church of giving Communion to the innocent party in a divorce, but this did not satisfy him. Innocent or guilty, she had married again and he did not wish to give Communion to a woman with two husbands living. If he gave me all the facts about her first marriage, would I tell him whether in my opinion the Roman Rota would have declared it null?

I wrote at once to say not only had I no authority to adjudicate in matters matrimonial, I was not even a canon lawyer. He said he quite understood that: he was not asking me to make a decision, but only to give him my personal opinion as to what the Rota would have decided. So I agreed. He sent me the facts. With scores of Rota cases seething in my head, I told him that I thought the Rota would have decided for nullity. He admitted the lady to Communion. I hope she prayed for me.

I have spoken of scores of reactions to the book scattered over the years. I kept no count of Catholics who wanted me to "take their case." I always gave the assurance that I had no standing in the ecclesiastical courts but would be glad to advise, I heard some heartbreaking cases, and helped a large number of people out of impossible situations.

But from all this I learned two things which the Rota reports of decided cases had not clearly shown me, especially the frequency of monstrous delays. Everyone who wrote to me seems to have suffered from them. Most had no idea how to cope with them. One who had was as close a friend as I ever had in the hierarchy, Archbishop MacDonald of Edinburgh. His Matrimonial Court had sent a case to Rome, recommending that the petition for nullity be granted. Months went by, years, I think. One afternoon he turned up at the Rota office and announced that he had come for the decision. He was told that the case was under consideration and that he might expect a decision quite soon. He said, "You don't understand. I have come for the decision. I am not leaving this building without it." They protested that the office was about to close. "I am prepared to spend the night here," he told them (waving, I believe, a packet of sandwiches). There was a hurried consultation: if they promised him a decision at eleven next morning, would he please go away now? He agreed. Next morning he got the decree and carried it home to the petitioner.

The slowness with which the Matrimonial Courts set about deciding cases so vital to human happiness could really be monstrous. One case in particular I remember. It concerned a man who had joined the Church in his twenties, just after divorcing his first wife for her adultery. His decision to become a Catholic showed a high degree of heroism, for it bound him to remain unmarried for the term of his natural life, so to speak—and a very unnatural life it promised to be. After some years he discovered, from my book *Nullity of Marriage*, so I am told, that he had grounds in Church law for having the marriage declared null, and sent the facts to the proper authority. For four years the proper authority did nothing whatever about it, simply let the document gather dust in his desk. At last he was forced into action, the case went to Rome and the decree of nullity was granted. The petitioner married again, most happily. I am told that at the wedding party one of the guests, "freely primed with huge potations," went about saying to all and sundry, "Sheed ought to be here. He made it possible." On that ground I should have spent a lot of time at weddings of people unknown to me.

I have spoken of heartbreaking cases. In some the heartbreak resulted from the heartlessness of the clerics to whom the bishop had entrusted marriage cases—prolonging the physical torment of the man and girl either by simply not getting on with the case, as in the instance I have just given, or sometimes by deliberately denying the petitioner his rights because the clerics involved disapproved of nullity anyhow! I was concerned with cases where the officials simply assumed that the petitioner was lying and told him so.

In some cases the heartbreak was caused by the law itself. A marriage requires the consent of both parties. If one of them went through the ceremony—through fear, for instance, of an angry parent —unwillingly, not consenting, then the marriage is null. If he said nothing to anyone at the time, how is he to prove it? How is the Court to know? Yet he himself knows, and knows therefore that he is not married. I read about such a case: it happened some centuries back. The man refused intercourse with the woman on the ground that he knew he was not married to her, so that intercourse would be for him the sin of fornication. The woman complained to the bishop that she was being defrauded of her rights: the bishop ordered the man to have intercourse under threat of excommunication: the man still refused; fornication, he insisted, was a sin. It was pointed out to him that he could set matters right by now giving the consent he claimed he had withheld at the wedding ceremony: but this would be a forced consent, of no use therefore to validate the marriage. I wish I could remember how the case ended.

Anyhow, the situation has been brought to my attention again and again where one party knows but cannot prove that there was no free consent, or that there was some other invalidating element. The marriage has in any event broken down. He wants to marry someone else. But no priest can marry him because his first union has not been declared null. It has been suggested that the case comes under the heading of "no priest obtainable" so that the parties are free to marry without one. My own feeling is that if a person of good character is prepared to affirm on oath that the situation is as he claims, his oath should be accepted. (Our Lord said of the Sabbath that it was made for man, not man for it. That is surely so of marriage.)

I have spoken of the rigorous logic with which cases are decided in the Rota. But can rigorous logic cover all the possibilities? For a long time now there has been a de-rigorizing tendency which in effect takes account of the diversity of men. It has always been obvious that the insane cannot make either a marriage contract or any other: it is being more clearly seen that insanity which shows only after marriage may have already existed before. Again it has always been realized that bodily impotence renders impossible the oneness which is of the essence of marriage. But there exist psychological defects equally fatal to genuine union. There is plenty of uncertainty here, but ecclesiastical courts are giving the matter serious consideration. Like the theologians who took the burning of heretics as being for the good of souls, canon lawyers of an earlier day can no more be blamed for not knowing modern psychology than for not knowing modern physics.

Insanity, psychological unfitness—these affect individuals, each case can be judged on its own merits. But there is a whole category of cases where the law itself seems to call for a closer look. A non-Catholic marries: his marriage breaks down: he becomes a Catholic, wants to marry. Is it to be assumed that he entered into his first marriage holding that marriage is made by God permanent, unbreakable? If he did not, then it is hard to see how the Church can bind him to a lifelong permanence which he did not intend, to which therefore he did not consent. It may be that a century ago it might safely have been assumed that all Christians saw marriage as the Church did. Can it be assumed now? This is the kind of case in which the rule of thumb simply does not work.

P.S. Because of its subject *Nullity of Marriage* had an effect on people's lives which one's other books were not likely to have. But a book I wrote and published about the same time did affect one life in a rather special way. I heard of it from a prison chaplain in Indiana. A Negro, sentenced to death for murder, told the chaplain he thought of becoming a Catholic. As there was no time for a full instruction, he was given a book of mine called A *Map of Life*. He read it, was baptized, made his first Communion. Then he was told that if he applied for a reprieve he would probably get it. He refused, saying, "If that book is true, I'm going." And he went.

CHAPTER 10

LECTURING IN AMERICA

I

A couple of chapters ago the reader may have been surprised to come unwarned on the publishing house we had started in America. I owe him a word of explanation.

Our publishing grew out of some American lecture tours. I had become a lecturer in America by chance, the chance that brought a Paulist, Father Elliot Ross, to Hyde Park one Sunday afternoon in the summer of 1924. When I got down from the platform he introduced himself and offered to arrange a lecture tour for me in the States. I said I was sorry but I was going back to Australia in a month or so. He pointed out that one way to Australia lay through the States. So that was settled.

In the same month two more chances brought American bishops to the same platform. Archbishop Dowling of St. Paul invited me to lecture in his diocese, Bishop Kelley of Oklahoma invited me to dinner in London. There he introduced me to two Mexicans, the Archbishop of Guadalajara and Msgr. Miranda, and Bishop Gherken of Amarillo, Texas. Bishop Gherken told me that he could accept as seminarians only men who would agree to do all the work of the seminary including growing the food—this was my first, and for a long time my last, intimation that an American bishop might be poor. The Archbishop told me a grisly story of the persecution then happening in his own country. He had not been expelled. But every morning the police would take him to the house of one of his Catholic people and threaten to blow his brains out on the doorstep unless a large sum of money was paid. After this had happened a few times, the Archbishop left the country to save his people from financial ruin.

During dinner Bishop Kelley, Canadian-born, naturalized American, asked me if I could read Latin. When I said yes, he offered to ordain me in a year. I asked, Would he also ordain Maisie Ward? He agreed there might be difficulty about that: but if I would come to Oklahoma he would see to my making a living as a lawyer.

I did go to Oklahoma, but only to give lectures and be on my way. Before I got there Father Elliot Ross had arranged lectures for me, mainly to Paulist parishes in Ontario, New York, Washington and Chicago. After that I talked my way to Portland, Oregon, and San Francisco, where I was rejoined by my mother, who had come as far as Toronto with me. And so back to Sydney, where I found the telegram from Maisie Ward accepting me as a husband.

She and I had two lecture tours in the States in 1931 and 1932, the second cut short by her mother's death. I have said that my becoming a lecturer in America was sheer chance. So was my becoming a publisher there. On the 1932 tour I lectured at Manhattanville, a college for women run by the Religious of the Sacred Heart. Father John J. Hartigan was at the lecture. He decided on the spot that Sheed & Ward must open a publishing house in New York, an idea which had never occurred to me. In January of 1933, with him as the magician in charge and me in a state of hypnosis, I signed a lease of the ground floor at 63 Fifth Avenue. Mark Twain had lived next door (I think he would not have liked us), Victor Herbert had written songs in the corner where my desk was to stand.

Up to that time all I knew of America I had learned from the indoor lecture platform. It was my novitiate as an American publisher. It has continued as my special way of contact with my new world. I shall dwell on it awhile.

II

It is in America that I have had most of my experience of lecturing to indoor audiences. I had talked (unpaid) to hundreds of audiences under the open sky before I ever found myself saying, "Reverend Fathers, Reverend Sisters, Ladies and Gentlemen," under a ceiling, for a fee. By now I have had thousands of audiences of both sorts, each experience helping with the other, but the outdoor vastly the more enriching.

One lesson in particular I had learned from it—never to assume the audience wanted me to go on talking. I have seen too many outdoor audiences walk away and leave me talking to myself, to think my personality is magnetic. Indeed I am more bothered with "holding" indoor audiences than outdoor, because the outdoor go when they've had enough, the indoor can only want to. If the outdoor crowd is still there, then you needn't worry: you're holding them.

Indoors how can you be sure? Dialogue is the essence of it. During the lecture the speaker must be aware of his listeners as saying to themselves after every sentence either "Yes" or "No" or "Maybe." When question time comes they write down their Nos and their Maybes. The speaker does his best to bring about a true sharing of minds. Ideally the meeting should be a small world of its own: the speaker never looks at his watch, that would remind the audience that there is a world outside in which they have commitments: he never drinks the glass of water thoughtfully provided for him, that would remind the audience that they too are thirsty.

The sane speaker never takes his audience for granted. The men in it have been dragged there by the women likely enough; you try to make them cease kicking themselves for having yielded to pressure. Colleges, high schools, not only expect to be bored, they start off hostile, especially if the lecture is in their own time, evening or weekend. I once gave three Sunday afternoon lectures at a convent. The hall was crammed. I remarked to the Reverend Mother that she must have put a lot of pressure on the girls. "No pressure at all. I simply told them noblesse oblige." The girls got the message. Already in the forties—long before Pope John and the explosion—I was conscious of the cynicism of the young: one could almost read in the rows of innocent faces the question "What's his racket?"

Seminarian reaction was more complicated—the students felt that the lecturer would not have been invited if the authorities did not regard him as part of the Establishment, yet he might have something of value for themselves. On the other hand they had been listening to lectures all day, and here was another: so any excuse for a laugh. In one seminary I had been talking of street corner crowds: a student asked, "Have you ever been hit by an orange?" I said, "No, but I have been missed by a lemon." That was thirty-one years ago. I still meet elderly priests who were there as students. They invariably remind me of the incident. And I wasn't trying to be funny. My answer was a model of precision—no orange was ever thrown at me, one lemon was.

A more interesting reminder of long ago came from a monsignor in the St. Paul Diocese. He claims that when he was a student—in Ohio, I think—I had given the advice, "Make up your mind whether you are preaching Christ or yourself. If you're preaching yourself, Heaven help you, for the better you do it, the worse it is." I cannot remember saying this. Perhaps it arose out of something I heard said of Bishop Schrembs—in Ohio as it happened: "He begins by saying something about Christ, then he says something about himself, and after a while you can't tell which of the two he is talking about."

To be remembered at all is something. You sometimes wonder if you're having any effect on anyone. After I had lectured in a convent, the Reverend Mother said as she led me to the dining room, "Your talk will have done the young nuns a great deal of good." The young nun who brought me my dinner said, "I hope Reverend Mother was listening." One of the root problems of the speaker is in those two snippets of dialogue. Everyone thinks the talk would be good for someone else. I doubt if there's a solution.

I had at least twenty indoor topics, religious and literary. I have already said that it was in Denver that I gave my first talk on the Catholic Intellectual Revival. I worked hard at a lecture about Thoreau, who is to me the greatest of American writers, showing (among other things, naturally) how splendid a religious meditation book could be drawn from the Notebooks: but I can't remember that any group ever asked me to give the lecture. One theme began to emerge in the thirties, shaping my own thinking and so my platform teaching. The theme was Sanity. In 1946 I wrote *Theology and Sanity*, seven years later, *Society and Sanity*, but for fifteen years before writing the first of them I had been—so to speak—obsessed with sanity. There is not a paragraph in either book that I had not talked out with scores of audiences, indoors and out, before I put it onto paper. All the difficulties they raised and my efforts to meet them are woven into both books.

Friends of mine, who had not read either—friends don't—were a little concerned for my mental state when the second appeared: they assumed I was writing about insanity—who writes whole books about sanity? I do. The insane stir my sympathy but I do not find their insanity very interesting, whereas sanity I find absorbing. It is a permanent preoccupation and a distant longing. I rate it too highly to think I have achieved it. Perhaps I may die sane—though I fear the betting is against it.

After this somewhat rhetorical outburst you may wonder what all the fuss is about when I say that by sanity I mean seeing what's there. Who doesn't? you ask. Who does? I answer.

If a man starts seeing things which are evidently not there we call him insane and do what we can for him. But a man may fail to see the greater part of reality and cause no comment at all. He may live his life in unawareness of God, of the spiritual order, of the unnumbered millions of the dead, and nobody thinks of him as needing help.

Once I was introduced to an audience in France. The chairman, who knew no English, took me aside and asked about my book, which he called *La Théologie et la Santé*: "*santé*" of course means "health." I tried to explain what "sanity" meant—living mentally in the fullness of reality. The French language has a word for "insanity," but if there is a French word for "sanity," my chairman did not know it. He introduced me to the audience as author of *La Théologie et l'hygiène mentale*. I decided to leave it at that.

For a Christian, seeing what's there means seeing what Christ saw, living mentally in the real universe he opened up to us. He saw God in all things. So should we, this not as a high level of sanctity but as a first level of sanity.

I discovered early that this distinction has constantly to be underlined. Several times I have paused in lecturing on Trinity or Incarnation to say, "I can read your minds. You are thinking, How holy he is." A roomful of embarrassed faces told me how right I was. I pointed out that they had, in Belloc's phrase, confused their categories. Sanity is the health of the intellect, sanctity of the will. All that they have learned about me is that my intellect sees clearly. But of my will, where charity resides or doesn't, they have no vision.

This was what *Theology and Sanity* was about. There is a well-known spiritual book, *The Practice of the Presence of God*, by Brother Lawrence. It is excellent, but its title has given the impression that living in God's presence calls for holiness. What we do about it may be holiness, but being mentally aware of it is simple sanity. Even people who believe in God can think of him as belonging exclusively to the sphere of religion; they would feel it a sign of religious mania to bring him into the practicality of life as life has to be lived. During World War II I lectured on it in Sydney. The Sydney *Morning Herald* carried no report of the meeting. The reporter had returned to the office in despair, telling her colleagues that I appeared to think that God could affect the outcome of the war: how could she possibly report that? Apparently they agreed with her that silence would be kinder to me.

In my book I had asked the reader to imagine himself riding in a car warning the driver that he was headed straight for a tree. If he answered, "It's no good talking to me about trees, I'm a chauffeur not a botanist," the passenger would be wise to leap out of the car: the driver is mad. For a tree is not only a fact of botany, it is a fact, and in a collision will knock out brains without regard to their knowledge or ignorance of botany. God, so to speak, is not only a fact of religion but a fact, an infinite fact. He made this universe of nothing, so that only his will holds it in existence from moment to moment. The formula for every created being, man included, is nothingness brought into being and held in being by omnipotence.

I apologize for dwelling so long on this matter. It has been the key to all my lecturing, it is at the center of the "I" who is half of this book's title, the "I" whose experience of the Church the book records. Having made this apology, I shall strain the reader's tolerance for another paragraph by mentioning one more illustration I used in the same chapter of *Theology and Sanity*—the illustration of a coat hanging on a wall, covering the hook by which it hangs. If a man is not aware of the hook, then he is wrong about the nature of coats, of walls, or gravity. He is not living in the real world. But everything whatever is held in existence by God: not to be aware of him damages sanity more than overlooking a hook.

I realize that, written down, these two illustrations may not be very impressive. I can but record that discussed with every sort of crowd, literally thousands of times, they had a kind of detonating power. One service I know I rendered crowds—I forced them to face the question, "Why isn't there nothing?" In the fifties and sixties, someone in the crowd (a university man of course) would be heard to say, superiorly, "That isn't a question." I would say, "Yes, it is. I've just asked it." He would then explain the philosophical sense in which he refused to grant it status as a question. To which I would say, "Whether it is a question or not, I still want to know why there isn't nothing."

Once that question is rooted in a man's mind—and I have rooted it in the minds of many—there is no way of uprooting it: it remains to nag him perpetually, the nagging being sanity's birth-pains. As that very able South African philosopher Martinus Versfeld phrases it, "Wisdom is that undeviating fidelity to the actual, that conformity to the primary wonder that there is anything of which we can say 'It is.' "

Right on into the fifties I did real lecture tours. In one of them I gave seventy-seven lectures in six weeks, seldom more than two in one place. Only the young can do that. Of recent years I like to do two or three or four and then head home. My wife too was lecturing. Usually we went our separate ways. I think Alaska is the only state in the fifty in which neither of us has spoken. Occasionally our orbits interacted and we had the fun of appearing on the same platform.

One such time she was staying in a convent. I was taken to her room. On the wall I found some lettering—

CEASE

THE HEART OF JESUS IS HERE

Cease what? I wondered.

When I began this chapter on our American lecturing I had just mentioned the founding of our New York house. It is hard to say whether I learnt more about the Church—that being my concern in this book—from the lecturing or the publishing. Certainly a couple of thousand lectures with an average of twenty or thirty questions after each, has taught me a lot about American Catholics. If there is anything bothering them that they have not asked me about, I can't imagine what it is.

III

But this is after a lifetime of it. I smile when I think how little I knew of America when I began publishing there. Three lecture tours amounted to little more than a crash course.

An incident floats into my mind as I cast back forty to fifty years. I had not been in Chicago's Harrison Hotel half an hour when a bootlegger was on my telephone offering to sell me a variety of strong drinks: the bootlegging in that area was in Catholic hands—Spike O'Donnell, I was told, was a most devout Catholic: he would not touch prostitution, and would kill only in defense of his right to make a living at a business which theologians had assured him was legitimate, since prohibition was against the Natural Law! I was not in Chicago for the Requiem Mass and practically regal funeral of Dion O'Bannian. By that time bootlegging was in the control of less concerned Catholics like Al Capone. Father Bede Jarrett, the English Dominican I have already mentioned, told me of a pleasing incident. He was to preach a retreat to a convent of contemplative nuns. He arrived on a freezing winter day. The mother superior asked what he would like to drink. He said coffee. She told the lay sister, "The Reverend Father would like coffee, Sister." The sister returned with whiskey. Father Bede Jarrett said, "No, Mother, I really meant coffee." The superior said, "The Reverend Father really meant coffee, Sister."

My sponsor, Father Ross, was the only priest I met who was convinced that the country was within its rights in forbidding the drinking of alcohol. But he was not the only priest who was horrified at the ecclesiastical silence about the corruption of the police by racketeers. I remember the anger of a small group of priests when they discussed what the Church authorities would do to any priest reckless enough to mention the topic at a Police Communion Breakfast. I had no means of judging how right they were in saying that only a notorious breach of the Sixth Commandment would bring ecclesiastical condemnation to a Catholic politician. But I was reminded of it when that colorful character, New York's mayor, Jimmy Walker, had to go—for a breach of the Sixth Commandment.

Yet precisely on the Sixth Commandment those earliest tours gave me some surprises. I have spoken of the assumption in my Australian years that priestly celibacy was really observed, the rare exceptions we heard about were seen as examples of poor fellows who had no vocation in the first place. And my years in England had done nothing to alter that assumption. America did.

A priest, an assistant in a big parish, had spoken very brusquely to a girl. He laughed at my startled look. "You see," he explained, "the three assistants before me have all got married. I have to be careful." Up to that moment I had thought Arthur Preuss had been exaggerating. He was a very notable lay theologian already known to me as translator of Monsignor Pohle's manuals of theology. He poured out a stream of stories, especially of episcopal turnings of a blind eye on clerical wrongdoings in the sex field, which took my young breath away.

Of Catholic life as a whole three qualities impressed me—nowhere had I seen such crowds at daily Communion, nowhere had I seen Lent taken so seriously, nowhere had I met such a devotion to the papacy. But there were less attractive qualities—I had never been in an obviously wealthy church before, and there was of course the whole relation of whites to Negroes.

Wealth first. Money did indeed flow, not to me of course. I sat at dinner with half a dozen Catholic businessmen. They were wondering what they could do for poor So-and-So (a name well known to me). I asked my neighbor what was the trouble with poor So-and-So. "He's down to his last four million" was the answer. Literally, I heard those words with these ears. You'll be relieved to hear he came out of it all right. With the clergy too I met opulence. There was a monsignor who entertained me in Chicago: he told me of the answer he gave to a Protestant minister who had expressed amazement at the splendor of his residence, "You ministers have better halves, but we have better quarters." Like St. Peter in the presence of a greater glory he did not know what he was saying.

Then there was the rector of a church I attended in New York: on the Sunday he preached on our duty to support our clergy "according to our means" (a phrase to which as a sort of lawyer I could attach no meaning at all): a few days later the rector and I crossed the Atlantic in the same ship, he first-class. I heard hair-raising stories of Polish Catholics who had been refused absolution in the confessional because they had not paid their Easter dues. I came upon another rector later who asked us to kneel while the collection was being taken up and recite with him a prayer of his own composition urging God to give us the grace to contribute generously, three dollars being mentioned as the lowest rung on generosity's ladder. But he was a well-known eccentric.

Not that a priest needed to be an eccentric to be driven to talk about money. The mere cost of the Catholic school system was frightening—and not only in America. I stood outside Blackrock College in Dublin while the staff (not the teaching staff) filed slowly past, each carrying a placard with nothing written on it but the amount of his weekly wage.

In another college I came down late for breakfast. The elderly layman waiting at table prattled on, I half listening. But I did catch one complete sentence, "Yes, it's a wonderful job. I get my weekly wage regularly once a month."

By chance I had a long glimpse of a curious episode. In a certain town a notably corrupt Catholic politician—protection rackets, brothels and such—presented a certain religious order with a very large sum of money. The father superior sent it back to him. The order was split in two, some feeling cleaner because tainted money had been refused, some furious at the thought of the good the order could have done with it. The superior was not re-elected. I knew him, but not well enough to ask him about it. I never met the politician, so had no way to find out what moved him to make the gift—hoping to win Catholic support perhaps, or relieving his conscience. I have referred to the episode occasionally in the long years since, and have found my fellow-Catholics divided in opinion along the same lines as the priests of the order. Those who think the money should have been kept used their own variant of the Latin tag *pecunia non olet*, money has no smell. Well? Has it or hasn't it?

Before I arrived in the States I had known there was a color problem. But one had to be there awhile to realize its enormousness, and awhile longer to realize its enormity. There is writing enough on it and I shall not attempt to add one more treatise. My concern throughout this book is with the Church as I experienced it, and the Negro problem forced me to look at the Church more closely. I jot down a handful of incidents that I had to build into my understanding.

It was a shock to find churches in which Negroes must approach the altar rail only when all the whites had received their common Lord. I assumed that things had somehow arranged themselves that way, no one actually insisting, until I met Monsignor —— no, I won't name him, he is dead and cannot explain himself. He was a cultivated man—after hearing Chesterton lecture he had published a furious article accusing Chesterton of taking money by false pretenses: I did not blame him for this, because the price of admission had been high and Chesterton had a habit of holding his notes close to his mouth and mumbling into them, laughing convulsively as he mumbled. What I found totally beyond my comprehension was his standing up in his pulpit and asking the Negroes present at Mass not to come again—they had a church of their own close at hand!

I had heard the story of Father Herbert Vaughan's conversation in the previous century with a highly color-conscious mother superior: as he was departing he said that he would pray for her to have a very high place in heaven: she purred, but stopped purring when he added "with a Negro on each side of you." Years later he came back and she begged him to take that prayer off her. It was just an odd story, it had happened long ago: but my monsignor was here and now.

To me it was strange enough that anyone at all who believed in the Church as Christ's Mystical Body should take such a line, but in priests, as I have said, I could make no sense of it at all. In one of the newly founded Catholic Evidence Guilds the priest in charge threatened to resign if Negro Catholics were allowed to become speakers. I was present when a Dominican champion of the colored attacked a Jesuit because the colleges of his order did not admit Negroes: "But," said the Jesuit, "we have ordained Negroes. You haven't." When one Catholic women's college decided to accept *one* Negro student, so large a majority of the alumnae raised a storm that the colored girl decided not to come.

I did my best to understand. I discussed it once with a group of educators of mixed religions. They were agreed that Negroes were intellectually inferior. I said, "I wish I could write English as well as James Baldwin." But of course no one is brought down by that sort of shot from the hip.

I remember one conversation in which I really tried to get a Catholic girl from the South to help me to see why she felt as she did. She did her best, I did my best. She could not convince even herself that she had said anything to convince me. I summed up our conversation—"if you have a very strong feeling for which you can't even state a justification to yourself, it might be either a neurosis or a psychosis." She was wholly unresentful.

To me the color question remains a mystery in Catholics who love their Lord. A mystery of what? Of ways of feeling too deep for up-rooting? Surely of truths not grasped in depth. Certainly of the plain truth that only the rare mind can question the familiar, the accepted. To the cliché "Habit is second nature" the classical retort is "Habit is ten times nature." And this is as true socially as individually.

IV

In those days the principal fact of Catholic life was the hierarchy. In my first lecture years I had a considerable experience of bishops. Most lived at a standard not known to me in England, but I remembered Bishop Gherken and his seminarians who had to grow their own food, and keep the seminary clean and in repair. And I was soon to meet a bishop on his way home from a meeting of the hierarchy in Washington, where he had gone to get a handout to enable his Rocky Mountain diocese to survive.

But rich or poor the bishops mattered enormously. It took me a while to learn that no bishop counted much nationally—Cardinal

Gibbons was dead, and no one took his place. But within his own area a bishop had absolute power. Yet even there one found exceptions. I was staying with Bishop Kelley in Oklahoma City. I came down to his Mass on the first morning, found some Mexican nuns there but no server. So I went up to the altar and served the Mass with no more than my normal inefficiency. At breakfast the bishop asked me not to do it again. The nun who usually recited the responses was upset. She would probably not come to Mass at all next morning: he would do his best to smooth things over.

Before we began as New York publishers I had already met quite a number of bishops. Archbishop Hanna of San Francisco had been wonderfully kind to me as a stranger. I remember Bishop Bennett of Lafayette, Indiana, for his fatherliness to his clergy, I had never met priests who so took it for granted that they would be welcome in their bishop's house. I met one or two notably scholarly bishops, a minority quite startlingly not so. Mother Dammann of Manhattanville told me of a bishop who asked her whether he could do anything for her in Rome. She told him she would like a relic of St. John of the Cross. He said that would be easy, the Passionists were his good friends. She said, "No, Your Excellency, not St. Paul of the Cross, St. John of the Cross." "Oh, are they different?" she says he said.

And I met one bishop—retired—who had neglected his reading to his own misfortune. He had reported one of his clergy to Rome for Communism and enclosed a list of the priest's revolutionary statements taken down as he uttered them from the pulpit. They were all quotations from Pope Leo XIII's encyclical *Rerum Novarum*.

Such accidents will happen of course. But barring accidents, the bishop's power in his own area was absolute: no one seemed to question it, certainly the bishop didn't. One bishop I met was known for his proclamation of the rights of the working man, he had built up a large organization to help the poor, but he would not let his own lay staff join a union.

I had the feeling that many of the bishops I met found me rather a puzzle. They showed small sign of sharing my concern with the millions who were not getting gifts Christ wanted them to have. Most of them thought I carried my concern to an unrealistic extreme: I thought they showed small sign of feeling it at all—beyond having occasional missions to non-Catholics. It was hard to think they were losing any sleep over it. About the criticism which once or twice slipped out from me of the teaching of doctrine in their schools and seminaries they were polite: but there too they felt I was going to an unrealistic extreme. What would they have thought a realistic non-extreme?

Anyhow, as a husband and father, a businessman given to the study of theology, I fitted into no category. Later they got used to me in this role. Archbishop Hallinan of Atlanta, for instance, wrote of my book *God and the Human Condition* as "a mystical martini"—I am a non-drinker but those in a position to know told me this was high praise. And Bishop Wright paid as neat a compliment to a book of mine as I ever expect to receive even as a joke. He told an audience that a theological difficulty had been sent for answer to the Holy Office in Rome. The cardinals could not solve it. They asked the Holy Father. He said, "As it happens I have just been reading a book called *Theology and Sanity*. It says . . ." The Pope doubtless had better reasons than this for making Bishop Wright a cardinal.

Another compliment was all the funnier for not being meant as a joke. A chairman described me as "Aquinas in a collar and tie." I caught the eye of a Dominican in the front row. He looked startled. He was wearing a collar and tie.

That incident was later. In the beginning, my status as a business-man with theological interests bothered people.

Nuns in a Chicago convent were discussing the news that André Gide's books had been placed by Rome on the Index of forbidden books. An older nun came in halfway through, heard that Gide had been banned, and said, "I'm very glad. Laymen should leave theology alone." She was disappointed to learn that it was Gide not Sheed—all the more so because she had never heard of Gide.

A customer in the Sheed & Ward bookroom refused a copy of my *Map of Life* on the ground that he did not want theology written by a layman. "You can't call Mr. Sheed a layman exactly," said the girl in charge. That "exactly" was the problem.

And of course there were those who doubted my theological competence. A Maynooth professor was heard to complain, "I teach my young men theology, and they go out and preach Theology and Sanity." And at a certain university there was a professor who hated the book so thoroughly that a student had but to mention it to launch him upon a tirade against it which might last for the whole period, leaving the class free to write their letters home or read their detective stories.

v

My topic is the Church, not the American Church, not the Church of any one country. The Churches of different nations have each their own ways of falling short of what their Lord wants. Any national Church can help one's understanding of the whole Church. I found the Church in America especially educational because I came new to it as a grown man.

As we began publishing in it forty years ago, it was a wholly ecclesiastical structure. The sacrificial-sacramental-doctrine-defining sphere was clearly priestly. There was not only no concept of a lay sphere of action, there was not even the feeling that there was a vast area of Catholic activity which did not require priesthood for its performance and could only sidetrack priests from their priestly work. Any area in which decisions must be made, power exercised, money spent, was as a matter of course to be controlled by the clergy.

But just as we were opening up at 63 Fifth Avenue, the laity were entering into three areas from which they were not banned by vested clerical interests. There was the living among the poor of Dorothy Day, Peter Maurin, and the Catholic Worker group; there was the living among the Negroes of Catherine de Hueck and the Friendship House group; there was the outdoor teaching of the Faith, first by David Goldstein and then by the Catholic Evidence Guild. In all these the laity were given the privilege (I am not being sarcastic, it was an immeasurable privilege) of doing work for the Church which the clergy did not feel to be theirs.

I remember 1933 as a year in which our own publishing agonies were beginning and in which Dorothy Day and I groaned together over the general hellishness of trying to serve the Lord: Peter Maurin lived in some sort of translunar sphere of his own. I gave talks at the Catholic Worker house on the Lower East Side, and at the Friendship House in Harlem. And I talked outdoors.

If my memory is right my first outdoor talking in America was done in Oklahoma City. There was no Evidence Guild there but Father Leven, who from the American Seminary in Louvain had come to speak at our meetings in London, took me out to talk on the courthouse green on two or three afternoons. It remains the only place in which I have been heckled by a man with a gun on each hip. He called me Brother and I returned the compliment. I can't remember a single amiable discussion with a man who called me Brother—something to do with Cain and Abel perhaps. As the meeting went on my Oklahoman grew less than brotherly, more like an English heckler.

For as we went on to join in the founding of Guilds in Baltimore, Washington and Philadelphia, we discovered how vastly more polite American crowds are than English. It was rare to be interrupted till one actually asked for questions. And I have never been called a liar at an American meeting—it used to be the normal way for an English heckler to indicate that he was losing the argument. How different was the man I had in Baltimore who raised his hat as he left the meeting, reminded me of the Inquisition, then went swiftly off.

The outdoor movement never caught on in America. I made several appeals to Catholic groups, was applauded, but could not get speakers. I got the impression that Americans are more self-conscious than English men and women. I have described some American outdoor incidents in Chapter 3. There were never more than half a dozen Guilds at one time, running only a few meetings a week, so that America does not provide me with the same flood of memories as England. But one New York meeting has a strong hold on my memory. It was outside the Treasury Building, just off Wall Street. It began farcically. A man wearing a clerical collar set up his platform a few yards from mine. He had a very small crowd and only one questioner. At a point I heard him say to the questioner, "Would you take the platform for a while? I want to go to the bathroom." The questioner obliged and talked no worse sense than the speaker, who returned in a few minutes, having evidently found the bathroom.

At the end of my own meeting a man stopped me and said, "You spoke of Dublin. That's where I come from. I used to be a Roman Catholic priest, now I'm an Episcopal priest. That shocks you, doesn't it?" I said, "I'm never shocked at anyone's sins but my own." I went on, "Tell me, do your Episcopal colleagues feel that there is anything in your priesthood that theirs lacks?" He went away without another word. I had asked the question in all seriousness, I really wanted to know.

I am reminded of an incident concerning Bishop Pike, who as a youth had left the Catholic Church. It was related to me years later by Bishop Wright. At an ecumenical sherry party or some such gathering he was approached by Bishop Pike, who said, "You don't think

I'm a bishop, do you?" Bishop Wright answered, "*You* think you're a bishop, don't you? Why should you care what I think?"

P.S. Graham Greene came into our Fifth Avenue office one day in the thirties, told me he was planning to visit Mexico, and asked could I give him an introduction to the Catholic authorities there— a persecution was on at the time, and they might be suspicious of a stranger. Bishop Miranda, whom I had met in London with the Archbishop of Guadalajara, was in New York. I introduced Greene to him as a Catholic of good will. *The Power and the Glory* was the fruit of that visit. I have not had the occasion to find out what Bishop Miranda thought of what Greene thought of the Church in Mexico: or indeed of what Bishop Miranda thought of me as a judge of good will.

CHAPTER 11

PUBLISHING IN AMERICA

I

I have spoken of the agonies of our American beginnings as publishers. The word is not too strong. We had not enough capital to start with. To make it worse, America went off the gold standard the week after we issued our first books, so that all the prices were wrong. And Nature has not built me for the solving of financial problems. Twenty years later I was at a reunion of my High School class in Sydney. It was agreed that if, back in 1913, we had had to choose the boy least likely to succeed in business I'd have had every vote, including my own. I shall not lacerate readers with the details of our woes. I shall say only that without the aid of John Moody, the founder of Moody's Investors Services, we should not have survived our first year.

To the best of my memory we were the only Catholic publishers who did not deal in statues, altarpieces, vestments and such—lumped together as Church goods, smiled at by the progressive as *bondieuserie* (make your own translation). It was axiomatic that a Catholic publisher could not exist without Church goods. We did not go in for textbooks either, that other necessary of Catholic publishing life. We wanted to get Christ's revelation out of the classroom into the living room—which shows how young we were.

At least I knew more about publishing in 1933 than I had known when we opened in London in 1926. I could hardly have known less, there wasn't any less to be known. I had seen pamphlets through the press in my last year in the Catholic Truth Society, but of publishing books I had had no experience at all. It would have paid me to work three years in a publishing house for nothing. As it was I used as my manual a book which had just appeared—*The Truth About Publishing*, by Stanley Unwin. The first time an American publisher —Bernard Benziger—came in to buy American rights of one of our books, I had to look up "American rights, sales of," or whatever the heading was, in my manual. When six years later we started at 63 Fifth Avenue Bernard dropped in with advice: it was to the effect that most businesses had enough capital for their first year, it was about the sixth or seventh that survival would become a question. I have told of our first year: by the seventh, World War II had begun and the shortage of things to buy meant that publishers could sell just about anything they had. So swollen inventories, the curse of publishing, vanished like snowflakes in a heat wave.

Back in 1926 we had seen publishing as a simple proposition. Authors would write books, we would publish them, the public would buy them. Belloc's sister, Mrs. Belloc Lowndes, told us of Methuen, a London publisher who had started with nothing and now owned a country estate with ten gardeners, or was it twenty? We ourselves never got as far as even one, full-time that is.

I thought I knew the kind of book I wanted to publish—namely the kind I wanted to read myself. But that covered too wide an area. It included an awful lot of rubbish and anyhow we weren't rich enough for it. We must narrow our choice to books which would justify our existence, i.e., books which would meet an actual need. After a lot of feeling around we came to the conclusion that we should be aiming just above the middle of the brow, and that is where we have been aiming for forty years or so. It has worked well enough. But there were times when it seemed not to be working at all. A friend introduced me to a business expert. He advised me to publish a line of books aimed at lower brows: with the profit we made from those, we could finance more valuable books. I said it seemed to me like running a string of brothels to raise money for a purity campaign. "Why not?" our expert demanded. Anyhow, if you publish books simply to sell, the chances are that you won't sell them. If you publish books you *want* to publish, you are more likely to find a public for them. Even if you don't, at least you've had the pleasure of publishing what you wanted to.

Within a month of beginning we had found an element new to us—the demand of priests and nuns for discounts from booksellers. I remember saying, "in my excess" as the psalmist has it, that discounts are to the clergy what sex is to the laity, an itch and a constant preoccupation. And it was not simply a request for charity, but an assumption that they were entitled to pay less than lay people. The limit, perhaps, was reached by a priest who wrote to a church goods house demanding a clergy discount on a chasuble. Related to this sense of entitlement was a letter we had from a nun saying that Reverend Mother was about to have her Golden Jubilee and would we please send a gift of money. We did not answer. A second letter said that as we were ignoring Reverend Mother's jubilee, they would order no more books from us.

In the sixties came a new financial oddity. Quite suddenly the Continent of Europe was ablaze with the discovery that the streets of America were paved with gold. Catholic writers who had been content with a little fame learned about a wonderful thing called a dollar. One of them sold the same book to four American publishers, getting an advance payment from each. When he had to pay back three of the advances he was confirmed in his conviction that money is the only value Americans recognize.

But in the normal way it was the Catholic bookseller, not the publisher, whose blood was being sucked. It was cruelly hard on people who at the best were barely getting by. But rich as the Catholic body was, almost all the Catholics who wanted to serve the Church found themselves reduced to playing airs on a shoestring.

II

There was another matter to which we gave a certain amount of thought—there were some in our new public who found us just too lighthearted. A Protestant magazine sent us its first number and asked for an advertisement. In the advertisement we took we congratulated them on the excellence of the articles but said we found the whole number rather somber, with not much air of enjoyment in being Christians.

It is a matter of wavelength of course. There was the heckler who accused Father Vincent McNabb of being flippant. "Not flippant," said Father Vincent, "just full of fun." We decided to go ahead and be ourselves, with our house organ especially. We had begun with a modest pamphlet *This Publishing Business*. We turned it into *Sheed & Ward's Own Trumpet*, on the lines of W. S. Gilbert's

> If you wish in this world to advance
> Your merits you're bound to enhance
> You must stir it and stump it and blow your own trumpet
> Or trust me you haven't a chance.

When the police came along and led away one of the girls in our Trade Department for some form of unbalanced sexuality (the police were sensitive twenty years ago), someone suggested that we

bring out a special edition of Sheed & Ward's Own Strumpet. But
we didn't publish that.

Our occasional fooling had not caused any surprise in England,
the English having a natural habit of laughing over things they take
seriously. I remember my own joy when I met—in England—the
phrase "They're a funny lot, as the devil said when he saw the Ten
Commandments." I have remarked how unthinkable it would have
been for a French Chesterton to have clowned as outrageously as
G.K. did. A friend of ours has just returned from Germany, where she
had enjoyed herself with a group of Germans in a seaside hotel. At
the end of the week it occurred to them to ask her what her job was.
"I teach theology," she told them. They refused to believe it. "But
you are so happy," they said.

That perhaps was in Yves Simon's mind. He had come to a
lecture I gave at St. Mary's, South Bend, with that great teacher
Bruno Schlesinger, who had known me long enough to be used to
me. Part way through Yves whispered to Bruno—"He is so funny,
but he is so right." I gather he had been particularly startled when,
having told of the agnostic lecturer Ingersoll and his habit of taking
out his watch and giving God ten seconds to strike him dead, I went
on to imagine Ingersoll's arrival at the gate of heaven and God as
saying to him, "Have you brought your watch?" Yves had taken me
for an intellectual, and no French or German intellectual would have
lectured like that.

Being ourselves meant being Maisie and me and Jean Charlot and
Marigold Hunt, who wrote the back page of the *Trumpet* for the
twenty-five years of its existence. A reader probably had all four of
us in mind when he wrote, "I find Sheed & Ward's publicity hard to
take. It reminds me of an elderly nun tipsy on sherry trifle."

It was left to a German, a refugee priest, really to let fly at us. Under the title *The Mass in Slow Motion*, we had published a series of
sermons preached by Ronald Knox during the War to schoolgirls
evacuated to Shropshire, where he was making his translation of the
Bible. The sermons were a rather notable combination of humor and
spiritual insight. So most people found them. But our German priest
preached, and published, a sermon in which he raged at both the
preacher and ourselves for making a mockery of Christ's redeeming
sacrifice in order to make money. He all but called Ronald Knox
Judas, me too.

III

But our deepest problems were in finding writers and readers. Take readers first. Catholic America was fascinated by the Catholic Intellectual Revival. It was in Denver that I first lectured on it. That was in 1933, and in the next dozen years I must have been asked for it at least twenty times a year. But not only did it not produce writers as it had in England: it did not produce any great number of readers.

If only the people who thronged to hear about the surge of new Catholic writers had been willing to read them, we should have had nothing left for avarice to dream about. But limitless as the interest in the writers was, it did not extend to their actual writings. I was forever receiving letters from boys and girls to say their class was studying the Catholic Intellectual Revival, and that the writer of the letter had been allotted me by the teacher: would I tell her (it was usually a girl) about myself? Usually I dropped these letters into the wastebasket. One I answered: it began "I am doing a research paper with you as my subject." She wanted any information I might think useful about my psychosomatic problems. I told her that I did not even know that I had any.

Most of these requests came from high schools. But one college graduate (the only one, I hasten to say) was given me as a theme for her M.A. thesis. She interviewed me at length and got her M.A. She was kind enough to send me a copy of her thesis. It opened, "Black hair crowns the strange paradox of laughing eyes and a sad smile." Naturally I read on.

Certainly the space we had chosen as our own—just above the middle of the brow—was not a congested area. It contained no reading public sufficient to keep a publisher even in that frugal comfort which Leo XIII saw as desirable for the working classes, to which we surely belonged. It seemed that other Catholic book publishers had written off that expanse of brow as unlikely to pay the expenses of exploitation. So we had to create our reading public or perish. The next forty years would have been easier if we had decided to perish. The thought never occurred to us.

We just tried this and that. In England we had tested out the Unicorn Series, the best then being written offered annually in a block of eight to be ordered in advance, quite literally at cost price. We were giving them away, and a reading public began to show. In America we tried the Catholic Tutorial Masterpieces, which I have already mentioned in relation to my first meeting with St. Augustine. We advertised eight books, priced a little above cost, each with a Tutorial Introduction (by me, I fear), showing how it might be studied by groups in four weekly sessions. We used as a slogan

A MASTERPIECE A MONTH
TO FORM A CATHOLIC MIND.

Cheap, you think? Slogans tend to be. Earlier we had published a series of Essays in Order. Reviewers had complained that they were too difficult for the ordinary Catholic reader. So we advertised them under another slogan

IF YOU CAN'T READ ESSAYS IN ORDER
YOU CAN'T READ.

The first year of the Tutorial Masterpieces was a solid success. I prepared a second lot but they were never published—prices of paper and printing had risen too fast for us.

We tried whatever we could think of; two sorts of effort stay in my mind. There were discussion meetings led by our authors in the Sheed & Ward office. And in conjunction with Catherine de Hueck we formed an Outer Circle of Friendship House, Negroes and whites meeting every week or so—in our Riverside Drive apartment, or at Earl Hall, Columbia. The meetings were conducted on Evidence Guild training lines. They were vast fun. But most of those who got most out of them had no spare money for the buying of books.

Then there was our house organ. Three or four times a year we gave away up to 150,000 copies of the *Trumpet*. As a literary periodical it was comparable with the best then on the market, the one difference being that it treated the books of only one firm. The articles were either written by ourselves or reprints of reviews. The illustrations by Jean Charlot showed a combination of wit and spiritual insight as surprising as Ronald Knox's: most readers reveled in them: the handful who didn't hated them. One review we reprinted was a very notable treatment by Evelyn Waugh of Ronald Knox's translation of the Bible. We received a demand from Waugh for payment —at a very large price. What made it just about bearable was that he instructed us to pay the money to the Catholic Worker.

Our idea in distributing such vast numbers of the *Trumpet* was
that it would lead to a sale of books sufficient to cover the expense.
The trouble was akin to what I found with my lecturing on the Revival—that too many people found the *Trumpet* so rewarding that
they saw no point in reading the books it described. All the same,
with one thing and another we had by 1960 built up a body of readers who made the business profitable. It continued so for another
seven years—till the Pope John explosion.

We were able to do something about readers. But Catholic writers of first quality continued in very small supply indeed. The European surge of new writers into the Church was not matched in
America. There was the Jewish psychiatrist from Germany, Karl
Stern, whose *Pillar of Fire* seems to me the greatest story of a conversion since Luke's account of St. Paul's; but Karl Stern lives and
works in Canada. No name comes to my mind of a convert already
known as a writer to the general public. There were what I have
called reverts—men like that very notable biographer William
Thomas Walsh, who had begun as Catholics, lost contact with the
Church and found the Church again. But there were no outstand-
ing writers being converted. As to why England should have had
them and America not, I naturally thought all the time, and naturally produced a sort of theory. My half-guess is that the closeness to
Europe meant for the English an acquaintance with French and German writing.

The main stream of writing in England for a generation or so before T. S. Eliot is as shallow a body of writing as you will find anywhere. Call it shallowness, call it thinness—a brilliant surface but
you couldn't swim in it or drown in it. In Bernard Shaw, for instance,
there was brilliant figure skating but on unbroken ice. "Out of the
depths I have cried unto thee"—every literature has that, but not
this literature: it had plenty of crying but precious little depth. It
was the high noon of human sufficiency. Men had lost God and felt
no loss, they were dying of inanition without the pangs of hunger.

French writing of that period was very different. It had, as England had not, what Wallace Fowlie calls "an insatiable need to in-
vestigate what torments men." England has had no Baudelaire or
Rimbaud, no *Flowers of Evil*, no *Season in Hell*. But France had
both, with Léon Bloy for a postscript. And France was next door to
England. America was further away. Henry James was an American
who knew France, but he gave himself to England. The postwar

American expatriates, much as living in Paris meant to them, stayed so wholly American.

All this may of course be fantasy. Anyhow convert writers were not there. With ex-Catholic writers the landscape was littered—Ernest Hemingway, Theodore Dreiser, Eugene O'Neill heading a long parade. I don't know them well enough to be sure if it is right to say they had left the Church—one heard it said, for instance, that if Hemingway happened to be near a church on Sunday he might drop in and kneel awhile in the back row on one knee. But of most of them it was evident that if they were not out of the Church they were not very effectively in it. And some, like Will Durant, graduate of a Jesuit college, were not only ex but anti.

My theory about the distance from France and Germany may have explained why America did not produce convert writers as England did. But what happened to the thousands upon thousands of Catholics pouring out gowned and hooded from our colleges and universities every year? There were classes in creative writing: why was there so tiny a trickle of men and women able to write creatively? "Creative writing" can't be taught, of course. You are born with the writing gift. If you haven't been, then all that a university can do for you is teach you to write competently, i.e., so that the reader will know what you are telling him. Had Catholic universities succeeded in this forty years ago, then on the law of averages the small percentage of their graduates who by birth had the gift would have been writing creatively. But in those days they were not always teaching their graduates to write even at that level of competence. It was not a question of education—graduates of high education had not learned to communicate on paper, as we discovered from many a doctoral thesis offered us for publication. We published quite a number of really valuable books—which had to be rewritten in the office. The authors were so little interested in their writing that they did not even notice what had been done to it. The only author I remember as refusing to accept our editorial rewriting had never been to college.

I was often asked to lecture to college students on writing. I gave two pieces of advice for the writing of good prose—study Latin, and read poetry. Latin teaches (inter alia, of course) economy; with poetry you learn to use not only the meanings of words but their energies. I used to quote Wordsworth's "With the young of both sexes, poetry, like love, is a passion," and support this with Omar Khayyám's

> A book of verses underneath the bough
> A flask of wine, a loaf of bread and thou.

But Omar was a thousand years ago and Wordsworth a hundred and fifty. To my purpose I would quote a modern rewriting of Omar—

> A jug and a book and a dame
> And a nice shady nook for the same.

A book, you notice. Not a book of verses.

There was poetry in the college reading lists, but not in the reading habits of most of those I met. For Catholics there was one exception. It is long enough since I heard anyone mention Francis Thompson. But fifty years ago, even forty, wherever I lectured I met him. Catholics who never read another poet raved over him. He was their only poet: not only that, he had but one poem, "The Hound of Heaven." Now I come to think of it, there was Joyce Kilmer too —but he did not have even one poem, just two lines—"Poems are made by fools like me/But only God can make a tree." So we can leave Kilmer out. I assume he did not mean that it would be foolish to read poems instead of going out into the woods, but the Catholic public acted as if he did. It's obvious that if people who are not poetry readers adore one poet, it must be for non-poetic reasons, since to poetry they are deaf. It was the spiritual message of the *Hound* that excited them. It excited me. But I had been steeped in poetry, all the more for never having written a line of my own.

My conviction that poetry *must* become a need again caused me to compile, and include in the Tutorial Masterpieces, a small anthology of Catholic poetry in English. It caused no revolution. As to the value of Latin for the writing of English, I have to face the fact that the hour and a half all priests had to spend every day in the reading of the breviary in Latin had small effect on their style. But as to that, it may be relevant to tell of my asking a priest well on in life what meaning he attached to "mons coagulatus, mons pinguis"—"curdled" and "fat" being adjectives rarely applied to a mountain. He had never heard the words. They were in a psalm of Matins on the previous day, and he had been reading Matins all his priestly life.

We found plenty of priest writers, first-rate in their own special fields—but the creative writing gift and vocation to the priesthood are not usually found together. Is there a priest *writer* of world class between Augustine and Rabelais?

The first creative writer we published in America, Father Leonard Feeney, was a humorist in the Knox class but different again—I don't think he thought much of Knox, rather disliked him in fact. Each enlarged my knowledge of the Church (I cannot too often remind the reader that that is what this book is about), Ronald Knox by his total acceptance, Father Feeney by colliding with it head on.

That Ronald Knox could make me laugh in conversation as in writing, I have already shown. So could Father Feeney. I remember long drives with him at the wheel "singin' all the while." I would give a great deal to have been present when he acted Paul withstanding Peter to the face, Peter being that more solemn Jesuit, Father John La Farge. I did hear his idea of Katharine Hepburn reporting a prizefight, and of Franklin D. Roosevelt being Franklin D. Roosevelt. The mimicry of the two voices was of a perfection, the utterance of the two characters was of Ruth Draper quality.

He was rich in stories of things he said had happened to him—as of the man who came and sat next to him in a train. "I'm sure you'll be pleased to know, Father, that I have a sister a nun."

"Of what order?"

"The Faithful Companions of Jesus, if you'll pardon the profanity, Father."

I still sing a limerick I heard only from him:

> There was a young man called McSweeney
> Who drank seven quarts of Martini.
> But the Paris police
> Sent a wire to his niece
> "Nous regrettons, McSweeney est fini."

We published several of his books, reveling not only in the fun but in the mastery of his English and the sheer precision of his utterance. We had become close friends—he took me out for my first speech on Boston Common, and had (like a priest in Baltimore) to convince a Catholic policeman that I really was a Catholic.

I was miserable about what I regarded, though he didn't, as his stepping out of line with Catholic norms. Miserable for him of course, but miserable, too, because of what his writing might have done for the Church from inside.

Most Catholics in conflict with the Church authorities find support in the world outside, indeed it is a certain formula for success. The point on which Father Feeney was in conflict excludes that support, for it seems to have been a literal assertion of the phrase Pius IV got from Augustine "extra ecclesiam nulla salus," no salvation outside the Church. In the early days of his movement, some of his followers would picket Catholic churches. There is a story of a policeman coming into the sacristy, where a priest was vesting for Mass, and saying, "They're being a nuisance outside, Father. Would you like me to rough 'em up a bit?"

"Who are being a nuisance?"

"Just those extra ecclesiam nulla salus guys."

In the handling of Father Feeney we hear a troubling echo of the handling of the Modernists at the turn of the century. Like them he was condemned but not answered. When Boniface VIII said in the bull *Unam Sanctam* that it was "altogether necessary for salvation for every human creature to be subject to the Roman Pontiff," he seemed to be saying not only what Father Feeney was condemned for saying, but what a vast number of yesterday's Catholics had grown up believing. Everybody would have been helped by a full-length discussion. Either Boniface did not mean what he sounds as if he meant—he was concentrating perhaps on one element, omitting others which also need to be taken into account; or else we are not bound to hold what he held. Even under Pius IX it was made clear that people who love God may be saved though they do not accept the Catholic Church, and the teaching to this effect has grown steadily in volume so that it may be said to be the universal teaching. That Boniface would have found this startling can hardly be questioned: there were seven centuries of history and psychology which had not yet happened.

But that raises the question of papal statements generally, especially the non-infallible ones. A discussion of this sort in the Loisy-Tyrrell-Von Hügel period, or even in relation to Father Feeney, might have diminished the violence of the explosion we are still living through, might even have prevented the explosion. And discussion would have been easier in the comparative tranquillity of those times. One understands the desire to avoid confrontation, which would involve the admission that earlier statements of authority need amplifying or correction, but experience suggests that confrontation can be only postponed. On this particular matter it still awaits us.

The one other writer we found early in the States who gave a special kind of joy in his writing was Father Leo Trese, a secular priest. He also had a power of being funny on paper, but the whole feel of his writing was different from Father Feeney's. I think the difference lay in the power of his compassion. No book has taken me deeper inside a priest in his sheer dailiness, than Father Trese's *Vessel of Clay* took me.

But in those first years our lists were largely built on transatlantic writers. And no book has taken me deeper inside a Catholic who is a novelist, both in his creativity *and* in his Catholicism, than François Mauriac's *God and Mammon*. It was not by any conscious planning that the two novels and one play we published in our early years were by Frenchmen. One was Mauriac's *Noeud de Vipères* (we called it *Vipers' Tangle*): I hope no lover of Mauriac will mind my saying that his novels are very much like one another, and this one I chose for translation as their archetype. Of Léon Bloy's *La Femme Pauvre* (*The Woman Who Was Poor*) I have already spoken. Claudel's *Soulier de Satin* was translated as *The Satin Slipper* by Chesterton's Father Brown, Monsignor John O'Connor. Claudel was that rare author who thought the translation better than his original (another was the Redemptorist Père Durrwell, who said the same about Rosemary Sheed's translation of his book on the Resurrection). I am inclined to think *The Satin Slipper* the greatest book we ever published. But the discussion of that would belong in a history of Sheed & Ward, which I am not writing.

CHAPTER 12

PRINCES OF THE CHURCH

I was sitting with Cardinal Cushing in his home in Boston. I told him of an incident on our Hyde Park platform. It concerned that notable priest Father Vincent Rochford, who once knocked down a heckler for obscenity about Christ's mother, was fined by a London magistrate, paid the fine, framed the receipt, hung it on the wall of his waiting room. He was speaking on sin and such. At a point he said, "The Catholic Church is the only place for a poor bugger like me." The Cardinal listened intently, sat silent for a while, then said, "The Catholic Church is the only institution in which a slob like me could be made a Prince."

I

For years I had been bothered about cardinals—of all the features of the Church's life, they are the one least imaginable in the Church of the first Christians. It struck me as strange that Peter's successor should be chosen not only by, but from among, holders of an office of a kind Peter had never heard of, an office not so much as hinted at by the Church's founder, an office which the Church had got along without for a thousand years.

As history reaches most of us—the spectacular bits prominent, the soberer realities left unmentioned—cardinals do not for the most part look their best. The only cardinal one hears of as having been martyred was St. John Fisher, and he was made a cardinal only as a last-minute effort to save him from martyrdom—surely, the Pope felt, no Catholic king would have a cardinal executed. Henry VIII's comment was that Fisher would have no head to put his cardinal's hat on, and the headsman saw to it.

What is worth dwelling on is that Fisher had said, only a while before laying his head on the block for Papal Supremacy, "If the Pope does not reform the Curia, God will." Pius IV had heard of the beheading; I wonder if he had heard of the saying. His predecessor,

Paul IV, had made a nephew of his a cardinal. Pius IV proceeded to a reform of the Curia by having this one beheaded.

For centuries the cardinalate had from time to time shown up as one of the Church's more distressing features. Saint Catherine of Siena had described a group of cardinals as "not men but devils, with their monstrous love for the filthiness of their own bodies."

The fifteenth century saw the Curia at its worst. The Franciscan Pope, Sixtus IV, made six near relations cardinals. To one of them he gave eight bishoprics and their revenues. This one was to become Pope as Julius II. In between, he helped to secure the papacy for Innocent VIII, the first Pope publicly to acknowledge the illegitimate children he already had and raise them to, or marry them into, princedoms. A child of one of these marriages became a cardinal at the age of thirteen, and in due course (if due be the word) Pope as Leo X. On his election he is said to have said, "God has given us the papacy, let us enjoy it." Part of the enjoyment was Martin Luther.

Holiness, of course, was not a bar to the cardinalate. That mystical master the Franciscan St. Bonaventure was raised to it, St. Thomas Aquinas would probably have been if he had not died on the way to the Council of Lyons. And even the worldliest of pre-Renascence cardinals were still Catholics and could react to holiness —sometimes disconcertingly, as if to something they did not know very well.

In 1294 the Conclave had met to elect a successor to Nicholas IV. There was much jockeying for position, and no prospect of a result. One of the cardinals received a letter from a hermit, Pietro di Murrone, widely famed for his ascetical life, adjuring them not to keep the Church waiting any longer. He read it to the others and these tough men suddenly seem to have felt that a saint was the answer. They elected Pietro, against his agonized protests, and he became Celestine V. The result could have been foreseen. The running of the Church requires certain qualities, certain skills, certain experience, for which holiness is no substitute—just as in a storm at sea the boat will be better handled by a sailor with a wife in every port than by a nun of whatever piety. As Belloc has said, "It is the mark of the educated man not to confuse his categories." Celestine V was a disaster. He built for himself a small hut within his palace, and in it lived his austere life. But he took the word of every blackguard who wanted office. In no time at all there was chaos. Celestine was only too pleased to retire. He died soon after, murdered probably.

Twenty years later, Pope Clement canonized him. Dante put him in hell.

We have been glancing at the office of cardinal as we meet it in history, with special regard paid to its condition as the Reformation was drawing near. It had never been as bad before, and never sank as low again. But through a great part of its history the popes seem to have regarded the cardinalate as part not of the Church Spiritual but of the Church Administrative, very much as the Roman Emperors had regarded the Jewish Sanhedrin—to be used, to be handled, certainly as calling for no reverence, simply as part of the practicality of government. The Emperor Caligula had shown his contempt for the Roman Senate by making his horse a proconsul. Pope Alexander VI could hardly have shown more acidly what he thought of the College of Cardinals as it had become than by appointing to it the brute he had himself begotten, Cesare Borgia (whom Machiavelli proposes to princes as a model).

Pius IV, beheading Paul IV's cardinal-nephew, had started cleaning house. And the Counter-Reformation did bring a beginning of new health to great areas of Church life. But the cardinalate continued for long to call for judging by political rather than spiritual standards. Christopher Dawson remarks somewhere that ecclesiastics in politics tend to be rather more corrupt than the average. Cardinal Wolsey of course came before the Council of Trent. So did Cardinal Beaton, whom the Scottish Reformers slashed to death and hanged from the windows of his castle at St. Andrew's, without causing much grief anywhere. But in the century after Trent Cardinals Richelieu, Mazarin and de Retz gave Catholics small ground for pleasure.

In the last two or three centuries cardinals have not been much on the world's political stage. There have been magnificent men among them, like Cardinal Pecci: out of favor with Pius IX he had been sent off to vegetate in Perugia for thirty years: as Leo XIII he was one of the greatest of popes, ushering in what, before the explosion, we used to think of as a new age.

II

I have told how I lost my awe of bishops. I lost my awe of cardinals too. Awe is not a feeling I lose easily. The first Cardinal with whom

I had much contact, Bourne of Westminster, held my respect to the end: so did the last, Cardinal Cushing. In between, some did and some didn't.

Cardinal Hayes of New York puzzled me: he was a new breed of cat, so to speak. I remember my surprise to hear him addressed as Pat by Mrs. Nicholas Hayes—but then she was a Papal Duchess. The nearest I had come to hearing a cardinal christian-named was when a Catholic layman, with Cardinal Bourne in the chair, spoke of him as "our much loved Cardinal, may I dare call him our Francis?" The Cardinal had never looked more glacial. I doubt if anyone dared do it again.

I was at a public dinner for Cardinal Hayes on his return from a journey round the Mediterranean on the yacht of George Mac-Donald. There had been much pulpit emphasis at the time on the duty of Catholics to send their children to Catholic colleges, with quotations from the Code of Canon Law about excommunication. It was not of this that Cardinal Hayes spoke but of the journey he had just had. He was quoting Byron, I remember—"The glory that was Greece and the grandeur that was Rome"—when there came a loud interjection: "Why doesn't George MacDonald's son go to a Catholic college?" There was a kind of stunned silence. MacDonald's son was indeed at Princeton. But no one interrupted bishops in those days and I fancy there was a confused feeling that the interjector was being disrespectful to the Pope, who had made George MacDonald a Papal Marquis. All those around me agreed afterwards that the man must have been drunk. Four men carried him out of the room. Cardinal Hayes went on with his Byron.

The next time I met him was at a Commencement at Manhattanville, the women's college at which my lecture the year before had led to my opening our New York house. The Commencement began oddly with his refusal to go on the platform till the poetess who was to give one of the speeches had washed the cosmetic off her face. Incredibly she agreed. All the same I think the incident disconcerted her rather—but not as much as the shriek of laughter which greeted her older-fashioned pronounciation of the word "ass" in a poem she was reciting.

My own talk went off without incident. But in his closing remarks the Cardinal congratulated the graduating class on their intelligence —they appeared to have understood my speech.

III

In 1932 Maisie and I went to Dublin for the Eucharistic Congress. The Congress has left me with a half dozen vivid memories, two especially, recorded by G. K. Chesterton in a book we published, *Christendom in Dublin*. One was the story of a man walking through a glen in the West of Ireland, meeting a beautiful woman and a small boy: overwhelmed with an awe he could not explain, he fell on his knees: the Lady said, "This is himself, and I am his mother, and he's the boy you'll all be wanting at the end." The other was a comment heard in a bus: the rain had threatened throughout the Congress: on the last day it looked its most threatening. One woman was heard to say, "Well, if it rains now I can only say He'll have brought it on Himself." Whenever I consider the state of the Church in one age or another of its existence I find myself repeating the last half dozen words. After all he needn't have built a Church of human beings.

But I am not writing about the Congress. My present topic is cardinals. On that visit I remember especially one Cardinal in being, MacRory of Armagh, and one Cardinal to be, Archbishop Glennon of St. Louis, who preached at the outdoor Mass in Phoenix Park. His sermon was as surprising as I have ever heard. For fifteen or twenty minutes it was exactly what I had expected to hear—a tribute to the Faith of the Irish of the sort no St. Patrick's Day celebration was complete without. My impression is that it was received with the half-smile with which the Irish of Ireland react to praise from visiting children of the Gael. Then came the shock. "Yes, your faith is wonderful. What about your charity?" In the thousands of talks I have heard, nothing was ever quite so startling as that. The Archbishop went on to give what amounted to an examination of the consciences of the half-million men present—a fearsome catalogue of the ways in which we can sin against love of neighbor. I doubt if many half-smiles were left. If for nothing but that sermon, he had earned his cardinalate.

I was reminded of it thirty or forty years after by a speech made to the novices and seminarians at St. Bonaventure, New York, by the Cardinal of Lima, with its key phrase, "You cannot have an apostolic laity without an apostolic clergy." He seemed to have no illusions about the immediate likelihood of the latter.

Cardinal MacRory drove us round Connemara with the Franciscan Archbishop Paschal Robinson, who had been Papal Nuncio in the Middle East. It was quaint to hear the Cardinal pontificating about Middle Eastern problems to the Nuncio, instructive to note the unruffled courtesy with which the Nuncio listened to what sounded to me like baby talk. By no flicker of the face did he indicate how it sounded to him.

I think it was on that visit to Ireland that I met a monsignor who had been sent from Rome on a visitation to a certain South American country, with a mission to inquire into the state of priestly celibacy there. He told me that one of the real difficulties of priestly celibacy in Latin America was the conviction of many Indian girls that there was a special blessing attached to having a child by a priest: they wanted that blessing: another thing he told me was that his visit was resented, he had just reached the border in time. What he said of the girls reminded me of the Illuminists, whose spread in the country districts of fifteenth-century Spain was one reason for the setting up of the Inquisition. Along with certain strange doctrinal ideas—such as that the communicant got more of Christ by receiving a larger host—there was a lot of occultism, and a lot of sex. One Illuminist claimed that it had been revealed to him that he was to beget another Messiah from a holy woman: forty-nine holy women had believed him before the Inquisition caught him. My guess—for the little it's worth—is that the next world-religion will build largely on sex rituals.

But back to cardinals. Two who helped me in my thinking about the nature of the Church were the two Americans Cushing and Spellman. They were as different as two men could be while both remained in the human race. It would have been unthinkable for Cardinal Cushing to have his biography written in his lifetime and choose his biographer as Cardinal Spellman did. The result was as might have been expected. Shane Leslie wrote in a review: "The statement that the Cardinal is not without faults will be found only on the book's jacket."

IV

I have told of my Commencement address at Manhattanville in 1933 and of Cardinal Hayes's congratulations to the students for seeming to understand it. My next Commencement appearance on the same platform brought no congratulations, I have seldom known such universal gloom. And no one ever found out why.

I had given my harmless necessary talk—I actually wrote "chat," but Shakespeare would not have liked it. Cardinal Spellman rose and gave ten minutes of incoherence. It was hard to know what he was saying: he was clearly in a rage, apparently with me. He refused to meet the parents of the graduating class and went back home leaving nuns and parents stricken and me dumfounded.

I was down to speak on the following Sunday at a Salesian house where he was to be. So I rang his secretary, said I had clearly angered the Cardinal, should I have a diplomatic illness and stay away on Sunday? The secretary answered, "I will ask His Eminence." He came back and said, "His Eminence wishes you to be there." I went. He was there ahead of me, put his arm round my shoulders, took me round and introduced me to all and sundry. To my talk he gave the kind of praise which might have seemed exaggerated for Cicero.

I wrote to him a few days later, expressing my regret for whatever he had disliked in my Manhattanville talk. His answer was in one sentence, "I give you my blessing." Over the years we met frequently, usually on platforms, but no more was ever said. My own guess is that, whatever the trouble was, it concerned me only indirectly. He had just preached a sermon—that very morning, if my memory is accurate—in which he had come out clearly for America's support to England in World War II. Given the state of American Catholic opinion, it must have been a considerable strain, and he may have been feeling the reaction. To be forced to listen to a British citizen prattling on about some trifle like Catholic Education may have been just too much for him.

He was a curious mixture. Who isn't? you may ask. Anyhow he was. Shortly after his appointment to New York two very different things happened, which were told all over the diocese and gave his clergy some "feel" of their new leader.

The first was his recall of an auxiliary bishop who had retired from the practice of the priesthood after a quarrel with Cardinal Hayes. He brought him back to his own house, had him once more officiating, gave him happiness the last year or two of his life.

The other concerned a priest who was sitting in his study one afternoon, reading a detective story perhaps. He was startled by the entrance of the Archbishop, inquiring about his health. He answered that his health was excellent. "Oh," said the Archbishop, "I thought you must have been sick. We had a telephone message at the Chancery to say you had been called to see a dying man and had not gone. So I went and anointed him, and I've come to see how you are." The priest, so I'm told, looked as if he could do with the Last Sacraments himself.

Over the years I watched with interest his relations with the *Catholic Worker*, and with our great friend Dorothy Day, its founder. It is not too much to say that the Cardinal accepted the capitalist system: he must have found the *Catholic Worker's* unending attacks on it trying, especially in a paper with Catholic in the title. But he took no action against it. Dorothy tells me that to her he was polite if not cordial. She wrote to say she had heard he thought her heretical: if so, as her spiritual father he was bound to tell her in what way. His answer was, "Some of the bishops are on your side. I am not committed." When the *Catholic Worker* decided to picket his chancery in support of the striking workers in the Catholic cemeteries, she wrote him a careful explanation and received a wholly amiable but unyielding reply. Naturally he gave no financial support to the *Worker*. Dorothy smiles over a circumstantial report, written by a friend of hers, that he had given them money. But he issued no condemnation!

What he did condemn was the movie *Baby Doll*. Naturally this caused the crowds to flock to it. Strange that he did not know that condemnation was the best advertisement the picture could have (indeed a lot of people thought the movie people had persuaded him to condemn it).

In some areas, indeed, the Cardinal appeared to be naïve to a point, and in others wholly sophisticated. The naïveté concerned his writing. For a time he was the most highly paid poet in the world —the *Ladies' Home Journal* paid him vast sums for his poetry. I doubt if it was ever seriously considered for any anthology of American verse. He wrote a novel, *The Foundling*, and offered it to Scribner's. Clutching at a straw, they said surely it should come from a Catholic publisher, Sheed & Ward, for instance. He pointed out that if the novel had a Catholic publisher, people would think the publisher had no choice but to accept, whereas if it bore a non-Catholic imprint it would be clear that the publisher really wanted it. So Scribner's had to want it.

On the public platform he varied between deadpan and benignity.

There was another side to him, a neatness of wit never shown to the public. Two quick stories. A layman thought to curry favor with him by saying that the U. S. Post Office ought to refuse to carry the Esquire girls, double-page colored ladies who left little unrevealed. The Cardinal listened gravely, then said, "Well, you know, I like them better than the Venus de Milo."

Towards the end of the war the Cardinal was dining at the American Army Headquarters in North Africa. The General had just returned from a visit to Rome. The Cardinal asked him how he liked the Vatican. The General said it had struck him as rather gloomy, it could do with some music and girls. "Well, you know, General," said the Cardinal, "that *has* been tried."

It was no unsophisticate who uttered those comments.

v

I have noted that Cardinal Cushing would not, like Cardinal Spellman, have wanted his biography written in his lifetime: I can't imagine his thinking it worth writing at any time. The two men were different, and naturally they differed. But there was reconciliation at the end. Cardinal Cushing built a high school in Boston, named it after Cardinal Spellman, and asked his distinguished colleague to perform the opening ceremony. Here is a snippet of a conversation I had with Cardinal Cushing just afterwards:

"Do you know what Cardinal Spellman said to me?"

"How could I?"

"He asked me who I thought would get New York when he died. Why should he care? I don't care who gets Boston after me."

But then New York was a diocese in which each new Archbishop was the man people felt his predecessor would have chosen—until Spellman himself, that is.

There never was a man in public office who cared less about his public image than Cardinal Cushing. Every year he hired a theater and had a party for the old men and women of Boston. On one occasion he partnered an old lady in an Irish reel. Television caught the moment. Pius XII saw the film. That, one was told, was why he was not made a Cardinal till John XXIII arrived. I imagine John saw the film too. I heard the Cardinal say at a public dinner that he could not understand Latin. He offered to pay for a translation system at the Vatican Council similar to the one at the United

Nations, where by pressing a button you can have the speeches in the language you want. This being refused, he simply went home, not pretending to understand.

His one vast weakness lay in his public speaking: his voice was ugly, his sentences were shapeless, he never knew when to stop. Privately he was a master of the terse phrase. Soon after his appointment he summoned a meeting of his clergy to announce changes. Some of the older clergy objected, Cardinal O'Connell would not have liked this change or that. He stood it as long as he could, then: "Cardinal O'Connell is dead. I saw him die." I was sitting in his room when someone telephoned to ask him to do something or other. "Come and ask me that to my face," he said, and hung up. At a Commencement at Newton College he said to the graduating girls: "If any of you gets engaged to a rich Catholic, introduce him to me."

Naturally he needed money, he used it so generously, at his death his private fortune totaled a few dollars. He appealed to his fellow bishops to spare priests for work in Latin America, and urged his own clergy to offer themselves. I could go on and on about him. I resist the temptation. After all, I never had to live under him. I might have drawn a less Arcadian picture if I had. In any event I have met other cardinals. I pause upon three Europeans.

Towards the end of the twenties I was invited to speak as England's representative at a Semaine Internationale in Geneva. The organizers wanted me to speak on Corporate Reunion, which they clearly saw as close at hand. I spoke of the difficulties—especially the simple fact that the Church of England, divided among High, Low and Broad, was not the sort of Corpus with which reunion would be easy. Next morning's paper reported me as saying the exact opposite. I went to see the editor and demanded that he print a correction. He explained that a very high Catholic authority wanted my speech altered because he was in favor of Corporate Reunion. The editor would not even accept a letter from me. Later that day I found myself wondering if the "high authority" could have been Cardinal Baudrillart. For I looked in at a meeting of the old League of Nations and he was speaking. I found it hard to believe I was listening to an adult—"The glory of a nation is its young, the glory of the young is enthusiasm—" He was the first member of the French Academy I had ever seen. It was a bad start.

During the War I had to pass through Lisbon more than once. I was introduced to the Patriarch of Lisbon, Cardinal Cerijera. We spoke in French. I had learned French in Australia without meeting a Frenchman, just as I learned Latin without meeting an ancient Roman. The one language is almost as "dead" to me as the other. I get no enjoyment out of spoken French. But Cardinal Cerijera spoke French no better than I, so we got along famously. He was a great reader of Chesterton, he told me, and he delighted in the personal stories I was able to tell him. I was fascinated by one thing he said. Portuguese men did not go much to Mass, because like all Latin men they were concerned about their dignity, and did not want to be seen in church with a lot of women and children: he thought the known fact that the Dictator, Salazar, was a daily communicant might change their attitude. I have never had an opportunity to check on whether or not it did.

By the mention of the Cushing suggestion of a translation system at Vatican II, I am reminded of Cardinal Pizzardo. At the Lay Congress in Rome around 1950 they had one. During Cardinal Pizzardo's speech a delegate arose on the platform to complain that the English translation was not coming through. He had not realized that the Cardinal thought he was talking English.

I conclude this first glance at cardinals with a pleasing story. The chairman introducing me to an audience in Boston concluded, "The next time I introduce our speaker, I hope it will be as Frank Cardinal Sheed." The audience was naturally amused. My own opening words were: "Frank Cardinal Sheed will never appear on this platform without Maisie Cardinal Ward."

VI

Late in the thirties I had a letter from Archbishop MacDonald of Edinburgh (not quite a cardinal, but his successor is) to say that he had been told I had a method of teaching the Faith, he would like to know what it was, because 50 per cent of the boys and girls in his primary schools gave up Mass and the sacraments on leaving. I wrote back what I now feel to have been an impertinent letter, to say that we of the Evidence Guild had developed a method of teaching religion but that as most teachers did not know the Faith it hardly mattered what method they used. He wrote back by return to ask what I could possibly mean and would I come to Edinburgh and tell him?

He had all his teachers—some 600 of them—come on four after-noons running, and himself sat behind me on the platform. After thirty-five years I cannot remember the details. My general idea was that the catechism answers are splendid summarizations, but of value only to those who have studied the truths summarized in them —they belong at the end of teaching not at the beginning, above all not as a substitute for teaching. My questions were aimed at find-ing how well the truths summarized were known.

I suppose that the teachers and I would have had quite different impressions of how it all went. For myself I should have been horrified, if I had not already known for years past how little was understood by men and women whose duty it was to teach the Faith, in schools whose reason for existence was that the Faith be taught. The teachers, whose politeness never flagged, may not have seen it so.

The Archbishop did. He said to my wife, "Your husband has a most expressive back." She said, "What is it saying?" He answered, "It is saying that I couldn't cope with the questions any better than these teachers." He asked me to question him as I had questioned them. I refused. He said, "I command you." I said, "You are not my bishop."

On the third afternoon two senior university students offered themselves as "vile bodies" (you remember the old rule—fiat experi-mentum in corpore vili—experiments should be made on cheap material). I treated them both as a class I was teaching, then gave them the sort of questions that go with the Evidence Guild teaching method. They did admirably. Both were converts. Their performance, I think, lifted everybody's spirits. If so, the lift did not last. For the final meeting I had asked that a class of primary school pupils should be brought in who had received a high mark from the diocesan in-spector of religious teaching. I examined them in the presence of the Archbishop and the 600. I was not heckling, simply trying to find out what the catechism answers meant to them which they gave so accurately, so confidently. It was very grim.

At lunch afterwards I was seated next to an elderly priest (the original, I was told, of the Monsignor in Bruce Marshall's lovely *Father Malachy's Miracle*). He hardly ate at all, but kept on repeat-ing that it was hard to expect children to think up answers to questions of such difficulty. I said that the questions were elemen-tary, if they did not know the answers they simply did not know

what the Church was actually telling them. I agreed that no one
could be expected to improvise the answers: my complaint was at
their having to improvise: the points should have been discussed in
class as a matter of course.

This happened just before the Hitler war. I think the teachers bore
me no malice. Well after the war they asked me to address their
convention in Edinburgh. A large contingent came over from
Glasgow. The chairman, welcoming these, said: "What came ye
out to see?" From all over the hall one seemed to hear, "A Sheed
shaken by the wind."

It may have struck the attentive reader that Archbishop Mac-
Donald was a rather unusual person. He was wholly surprising. I
have already told how he descended on the Roman Rota, which had
been too slow in giving a decision on a petition for nullity of marriage. Three other incidents I recall, the first told me about him, the
others told me by him.

The Catholic schools of Scotland had a different arrangement
from those of England with the Ministry of Education in London.
On one occasion there was a row on between the Scottish bishops
and Whitehall. Whitehall asked an English bishop to intervene. He
wrote a letter to Archbishop MacDonald in support of the government's position. The Archbishop sent the letter back with "Mind
your own business. A.J.M." written across it in red ink. When I heard
the story I remembered happily how the Scottish Truth Society had
turned on me when they thought (rightly) that the English Society
was trying to absorb them.

He was asked to baptize a baby of a very rich, very important,
Catholic family. They wanted the baptism to be in their own house,
not in the parish church. He said it must be in the church. They said
the godmother was too ill to come to the church. He expressed concern and said he would like to visit her. They said that was impossible because she was coming from abroad just in time for the
baptism. He stuck to it that other people had their babies baptized
in the church and there was no reason why they should not. They
asked could not an exception be made? His answer was that exceptions were indeed allowed for families which had rendered special
services to the Church, but there were no such in this instance. One
is reminded of an incident which happened just after Manning was
made Archbishop of Westminster. A socially important lady called

on him and gave him a check for £5000. He said thank you and laid it down. The lady was nettled at so cool a reception of her gift and said so. He replied, " 'Twill serve to cover a jam jar." Clearly he thought it important to show right at the beginning that he was his own man. She took her check back.

I report from memory a conversation Archbishop MacDonald had with Pius XII. It went something like this:

Archbishop: Would Your Holiness not agree that English-speaking Catholics are among the most devoted supporters of the papacy?

Pope: Yes, indeed.

Archbishop: Would Your Holiness not also agree that the friend-ship of the English-speaking nations is of tremendous value to the Church?

Pope: Certainly.

Archbishop: Then does not Your Holiness find it strange that no member of the Curia can speak English?

There never was a man in high position so incapable of not saying anything he thought.

Another man given to speaking his mind is my friend that notable poet Allen Tate. Soon after his conversion he was in Rome, determined to tell Pius XII all that needed correcting in the American Church. He made full notes of what he meant to say. Day followed day, with no summons to the Vatican. Suddenly the call came very early while he was still in bed. He rushed to the Vatican in such haste that he forgot his notes. So the Pope never heard what was wrong with the American Church. I doubt if it would have made any difference. We discovered that Pius XII's English was like my French—we understood him but it was clear that he did not under-stand us.

I have one other memory of Scotland and the Church. Archbishop Godfrey, who would later be a Cardinal, was the first Apostolic Delegate to visit Scotland since the Reformation. I was the other speaker at a vast meeting he addressed in Edinburgh: all Edinburgh's ecclesiastical and civic leaders were there to do him honor. He gave a talk on the Marks of the Church as proof of her divine origin. It was a talk which the Catholic Evidence Guild would not have al-lowed a junior speaker to give on one of our street corner platforms. By any standard it was baby talk. From where I sat I could watch the mounting incredulity on the faces of the audience, the Protestants especially. I think they decided that they were witnessing a typical piece of Roman diplomacy—the guileless front masking the subtle mind! The story goes that Cardinal Ottaviani, archest of Conservatives, pointed to Cardinal Godfrey on the opening day of the Council, asked who he was, and said, "He looks pretty reactionary, doesn't he?"

After publishing some parts of this chapter in various newspapers, I had a couple of letters from angry Catholics who thought I was letting down the Church—we should leave criticism to the Church's enemies, they said. One of them said: "You have lost your awe of Cardinals. I have lost my awe of you": but no one who knows me has ever held me in awe (when I was doing my compulsory military service as a boy in Sydney an officer called me "the worst bloody blot on God's otherwise beautiful universe"). The other writer asked if my earlier pose as a loyal Catholic had been only a pretense: but no one who knows my writings would think I had ever soft-pedaled ecclesiastical ill-doing—though I never used words as violent as the words I have quoted of Catherine of Siena.

In the columns under attack I wrote of Renascence cardinals. I have just come across something in a book we published, *The Church of the Word Incarnate* by Charles Journet. In advertising that book we quoted Jacques Maritain's opinion that the author was the greatest living Catholic theologian. This opinion was challenged—some saying that there is no way of grading theologians, some selecting another theologian as greater, some writing him off as too orthodox! Orthodox he certainly was, all the same he did not stop at criticism of Renascence cardinals, he thought the Renascence popes "were fascinated by will to power and absolutism." And he wrote, "A war does not become holy just simply because it is the Pope who declares it, for the person who holds the pontifical authority can be led into injustice, ambition, revenge and other faults of the utmost gravity."

Rome did not seem to mind either criticism. It canonized Catherine of Siena. And Paul VI made Charles Journet a Cardinal. Long ago my wife and I had lunch with him in Fribourg. I remember a faint beginning of awe of him. I have not lost it.

CHAPTER 13

BOOKS AND CENSORS

I have written of the Roman Curia in its handling of matrimonial cases. I proceed to the Curia as censor of books. The matrimonial cases concerned me only as an interested spectator, my own marriage not calling for remedial treatment. But censorship was different, for censors ban books and we were publishers. A few years ago I wrote an article summarizing forty years' experience under the heading "Nobody Loves Censors." There have been occasions when a censor did not know how close his throat came to being cut. Yet over the whole span I have not suffered much from them, and some of what suffering I had now seems comic.

I

Imprimatur is a grim-sounding word, suggesting rack and thumbscrew and truth throttled. It means "It may be printed." Printing indeed brought it into being. Before the invention of printing, books were few, the handwritten copies of each so few that they did not call for general legislation. Indeed printing had been in operation for a century before Pius IV thought up the imprimatur.

By my time this "permission to print" had to be asked for on books whose *main purpose* was to deal with Scripture, theology, Church history, Canon Law, natural theology, religious and moral science. Books which treated of such matters here and there but not as their real theme did not need it. *All* prayer books had to have it: this did not trouble us, we did so few of them: but the rule saved the Catholic public from some—alas, not all—pious grotesqueries. In the eighteenth century the invocation to Our Lady as "Queen of the Sacred Heart" was forbidden absolutely. Rome has recently ordered censors to be specially careful about accounts of miraculous answers to prayer at this or that shrine—one order from Rome which has not been rigorously observed perhaps.

The publisher sends the manuscript to a diocesan Chancery. He has three choices of diocese—the one in which the author lives, or the book was printed, or the publisher has his office. This last meant for me further choices, between England and America. From the Chancery it is sent to a priest, the *censor deputatus*, who reads it. In nine cases out of ten he reports *Nihil Obstat* (nothing stands in the way) and the bishop or his representative, the vicar general, sends on the imprimatur.

The England-or-America possibility led to one of those incidents I have called comic. We had translated a small book of Karl Adam's under the title *One and Holy*: it dealt with the appalling state of the Church in Germany when Luther made his breakaway. By chance a copy was sent for imprimatur both to Boston and to Westminster. The Westminster vicar general refused the imprimatur. The Boston censor granted it. So we published the book in both countries with Boston's imprimatur. The Westminster censor wrote to say that an American imprimatur was valid only for America, that for an English publication an English imprimatur was necessary. Cardinal Griffin, he told me, was angry at our flagrant disobedience to Canon Law. I wrote back that Canon Law required an imprimatur for each different language, not for each country, that America was flooded with Catholic books bearing Westminster's imprimatur, and what of Canada, Australia, New Zealand? He did not answer the letter; Cardinal Griffin, with whom I had always been on the best of terms, never mentioned the matter at all. As I say, the incident was comic. Rome's command that we withdraw Karl Adam's earlier masterpiece *The Spirit of Catholicism* was not comic. I shall talk of that later.

To return to the normal procedure. I have said that the deputy censor reads the manuscript. I sometimes wondered about this. There was one censor who never did. He regarded Catholic publishers as so trustworthy that reading was not necessary. We loved him. Once he nearly ran into trouble.

A priest had written a review attacking one of our books for just about everything from heresy to blasphemy. A bishop, who had not read the book but *had* read the review, wrote to the censor (who had not read it either) and to me (who had), to say that he intended to preach against the book, the censor and me. The censor accused me tearfully of having proved unworthy of his trust! I told the bishop that the reviewer whose word he had so innocently taken was an unfrocked priest, and sent him copies of laudatory reviews by half a dozen frocked priests. I persuaded him to read the book and he found it harmless. The episode was comic of course: it reached high comedy in its final phase. For the bishop's last words were, "I hope this will teach you to be more careful in future."

Under the head of comedy I might list:

(1) A demented censor who demanded a couple of hundred changes and was withdrawn from his duties and sent to a psychiatrist when the authorities learned that in the confessional he was giving his penitents *for their penance* to buy and read a book he had written himself;

(2) A censor who refused the nihil obstat to a perfectly respectable theological work on the ground that the publisher had published an over-sexed novel by somebody else the year before;

(3) A priest who told me that he had once written a letter to Rome delating me for saying that as members of Christ's Body we were more closely related to Christ than his mother was simply by conceiving him. He had not sent the letter because a friend reminded him that St. Augustine had said very much the same— "More blessed was Mary for receiving him in her heart, than for conceiving him in her womb." Actually he had known Augustine's phrase—but in Latin. He had not translated it to himself;

(4) A censor who made large grammatical and stylistic corrections, and sent the publisher a bill for the editorial work he had done. Not being a Catholic, the publisher did not know what a censor's rights are. He paid the bill.

II

The *Index Expurgatorius* was established by Pius IV, the one who beheaded Carlo Carafa, the deplorable young man whom his uncle Paul IV had made a Cardinal. It is issued by what until recently was called the Holy Office, and lists books which contain doctrinal errors which might mislead Catholics about the revelation of Christ. I have spoken of Rabelais as the first great literary figure the priesthood produced in the thousand and more years after Augustine. The Franciscan order and the Benedictines are each entitled to boast of him, neither does. Of all the world's great writers he is the most obscene, the body's privacies are spattered all over his pages: celibacy he found "as unattractive as Lent": he hated monasteries and slammed Rome (slammed Calvin too). He sounds like Index Candidate No. I; most people assume his works are on it. But they are not. The Index was set up to protect Catholics from errors concerning the revelation of Christ and Rabelais never attacked doctrines. On the same principle the Spanish Inquisition refused to condemn a book which said that most of the monks of Spain had concubines. This was not true, the Inquisitors said primly, but it involved no false doctrine. A generation ago the Holy Office was concerned about Catholic novelists who showed the sexual troubles of priests in too much detail. I have not observed much diminution of detail in this area.

When a book is placed on the Index, Catholic booksellers may not sell it, Catholic readers may not read it without permission, all this under pain of grave sin. I have already spoken of what we may think of as flood height, the fourteen books a year "indexed" under Pius X, when there was panic about Modernism at the beginning of the century. The number fell to three a year under Benedict XV and has not risen since to flood height (though out of the thousands of books published annually by Catholics throughout the world, fourteen seems a pretty modest flood).

The Index exists not to keep an iron hand on the progress of human knowledge, which is the product of human reflection upon human experience, but to safeguard divine revelation. If Christ had not given his revelation it would not be there for human minds either to develop or to distort. The human mind has shown astounding ingenuity in both activities. Theories are constantly being thought up or churned up—profound, wild; constructive, destructive; illuminating, distorting. The reader not trained in theology and Scripture cannot so much as follow, much less judge, the arguments on which the writers base their theories. Even vast learning gives no certainty, with able theologians differing in rich variety. One hears patronizing talk of protecting the faith of the simple Catholic, but the faith of the complex Catholic can do with a little safeguarding too.

God gave his revelation because he wanted men to have it; for the same reason he is concerned about its exploration. It would be odd of him to reveal truths and then not care what men thought he was saying. He had given the revelation through men, he guards it through men. He founded a Church to teach what he had revealed, and an essential element in teaching it is the power to declare what is or is not in harmony with it.

That is the principle of censorship. I do not see how one can object to it save on the highly mystical idea that if you don't interfere the truth will emerge triumphant and the errors wither and die. It would not work with weeds in a garden; it would not work in any field at all. But if the principle of censorship is sound, the practice may be anything from inefficient to awful. In relation to the Church at large I shall look at this later.

For ourselves as authors we had nothing to complain of, as publishers very little. In forty-seven years we have never had a book put on the Index, but four were withdrawn by command of the Holy Office. Four in half a century is not much of a flood either. And on two of them—Karl Adam's *The Spirit of Catholicism* and Alfred Noyes's *Voltaire*—the veto was lifted pretty quickly. Of the two that stayed banned I know very little. One was by a German secular priest, the other by an English religious. Neither wanted to take any action, so we simply swallowed our losses.

I cannot remember the date—it was ten years ago, perhaps—of an incident in the Catholic students' chapel at Cambridge (England). The Apostolic Delegate, Archbishop O'Hara, was to preach at Mass there. He came out from the sacristy waving a copy of a London Sunday paper which accused the Holy Office of strangling thought in the Church. He seems to have called the article a pack of lies and eulogized the Holy Office almost beyond human possibility.

A few days later I was lunching with him and he was still fuming over the article. I found that though he had held high office in Rome's diplomatic service, including the nunciature in (I think) Yugoslavia, he was quite literally unaware that there was any possible ground of complaint against the way Rome handled the books it disliked. He had never even heard of writers condemned unheard! I told him the story of Noyes's *Voltaire* and Karl Adam's *The Spirit of Catholicism*. I think he found both stories educational. But not long after he reported an English bishop to Rome for having written a letter to the *Universe* saying that the Curia was dragging its feet about the implementing of Vatican II. Rome wrote to the accused bishop demanding an explanation. In fact there was no such letter.

III

We had published a large—and largely laudatory—book on Voltaire by Alfred Noyes. His scholarship was vast, his interpretations subtle and carefully argued. We were offered a new Voltaire, not exactly a Father of the Church, but a genuine believer in God and

fundamentally a better Christian than some of the Churchmen—
one got the impression that he lashed them very much as Christ
lashed the money changers! The book had a considerable press and
a considerable sale. But when the sales were beginning to peter out,
our own Cardinal Hinsley received an instruction from the Holy Office that the book must be withdrawn and the author must make a
public apology for having written it!

I won't go into all the details of what followed. It would be amusing, for instance, to tell of the difference between Alfred Noyes and
me as to the best way to handle the matter which had us writing against each other to the London *Times*. But I am not writing
his biography or my own, my topic is the Roman censorship. Cardinal Hinsley wrote to Rome, defending the book and demanding
an explanation. But no one in the Holy Office seemed to know anything about it. Apparently a lady had bought a copy of the book in
the Catholic Truth Society bookshop in London and had written
her indignation to Rome. Cardinal Sbaretti had reacted to her indignation with his own, wrote to Cardinal Hinsley and died. So
Rome told Cardinal Hinsley to settle the matter as he thought best.

But Alfred Noyes did something without parallel in the history
of censorship: he began a civil suit against the Cardinal for infring-
ing his rights as a British citizen by sending on the Roman document
to Sheed & Ward instructing them to withhold his book from continuing publication. It would have been a comic law case, I fancy.
A cleric sent by the Cardinal to reason with the author used the
phrase, "Of course Cardinal Sbaretti was——." It was a rude word
which might have meant anything from ill temper to homosexuality.
The rumor went around that Noyes's lawyer was going to cross-
question the cleric as to what exactly he meant by the word! Anyhow the case was withdrawn, Rome having withdrawn the
condemnation, only asking that the author write an Introduction
explaining in his own words why he had written the book. As written, the Introduction would have pained the spirit of Cardinal
Sbaretti if it came his way.

But there was a sequel which might have consoled the dead Cardinal. The book had contained a long idyllic section on the devotion
to the aged Voltaire of the niece he called Belle-et-Bonne. It seems
now to have been settled beyond doubt that she was his mistress.

There was another sequel which might have cancelled the consolation—Cardinal Hinsley's successor, Cardinal Griffin, secured

from the Holy Office an assurance that no English Catholic author would ever again be condemned unheard—the bishop on the spot must be told and the author allowed to state his case.

IV

What happened to Karl Adam's *The Spirit of Catholicism* was, if anything, even less comprehensible. We had a letter from the book's German publisher telling us that the Holy Office had ordered it withdrawn from circulation for *grave errors*. I wrote at once to Rome asking whether the ban extended to the English translation, which differed from the original at many points: if it did, might we be told what the serious errors were, that we might ask the author to correct them? The reply was that the ban covered every translation: about the errors nothing was said.

For two years there was silence. But protests had been reaching the Holy Office from all over the world. Archbishop Williams of Birmingham called at the Holy Office, said the book was his own spiritual reading, wouldn't they please do something about it? Quite suddenly Rome wrote to the author and asked him to make his own corrections, still not telling him what was wrong. So he altered some sentences, and the book was once more in circulation, as it has been ever since. Once again, no one in Rome seemed to know what it was all about. There was not even a dead Cardinal to be called a rude name.

Both incidents are a reminder that the daily work of running the Church has to be carried on by officials, in offices. There has to be a bureaucracy, and there are certain strengths and certain weaknesses common to all bureaucracies everywhere. I do not mean small human weaknesses—envies and jealousies, one man's wanting the other man's job, for instance. These are so universal that they are not worth lingering on. My interest is in weaknesses inseparable from bureaucracy itself: one in particular.

It is not only self-seeking, power-seeking, that causes officials to draw more and more things into their circle of authority. In the nature of the case modern life is so complex that in any event the orderly conduct of affairs is difficult. If everybody can make his own decisions, the people in control feel that running the show is impossible. The more decisions that can be drawn into their own power, the easier for them. So they feel. But the result is that they bite off more than they can chew. With such a mass of details to be handled, some get overlooked. There is chaos inside the bureau to match the chaos outside. I think that that largely explains the banning of *Voltaire* and *The Spirit of Catholicism.*

Yet officials there have to be. The Church no more than the State can function without a Civil Service: and in the Church as in the State the Civil Service can get on the nerves of the citizenry. And not only of the citizenry. To a visitor Pope John spoke in praise of a book just published, about an Italian parish, I think. "But," said the visitor, "the Holy Office has just banned it." "Oh," said the Pope, "those old horrors don't like it, don't they?"

Father O'Connell, S.J., head of the Vatican Observatory, told me of an incident concerning a Conference of Astronomers to be held there: he was instructed that he must not invite Professor Hoyle, because of his notorious atheism: he appealed to Pope Pius, who insisted that Hoyle be invited and walked and talked with him.

A more recent happening has given me a warm feeling about the Curia. In a missionary country there was such a shortage of priests that one of them said five Masses on a Sunday—three being the normal limit. The high ecclesiastic in charge in that country reported him to Rome. The reply came that if the high ecclesiastic and his secretary would each say a public Mass then the accused priest need not go beyond the permitted three.

To return to the two-year interdict on Karl Adam's *The Spirit of Catholicism:* earlier we talked of the refusal of a Westminster imprimatur to his *One and Holy.* Can we learn anything about censorship by studying the work of a man who thus stirred the censors into action in two incidents a quarter century apart?

Karl Adam was born in Bavaria in 1876, one of a family of ten (which in our world raises the question whether he ought ever to have been born at all). After ordination he worked for two years as assistant in a parish. He reveled in the work and judging by certain stories which have come down to us had something of a gift for it. There was the woman who was having a row with the parish priest. She was ill. Father Adam called on her. She showed her contempt for him by turning to the wall and presenting her bottom to him. He smacked it, hard. A few minutes later he was hearing her confession.

He was too good a student to be left in parish work. He was sent to Munich to study the history of dogma. He was Professor of Moral Theology at Strasbourg when the French Army arrived. Alsace was French again. He had to go. He became Professor of Dogmatic Theology at Tübingen, famous for having two Theological Faculties, one Catholic, one Protestant. He was fired under Hitler for a very outspoken speech on the Jewish contribution to Christianity: was reappointed; was fired again. To have been banned by the French, by Hitler, by Westminster, and (more temporarily) by the Vatican, constitutes a kind of record perhaps.

The book which carried his message all over the world was *The Spirit of Catholicism*. One has met it in translations everywhere. We brought out the English version in 1928. Its aim was "to render the spirit of Catholicism intelligible to the contemporary mind." It may seem ridiculous to say that had already for ten years been the aim of our outdoor speaking in the Catholic Evidence Guild. I am not even hinting that we did it as well, only that in fact it was what we were trying to do, and we fell upon his book as nourishment for which we were craving. We had been in our lesser way forerunners of the New Apologetic. He became its standard-bearer.

He was not trying to prove other religions wrong. He was not even trying to prove the Church right, only to make it intelligible. He was not stating the case for Catholicism, only *showing Catholicism* (*Wesen* was the German word which was translated as Spirit in the English title). What it is—what difference it can make, what it can do for us, what we lose by not making it our own.

As I wrote at the time, "the essence of the formula was in Newman, but it *could* not be applied in Newman's day: some alloy of controversy there had to be." But there is no controversy in Adam, except in his more technical works, written to be read by scholars. What he wrote on the development of dogma, especially on the Sacrament of Penance in the Early Church, stirred controversy, not always peaceful; the banning of his book by Rome may have been a last spurt of these controversies.

But what he wrote for the public is all exposition, showing. He relies on the power of the truth to hold the reader and nothing else, no epigrams, no paradoxes, not the hint of a joke. So many preachers I have heard who feel that they cannot hold the audience unless they can make it laugh.

Two doctrines Adam spent his life in "showing"—the Incarnation (on which we published *The Son of God* and *Christ Our Brother*) and the Mystical Body (which is what *The Spirit of Catholicism* is about). He did not think that with any given man, the truth is necessarily a winning argument for itself, but it is the only finally valid one. He writes, "A man who, when confronted with the paradox of God the all-perfect, all-holy, eternal, becoming a man, a carpenter, a Jew, haled before the court and crucified, feels that he simply cannot take it, may be actually less remote from a living piety than one who coolly accepts all this and glibly repeats his *Credo*. But at the end of all things can man's power to accept really decide the limits of the possible? Is not God greater than man's conception of God? In the infinite possibilities of God all conceivable possibilities are included, even the possibility of a Bethlehem, the possibility of a Golgotha. We cannot ignore Jesus. He is a possibility of God's."

I began this glance at Karl Adam in the hope that it might shed light on censorship. I can't say it sheds much for me.

The real problem in censorship cannot be finally solved. It lies in this, that the bishop's right to object or protect, cannot be defined mathematically. In *Is It the Same Church?* I wrote:

A Catholic needs to know when a given teaching is out of harmony with the truths, doctrinal or moral, entrusted by Christ to his Church. And it was not Pius IX but Newman who said that truth may be error to minds unprepared for it. Authority can swell into tyranny certainly. But freedom can collapse into muddle.

My own feeling is that something like the Index may continue, but for information. Authors perhaps will be under no obligation to withdraw "indexed" books, readers under no obligation to shun them. But at least if a Catholic chooses to read one, he will have been warned—he will not be misled into thinking he is getting the Church's teaching.

Things may work out quite differently of course. But I think one simple psychological principle is now grasped—to force protection on people who don't want it is not protective.

CHAPTER 14

KARL MARX AND I

At any given moment one or other special problem looms to complicate things for the Church, looms and fades. But throughout my life two have shown no sign of fading—Marxism and Nationalism; Sex has been there throughout the Church's life, and the future offers its permanence no threat. I shall give a chapter to each. I begin with Marxism because, of the three, it was the first I was aware of.

I

I have told how my father, a true believer in Karl Marx, turned every meal into a monologue on Communism. By the time I was ten I had heard—it would be unfilial to say ad nauseam—about the Theory of Surplus Value, the Materialist Interpretation of History, the Class War, the Classless Society, Religion as the Opium of the People. My father was convinced that with religion dying, the real opium of the people was sport; he hadn't a notion of what use Russia would one day make of it.

I was not the first son to let his mind wander occasionally. But in nine years I followed enough to convince me that I had hit on Marxism's root fallacy, the notion that the right system of production, distribution and exchange would mean all men's needs met and society wholly harmonious. Had I heard this only once or twice or thrice I might not have seen its unreality: but by the twentieth, thirtieth, fiftieth repetition, I hadn't a doubt.

Every element of Marxism as it came from my father's mouth I tested privately by applying it to my father himself, wondering what difference it would make in him, finding it impossible to see him not talking back bitingly at those above him, or doing anything he did not feel like doing, in any system whatsoever. There was my headmaster too—what could Karl Marx do about him? Whom would he flog in the Classless Society, and how would he be happy not flogging? It was not till years later that I saw myself as part of the prob-

194   THE CHURCH AND I

lem that the Classless Society, or any Society—the Church, for instance—would have to cope with.

But at least this one thing I got from nine years of Marxist monologue—that people are the problem, not systems. It was all very superficial and small-boyish. But it was the point. To this day when I lecture on Marxism, or that other great international the Church, I invite my listeners to glance at the people on each side of them and ask themselves how either Karl Marx or the Pope would make an ideal society out of them. That is what sociology is all about.

Edmund Clerihew Bentley once wrote of the difference between Biography and Geography—

> Geography is about maps
> Biography is about chaps.

Sociology is about chaps too. It seemed to me that Marx, as I met him at meals, and later in his writings, had simply left chaps out of his system.

When I was twenty, the Bolsheviks took over Russia. I watched the takeover with a delight special to myself. It would settle whether I was right or wrong in my conviction that Marxism would not work with people—however well it looked on paper, which will put up with anything.

But it settled nothing. I remember my mounting indignation—on Marx's behalf—at what the Soviet rulers were doing with Marxism. I still thought the old man wrong, but not wrong like that. How it would have worked out under Lenin one cannot know. But Lenin had only five years. Stalin came. And Stalin was one of the realities, one of the chaps, so to speak, that Marx had made no allowance for. He was not a Marxist, of course: Marx he would have disposed of very early. Ideology was not for him. Power was his obsession, an obsession commonplace enough. But it was his gift too, and there was nothing commonplace about that: it ranked him with the Emperor Diocletian.

Franklin D. Roosevelt was a master of power, Western style: but living in a liberal democracy he had to get his own way by persuading. Stalin had only to will. At Yalta the persuasive man met the man of will: and the arts which had the head of the Teamsters' union jumping through hoops were of no use at all against the will which had watched ten million Russians die of starvation because the purchase of wheat from abroad would have weakened the Russian ruble.

The phrase with which Roosevelt covered his failure to cope with the greatest natural force he had ever met was, "The way to make an untrustworthy man trustworthy is to trust him." It was the kind of sheerly farcical remark that Stalin would have seen the richness of. I wonder how it sounds in Russian.

To the Russian experiment with Marxism we might apply Chesterton's remark about Christianity—that it was not tried and found wanting, it was found difficult and left untried. If I am right about this there is irony in it, for the clear result of Stalin's thirty years has been to convince the rest of the world not that Stalin was bloody, but that Communism is.

Would it have been different if Lenin had lived? That he would have eliminated Stalin is fairly certain, for he too had a will of steel and he held all the cards. But he would have had to face the same problem—that only a highly industrialized nation can fight a modern war. Russia was wholly agricultural; it was forced to industrialize itself almost overnight to save itself from destruction. That sort of conversion would in any event have called for the limit in compulsion, tyranny using slavery. Would it have meant the same amount of bloodshed, or were the rivers of blood Stalin's individual contribution? Anyhow I still have no actual evidence to support my teen-age conviction that Communism would not work.

Through the twenties of this century and most of the thirties I kept an interest in Communism but not a very vital one. My father's mealtime monologues, whatever they may have been doing in the depth of my mind, were no longer very actual in my mind's front. The brief hope that Marxism would be given a thorough workout by Soviet Russia had flickered and died. At least I never saw the Russian bloodbath as disproving Marxism any more than I saw the Mediaeval Inquisition as disproving the Church.

Meanwhile I was fascinated by the social teaching of Pius XI and spoke on him at the meetings of various non-Catholic societies to which I was invited:

> From the factory dead matter goes out improved, whereas men there are corrupted and degraded.
> The State which should be the supreme arbiter, intent only upon justice and the common good, has become a slave, bound over to the service of human passion and greed.

The denial of the right of workers to form unions for protection against oppression by the employing class is criminal injustice.

Certain forms of property must be reserved to the State, since they carry with them a power too great to be left to private individuals without danger to the community at large.

Every effort must be made that a just share only of the fruits of production be permitted to accumulate in the hands of the wealthy.

Working men are surrendered, isolated and helpless, to the hardheartedness of employers and the greed of unchecked competition.

With the spread of industrialisation to America and the Far East, the number of needy proletarians, their groans rising from earth to heaven, increased beyond all measure.

The Church has lost the working classes. The Pope says that many Catholics have embraced Socialism, feeling that the Church and those professing attachment to it favor the rich and have no care for the workers.

All these quotations are from *Quadragesimo Anno*. In *Divini Redemptoris* Pius XI looked even deeper—into the way "an avaricious and selfish priest" can come between the poor and Christ. Seven years after *Quadragesimo Anno* Cardinal Mundelein of Chicago translated those last words about the feeling that the Church favored the rich into plain English: "The trouble with us in the past has been that we were too often drawn into an alliance with the wrong side. Selfish employers have flattered the Church by calling it the great conservative force, and then called upon the police to act while they paid but a pittance of wages to those who worked for them . . . our place is beside the poor."

The Pope's words seemed to me wholly realistic, meeting the actual situation of the workers. I could not see how Karl Marx improved on them by denying God and a next life. All the same I was tickled by the title of the greatest of these encyclicals—*Quadragesimo Anno*, in the Fortieth Year, issued to celebrate the fortieth anniversary of Leo XIII's *Rerum Novarum*, on the rights of the working class. It struck me that *Rerum Novarum* itself might well have been called *Quadragesimo Anno*—forty years after the *Communist Manifesto*: if only it had come forty years before it, instead of forty years after!

How *did* I see Communism in those years? On the way to one of our own platforms I would pause and listen to other speakers. Being a speaker I was interested in their techniques, weighing their ways of communication against my own. I found the majority concerned with attack, not much given to exposition of their own case! This was true particularly of three platforms—the Protestant Alliance, the Communists and the men with something to sell—a patent medicine usually. For the Protestant Alliance, a strange underground of which normal Protestants had never heard, it was all attack, on the errors of Rome naturally. Apart from that they seemed to have no case. The other two were definitely *for* something—an ideology to be spread, a bottle of medicine to be sold.

It may seem frivolous of me to mention a thing so small and a thing so vast in the same breath. But it was the medicine sellers who helped me to see what the Communist speakers were doing. Each lavished all his skill on the disease to be cured—cancer, Capitalism—with a minimum of talk about the remedy. The techniques were precisely the same, but easier to see when stripped to the bone by men who had to have quick sales or starve. Certainly most of the Communist propaganda one actually met was about Capitalism. By the time the speaker had dealt faithfully with all that the poor suffered, he felt no need to show the values of Communism —it had the one all-sufficing virtue, it was not Capitalism. And while most of the horrors of Capitalism belonged in the previous century there were plenty still.

The result was that most of the Communists, the rank and file and even many of the active speakers, hardly knew Marxism at all. Lenin had said that without Hegel Marx's *Das Kapital* is unintelligible. I could count on the fingers of one hand the Communists I've met in fifty years who could talk three intelligible sentences on how Hegel clarifies things for the student of Marx.

But it did not seem to make any difference—the horrors of nineteenth-century Capitalism were enough. *Any* criticism of Communism, any questioning even, was taken as proof that one was pro-Capitalist. So deep-rooted was this reaction that the anti-Capitalist encyclicals of Pius XI produced no effect on it.

I should have gone on at this level of interest in Communism— real but detached. But two things of very different sorts forced me to a closer study, turning me from a mere spectator into what I may call an active observer. One was the contrast between the apostolic fervor of the Communists and the apostolic unconcern of Catholics. The other was the Spanish Civil War.

II

The apostolic unconcern of Catholics was at all levels. I could never get used to the successors of the Apostles teaching algebra to Catholic teen-agers while millions were starved of the food Christ wanted them to have. The Catholic Evidence Guild in New York was never more than twenty lay speakers out of a million or more Catholics, but it simply could not get priests to speak in Times Square. The clergy said Cardinal Spellman would not allow them to speak outdoors. So my wife asked him and he said, Yes, they might. But they didn't. Two or three did, once or twice. The one who wanted to continue speaking knew so little about the Faith that he was an embarrassment. The Guild is now reduced to five speakers, who just will not give up. And a priest has begun to speak with them.

But the unconcern was everywhere. In any group in which I found myself, by plane or boat or merely at dinner, two rules were absolute. (1) If there was a Communist in the group everyone knew it within three minutes; (2) if there was a Catholic in the group, no one ever found out at all. In other words, only among Communists could we of the Catholic Evidence Guild find an urgency to communicate like our own.

It may be that the Communist insistence on propaganda at every instant alienated more people than it won; I was not suggesting that a Catholic turn to the strange lady next to him at a dinner party and ask, "How is your soul this evening?" I was not contrasting techniques of communication; my problem was why the Communist was so blazingly on fire with his system and the Catholic so cool about his. It was clear that Communism mattered to those who held it. Why didn't the Faith matter to Catholics?

In a train crossing Nebraska I came across a phrase of Bernard Shaw's which I have increasingly seen as the key to man's likely future. That part of Nebraska does not solicit the eye, so I read my book. It was *Back to Methuselah*. Shaw, I suppose, was as talkative a man as ever existed. I don't know at what age he uttered his first fallacy—six months, perhaps—but till his death at ninety-three he hardly stopped. Now, a man who utters as much as that can hardly help occasionally saying something pretty good. In the Preface to *Back to Methuselah* I found my light-bearing phrase: "The Class

War of the future will be a war of intellectual classes. And the conquest will be the souls of the children."

It was a road to Damascus flash like the one that had almost hurled me to the ground when Shane Leslie told me of the old ladies in Dublin and so showed me the essence of prejudice in myself. And I recognized the "war of intellectual classes." I saw in that instant that it mattered more than the two World Wars we have had: if World War III does not send us all into outer space, it will still matter vitally: for the souls of the children are truly at issue.

I recognized the war instantly, a war of minds. On one side were those who hold that all the world's problems must be solved within the boundaries of this world. On the other those who hold that without God and his Christ and the spiritual soul and the world to come, no problems *can* be solved. In between lies a great soggy mass of people who do not even know that there is a war on. Of those who do, one side is spearheaded by the Communists. Who spearheads the other? Has it a head or even a spear? In any war, if one side doesn't fight, there is no question of who will win. And I got the impression that the Church did not want its rank and file to fight, thought its Faith would be safer if it didn't! Anyhow, since there *was* a war of minds, I felt I had better use my own mind—on the spearhead.

III

I might have gone on moaning about Catholic unconcern without being driven to an actual study of Marxism. It was the Spanish Civil War that detonated my interest.

Like the majority of Catholics of the English tongue I wanted Franco to win. We did not know much about conditions in Spain, but as between people who murdered priests and nuns and people who didn't, we preferred those who didn't. It was practically a reflex reaction.

Certainly I had no expectation that Franco would be any better than the average of military men turned ruler. I was interested in his taking over of anti-government Spain because a man I knew, Douglas Jerrold, played a part in it. The Republican Government had sent Franco off to the Canary Islands, from which he had no way of getting back to Spain. Douglas Jerrold, in England, had hired a plane, ostensibly for a joy ride: he had flown it to the Canaries and had got out for a stroll: while he was away Franco and a friend

200 THE CHURCH AND I

climbed into the plane and flew to Spain. I never thought to ask Jerrold if the story were true.

Anyhow he was a Franco supporter; and though I liked him, I would not have been enthusiastic at the prospect of being ruled by him. He was Managing Director of a large London publishing house, Eyre & Spottiswoode, and he wanted to buy up Sheed & Ward. I said, "No, I like small businesses." "So do I," he said, "that's why I wanted to buy Sheed & Ward." I felt I knew exactly how Red Ridinghood's grandmother felt. From what I had heard of his friend Franco, I doubted if I'd have much liked being ruled by him either, he must have caused a lot of people to feel like that same old lady. But then again I could think of friends closer than Jerrold I'd have disliked being ruled by. Anyhow, for better or worse I saw Franco as one more politician, the point clearly in his favor was that he did not massacre priests and nuns.

But most of my Catholic friends saw Franco as leading a crusade: after the marvelous defense of the Alcazar at Toledo, one of them had his baby daughter christened Alcazar. A group of Evidence Guild speakers felt that we should do Franco propaganda from our platforms. I had resisted our campaigning against Communism: I now resisted campaigning for Franco. Both sides put their case to Cardinal Hinsley. He decided for non-intervention.

It was only slowly that I came to see that we had oversimplified in making the killing of priests and nuns the only matter to be considered, just as it would be if, in an election in England or America, we made aid to Catholic schools the sole consideration. The killing of non-priests and non-nuns is also evil. And there are social injustices pressing millions to the earth year in and year out which cause a greater mass of human suffering than the slaying of religious men and women. I am not saying, or even suggesting, that in the balance Franco was worse than the other side, as I fancy Jacques and Raïssa Maritain thought, and the French Dominican weekly *Sept*, and perhaps England's *Catholic Herald*. I am saying that we had not the evidence to enable us to judge.

It was not our work as teachers of the Faith to campaign against Communism. But with our crowds strongly against Franco, particularly after the "bombing" of the "sacred oak" at Guernica, one had to know Communism better. As a social-economic system it was not our topic, but as atheism it certainly was. Just as the Marlborough and Marconi nullity cases had driven me to study the Church's Law of Nullity and write a book on it, so under the same kind of pressure I plunged into the study of Karl Marx, grateful to Lenin for the hint that I must begin with Hegel.

In 1939 I gave our speakers a long course of lectures on Communism. Dorothy Collins, who had been secretary to G. K. Chesterton until his death, reminded me that he had dictated books to her typewriter: why shouldn't I? So I turned the lecture course into *Communism and Man*.

IV

The book made an effort to cover—deeply in some parts, sketchily in others—the whole shape of Marxism, beginning as Lenin would have required with a chapter on Hegel. Putting Hegel into a chapter sounds ridiculous of course, considering that Hegel is said to have said on his deathbed, "Only one man ever understood me, and he didn't" (I wonder if that "one man" who did but didn't was himself?). My aim was more modest than it sounds. I concentrated on the dialectic—thesis and antithesis and synthesis—the conflict of opposites producing progress. I concentrated on it because it was the principal idea that Marx drew out of Hegel. Even to get that into a chapter sounds improbable enough. Here again I reduced it not to what Hegel meant but to what Marx thought he meant. I was studying Marx, not Hegel.

The Marxism of Marx was atheist. I don't mean simply that Marx was an atheist but that his system was. That all man's needs can be met within the boundaries of this world was essential to it: everything was moving towards the Classless Society, in which all men's needs would in all literalness be met. If there were any being outside the universe, God, let us say, who could affect what happens here, if there were any life after this, his system would have been wrecked. That is why he reserved his most powerful invective for those who thought they could accept his social-economic system while believing in a religion. Religion was a "yoke," it was "opium" —which Lenin reworded as "a crude kind of spiritual vodka." Those who would bring their own more rarefied religion into Communism Lenin called "ideological slaves of the bourgeoisie, clericalism's flunkeys."

Man's highest activity, as Marx saw it, was economic, which included everything that has to do with the production and distribution of all that earth and sea and sky contain in them for men's use. Defective production, defective distribution, mean needs unmet, men unhappy. In production the individual can only scratch the surface; the group, the collective is the producing unit. Because it is the unit of production it is the unit of society. "The human essence is no abstraction inherent in each single individual. In reality it is the ensemble of the social relations." The individual man or woman has no meaning whatever save in the collective. For Marx Economics governs every human activity—not being mad, Marx did not, as some of his opponents seem to think, hold that men act for no motives save economic. They act for myriad motives; but economic reality, the mode of production, shapes everything decisively—history, sociology, politics, philosophy, science, art, religion: as that changes, these all change with it. And whoever is in control of the means of production rules society; in the past this has meant a succession of governing classes, but one unvarying class of governed, the proletariat, those who have nothing to contribute but their labor. Whoever rules, the proletariat are exploited. We have reached the point where there are only two classes left, bourgeois and proletariat: the dialectic of the Class War makes it certain that ultimately the proletariat alone will rule.

They will then be on the threshold of the Classless Society. But they cannot at once cross the threshold, because in their millennia of servitude they have been stained with, or at least tinged with, the faults of their masters. There has to be a period of cleansing—a purgatory, in fact—before they can cross the threshold. The purging will be done in the Dictatorship of the Proletariat. By instruction, by coercion, by terror, all men will be purged of whatever residual stains may be still on them. The coercing completed, the Classless Society will have arrived; wholly socially conditioned, men will be incapable of functioning otherwise than perfectly for the collective well-being. The state will have withered away, for the state means coercion and men will not need to be coerced.

Since the denial of God and survival were for Marx at the root of all else, one might have expected him to devote a vast amount of effort to disproving them. Incredibly he devotes none at all. He simply says there is no God, no afterlife. He accounts for the belief in a next world by the inadequacy of all economic systems that ever have been. Freud accounts for it by unsatisfied sexual needs, Marx by unsatisfied economic needs. For both, belief in the next world is a shadow cast by unsatisfied needs—as the needs are met, nothing remains to cast a shadow. There is no need to disprove a shadow which is no longer cast. There is something Ajax-like in thus simply flipping aside beliefs of which mankind has so recurrent a habit. But Marx is an Ajax who does not know the power of the lightning he defies. He shows no sign of realizing what religion had in fact accomplished. Consider, for instance, how Christopher Dawson describes Islam—"A new attitude to life which first arose in the arid plateau of Arabia, transformed the lives and social organization of the Slavonic mountaineers of Bosnia, the Malay pirates of the East Indies, the highly civilised city dwellers of Persia and Northern India, and the barbarous negro tribes of Africa." Marx must have known this, but seems to have drawn no moral of any sort from it.

I have talked of the great mass of Communists who have never studied Marx: their embrace of Communism is simply a resentment of Capitalism. But in every country there is a minority who have given their minds to what Marx taught: they are the brain, the energy center. I am convinced that the Classless Society is what draws them and holds them. Their common quality is that they have active minds. Because of what a mind is it needs to find two things particularly—order (how much should a man do, for instance, how much should he get?) and purpose (what is the goal of his own life, towards what goal is the human race moving?). It cannot be content without them. In the world as they see it run they get neither.

How much should a man do? As little as he can get by with. How much should he get? As much as he can lay his hands on. This is not order but chaos, with the state standing by to pick up the pieces. The goal is no better seen. The individual man is not going anywhere: at death he returns to the bosom of matter from which he had so briefly emerged. The race is not going anywhere either: the materialist tells him that the material universe is moving towards a state of maximum entropy, which means the total cessation of activity: even any religion he may have probably sees no goal towards which the human race is moving—God will simply end it. To be members of an army marching nowhere, of a society going nowhere, means a great diminishment of human dignity, a corrosion of energy, if one has enough mind to be aware of it. The Church has from Christ answers to both: a society is united by agreement as to what its members love and the only love which cannot divide is love of one's neighbor as oneself: the race is moving towards the building of Christ's mystical body. But no Catholic is likely to give anyone those answers—most of us have hardly glanced at them ourselves.

Marxism offers answers, and Marxists are only too eager to state them. On order, for instance: how much should a man do? From every man according to his capacity. How much should a man get? To every man according to his need. And there is a goal, the Classless Society, all needs met, all men happy and fulfilled. About both the order and the goal there is in fact something dreamlike—a perfect system, hypnotically coherent. But one marvels how it could stand up to the examining mind—dreams and hypnosis aren't expected to, of course.

"All needs met by production, distribution functioning perfectly, men thus fulfilled incapable of acting un-socially"?—the first man one meets could dispel that dream: here as so often, ourself will do. Indeed Marx would have done: for outside his family this herald of the collective could never find a collective he didn't detest. When the good Socialist Proudhon wrote *The Philosophy of Poverty* (with its echoing slogan "property is theft") Marx had to tear him apart with *The Poverty of Philosophy*. For Marx's "Dictatorship of the Proletariat" we have to wait for his *Critique of the Gotha Programme*—Socialists had held a conference at Gotha, Marx was not there, he had to criticize them.

If the faults of men had been to him as relevant as the faults of systems he might have been a very great sociologist. But he was in love with his system, and not much given to loving men. The upshot was that he was not a sociologist at all, because societies are made of men and he left out man's incalculability. In those boyhood days when I was testing Marxism by my father and my headmaster, I was sometimes called upon in school to do a sum which, as I saw only later, provided a working model for Marx as a sociologist. It went something like this: If one boy can mow a lawn in two hours, how long will it take two boys to mow the same lawn? This was one sum I could do. If one boy can do it in two hours, two boys can do it in one. That is the mathematical answer. It is not true of course. The two boys will start chatting, start arguing, wrestle a bit, race their lawn mowers against each other, raid the icebox for a Coke, forget to come back. How long will it take two boys to mow the lawn? Heaven knows. That is the sociological answer.

Marx solved the problem by leaving out the boys. At any point in human life we come up against the self—clutching at what it wants, evading what it finds unpleasant. Marx makes no allowance, leaves no margin, for the self. Camus can write, "Paris is a magnificent dummy setting inhabited by four million silhouettes with two passions, ideas and fornication . . ." A single sentence will suffice for modern man—"he fornicates and reads the papers." Camus is not writing demography, of course, just relieving his feelings, but he has at least looked at men. Marx, to repeat, had not. The proletariat guiltless of original sin would not have survived—say—the reading of Dickens, or an occasional evening in the nearest pub.

v

Communism and Man sold well enough in America, very well in England. In America it is long out of print, in England it is still in print thirty-five years later. I think it may have been the chapter on Hegel which made the difference—with English readers willing to live through it, Americans not. As publisher I should have liked to leave it out in the interest of sales, but as author I had no choice. It was not only that Lenin had said the study of Hegel was essential, but as I came to study him I saw it so. There is so much in Marx's system which is understood better if we know what Hegel had at the corresponding part of his.

And of course reading Hegel had its occasional compensations— as with his statement of the three religious vows: "The pernicious ecclesiastical institutions of celibacy, voluntary pauperism and laziness." If I were a monk I might meditate on that. I smiled often enough at his trick of sprinkling his most unchristian passages with the great Christian words—Trinity, Holy Spirit, Incarnation, Creation, Revelation. I once read out such a passage to an audience of nuns. They found the sound of it so edifying that I hated to have to tell them what he was actually saying.

In a general way, no one seems to have disliked *Communism and Man*. I heard of Communist groups who were instructed to study the first sixty pages, which are as clear a statement as I could make of what Marx taught: the critical part which follows they were advised they could ignore. We had learned early that you cannot interest a man in your own point of view, unless you can state his as well as he could state it himself. That indeed is a bare minimum. You cannot win a man from his belief, political or religious, unless you can see why it attracts him and can almost imagine yourself holding it. George Orwell wrote a review which gave me the liveliest pleasure. He approved of my treatment of Marx, his only reservation was about my treatment of the Church's answer to the problems Marx raised.

The accuracy of my presentation of Marx was a solid asset. I always told audiences of my hope that if Karl Marx had been there he would have said, "Yes, that is what I held." I remember a meeting in the town of Dundee. I was to lecture on Communism on the Sunday night. On the Sunday afternoon the organizers told me that they had learned that 300 Communist miners from Fife were coming to wreck the meeting. Should we cancel? We decided not to, of course. When I came onto the platform the miners were there, in a great stretch across the center of the hall, wearing their caps. I announced that I should begin with a statement of Marx's teaching: if at any point they found I was stating it wrongly, they should correct me. By the time they had absorbed thirty minutes of pure Marx, without finding anything to object to, they seem not to have felt like reacting angrily to my fifteen minutes of criticism. Even at question time there was no sound from the men of Fife. But they kept their caps on throughout.

That was a special occasion. But at scores of meetings the exposition of Marx had the same mollifying effect. I usually like the Communists I meet, they lack the arrogance which makes it so hard to warm to Fascists. And I found a real link with them in my feeling that Joe Hills, the author of "Pie in the Sky," had had a raw deal. He was an American, a member of the Industrial Workers of the World, executed for the blowing up of a house which he almost certainly did not blow up. I seldom met a Communist who knew the words of his song, and I have kept no count of the crowds to whom I have taught it:

> Long-haired preachers come out every night
> Try to teach us what's wrong and what's right.
> But when asked How about something to eat?
> They will answer with voices so sweet:

> You will eat by and by,
> In that beautiful land beyond the sky.
> Work all day, feed on hay,
> There'll be pie in the sky when you die.

KARL MARX AND I

After that they were less disinclined to listen to the social teaching of Pius XI.

I have talked of the general lack of rank-and-file knowledge of Communism, the hatred of Capitalism which does duty in its absence, and the assumption that anyone who questions Communism must be pro-Capitalist. Just after the War I was asked to speak at a meeting in Richmond, Virginia. The other speaker was a trade union leader: the chair was to be taken by "Ma" Johnson, Franklin Roosevelt's Secretary for Labor. Only when I got there did I learn that the organizers had planned it as a debate—the union leader for the Workers, I for the Employers, Miss Johnson holding the balance. I began by disclaiming the role allotted to me. For ten minutes I painted the faults of owners and managers. The audience clapped me excitedly. When my criticism of the employers had reached its climax, I said, "In fact they are every bit as bad as the workers."

Human nature is the point. I invited my audience to picture the two sides of the table in any industrial dispute: could anyone decide from the faces which side was which? The proletariat innocent of the original sin of exploitation was a dream. As Augustine said of babies, their innocence is only lack of opportunity.

What bedeviled all discussion of Marxism in the thirties and forties was Russia. One practically never met a Communist who was not an idolater of Russia: indeed there were a whole mass of Communizers who were not even sure they were Communists but felt that there was something charismatic about Stalin—one could weep to think of the splendid young idealists I met everywhere to whom he was Uncle Joe. Churchill had called him "a bloody baboon." We know what Khrushchev was to tell Russia and the world about him.

I found among a lot of papers whose existence I had forgotten something I wrote just before World War II, about an article by a British Labour M.P., John Strachey (Member, I think, for Dundee!) and at that time a Communist. His article was a perfect example of the habit so many Communists had of devoting so much skill to depicting the horrors of the disease that they did not find it necessary to show that their remedy would cure it. It was a three-page attack on Nazism and Capitalism, with only two sentences on Communism.

"The core of Nazi doctrine," he wrote, "is the denial of humanity. And whether we like it or not, it is an historical fact that the concept of humanity appeared in a religious form; it appeared above all in the specific form of the Christian doctrine of the infinite worth of every soul. . . . This doctrine was the dissolving agent—the unsaying 'word'—which undermined the institution of slavery."

This was admirable. For a Communist to admit that a Christian doctrine dissolved the institution of slavery might make Karl Marx writhe in his grave in Highgate Cemetery, but it is a splendid piece of truth. Mr. Strachey was right in seeing it as standing between us and the return to slavery. But how can a Communist hold it? He does not believe in the everlasting value of the human soul, since for him it ends at death. What individual value of any kind can be attached to man if he be (as the Communist holds he is) merely a product of matter, emerging from the bosom of matter for no particular reason, held briefly above the bosom of matter for the space of a lifetime as a cog in the collective, plunged back again at death into the bosom of matter for ever, his place in the collective taken by another cog as meaningless as himself?

Not long after, I met John Strachey. I was asked to debate with him before the students of London University on the desirablity of Catholics co-operating with Communists in fighting for those principles they held in common.

I had long been against debating as a means of clarifying issues. A debate is almost invariably won by the abler speaker. The fact that I sometimes filled that role myself did not alter its irrelevance —for the ability of the speakers is not part of the question under discussion. Not only that, important matters cannot be settled in an hour or two of bright talk. However, I agreed to do it. Mr. Strachey stated his case for collaboration-up-to-a-point. The case against it called for no very subtle argumentation. I had not then heard Winston Churchill's definition of appeasement—feeding the crocodile in the hope that it will eat you last. But I did say that it was dangerous to work with a party which made no secret of its determination upon world conquest. That took about three minutes. So I filled in the remaining time with the reasons why a Catholic could not be a Communist. Mr. Strachey was scornful—I had missed the point: of course Catholics could not be Communists, the question was, should they collaborate? I was wholly happy to have one of Communism's leading spokesmen assuring Catholic students that Communism was not for them.

From that time on I had only the chance meeting with Marxians. I got to know Trotskyites fairly well, and found no reason to question their loathing of Stalin. Communist hecklers still turned up at our street corner meetings, and we found them more and more cut to a pattern. They were utterly predictable. One time I had been saying that the notion of happiness resultant from the meeting of all man's needs left out too much. Some of our greatest miseries can co-exist with high material prosperity. A poet, for instance, whose poems are despised is not to be consoled by money, nor a man whose wife has gone away with some other man. A questioner interjected: "There you go, treating a wife as a mere chattel." It was as mindless a remark as I have heard. One's reaction to the stealing of a chattel —a piano, say, or a lawn mower—may be anger. But it does not compare with the anguish of losing a loved woman. One would not feel like dying of it, one would not want to kill for it. All this I said. I might have saved my breath—his last words were "mere chattel."

But in the sixties I had a different sort of experience. My wife and I were lecturing in the Philippines. In prison at the time were Luis Taruc, second in command of the rebellious Huc forces, and Alfredo Saulo, their chief of propaganda. They asked me to visit them in prison. Taruc, whose English was excellent, told me that they had both been reading my *Communism and Man:* they found it convincing on two points especially—that Russia was simply making use of Marxism, and the Hucs, as pawns in its own game: and that the social teaching of Pius XI was essentially what they had been fighting for. I have never seen a book so underlined and marginally written in as their copy of *Communism and Man:* we discussed points in it for some hours. Both had returned to the sacraments: both were as determined as ever to fight for what they thought the Philippines should be.

The oddest of all my contacts with Communism was not exactly a contact and I was told of it years after its happening. When Mao took over China, the Church was not immediately crushed out. The Jesuit university in Shanghai stayed open. In that period a translation of *Communism and Man* was printed—under the harmless title *Trends in Western Philosophy*. The first edition attracted no notice. But when the second was being printed, the printshop was destroyed, the printer not seen again. The president of the university was compelled to assemble the students and warn them not to read the book. I hope his warning had the kind of effect warnings from authority usually have on the young.

Purely Personal P.S. I have never met the top men in Fascism or Communism. But of the people I do meet, I find friendship with Communists easier than with Fascists—one feels an arrogance in the men of the extreme political right which makes them less companionable. I was on a panel discussion in Rome with Signor La Pira, the notably Socialist Mayor of Florence, and enjoyed him vastly.

VI

Marx had dismissed philosophy—"the problem is not to understand the world, but to change it." The idyllic ending of all human conflicts in the bliss of the Classless Society suggests a sentimentalist, whereas he was a hard materialist. His ignoring of man's incalculability was surely carrying non-understanding rather far. Why did Marx not see it? I think Christopher Dawson provided the answer in *Religion and the Modern State*. Marx was of the blood of the prophets. On his father's side and on his mother's he was descended from a long line of rabbis. The baptism his father had imposed on him along with the rest of his family when he was six was purely a way of securing promotion in Russia's Civil Service.

Christopher Dawson writes:

> The Messianic hope, the belief in the coming destruction of the Gentile power and the deliverance of Israel were to the Jew not mere echoes of Biblical tradition, they were burnt into the very fibre of his being by centuries of thwarted social impulse in the squalid ghettoes of Germany and Poland. . . . The three fundamental elements in the Jewish historical attitude—the opposition between the chosen people and the Gentile world, the inexorable Divine judgment on the latter, and the restoration of the former in the Messianic Kingdom—all found their corresponding principles in the revolutionary faith of Karl Marx. Thus the Bourgeois took the place of the Gentiles, and the economic poor took the place of the Old Testament Jews . . . while the Messianic Kingdom finds an obvious parallel in the dictatorship of the proletariat, which will reign until it has put down all rule and authority and power and in the end will

deliver up its kingdom to the classless and stateless society of the future which will be all in all.

Only on the last point am I not convinced by Dawson's explanation—the delivering up of the Kingdom to the classless society which will be all in all. That sounds not like the Old Testament, but like a straight echo of St. Paul's statement of Christ as handing over the Mystical Body—the Church grown to the stature of Perfect Man—to God who will be all in all.

As Dawson saw, Marx displayed in himself the power of religion which he so rigorously denied in his system. That he should make his own a theory thus rooted in the Old Testament is not perhaps surprising: that it should involve him so deeply that he failed to consider its want of relation to any human beings, to any proletariat, known to history, goes with the grip a doctrine can have on its creator. But what of his disciples? Lenin was not a Jew, neither was Bernard Shaw. Both saw that the Classless Society would not fit the humanity known to us.

Lenin dismissed the problem with a wave of his wrist—"By then men will be different, not the present man in the street." What will produce the difference? The purgation period, the Dictatorship of the Proletariat. Marx surely got that from the Catholic doctrine of Purgatory, the period of cleansing when cleansing is needed, before entry into that heaven where "nothing defiled shall enter." That Lenin should see it so is natural enough: he was cut out for the role of interpreter to itself of the will of the proletariat. And Hegel had shown him what this implied. "The will of the state is morality," said Hegel. "The good of the proletariat is the test of morality," said Lenin, "the consciousness of the proletariat is the test of truth." But Hegel also said, "The people stands precisely for the party that does not know what it wants, its will must be interpreted to it." For Hegel this interpretation must be the work of "world historical individuals." For Lenin it must be Lenin.

Bernard Shaw was at once more realistic about man than Lenin and more in adoration of the Marxian system. "If man will not serve, nature must try another experiment." In other words the system is an absolute: if man does not fit it, man must go: nature must evolve some race that will. That the Dictatorship of the Proletariat suited Lenin, whether he believed in it or not, is natural enough. What of Shaw, what of thousands of honorable men with no axe to grind?

Thirty-five years ago I produced an explanation. It still seems to me sound:

> There is a quality in that one man Marx which all the professors combined do not possess. For they remain professors, but he has changed the world. There was an elemental force in Marx, which makes his admirers look faintly ridiculous when they criticise him. Marx can finally be met only by a personality greater than his own.

I assume when I wrote the above that I saw the greater personality as Christ Our Lord. I am more sure of that now than ever.

CHAPTER 15

CATHOLICITY AND NATIONALISM

Traveling over the Catholic World, writing about it, publishing books about it, I have everywhere seen the Church's Catholicity writ large and unmistakable. Yet it is gloomy to note how often one finds it shot across with nationalism, at any level from nuisance to curse.

I

Nationalism should be at the opposite pole from Catholicism, yet it is a vice to which Catholics are liable because it is a parody of the virtue of patriotism which the Church has steadily taught, and it can so easily slip on patriotism's mask. Rulers are skillful in whipping up their people's patriotism in the service of their own nationalism. In our world especially it is vital to distinguish them.

Patriotism means love of one's country—not necessarily of its administration. People singing "America the Beautiful" are not thinking of the Senate as beautiful or the Supreme Court—or even the President: they may indeed dislike all three quite violently.

A man who loves his country might find it hard to say just what it is that he loves. So much of it is deep inside him. If you ask him, his mind may fly to some episode of his boyhood, or to some piece of scenery in which the whole seems implicated—Swanee perhaps, or Dixie—or Belloc's Sussex, or Echo Point in the Blue Mountains near Sydney. Nothing of this sort can be put lucidly into words, yet it may carry a rich charge of contentment and certitude. He probably makes no effort to state it.

In his own country a man feels at home, at ease, feels he belongs. Having lived most of my life outside Australia, I still feel fully myself there, as nowhere else. I belong, I can say "We." A man *is* himself in his own country, nourished, warmed; even if he is physically un-nourished, un-warmed, he will blame the politicians or the rich. The love of country may be unsayable, but love it is. He will lay down his life for his country, yet find it hard to say what it is he is dying for —not President or Congress or Supreme Court certainly. Something in his soul, something in his blood and bones, responds to something in his country.

It is an error to think that men will love mankind more if they have not this special love for their own place and people. The internationalists we come across do not strike us as especially loving—Marx, for instance, loved his own family wholeheartedly but few others seem to have felt love in him. Such men have their own sort of dedication to mankind, but mankind is too large and unpicturable to stir love; their dedication tends to be to the system, for which no sacrifice is too great.

Under the title "Patriotism and the Christian," I spoke on this at the Bombay Eucharistic Congress to the largest crowd I have ever looked at from a platform. The special point I tried to make was that we are so built that we love most intensely those close to us, less intensely as we move outwards. The family is the natural, all but irreplaceable, school of love. Christ's injunction to love neighbor as self sounds impossibly unrealistic: yet in families it is normal to find mothers (and not wholly abnormal to find fathers) loving children *more* than themselves.

The greater the love at the center, the greater the radiation. Man grows by loving and the range of his loving-power grows. The man who lacks love for his country is a diminished man, not so diminished as if he lacked love for his family, but there is less to him all the same.

All this I said to the Bombay audience. The next speaker was Captain Cheshire, who, as a penance for the guilt he feels for having been an observer on the plane which atom-bombed Hiroshima and Nagasaki, has devoted his life to the marvelous remaking work of the Cheshire Homes. (It was in India too, but later, that we met the work of a German charitable society, Misereor, which has set itself to rebuild as much as Hitler's Nazism destroyed.)

Patriotism is a great virtue. Nationalism, its parody, is a great evil. George Orwell has written a long essay on the two -isms: he deals justly with nationalism and its desire to conquer, but fails to grasp the point of patriotism because he has not sufficiently looked at love, which is the whole point of it. Patriotism he describes as thinking one's own country better than others, without desiring to absorb or destroy them. But patriotism does not imply thinking one's country superior to others, only loving it better.

At that same Bombay Congress I was called upon at fifteen minutes' notice to give a talk (it was listed but I had not seen the list) on "The Church in the Underdeveloped Countries." Rushed there in a car, I explained that I had never lived in any of what are called the underdeveloped countries and could not talk about them. But I had spent most of my life in countries spiritually underdeveloped and had begun my life in one. If they didn't mind I would talk about Australia and England and America under that head. They did not mind. Nor did my Australian friends.

Love of one's own land, I have said, no more means thinking other lands inferior than love of one's mother means thinking other mothers inferior. The question simply does not arise. It is a totally different matter. Patriotism bears exactly the same relation to nationalism as family affection to snobbery. Patriotism like family affection is an expression of love. Nationalism like snobbery is an expression of egoism. Love of country can be perverted into nationalism just as love of family can into snobbery and love of women into promiscuity. But the cure for all three is the same, not to abandon the love but to rectify it, cleanse it. It is hard to say in which of the three the rectifying is hardest. Or most necessary.

II

When Catholics are bitten by Nationalism they can have a bad attack. Yet it need not be virulent. There is no doubt that for many Irish Catholics the Church is only fully itself in Ireland. I was once accused of theological error by a man with an Irish name: he said he had an ancestral right to correct me. I pointed out that I had the same ancestral right to reject his correction: we must settle the question some other way. In my boyhood Irish Australians, as I have shown, were ardent Irish nationalists: their rejection of conscription in World War I, Archbishop Mannix's description of Britain as fighting a "sordid trade war," these and a dozen other things were part of a war for Ireland's freedom. There was the same fighting of Ireland's battle in America. Long ago in California I heard of a very notable priest, Father Yorke, who had fought the battle so very vigorously that his archbishop thought it better to cool him down by appointing him to a Portuguese-speaking parish. In three months he was preaching on the wrongs of Ireland in Portuguese.

Once freedom was gained, the Catholics of Ireland could at last be themselves. As themselves they have done something without parallel: four times they have had to elect a President, twice they have chosen a Protestant—Douglas Hyde and Erskine Childers—add the Jew they chose as Mayor of Dublin, and you have a degree of religio-political maturity not to be matched anywhere. It was not matched by their Norman conquerors eight centuries ago—the Irish were not accepted as monks in the monasteries the Normans founded in Ireland. If the only English Pope, Nicholas Breakspeare, who was Adrian IV, really did give Ireland to England's suzerainty, one can hardly fail to suspect that Nationalism had something to do with it.

The Italian popes at least have shown an astonishing freedom from nationalism, even after there was a nation of Italy to be nationalist about. Partly of course the rulers of the new Italian nation were seen as *the* enemy. Even when the concordat between Mussolini and the Vatican was on the point of conclusion in 1929, Pius XI could say to clerical students at Mondragone, "I would make a concordat with the devil, if it were for the good of souls."

Yet what but plain nationalism could have caused him to bless the Italian guns when Italy invaded Abyssinia? He hadn't a notion of the trouble he was to cause us in Hyde Park! I remember telling the crowd what a blessing was—a prayer to God that the object blessed should be used in God's service. Blessing guns did not mean "Good shooting: go on and conquer"—if God were not being served the blessing would work the other way. It was all perfectly logical. But I wonder if Pius XI had that wholly in mind? Would he, for instance, have blessed Abyssinian guns?

And one suspects nationalism in the Duke of Norfolk's persuading Rome to condemn the Plan of Campaign towards the end of the last century. I don't know how many remember it. Irish tenants, cruelly overcharged by landlords whom England had imposed on them, tried to negotiate for more reasonable rents. They got nowhere at all. So someone thought up the Plan. The tenants would each pay a reasonable rent into a bank: the landlord could have it if he would agree to its reasonableness. England's most highly placed Catholic, the Duke of Norfolk, convinced Leo XIII that the Plan was immoral, a breach of contract! The Pope issued a statement to this effect. Hilaire Belloc summed up the Irish reply—"Prostrate at the feet of Your Holiness, we wish you would mind your own business."

So far I have talked of Irish Catholics. French Catholics have a vast reputation for what we may call Frenchness: as they have not been as continuously enslaved as the Irish, their nationalism has affected others a great deal more. When I was younger I often heard on French clerical lips the phrase "France, eldest daughter of the Church." On one such occasion a man said, "Let me see, was that Goneril or Regan? I've not read King Lear recently." One smiles, but the French are not the only people that sees its own Catholicity as special.

As it happens, my first contact with French priests was with French missionaries whose vast dedication and willingness for sacrifice had spread the Faith rather wonderfully. I was baptized in St. Patrick's Church in Sydney by a French priest of a French order, the Marists. I had my first confession and Communion from French priests of another French order, the Missionaries of the Sacred Heart. These men meant everything to the Faith in Australia and the South Pacific. In a most extraordinary way they Australianized themselves. The transition was painless.

But it was not everywhere so. Our own first experience of something different came when Maisie's brother Leo went to Japan not as a missionary, but as a diocesan priest. He worked hard not only for a Japanese clergy but for a Japanese hierarchy. When a Japanese, Doy, was made Archbishop of Tokyo, the French priests withdrew: Leo had to take a parish. He protested to Archbishop Doy that his Japanese was pathetic—and indeed we learned when we were in Tokyo of a sermon he preached on humility: the word is very close to the word for diarrhea (about which there is indeed something humbling): and it was the virtue of diarrhea he was urging them to practice. Anyhow, the Archbishop had no choice: Leo took the parish.

The situation in China seems to have been a great deal worse. We were brought to awareness of it by publishing a book on the Belgian Père Lebbe, who devoted his life to winning a Chinese bench of bishops for China. As it was described in the book, Chinese priests were indeed ordained by the French while they ruled the Church there, but were treated as servants, not even sitting at table with their European fellow-priests. (I get a certain pleasure from remembering that in the nineties, a Chinese, Quong Tart, was several times elected Mayor of Sydney.)

I was never in direct contact with Frenchness in any of the missionary countries. I met it in Canada, the one country where English and Irish Catholics live in happy amity, forced into each other's arms by their French co-religionists of Quebec and Montreal. Of the grievances of French Canadians I have no knowledge whatever—I speak only of the fact of difference as I saw it, offering no hint of judgment.

I think I was first made aware of it at a meeting in London to honor Cardinal Bourne of Westminster. A leading Catholic layman congratulated the Cardinal on all he had done to reconcile English-speaking and French-speaking Catholics when he was in Canada. A chill filled the room. The speaker must have been the only one there who did not know of what had actually happened. The Cardinal had stated the English case to a French-speaking audience! The moment he finished, Henri Bourassa, spokesman of French Canadians, was on his feet: "Eminence . . ." It had been all very electrifying.

Towards the end of World War II Archbishop Charbonneau of Montreal invited me to talk there. I have forgotten the subject, something Catholic, nowhere touching the French-English issue. He had issued a notice that he expected all the clergy, of both languages, to attend—the first such meeting, I was told, that anyone could remember. It all went off agreeably. I went on to address the (French-speaking) seminary. They did not seem to dislike it.

I had particularly liked Archbishop Charbonneau—like Cardinal Cerijera in Lisbon, he was an enchanted reader of Chesterton. Soon after, he was on his way to Vancouver when a statement appeared in the newspapers that he had resigned as Archbishop of Montreal because of ill-health. Arrived in Vancouver, he was asked about his health and said it was excellent. But his successor was appointed in Montreal. (I have just read that another Canadian Bishop Charbonneau has been forced by ill-health to resign!)

Once more I met the problem, this time in Rochester, New York. There Catholics were evenly divided between Irish and French Canadian. As I am told, they were like two opposed Churches: if a French-speaking girl insisted on marrying an English-speaking man, it was treated as a mixed marriage and took place in the sacristy. The new bishop—John Wright, for whom so spectacular a career was beginning—wanted me to lecture there. On Joan of Arc. I would not dream of accusing the Bishop of diplomacy, but in fact Joan was the one topic equally attractive to French and Irish, since she defeated the English.

The situation in India was special, because of a long-standing treaty by which the Vatican agreed that every second Archbishop of Bombay should be a Portuguese. The last Englishman to hold the chair was Archbishop Roberts. India was already an independent nation and it was clear that Indians must fill the episcopal chairs. It was all very well for an Italian to be the greatest Archbishop Canterbury had ever had, St. Anselm, but that was back in the twelfth century, before nationalism, or even nationality, had properly emerged: with a Norman as their king, why should the English worry about having an Italian as their primate?

Archbishop Roberts pointed out the impossibility of Europeans ruling over an Indian Church. The Pope saw the point: he had asked the Portuguese to forfeit their claim: but they had stuck to their rights under the treaty and the Pope did not see how he could break it unilaterally, by appointing an Indian. Archbishop Roberts then asked if it would be a breach of the treaty if the Pope appointed an Indian as his auxiliary. Evidently it would not. So the Archbishop recommended the Goan Father Gracias. Then the Archbishop applied for leave of absence, leaving Bishop Gracias to run the archdiocese. At the end of four years the Portuguese knew the game was up. They agreed to the ending of the treaty: Archbishop Roberts resigned; Gracias became Archbishop of Bombay, and in due course a Cardinal. It was he who welcomed Paul VI, the first Pope to visit India, to the Eucharistic Congress in 1968.

But that raised the question of rites even older in India. Cardinal Gracias belonged to the Latin Rite. There had been Christians of the Syrian Rite in India for 1,800 years—convinced that they had been founded by St. Thomas the Apostle. Compared with them, Gracias and the Latin Rite men were only of yesterday. Rome solved the problem by making the head of the Syrian Rite Christians a Cardinal too. They were both on the platform at Kerala when I had the unnerving privilege of addressing the eighty bishops—and two Cardinals—of the Church in India.

Yet with all I have seen of nationalism among Catholics, I have been startled by their invariable Catholicness, within themselves, so to speak. National differences might prevent their seeing Christ in other Catholic peoples—when the Orthodox think of Catholics they can hardly help thinking of the Crusaders who repaid Constantinople's welcome by plundering the city; Russians are not likely to forget the Baltic knights. But *within themselves*, all Catholic peoples feel the Church as theirs. To Anglicans, the Catholic Church in England these last centuries might seem an Italian mission; but not to its members. And this is a universal experience. In whatever place I met the Church, its members seemed to be at home in it, as in another kind of *patria*. Not only that. Wherever I met the Church I felt at home myself.

I have already talked of the negative proof of the Church's Catholicity arising from my experience that any statement of Catholic doctrine anywhere draws the same criticisms, and the same reactions to my answers. Place, color, education, seem to make the minimum of difference. When I first had to speak to street corner crowds in America, for instance, I walked warily, thinking it would be necessary to discover a wholly new approach: it was not. Far stranger was the feeling I have inwardly had of myself belonging, no matter where I met the Church.

That Mass and Eucharist should have been the same everywhere was not surprising—there was a Mass in Cuernavaca with a mariachi band and the whole Church singing the Gloria and Credo and Sanctus and Agnus Dei in Spanish. There was a Mass in Andra Pradesh, northwest of Madras, with a congregation of outcasts listening, avidly is the only word I can think of, to a long sermon in Telugu. There was a High Mass in Haarlem near Amsterdam three years back, with the whole congregation singing it in Latin. There were what one thinks of as mass Masses, with congregations in scores of thousands, at Congresses in Dublin and Bombay and Kerala. I have been at a dozen other memorable Masses here there and elsewhere. And at all of them I was wholly there with priests and people. One might have expected all the ritual changes, all the doctrinal explorations, to alter the at-homeness. But they have not—provided they have not removed Our Lord Jesus Christ. As I read this over it struck me that I had exactly the same sense of belonging, when I met the first Christians in the Acts and the Epistles.

But given my lecturing habits and my publishing habits, I have not been confined to meeting Catholics of other countries only at Mass—though one cannot exaggerate the value of this, Mass being the one action in which we approach God *as his people*: as individuals we can speak to him, listen for him, any time, any place: but only at Mass as his people. I have lectured just about wherever the English language is understood. I remember the startled looks on audiences—in Holland and Germany especially—at my opening remark, "You are about to hear English spoken as only an Australian can speak it." In Holland it was assumed that everyone in my audiences knew English. In Germany and Japan translators were there for any who might need them: but again and again I noticed that any mis-translation would be corrected by half the audience.

I gave very similar talks to a Pax Romana group in Amsterdam and to the Women's University in Manila on the problem of specialization grafted on an insufficient general education (the result being that the specialist lives not in a rut but in a hole, a brilliantly lighted hole but a hole unmistakably). In the Manila talk I claimed that I was better entitled to the description oriental than they, Sydney being to the east of Manila: and I could not help adding that rather more of my books had been translated into Asiatic languages than European—Chinese, Japanese and two Dravidian languages, Telugu and Malayalam.

In Teheran I had an unusually ecumenical luncheon at the home of the Internuncio Salvadore Asta, Administrator Apostolic of the Archdiocese of Isfahan of the Latins. He spoke gloomily of the beginning of American intervention in Saigon, where he had been. Among the guests were the Armenian Archbishop, the Chaldean Bishop, the Russian Orthodox Father Victorin, whose view was dim on the subjection of the Orthodox Church in Russia to the Soviet Government, the American pastor of the Community Church, the head of the Presbyterian Mission, an Australian Anglican clergyman stationed in Teheran, two Catholic missionaries, the Canadian and Australian ambassadors, and Ted Heffron, who had spoken with me for the Catholic Evidence Guild in Washington. I have seldom been at a meal where everyone seemed so pleased with everyone else.

About my lecture that evening on Fresh Air in the Church, I can remember nothing save that I think no Mohammedan came, and that after it I met a Catholic missionary and a Protestant who went about in the same car.

Surprisingly, I have found that the generation gap makes no unbridgeable gulf—even when united with differences of color: speaking to, and taking questions from, seminary students at Kerala in India, high school boys in Trinidad, pupils of the Ateneo in Manila, Sacred Heart Academy girls in Tokyo, nothing happened to remind me of age or color or race.

I have already mentioned my talk to India's National Hierarchy in Kerala. India, as I need hardly remind anyone, is a continent not a country, it has hundreds of languages spoken by large numbers, hundreds more spoken by a remaining few. I gave the same kind of talk to its eighty bishops and two Cardinals as I had given to bishops, priests and lay people in America, England, Australia! Here as everywhere I felt I was talking to fellow-Catholics sharing one same heritage.

The essence of the talk was the dimming of Jesus—so many Catholics who would die rather than deny him yet do not find him very interesting, do not try to grow in intimacy with him through Gospel reading, remember only the most obvious things he said and did without having really used their minds on any of them. I went on to take a sort of quick hand gallop over five matters I never heard mentioned in sermons.

Christ himself as Son of God and Redeemer, not only in paraphrases of the Gospel of the Sunday;

The distinction between Christ, whose Body the Church is, and the people who at any given moment constitute the Church on earth;

The Mass as Calvary as Jesus now offers it to his Father in heaven;

Morality, not only sexual but at all the points where his morality challenges the world and the flesh and the devil *in us*;

Heaven as the goal towards which all are moving.

I told the Indian bishops that on all these matters I had met nothing but silence in the churches I attended. There was a long question period, with nothing much to suggest that this silence was often broken in India. At the end of my talk I suddenly felt like saying something I had never said before save in conversation. I prefaced it with the remark that what I was about to say did not really belong in my talk, I was saying it only because it was much in my mind and they were there! It was to this effect:

Our Lord was continually accused of keeping company with bad characters. I have never heard this accusation launched against a modern Catholic bishop. I wonder if this is not part of the imitation of Christ that might be restored. The impression one gets everywhere is that bishops are accessible only to those of their flock who approve of them, which means that they are out of touch with the world in which their flock has to save its soul.

To show what I have in mind, I take James Joyce. No Catholic in our century has had more effect upon the world than he. Everyone who can write has read him and been affected by him. He has made a vast change in the literary world, and that world affects the rest most powerfully. James Joyce had been at a Jesuit school in Ireland. A friend of mine has hanging on his wall the certificate of his admission to the Sodality there, signed by James Joyce as the president of the Sodality. Out of school, writing brilliantly in Dublin, he was losing contact with the Church. Two things I regard as highly improbable—one, that Joyce should have wanted to call on the Archbishop of Dublin and talk to him; two, that the Archbishop of Dublin should have wanted to see Joyce.

If I am right about this, there were two results: one, that Joyce never really knew grown-up Catholicism; two, that the Archbishop kept himself from one of the influences from which his flock had no way of keeping itself.

This postscript to my talk to the Indian Hierarchy has no particular connection with nationalism, which is what this chapter is mainly about. But it does relate to the other word in the chapter's title. The Catholic who is different and therefore difficult is felt to be a nuisance. My son has spoken of "the unwinking and beady-eyed suspicion" with which the Establishment Catholic regarded Teilhard. Men like Joyce who raise moral problems are an even more searching test of the Church's Catholicity. To the extent that it has nothing to offer them, that it does not give its mind most specially to them, its Catholicity is lessened.

After a lecture in a Catholic college on Sex and Marriage, one of the students questioned me more closely about Birth Control. The following week he came to see me. He had been expelled.

Thinking of Joyce set me to thinking of a far more extreme case, Baudelaire. French readers will regard it as an honorable confession on my part of gross weakness when I say that for me French poetry goes underground after Ronsard and emerges again with Baudelaire. But that is not my present concern with him. He had turned from God, not denying his existence but simply refusing him, though he had an awareness of his majesty such as great saints have had. Neuralgia brought him close to madness: but so did his felt need for the God he refused. Catholics saw the sinfulness of his life and heard the blasphemy with no suspicion of the spiritual elements struggling within him. His was an extreme case, but there are plenty of Catholics with some measure of his conflict; and the Church does not make any very obvious provision for them: any more than Marxism does.

Marx seems not to have known about "the impassioned and tumultu-
ous dynamism of human nature" which Dostoevsky sees under the
"thin crust" of every social order. The Church knows it, but does not
make any very clear provision for helping those who seem to be mastered by it. But at least for Baudelaire there was God at the end.

I conclude this chapter with one instance of a surprising absence
of nationalism. Only four English Catholics have ever made any impact on the Catholicism of Europe. One of them is Newman, of
whom Europeans are vastly more aware than Englishmen. Every four
years, for instance, Luxembourg has a Newman Conference attended
by scholars from everywhere. At two of these conferences my wife
was asked to read papers. I went along for the ride. It was in Luxembourg that I realized how almost totally forgotten in their own country are three eighth-century Englishmen who affected Europe
profoundly—St. Willibrord, St. Boniface and Alcuin.

Of St. Willibrord I had not so much as heard. He was an English
Benedictine monk who converted to Christianity what we now call
Holland, Flanders and Luxembourg. I am not likely to forget him.
Every year at Echternach there is a ritual dance in his honor. We
watched it for a couple of hours—people, priests, nuns and laymen,
in linked lines of five, solemnly dancing a curious pattern—three steps
this way, two that—with a brass band every thirty or forty lines, all
playing the same tune, beginning (I think) with the words "Adam
had three sons." The dance, I was told, was a stylization of epilepsy,
St. Willibrord having cured sufferers. As the procession was nearing
its end, came a line with only four people in it. I took the place of
the absent fifth and danced my way to the cathedral, up the aisle,
down into the crypt and up again to a place on the other aisle. I was
surprised to learn that Willibrord, like my confirmation saint, Gerard
Majella, was and is much petitioned by pregnant women.

Of Boniface and Alcuin I did at least know the names, if only
because they had come into books published by our firm. Boniface,
who had worked with Willibrord, went on to become the Apostle of
Germany. English Catholics might overlook him, German Catholics
cannot: in any country he would have counted as one of its towering
men. In a brilliant essay on Alcuin, Douglas Woodruff notes that
to an Englishman the phrase "Yorkshire schoolmaster" suggests Dickens's appalling Squeers. But Alcuin *was* a Yorkshire schoolmaster,
who from Charlemagne's court was to become schoolmaster to all

Europe. With the trivium and quadrivium he established the educational curriculum for the whole Middle Ages.

It is strange that England thinks so little of these three. But then I have not found much excitement in Ireland about John Scotus Eriugena, the one Irishman who could not be left out of any history of Western philosophy.

CHAPTER 16

THE CHURCH AND SEX

I listed three main problems the Church has had to cope with in my lifetime. Marxism and Nationalism we have looked at. One sees a possible fading out for both. But not for Sex. It is in the marrow of the bones as the other two are not.

I

In maintaining its teaching on sex, the Church throughout the ages has had plenty of trouble from human nature and its cravings. But apart from divorce and contraception, people had in a general way accepted the moral standards their ancestors learned from the Church. It seems only yesterday that agnostics and atheists—Thomas Huxley for one—were rejecting as scurrilous any suggestion that they were not as deeply committed as any theist to the highest sexual standards. Now we find ecclesiastics, including some of our own, almost equally indignant at any suggestion that sexual standards should still be maintained! One Catholic society informed its members, "For Christ the only sin is legalism."

I need hardly say that the acceptance of moral standards did not imply their rigorous observance in any class of any country. As Belloc once remarked to me, "The English aristocracy is promiscuous." He added that when one Prime Minister got married five men claimed to be his father-in-law, so generous had been the bride's mother. That model of rectitude, England's Prime Minister Gladstone, could say that he had personally known thirteen Prime Ministers and eleven of them were adulterers (I have heard the numbers quoted as eleven and seven respectively—a solid percentage still). A titled lady told Robert Browning of another titled lady who had "popped two chicks" before she married.

Family life in the middle classes seems for long to have been under better control.

The family father of Britain
Is a model of all that is good.

That was said in fun but by all accounts it was close enough to the fact, perhaps because the middle classes had neither the leisure nor the money of their social betters. But promiscuity is no longer the privilege of the aristocracy. "Freedom slowly broadens down," said Tennyson. He would not have liked this particular broadening.

There is today no discernible public feeling against self-abuse or fornication or prostitution or adultery or wife swapping or sodomy or lesbianism or abortion. A Congregational minister in Australia recently celebrated the wedding of two lesbians, sure that Christ would want him to bless their love. A few years ago a priest in Europe similarly joined two men in holy wedlock. I think his bishop suspended him: today a bishop who took a line so unconstructive would probably have his house picketed in the name of gaiety. The four-letter words are everywhere, all but one. The word "lust" is no longer heard—its territory has been taken over by "love." A couple of strangers casually linking their bodies in a bus station are described as making love: in fact they are making lust.

Just twenty years ago I wrote in *Society and Sanity* of schoolgirls who would feel socially inadequate without a contraceptive in their handbags. A minister reviewing the book scolded me as unjust to my juniors—one had only to watch a lot of jolly girls playing hockey to realize how morally healthy they were! I hope he still thinks chastity morally healthy, but I wonder if he would still be so sure of the hockey players. There floats into my mind a hockey match between a convent school at which I lectured and a Quaker school. At the interval the mistress in charge of the Quakers said to the nun in charge of the Catholic girls, "If your girls continue to take God's name in vain, I shall withdraw my girls from the field"—but profanity of course is not unchastity.

If the standards were not always—or often?—observed, they were accepted. Was the acceptance of any value? I think it was of solid value. The individual making his own struggle against his craving body has no chance at all in a society where no one attaches importance to purity or fidelity. The one test held to cover all the uses of sex is sincerity, which in practice may mean nothing more than the urgency of the craving. It is a maxim of English law that the King can do no wrong. Now sex is king. With no help from public opinion, people are cast back upon self. What is self's history in this area?

II

In all times and places self has found sex close to irresistible, and this even apart from the relief of bodily craving. Sexual union is the one activity in which a man can feel wholly himself, having his way, neither God nor man intervening, the woman responding. In the four-thousand-year-old Sumerian *Epic of Gilgamesh*, the prostitute, having seduced the virginal Enkidu, says to him, "Now you are like a god." So any man might feel, for about ten minutes. What else in our world makes a man feel godlike, even for ten minutes? There is a mystical, magical element in sex which survives any number of un-magical, un-mystical experiences of it. This element the moral theologians seem not sufficiently to have considered. But neither have the rest of people. The mystery and the magic have to be worked for, grown into; they are not there for the grabbing.

As I wrote in *Society and Sanity*, nobody thinks about sex. People long for it, ache for it, drool over it, dream about it, but longing aching drooling dreaming are not thinking. Thinking means concentrating the whole power of the mind on it, asking what it is in itself, asking why it is there at all. There is precious little sign of that.

That was twenty years ago. In the new world of "anything goes," the mind is still not brought into action. Decisions are made by desire, the blood, the sex organs. Feeling is all. Yet sex-at-will quite obviously does not bring freedom but the certainty of servitude.

The adolescent boy feels powerfully drawn both by the sense of sex's mystery and by the stirring of his own body. He has daydreams of girls following him down the street with mattresses. If he has metaphysical interests, notes Albert Camus, "he loses them with his first mistress." (Abelard didn't.) The sexually experienced among his friends he sees as the sophisticated ones. The one who boasts that he can barely totter from one woman to the next seems the very essence of virility, mastery, maturity. It is all illusion. The craving grows stronger. But strong cravings do not mean strong men. They eat into strength. That sort of sexing may be great fun. But there is no sophistication or maturity in doing what any alley cat can do, no mastery in being mastered, no virility in being unable to say no. For that is the situation. One remembers Jenny, the heroine of the musical *Lady in the Dark*.

Jenny made her mind up when she was twelve
That into foreign languages she would delve.
At seventeen to Vassar it was quite a blow
That in twenty-seven languages she couldn't say No.

One need not be a specially spiritual person to see how far from reality is all the talk of maturity in sex decontrolled. The obliging young woman in the musical *Oklahoma* can say

Supposin' that he says you're peaches and cream
And he's gotta have cream or die—
What are you goin' to do when he talks that way?
—Spit in his eye?

But she just liked men. The writer of the song was in no illusion about the amount of virility involved in having to "have cream or die." But then comic songs have always been admirably realistic about sex. I don't say that they are a surer guide than psychiatrist or dramatist or preacher. But all three would be wise to sing them to themselves occasionally.

Robert Burns, who had tottered from a great many women to the next, stated the reality in all its bleakness. In his "Advice to a Young Man" he writes

It hardens all within
And petrifies the feeling.

In the almost agony of craving for physical release, the other party can too easily become a mere object, depersonalized into a piece of machinery for the relief of one's own tension, humanity barely there. When Jesus lists fornication among "the things that defile" he may well have been thinking of these two facts of life—the self reduced to a craving, the other person reduced to a convenience—which are plainly evil, whether or not one believes in Jesus or believes in religion at all.

What of clerical celibacy? Merely on experience I am a strong believer in the value—*to the Christian people*—of a celibate clergy. But if the pressure on the priest is too great, it is not for me to tell him to set his teeth and bear it. And my friends among Uniates here in America have found no want of dedication in their own married priests. But there is a tendency to discuss clerical celibacy as if the whole case for it lies in St. Paul's argument that wife and family distract from total service of God. There is something else. The committed celibate has not to contend in himself with the danger always present in the marriage act of "the self reduced to a craving, the other person to a convenience."

Anyhow it has always been felt, and today is everywhere proclaimed, that sex copiously indulged is the hallmark of the red-blooded man. Those of lesser sexual energy can but envy him and do their poor best. Or they can make a virtue of their anemia and call it virginity!

A high point of sex's glorification was reached by Mark Twain. His *Letters from the Earth* were not published in his lifetime. He died in 1910 and they were not published till 1960. In the years between had come the sex revolution. There seemed no possibility left of shocking anyone. Yet if he did not shock any but a devout few, he did at least startle all his readers with the attribution of sexual activity to the Supreme Being. He certainly startled the audiences for whom I reviewed his book, one of them I remember in Dayton, Ohio. The pagan myths of the world in which Israel was born show the gods as sex gluttons: it is a uniqueness of Genesis that its Creator-God has no consort, sex is for men and animals. In one stride Mark Twain went back not only beyond Genesis but beyond the myths. The liveliest of the old gods had not advanced to the idea of a sex act that never stopped at all.

These are the fantasies of dream, and sex has always been rich in them. Men who have lived a full and satisfying sex life do not need them. I know nothing of Mark Twain's private life, but it is at least interesting that three men who have in very different ways helped to bring about the sexual revolution were themselves not notable performers. We heard his fellow-Irish Protestant St. John Ervine state roundly over the BBC that Bernard Shaw was impotent: D. H. Lawrence and Havelock Ellis appear to have been something less than adequate. And one remembers the curious matter of Swinburne, which I came to know about only because of a notable poem of G. K. Chesterton's.

Swinburne was the best-known erotic poet of the end of the Victorian age, a poet least likely of all to have amused Queen Victoria. Almost his most widely known poem was to "Dolores" with its lines:

> The lilies and languors of virtue
> And the roses and raptures of vice.

As we now know Swinburne knew as little of the "roses and raptures" as of "lilies and languors." He was a masochist who got the whole of his sexual stimulation from being scourged (he had broken school rules at Eton in order to be flogged). Raptures he may have had but scourges are not roses. His friends, hoping to win him to better ways, imported from France the American Ada Mencken, who had had Théophile Gautier and Victor Hugo as clients. It was to her that Swinburne wrote his triumphant poem. It was wholly illusion. In no time at all Dolores was back in France, saying of Swinburne, "He was my only failure."

As I say, my interest was aroused by the poem in which Chesterton had Dolores answering Swinburne, with its concluding lines

> If you think virtue is languor
> Just try it and see.

Had I had the ordering of Chesterton's tombstone, those lines would have been on it. They summarize Chesterton's teaching on virtue and vitality, a medicine our own age most urgently needs. The notion that virtue, any virtue—virginity, for instance—is pallid and devitalizing could be held only by one who has not seriously tried it. Virtue is not the absence of wrongdoing, which might be no more than lethargy, but the right direction of energy, which only too often means the reversal of its wrong direction. The special energy that virginity must direct is the energy of love. It was Caryll Houselander who described virginity as "The willed leaving of one part of life empty that God may fill it with himself"—one sees why Ronald Knox wished she could conduct a school of spirituality. I think, but am not sure, that it was she who said, "Chastity makes the other virtues sparkle, makes them gay. But there must *be* other virtues. Chastity shining on vice makes it cruel and cold: a chaste liar, a chaste thief." All of which is a happy gloss on William Langland's "Chastity without charity shall be chained in hell." Certainly the efforts and resistances virginity calls for can be very muscle-building indeed.

I have often had to discuss this with men who have derided virginity as anemia. The discussion always takes the same line. I ask, "Supposing, for any reason that seemed sufficient, you decided you ought to stay away from women, would you admit that it would take strength?" If you can keep the other man to that single point, he will end by admitting not only that it would take strength, but that it would be beyond his own strength. Sexual indulgence calls for no effort, simply a going with the stream of inclination: in itself it is de-energizing, devitalizing. I remember Belloc asking me what I thought a strong will was—a will which is determined on getting what it wants against every obstacle, or a will which has itself under total control? Certainly all experience seems to say that the sex glutton no more gets the full richness of sex than the food glutton of food. In Henry VIII or Casanova sex is not glorious but comic rather. It is always in the love of one for one that sex is seen as glorious.

III

Given the vanishing of sex standards inside and outside marriage in the world in which Catholics have to live, what is the Church doing about it? Neither I nor any of the Catholics I have asked can remember when they last heard a sermon on chastity or sexual purity. Yet in every area of life chastity is under attack. There is something eerie about the silence. All the eerier if one is old enough to remember how our pulpits once rang (and our confessionals groaned) with condemnation not only of divorce and adultery but of any kind of what used primly to be called "familiarities" even between engaged couples—one priest was famous for his advice on how to keep kissing chaste (it was a matter, I seem to remember, of latitude and longitude, the area covered and the time occupied—work that out for yourself). The Sixth Commandment, which forbids adultery, was given two extensions. By the first it was treated as covering any and every misuse of sex—this extension was natural enough in the order of practicality, since sex ought not to be misused and it was of pastoral advantage to bring every misuse under the ban of a Commandment. But the second would, I think, have startled Moses—the assertion that against the Sixth Commandment *there are no venial sins*, which seems to mean that the slightest variation from sexual rectitude could damn the soul.

As I have said, the pulpit condemnation was strong and continuous, and it was carried through into the confessional. But it was condemnation and nothing beside. There was, in fact there still is, no effort to show what is right with sex when it is right, what is wrong with it when it is wrong. There was no effort to show why fornication or masturbation, for instance, was wrong, their wickedness was simply assumed. We were told indeed of bodily and mental diseases said to be resultant from them. But there was no effort to show why they were wrong *in themselves*. The whole case for chastity seemed to be the example of the Holy Family at Nazareth. We could hardly be blamed for not finding this very helpful: two virgin saints with a son who was God—that was not exactly our situation. I once said this in a lecture, with a bishop in the chair. I thought his manner afterwards rather reserved. I learned that his Pastoral Letter, read that morning at every Mass in his diocese, had used the Holy Family as the whole case for chastity.

Inside the Church as outside, one got the same impression that no one ever actually used his mind on sex. There was plenty of *feeling* about sex, for and against: within the walls of the Catholic Church and school it was wholly against. We had a book jacket showing Michelangelo's Creation of Adam. A priest preached against it as too overtly genital. I wrote to remind him that it was from the ceiling of the Pope's own chapel, the Sistine. He answered, "If the Pope had heard as many confessions as I have, he would know better." The ordinary Catholic could hardly help feeling there was something necessarily nasty and brutish about sex. Some of our teachers seemed to feel it faintly shocking of God to have created a race which could propagate itself only by sexual intercourse. Indeed there have been Catholic writers who tried to clear God's character by teaching that intercourse was a result of the Fall: if Adam and Eve had not sinned, generation would have occurred without bodily contact! Even where this particular oddity was not taught, there was a sense of uncleanness about sex. One heard of girls taught that they must somehow wash their bodies without actually uncovering them, lest they be an occasion of sin to their guardian angels.

Given today's freedom of speech, it is strange to realize how recently Catholic tongues were hobbled. Just forty years ago I approached an archbishop about the numbers of Catholics who married without any knowledge of the mechanics, so to speak, of the marriage act. There were plenty of non-Catholic manuals available, but they all had chapters on birth control. So the archbishop told me to go ahead and have a book prepared. We translated from French a most admirable book, in which the bodily union was explained and the spirituality of marriage wonderfully shown. The archbishop said he could not possibly grant his imprimatur: it was too outspoken: could I not "modify" it? I answered that this would mean leaving out sex altogether: but as God had not left sex out of marriage, I didn't see how we could. The book was not published. Soon after that we did publish one, by Dr. Halliday Sutherland. It was banned in Ireland, though it carried the imprimatur of Cardinal Hinsley.

Which reminds me of a lunch I once had in Dublin with a member of the Board of Censorship. That morning the newspaper carried the announcement of the banning of Seán O'Faoláin's *Bird Alone*. I asked my guest what possible ground there was for banning it. He did not make a very convincing case, but ended triumphantly, "O'Faoláin is a puppy anyway."

In the thirties and forties I was often a member of a panel speaking about sex and marriage to mainly Catholic audiences. Invariably I was the only married man on the panel. I sometimes caused a certain discomfort to my fellow-members by saying that the only way to arrive at a full understanding of marriage is to study all that the Church has to teach on the subject and then get married. I sometimes added for good measure that that superb Irish-born Dominican Father Vincent McNabb told me that whenever married people came to him with any of their problems he himself always consulted a married man before replying.

Some of my co-panelists seemed to know nothing about the more urgent realities of the matter. One priest, head of marriage counseling in his area, was expressing distress at mixed marriages: "A young man with a good Catholic education marries a Protestant. *How can it happen?*" he almost wailed. "Perhaps sex has something to do with it," a loud voice (mine) interjected. The speaker looked pained but disregarded the interjection as irrelevant, if not actually obscene.

One priest I remember as really knowing the problems of sex and marriage in depth was John Augustine Ryan. He prefaced a wholly practical treatment with the words, "Although my second name is Augustine, I haven't a mistress." The least I could do when I followed him to the speaker's desk was to say, "Although my second name is Joseph, I am not a virgin." We had a glorious meeting.

There is of course one way of knowledge open to priests and not to the rest of us. They hear confessions. I once read a description of the public confession practiced at Moral Rearmament meetings. It concluded, "I heard the word 'lust' once and the word 'adultery' twice: but I heard nothing that was not in perfect taste." I quoted this to Father Leo Ward, Maisie's priest-brother. He said, "I was in the confessional on Saturday night. I heard both words many times. And all I heard was in quite abominable taste."

So I imagine most priests could have said. They must know what pressure of sexual temptation means to their flock. Things felt in blood and bone and sinew, pictured in imagination, agonized over in emotion have an intensity, a driving power revealed truth cannot easily match. Chesterton writes of "sin powerful as a cannonball, enchanting as a song." For the saint virtue has both the power and the enchantment. But not for most of us. Yet in the books of Moral Theology the clergy write they show small sign of it. I have just finished reading an excellent book of this sort, wide-minded, charitable—but without a trace of the male sex organ anywhere in it. It is the same with sermons, while one heard so much from the pulpit about the sinfulness of sin, I cannot remember a preacher showing any sense of the agony there can be in resisting it. The result was that many a man came away saying, "It's all very well for him. He hasn't my temptations." In fact the preacher may have known them in all their fierceness, may be in their grip even while he is preaching. One can see why he could hardly have conveyed this to the congregation. But what a difference it would make if he had.

One afternoon I was walking up Fourth Avenue in New York. In a bookshop window across the avenue I saw a huge white placard with a book attached to it, and in blood-red letters the two words "sex drenched." I went across and found the book was my own translation of Augustine's *Confessions*. A purchaser who bought it in the hope of a drenching might well have demanded his money back: it is part of Augustine's genius that he can convey the power of sex and the evil of sexual sin without any of the detail without which a modern novel would be incomplete. For though the book was not drenched in sex its author had been.

He tells of the anguish he had at sending his mistress away, tells it so rendingly that one wonders why he did not marry her (my guess is that she had a husband living); he tells how his mother got him engaged to a girl two years under the legal age for marriage, so that he was constrained to take another mistress. A bishop when he wrote it, he tells the dreams he still had—"to the very completion of the act"— and we would hardly need to be told that to the end of his life he felt the urge of sex. It is one great value of the *Confessions* that no one ever laid it down saying, "It's all very well for him."

I was discussing all this at a meeting during the Bombay Eucharistic Congress. In the first seats sat seven bishops in a row. I carefully avoided looking at them as I remarked that, while I did not exactly urge bishops to preach with that candor, I merely assured them that if they did no church would be large enough to hold their congregations, and that I should be enchanted to publish their sermons.

IV

The reason for the Church's delicacy in the handling of sex lies of course in her realization not only that there is sacredness in sex but that there is dynamite in it. Sex can take total possession, absorbing and concentrating every energy to the ruin of character and action, people will die for it, the mildest people can kill for it. The early Church Fathers did at least see that. Sex had run wild in their age and we can see why all their concentration is on its dangers. They knew that sex is not unclean, but it can be used uncleanly: and their world had rotted with sex's uncleanness. The Church's laws can turn from being a hardly noticed rule of normal living into a coercion and an anguish. Only people of weak passions, easily controlled, could fail to see that sexual love can be corroded more easily than any other power, and itself needs the control of law. "There is in sex a fury," Chesterton hardly needs to remind us, "that we cannot afford to inflame."

What are you going to do when the world's on fire? asks the revivalist hymn. What is a man going to do when he's on fire himself? The educators who say that the young should be taught to discuss their sexual mechanisms as calmly as the mechanism of their car, seem to be a long way removed from sex's reality. Any concentration on sex is playing with fire near a powder magazine, the possibility of explosion is always there.

In one same Epistle—the First to the Corinthians—Paul can say, "it is better to marry than to burn" (surely the poorest compliment ever paid to marriage), and can describe marriage as a symbol of the union of Christ and his Church (what compliment could be greater?). In *The Bow in the Clouds,* E. I. Watkin phrases this admirably: "The sexual combination of biological union with natural life and consequent procreation is the best reflexion on the natural plane of the spiritual union and fecundity in which spiritual life culminates."

How to instruct the young without setting them alight is a problem one cannot feel that either the Church or anyone else has wholly solved. But it would seem that the principles are best taught before sexual passion is stirring. I can remember a nine-year-old boy whose first reaction on learning of his own production from the bodily union of both parents was delight that there was something of his father in him: he had already been told that he came out of his mother's body, which accounted for his relation to her, but he hadn't been able to see how he was related to his father.

How, essentially, should sex be seen? Assuredly, of course, as God's provision for the race's continuance. But certain truths flowing from this should be shown very early. The first is that it is an action in which God asks for our collaboration; our life is from him, but he does not bring it into being unless a man and woman each give what is in them to give: if there is no sexual act, no new life is generated: procreation is in fact pro-creation, deputy creation. In the phrase of the Franciscan Father Alan Keenan, "It is the biological echo in us of God the Father's desire to create." That is why our use of it must concern God. The second is that it is the power to create a being, of our own order indeed, but made in God's image and destined for eternal union with him. There is no clearer proof of the present contempt for man than the dismissal of the place of sex in the production of new life as the "merely biological element." The Church steadily reminds us both of why God gave humanity the powers, and of the wisdom of finding out how he wants us, his collaborators in the creative act, to use them.

Sex does not live on illusion but illusion is what it tends to breed. As Shaw says: "There is less difference between one young woman and another young woman than the average young man thinks." This has always been so, but among today's believing Christians there is one illusion sex has not often bred before. I must have read hundreds of articles and letters written by Catholics in protest against the papal encyclical on Contraception. What interested me most was what the writers thought not about the encyclical but about sex itself. For the most part they struck me as of a purity so refined I felt coarse and earthy in comparison. The sex act they saw as love's highest expression. The ruling purpose in their own intercourse seemed to be the enrichment of their partner's personality. One wondered how refinedly they bore the discovery that she did not want her personality enriched that night. I mentioned this particular point to a couple of thousand women at a luncheon in Los Angeles. They laughed and laughed. I got the impression that each of them was seeing one special face, not looking its best. Cardinal McIntyre, who was sitting beside me, insisted that I give the same talk to his seminarians.

I have returned more than once to the fine art of kidding oneself. In no area is autokiddery so active as in the sexual. One marvels how anyone can think that bodily union is love's highest expression. The essence of love is precisely the giving of oneself to the other. But in bodily union the body's own need for physical release can be urgent to the point of anguish, so clamorous that it is hard to remember the other person *as a person* at all. A full rich bodily union is possible, with a true balance of delight for oneself and love for the other—this last not drowned in the excitement without which the act can hardly happen at all. This sort of union can be worked for, grown towards, but only if the whole of a shared life is experienced in it. Mere bodily release need be no more emotionally valuable than vomiting after seasickness.

In marriage there is a unity of shared lives—shared joys, sorrows, difficulties, problems, fatigues, exaltations: the marriage act arises naturally as the expression of that unity, draws richness from it and enriches it in return. But in the unmarried there is no such sharing of the whole of life. There may be a shared interest—in art or music, say—or no more than a shared desire for the act. There is no shared life together for the act to express or enrich, it expresses nothing but itself and has no issue beyond itself. And itself simply is not enough. It flickers and dies. It may have been entered upon solely because the body would not be denied. It may most piteously have been clutched at for relief in the desolation of a marriage from which love has drained out. It is still only a shadow of full union.

As it involves collaboration with God, and in its power to produce beings destined for eternal life, a boy may be brought to see the sacredness of sex, before the turbulence in himself has arisen to cloud his vision. And in preparation for the turbulence, one other thing can be shown, namely that *if human beings were not meant to have children, the generative mechanisms—so different in men and women —so meaningless without each other—would not be there at all.* None of this will prevent puberty being troubled, and the following years stormy. But at least under the strongest temptation the young will know why yielding is wrong—instead of knowing only that Father So-and-So says it is a sin and wondering what he knows about it anyway.

I may be wrong in thinking most Catholics are not given this teaching. That I have never heard any of it from a pulpit myself may be mere chance. What I am not wrong about is how sexual sin was treated by the Church's ministers. Under the statement that there are no venial sins against the Sixth Commandment, any misuse of sex was treated as mortal sin excluding from Communion, masturbation especially, and any dwelling in thought on sin's pleasures. The result was that confession became a torment. The story was current when I was young of the boy who confessed that he had had bad sexual thoughts. "Did you entertain them?" asked the priest. "Oh no, Father. They entertained me." It was a joke, but many of those who smiled at it could remember a time when it was no smiling matter. In those places where the whole school went to Communion, many a boy—afraid to confess, afraid to stay away from the altar rail—received his Savior feeling that he was in mortal sin.

The teaching that there are no venial sins against the Sixth Commandment cut a wide swath of disaster. I raised the matter with so wise and compassionate a priest as Father Martindale, and he could only say helplessly, "All moral theologians teach it."

My own feeling is that the phrase "mortal sin" was thrown around too carelessly, cheapening it for the tough-minded, causing panic in the morally sensitive. There are now those who hold that the old distinction between mortal sins and venial needs rethinking. What are called venial sins are hardly sins at all, I doubt if the word "sin" is ever used in Scripture of the sins we call venial. Sin being rebellion against God, it is misleading to use the word of small failings in perfection—they simply do not belong in the same order of experience. Not only that: the sins we now call "mortal" seem to be ranked without sufficient awareness of psychological reality. There is a world of difference between sins of weakness—a man disobeying the law because he feels he has not the strength to keep it—and sins of viciousness—cruelty, treachery, blasphemy. To put things so totally different under cover of the one word "sin" is to rob the word of meaning.

I do not pretend that I can work out a new Moral Theology. But I can at least think aloud in the general direction of one. There are three elements which are held to make a sin mortal—serious matter, full knowledge, consent of the will. From an early age I found it hard to see how eating meat on Friday could be "serious matter." I found it even harder when I heard Our Lord saying in so many words that it is not what goes into the mouth that defiles a man. What "full knowledge" means is also worth longer thought than it always got.

But it is about "consent of the will" that I was most troubled. The rule of thumb seemed to be that a sudden temptation yielded to without time to think was not a mortal sin, since there had been no deliberation. Yet a man faced with a craving, resisting it day by day night by night till at last he breaks down and yields to it, was held to have fulfilled the third condition for mortal sin: he had had time to deliberate, therefore he had consented. It was much as if a man hanging on the edge of a cliff, letting go when his fingers will support him no longer, were said to have "consented" to his fall into the abyss. Let us agree that God's grace was available to the man tempted—if he had asked for it with heroic faith. All I am saying is that a failure in heroic faith is not quite the same thing as deliberate consent to sin: it is not at all the same thing as rebellion against God.

Should it exclude from the reception of the Eucharist? To take a concrete example. A man has been deserted by his wife, who gets a divorce and sets up with a new husband. He lives with the craving as long as he can. It is not like martyrdom, which a man suffers rather than deny Our Lord: for martyrdom usually ends fairly soon in death, whereas the craving is endless and continuous: we have already noted that even so great a saint as Augustine had to live with it somehow to the end. If our man ends by taking another wife there is no rebellion, no viciousness, no individual wronged. He has played his own tiny part in the weakening of the institution of marriage, certainly, for every dissolution of a marriage makes marriage itself more dissoluble. But it is hard for him to think he has harmed Our Lord, he has not denied him, only yielded to his own weakness. If he wants to receive him bodily, he finds it hard that Christ should be refused as food to one whose weakness needs him so urgently.

v

My mind goes back to what I have called the Indian Summer of the twenties and thirties of the century, when there was such a riot of high spirits among Catholics: we were sorry for those who were not in the Church, made fun of them rather. Round 1928 the Lambeth Conference decided that contraception was permissible for Anglicans who had good cause to limit their families. Arnold Lunn had just joined the Church. He said, "The Church of England has made its first infallible pronouncement. It has defined the Dogma of the Immaculate Contraception."

We found this neat, its neatness verging on the exquisite. It was repeated everywhere. We had not a notion of what lay in wait for Catholics on this matter of birth control. Up to 1960 or thereabouts it was assumed by everyone that the Church taught definitively and unchangeably that artificial contraception was a grave sin.

What had she in fact taught? As magisterium—Pope or General Council—she had taught very little. In 1588—year of the Armada, one notes irrelevantly—Sixtus V issued the bull *Effraenatum,* making death the penalty for using contraceptives: the bull was repealed within a couple of years by the next Pope. That was all till *Casti Connubii* in 1930. But if there was nothing that even looked like an infallible pronouncement, there was a steady stream of teaching and legislation, curial and local, based on one single, simple statement about the marriage act—namely that if intercourse took place, the act must have its total integrity, not interfered with, not mutilated. The act was seen, on the lines we have discussed, as too sacred to be played with, which it is.

It was the vulcanization of rubber round 1860 that made contraceptives a new threat, practically a new thing. Yet the papacy did not respond at once to the newness of the threat. In 1880 Leo XIII issued *Arcanum Divinae Sapientiae,* a full-length encyclical on Marriage: it did not mention Contraception. Some time after that, the Curia gave a decision that a Catholic woman whose husband was using a contraceptive should resist him as if she were being raped. "Rush to the window and call for help, I suppose," said a man I knew. But in this century she was not called upon to resist physically, "being more sinned against than sinning."

In 1930 came Pius XI's *Casti Connubii,* the first full and formal statement. It left no opening for any conceivable use of a contraceptive, since all the contraceptives then known did interfere with the integrity of the marriage act, in itself, in the preparation for it, in interference with its consequences. Thus the integrity of the act was still the test.

It reads like a sufficiently moderate requirement, but there are situations in which the demand it actually makes is tremendous, to be met only at great cost. A mother may have been warned that another child may mean death; or the family's finances may be strained thin to support the children already born, and the prospect of another may truly terrify. Yet the body remains urgent, the soul too—for the marriage act involves the whole person.

Totally to abstain from the marriage act would be an answer: but the strain, the unrelaxing tension, can mean a degree of suffering beyond the imagination of those who have never had to face it. Even some of those who, with prayer and sacrament, have maintained the iron control that it calls for, seem to bear the scars of it for long after.

Then there is rhythm—performing the act only at times when conception cannot take place. Modern discoveries are making it possible to decide ever more accurately the very few days in each month on which conception is possible. For a long time Catholics were doubtful about the rightness of continuing to have bodily union while avoiding those times. But Pope Pius XII settled the doubt. He said to the Congress of Catholic Midwives in October 1951: "The limitation of the act to the times of natural sterility" is morally lawful if it "is based on sufficient and reliable moral grounds." A month later he said to the Family Front: "One may hope that science will succeed in providing this lawful method with a sufficiently secure base."

To many a Catholic it sounds like cheating. The use of contraceptives, the restriction of the act to infertile periods—both have exactly the same purpose, namely to have the pleasure of the act and to prevent conception: it is simply a mockery to say that one is sinful and the other virtuous. And indeed if limitation of one's family were a sin, then both methods would be equally guilty of it. But the Church has never said that it is. The sin she is concerned with is the desecration of the marriage act: in the infertile period the act is not desecrated but performed in its completeness.

A rough analogy would be the ways open to a man who needs money: he might steal it, or he might ask a friend to lend it. It would not occur to anyone to say that these ways are equally wrong because they have exactly the same purpose, namely to get money. To get money, to limit the size of one's family, may both be permissible; but the ways of achieving either may or may not be.

This roughly was the position when Paul VI set up a commission to study the whole question. There was one new element, the invention of the pill to be taken in the mouth. Did this too affect the integrity of the act? Paul VI's encyclical *Humanae Vitae* is as absolute as Pius XI's *Casti Connubii* on the wrongness of artificial contraception—"it is in contradiction with the will of the Author of Life" —it is not what God wants. But on the question of the degree of guilt the new document is a whole universe from the earlier. It has nothing remotely approaching Pius XI's "God detests this crime with unspeakable loathing." It is not called a crime at all. The word used is "illicit"—it and "licit" are used a dozen times—as a way of saying it is not what God wants. The word "sin" is used only once, close to the end, and not very clearly: "grave sin," "mortal sin," are not used at all. There is no threat, or even hint, of damnation.

It may be a mere chance that the encyclical contains no command, no "Thou shalt not." It does not even say that those who continue to practice contraception are excluded from the Eucharist. If the Pope did mean to debar millions from the Eucharist it would be odd to leave so vast a deprivation to be assumed from his silence. Pause upon this. As to who actually receives Communion, the decision lies with each man and woman. In big parishes the priest may never have seen hundreds of those to whom he gives his Savior and theirs. He cannot judge their worthiness to receive, nor is it normally his affair. I remember the newspaper uproar forty years ago when Ronald Knox, on the instruction of the Archbishop of Birmingham, refused the host to a young man who had written a novel about homosexuality. In fact the refusal of Communion is a rarity to one actually kneeling there expectant. As a Cardinal put it to me, he had no "metaphysical surgery" enabling him to enter into people's minds, no way of knowing the state of their conscience there and then. Cases were thinkable in which he would withhold the host, as for instance from one he knew to be a Satanist who might want it for a Black Mass. In a general way, it remains that the Church lays down rules for reception, but the individual answers to God about their application to himself.

It may be pure chance that exclusion from Communion of those who use contraceptives is not mentioned in *Humanae Vitae*. Yet—considering how many bishops and confessors in so many parts of the world had been saying they were not excluded necessarily—we might find it a curious kind of chance. All the same there *is* something, not exactly chancy but unfinished, about the whole document. A Cardinal (a different one!) told me that as it was prepared for publication, it was held by the Pope's advisers to be too long for the public's reading habits: a document half as long would be more likely to be read. But instead of being rewritten at the new length, it was chopped about till it was short enough. Even on a Cardinal's word I find this hard to credit. But it would certainly explain the result.

There were three burning problems for those immediately concerned with not having another baby—namely the woman who will die if she has another baby, the family already at destitution level, the denial of the Eucharist to those who use contraceptives. Not one of these three is mentioned at all. The Pope's whole concern is with those who could very well have more children but prefer a higher material level of life to bringing new life into being.

There was one vast problem for all—namely the possibility of the world's population outgrowing its food supply. This problem too is rather glanced at than examined. Clearly if artificial contraception is "in contradiction with the will of the Author of Life," it is always better to follow his will, whatever the present cost: the long-term cost of ignoring it will be worse for the human race.

But this principle is not exactly stated, only assumed. In forty lines the document applies it to poverty-stricken countries with exploding populations. A main point made in the encyclical—and many non-Christian Indians have made it—is that contraception is not the solution of a problem which arises from the greed of the rich and the incompetence of government.

A lengthier treatment would have helped. More questions are raised than could be answered in forty lines. Nothing is said, for instance, of the starving who will still be below destitution level while a just social economic system is under construction. If contraceptives can ever be used without serious blame—and this seems to be in the Pope's mind—it would surely be by the destitute.

CHAPTER 17

WORLD WAR II

I shall write of the War only as it affects the theme of this book, my growth in understanding of the Church—principally as I saw it in action in and upon its own members.

I

In a crazy effort to work with both Sheed & Ward of London and Sheed & Ward of New York I crossed the Atlantic fifteen times during the war. One of these crossings was in a bomber—I got that privilege simply because a friend in a government office used his influence. There were a dozen men who were entitled to be there, Very Important Persons, crossing on government business. They all knew one another. None of them knew me. While we were waiting in Newfoundland to go on board one of them detached himself from the others, came over to me and said, "Why are they sending you?" I said, "History will tell." He seemed impressed, so did the others when he reported back to them.

All my other crossings were on ships. Once at least I had reason to be grateful to a VIP. I had gone to the pier at New York as instructed. I went onto the ship berthed there, the *Western Prince*. They were full of apologies, but my berth had been given to a VIP: I must wait for the next ship. The *Western Prince* was sunk.

The journeys I actually took—mostly in convoy, sometimes alone if the ship was fast enough—could not have been quieter: I never heard or saw an enemy on the Atlantic. Once indeed we were at tea in the lounge, when there came shattering gunfire. We all maintained the correct British phlegm—"went on cutting bread and butter," so to speak—only it was margarine. The officers watched our act of heroic unconcern with amusement: finally told us that what we were hearing was the ship's own anti-aircraft guns practicing. On that trip our engines broke down, the convoy left us and we wallowed for twenty-four hours till the engines were set working, then limped across to the Azores for proper repair—sitting duck, waddling duck, we remained untouched.

But if we never saw the enemy ourselves, we had one reminder of him. As brave a thing as any recorded in the war was done by Captain Fogarty Fegen. He was in command of *Jervis Bay*, an armed merchantman, convoying a group of ships. A German warship appeared. Fegen headed for it, firing with his pathetic handful of guns. His ship was sunk, of course. But the delay gave time for the convoy to scatter and in the end the raider sank only four out of the thirty-eight. The ship we were on picked up some of the crew of one of these. I remember one old sailor particularly—he had clung to a raft for two days and nights in the Atlantic in winter. He looked very hale and sounded very hearty. I mention this incident because on a visit afterwards to Halifax I met a priest who knew Fegen and learned that he had been a daily communicant and had spent a long time praying before the Blessed Sacrament before going on board for his last journey. I found myself thinking of a comment Newman made soon after he joined the Church: "This is a religion."

It is strange how little remains in my memory of my fifteen crossings. On the bomber, one of the officers gave us each a parachute and explained its use. I went to him afterwards, said I hadn't understood a word of it, would he explain it to me in words of one syllable? He said, "I wouldn't bother if I were you. If you are going to fall into the North Atlantic in winter, it makes very little difference whether you fall quickly or slowly." I thanked him and went back to the bomb-rack in which I was to spend the night. I remember hoping drowsily that no one would press a button by mistake and release me into the Atlantic, quickly.

There was not much of religious interest on these voyages. On one of them I shared a cabin with an Irish Holy Ghost father, a missionary in Nigeria. He was full of enthusiasm for the fairness with which the British Colonial Office treated the Africans, and had seen enough of the local whites to look forward with horror to their taking over.

On another voyage I had much talk with a former secretary of Lloyd George. He did not need to tell me (but he did) that he was Eton and Oxford. We had begun coldly. We were both leaning over the rail watching bales being loaded into the hold. At the end of a silent half-hour he said, "It's bacon, you know." I said, "I still think it's Shakespeare." Nothing more was said that day. But we settled into much conversation. He was urging the value of Faith. I kept saying, faith in what? I think he did not believe very much in God, but did not seem to think God had any bearing on faith. We simply could not communicate. I think he thought me fundamentally irreligious. At the end of the voyage I had not the faintest notion what he meant by faith: it was a virtue one ought to have, but a virtue complete in itself, one did not need anything to have faith *in*. I am reminded of a conversation I had with an educator.

Educator: Religion and education are incompatible because religion claims to be an answer, whereas education can only be a search.

I: Then if you ever find what you're searching for, education will have to stop?

Educator (beaming): Ah, but we never will.

The wartime atmosphere of England has often been described, there is no way of exaggerating its magnificence. What still surprises me as I look back was the absence of hatred: I never heard hate-talk. I did hear of an occasion when a German bomber pilot parachuted into the midst of a factory he had set in flames. A policeman asked for volunteers to come with him to carry the man out. "Let the bastard burn" was the consensus. So the policeman went in alone.

In the first fire-blitz on London at the end of 1940 Sheed & Ward's office in Paternoster Row was totally destroyed. (I had slept in it the week before.) When I came in next morning, there was nothing there but a vast hole in the ground. One of our packers gave one look at it and brought up his breakfast—a sensitive type obviously. Three hundred titles went out of print that night.

In general it was curious the way the bombing came to be accepted as a fact of life—daily life had to be arranged around it: it wasn't just the act we had put on when we heard the gunfire on the ship: it had become a settled habit. I was in the office one Saturday morning with only a secretary: three bombs fell over a wide arc a couple of miles away (one of them we learned in that night's paper had fallen on a Woolworth killing hundreds). She was a lot less concerned than I was—she was there all the time, I was only an occasional visitor.

That morning was a reminder of the miracle of Sheed & Ward's continued existence in London during the war. Edward Connor, the director-on-the-spot—he had been an Evidence Guild speaker with a vast knowledge of the New Testament—had to find new premises after the bombing of Paternoster Row. Not only that, with conscription robbing him of most of his staff, he had to do just about everything himself—production, editorial, advertising, salesmanship, even packing. Under so many pressures, he did them all with vast competence, editorial especially. I wondered how he managed not to go out of his mind—"go crackers" was the slang of the moment. I didn't actually ask him, but he sent us the answer in a poem—Kipling fathered it, but I don't know who brought it to birth:

> If you can keep yourself from going crackers
> At all the things that you are told to do
> When Hitler sends along his air attackers
> With squibs and bombs to try to frighten you,
> If you can hear the hellish banshee warning
> Without that sinking feeling in your breast,
> If you can sleep in shelters till the morning
> And never feel you ought to have more rest,
> If you can laugh at every black-out stumble
> Nor murmur when you cannot find a pub,
> If you can eat your rations and not grumble
> About the wicked price you pay for grub,
> If you can keep depression down to zero
> And view it all as just a bit of fun,
> Then, Sir, you'll really be a bloody hero,
> And what is more you'll be the only one.

One night a bomb fell about a mile away from where I was staying. The blast lifted my hostess into my arms. The whole family was consumed with amusement—couldn't stop laughing. Next day her baby was born.

This coolness was part of the national temperament. But the Faith added a dimension of its own. Priests knew what they had to give, the laity knew their own need for what priests had to give. It was the kind of pressure in which the Church is always at its best. The chapel in our garden at Horley had been served by four priests from the Southwark Chancery—two of the four, Father Barry and Father Dockery, were killed looking after their people.

A priest I heard of visited twenty or more air-raid shelters every night. In each he would give a few minutes' talk, then say the Our Father, Hail Mary, Creed and Memorare: all the Catholics and many of the others joined in the prayers. Everyone listened. Then the priest asked them to recite an act of sorrow for their sins, gave them a general absolution and blessing. After that the people could lay them down to sleep—"snoring away in minor and major keys, in hundreds of tempos." My wife described all this in a lecture in the States. At the end of the meeting a non-Catholic stood up and asked, "Would Monsignor give us an absolution?" He gave them a blessing.

I am reminded of one Christmas Eve. I had planned to spend Christmas in Southport, which meant taking a train to Liverpool, walking a mile or so across Liverpool, then taking another train. When I got to the second station, I learned that the line to Southport had been blown up as far as Bootle, the second station down the line: a bus would take us to Bootle, where we could catch the train. The bus kept on not coming, the queue grew longer and longer, the crash of buildings under the bombing seemed to be coming closer all the time. The air-raid wardens begged us to go to the shelter. "But if we do," we said, "we should miss the bus to Bootle"; and that phrase kept sounding like a litany until the bus came. The bus to Bootle stays in my head as the symbol of quite a lot of buses the Church has missed—I too of course—by preferring to look for shelter.

II

When Arthur Hinsley was appointed to succeed Cardinal Bourne as Archbishop of Westminster there was the same rubbing of eyes as when John XXIII succeeded Pius XII. It could only be an interim arrangement and what anyhow was the point? Hinsley was an old man, hardly known in England: he had been head of the English College in Rome and was living on there in retirement, his lifework done. It sounded a lunatic appointment. I still can't make sense of it. But it made sense. For Cardinal Hinsley proved to have a radio personality second only to that of Winston Churchill. Certainly no religious leader so gripped the people of England.

He may have been helped by his voice. Outsiders find what is called the Oxford accent very puzzling. Having heard it only in Australia, I took for granted that it was a deliberate affectation, no one could naturally use the human voice like that. But in England I heard small children talking it, so I had to accept that it was a genuine dialect, not an affectation. It has one drawback, that whereas one may have this accent and be sincere, it is less easy to have this accent and sound sincere.

Cardinal Hinsley hadn't a trace of it. He never tried to rid himself of the Yorkshire burr. We hear of a scene in an officers' mess. When the Cardinal came on, the others began by leaving the chair near the radio for the Catholic chaplain: in no time they were all listening in utter stillness. At the end he said, "And now, on your knees." And on their knees they all went, as he prayed.

When the See of Canterbury fell vacant, Winston Churchill as Prime Minister had to appoint a new Archbishop. He is said to have said that he would have liked to appoint "the old boy at Westminster," Cardinal Hinsley. The Cardinal was asked if he would have accepted. "I'd have had a stab at it," he said. I wonder how it would have worked.

The Sword of the Spirit was the idea of Christopher Dawson and Manya Harari, a wonderful Russian Jewish convert married to an Egyptian. Under Cardinal Hinsley it did for a little while make reunion one shade less unthinkable.

The phrase Sword of the Spirit was from the end of Paul's Epistle to the Ephesians. He was a prisoner in Rome when he wrote it, living in a private house under guard of a Roman soldier. He must have been watching the soldier piece by piece put on his equipment, as he urged Christians to see to their own! "Take the whole armor of God, gird your loins with truth, put on the breastplate of holiness, on your feet wear the Gospel of peace, take the shield of faith, the helmet of salvation, and the sword of the spirit, which is the Word of God."

This was an updating of the verse in the Psalms—"hi in curribus et hi in equis, nos autem in nomine Domini," which we may update further as "Those trusting in their tanks, those in their planes, but we in the name of the Lord."

The Sword was a society of a special sort—not for direct action, but for that preparation of its members without which direct action always loses itself in indirection. There was the examination of moral principles everywhere under attack, the cleansing of oneself for the Lord's service. There was the use of the mind on the problems of the war and the far more complicated problems which must come with the peace. And there was the continuing union with God in prayer. The Sword produced spiritual writing in all these fields, especially in its fortnightly magazine.

Catholics of the conquered nations who had managed to get to England—Frenchmen, Belgians, Poles, Czechs—began at once to form their own groups within the movement. The magazine appeared as *Le Glaive de l'Esprit* for the French, as *Miecz Ducha* in Polish.

Its aims could be summarized as

(a) A campaign of prayer, study and action for the restoration of a Christian basis of public and private life, and a return to the principles of international order and Christian freedom;

(b) To bring the idea of God and the idea of Morality into every field of human activity, national and international, politics, business, private life, education.

The movement was not political. Christopher Dawson, one of its most powerful intellects, defined it as being "to bridge the gap between religion and politics." What is the gap? That politics has proceeded (and of course still proceeds) without asking the necessary questions about life, which is the framework within which politics has to be conducted, and about man, who is at once the raw material which politics has to handle and the reason why politics has to be.

The two foundation activities of the Sword were thinking and praying.

Thinking: at that time it may to many have seemed wholly impractical to be discussing philosophy while the world was reeling towards chaos. But men had probably already passed the high point of that glorification of the "practical man"—i.e., the non-reflective man—which was one of the curiosities of English thought for so long. In that mood the practical man was seen, and seen with delight, as the man who when something had to be done did something—not necessarily the right thing, for time would have had to be wasted in discovering what *was* the right thing—but something, anything. Our age has had its stomachful of that sort of practicality.

Politics and sociology are concerned with the relations to one another of men in this world. But men were made by God, and this world was made by God. Nothing could be more impractical than to discuss politics and sociology without reference to God. Or to approach the same principle in another way: politics and sociology concern the relations to one another of men. Therefore the most practical question possible for the politician and sociologist is, What is a man? And the decisive word upon that must come from God who made man. That question was what the war was about. It was the Nazi view of what a man is, against the remains of the Christian view of what a man is. The Nazi view was quite clearly held and applied with the most rigorous logic: the Christian view is by most held half instinctively, not at all clearly grasped, and applied spasmodically and without logic, is indeed in too many of our working institutions betrayed by us rather than applied. It survives with a remarkable tenacity as a residuum that we will not give up. But it is half instinctive: we no longer remember where we got it: we cannot defend it or even very competently state it. For millions of us it is little more than a prejudice.

But the questions Hitler raised as to whether the human person has any right against the State, whether one particular bloodstream gives a right to world dominance, whether brutality does not befit a man more than gentleness—these questions can none of them be answered until we can state quite clearly what a man is and what a man exists for. Short of such a clear statement in our own minds, we can exchange prejudices with a tyrant or exchange bombs with him but we cannot really answer him. And if our exchange of blows is fortunate, and we beat him into silence, we are still left with our own half-comprehended, half-uncomprehended view to face world problems of breathtaking magnitude.

Praying: ultimately the will of God is the one constructive dynamic in human affairs. Man is concerned with the will of God in two ways: to harmonize his own will with it, and to beseech God's providence and the inpouring of God's Spirit. For both these ends, prayer is the vital means. To call upon God without making the most intense effort to live by the will of God would be a mockery. To ask God to get us out of the present mess while continuing the line of conduct which helped to produce the mess would be a kind of insanity. Therefore there must be a strong effort, a kind of asceticism, aiming at personal reformation.

The Sword was not concerned with forming the minds and hearts of an elite, but with working upon the minds and hearts of the whole people. Now, obviously it would have been unrealistic to the last point to think that the whole people could in one act be set to praying. Too many had been away from prayer too long. But though the movement was not aimed at the few, it had to begin with the few and work outwards. That meant that the members of the Sword of the Spirit had, in a sense, to pray on behalf of the whole community until such time as the community itself returned to prayer: but meanwhile to use every means to reach the minds and hearts of men not yet ready for prayer. And in this the Sword of the Spirit was not working upon a religious instinct that was altogether dead. If the people of England were not all very much given to thinking about God, there had for most of them been no definite rejection of God. God remained, unnoticed perhaps, but unrejected too, in the background of their minds; God was not absent from the souls of men even if he was not very much present on their lips or even perhaps in their conscious thoughts.

The movement drew men of all religions. There were two mass meetings held in London—one presided over by Cardinal Hinsley with the Anglican Bishop of Chichester as principal speaker, the other presided over by the Archbishop of Canterbury with a leading Free Churchman and Father Martin D'Arcy, S.J., speaking. These provided a model for a great series of huge mass meetings and smaller community meetings all over England.

I remember my sick feeling and Cardinal Hinsley's sick face, as he told of the directive from Rome that only Roman Catholics could be full members. Something vital and hopeful withered in that moment. The Sword continued, an Anglican society was formed with the name Religion and Life. The Sword is still, thirty years after, doing excellent work. But, as a movement drawing all men of good will to "the unity of the Spirit in the bond of peace," it was over that afternoon. I never think of that time without remembering the bus for Bootle we might have missed if we hadn't been willing to take a risk. If only John XXIII had been Pope!

III

My wartime wanderings were mainly between America and England, with detours. But I managed also to get to Ireland several times and once to Australia. My chief memory of wartime Ireland is of a visit I made in order to address a group called The Common Cause. Most of the Irishmen I knew seemed to be in the group. I gave my talk, which they received politely and questioned me politely about. Politeness satisfied, they settled down to what really interested them —namely the state of the Church in Ireland. That seemed to be the common cause, for which they had named their group. I listened for a couple of hours while they painted their picture. As I understood it, their main complaints were three: (1) the economic gap between a comparatively affluent clergy and the really poor rest of Ireland; (2) the mediocrity of the religious teaching in an Ireland where the educated laity were for the first time outnumbering the seminary priests; (3) the clinging of the clergy to authority—in education, for instance—which they had had to take over when there was no educated laity.

It was my first large-scale meeting with a phenomenon new to me, the anti-clericalism of daily communicants. I remember offering my own definition of anti-clericalism, namely wishing the clergy were better. The episode left me with a feeling that there was no risk of a schism in Ireland, but a solid risk of a fading away of the faith, when the English tyranny was no longer there to pump artificial life into it. On the morning after, I was drinking coffee in Grafton Street, Dublin, with Seán O'Faoláin. He tore Ireland apart as only a patriotic Irishman can. After a while I said, "If life in Ireland is so grim, why do you go on living here? You're not a poor man." He reflected a moment then said, "Ah well! A flea gets used to the one blanket"— not a bad definition of patriotism perhaps. But there *is* a grimness underlying the brilliance of Irish conversation. It was Thoreau who said (in *Walden, Economy*), "The mass of men lead lives of quiet desperation. What is called resignation is confirmed desperation. From the desperate city they go to the desperate country." I met the opening phrase for the first time not in Thoreau but on the title page of Daniel Corkery's *Threshold of Quiet*, a novel about life in Cork, which is by way of being a Catholic city.

Of English tyranny there seemed on that wartime visit to be little trace left in the Irish memory. Maybe I am not allowing enough for the personal effect of John Betjeman (now the Poet Laureate). He was the representative in Ireland of the British Ministry of Information. He had immersed himself in Dublin—art, architecture, culture generally. I was invited to a farewell party given him on his resignation by the Irish journalists. His health was proposed in a warm and witty speech by Eamon de Valera's Chief of Propaganda— Britain's representative toasted by De Valera's, that was really something.

I met a change of roles just as surprising when I went to Australia during the war, to find Archbishop Mannix as Senior Chaplain to the Australian armed forces. Prosperity can make bedfellows as strange as adversity ever made. I had crossed the Pacific on a neutral vessel which, as I was assured afterwards, was loaded with war materials of one sort and another. My cabin-mate was Bishop Vesters, member of the Missionaries of the Sacred Heart. He looked a million years old—I heard a girl passenger describe him as a decayed buzzard. But he won the hearts of all, on the second day out, by ordering beer for the thirty or forty passengers. He was not a back-slapping type but as kindly, priestly a priest as I have met.

I cannot remember if there were any other Catholics among us.

I know that I served his Mass every morning in the lounge. On Easter
Saturday the whole body of passengers asked would he not give them
an Easter Sunday service. So he and I put together a service, Epistle
and Gospel readings on the Resurrection read by different passengers,
hymns common to Catholics and Protestants.

I no longer remember all the details. What I do most clearly remember was selecting a man and a girl with lovely voices—the girl
being the one who had thought the Bishop a buzzard—and teaching
them to sing the *Victimae paschali laudes* in Latin. I introduced their
rendering by giving the "congregation" an English version of what
they were about to hear. After the Last Gospel the Bishop gave his
blessing. The whole was as ecumenical as one could have had in those
distant days.

In Sydney I found the Church I remembered from eighteen years
earlier still euphorically in possession. One could, and I did, luxuriate
in it. There was not a hint, not to be discerned by me anyhow, of
the explosion to come in the sixties. Nor did I find any sign that
the seminaries were taking their students under the skin of the dogmatic and moral formulas. This does not mean that I foresaw the
violence of the explosion, or indeed any explosion at all: but we had
been saying for a long time that the bearing of doctrine on life, and
the interaction of life and doctrine, were all but totally neglected,
and that with the growth of an educated laity the truths as provided
would not prove sufficiently nourishing.

I felt this especially at Werribee, the Melbourne diocesan seminary, conducted by Jesuits. The rector was definitely a character,
"tight-mouthed Bob," I found him charming and learned. But it was
still theometry that I felt was being acquired by the students instead
of theology. It may seem that I am selecting Werribee as a bad example: on the contrary it was because of its excellence in what it
set out to do that I was disappointed to find it not sufficiently different in kind from seminaries I had met elsewhere. Twenty years
later I visited the seminary again and found it incredibly and beauti-
fully changed. The students were a different breed. They divided into
two groups—one round my wife, one round me. Their questions and
their replies to our answers showed men who had indeed been taken
below revelation's surface.

Before talking further of Melbourne, I must linger on one or two
special experiences. In Sydney I met the Missionary Bishop Gsell,
who could boast of I've forgotten how many aboriginal wives. "Buy-

ing" them, paying their parents a dowry, was the only way to save his Christian girls from being married off to all and sundry, and giving them a chance to marry a man of their own choice when they were older.

Between Armidale and Toowoomba I passed a small settlement called Dorothy's Doubtful. I don't know why I mention this, save that it pleases me.

In Brisbane I lectured in the stadium, standing right in the middle of the ring. The acoustics were amazingly good—I imagine that when a fight was on the patrons against the furthest wall got full value for every thump. If I remember aright I gave the same sort of talk on Communism as I have spoken of giving in Dundee. But the night is memorable to me because of the excitement the crowd and I combined to stir in Archbishop Duhig, a veteran of the old horseback days. He took me home with him and insisted on feeding me canned crab (I never willingly eat any sort of crab), actually opening a new can, spooning it into me. The crab walked sideways inside me all night.

What was specially notable about the Archbishop was his relation with the state university. The officials there told me of his generosity, for instance, in securing manuscripts from Italy for them. There had been nothing like this relation in Sydney, in my time as a student there at least. I was to meet it again with Archbishop Mannix in Melbourne.

So once again we meet Archbishop Mannix. He was kind enough to let me see much of him on this visit. He became then, and remained to the end, a puzzle to me—really vast intellectual gifts not used to the full in the spread of the Faith. The only time I heard him he spoke on politics, and he was as gifted a speaker as I have ever heard. Yet I was told that he had hardly ever preached in his own cathedral, and I never heard him speak on the revelation of Christ outside it. I had been tempted to say that if he had had religion he would have had everything. But all epigrams get their effect by leaving out too much—this one left out the hours he spent hearing confessions every Saturday.

It left out also an odd episode. I was lunching with him, just he and I. He told me of an occasion on which he was lunching wholly alone, when a stranger entered unannounced, stood looking at him, and said, "Christ wasn't crucified on a cross of gold and ivory." With his fingers on the crucifix he was wearing, the Archbishop sat deep

in thought. I made no comment. When at last he spoke it was of
something else.

In one area he provided an example of a curious sort of sickness
in the Church's structure which I had already met and was to meet
further—namely, the tendency of high ecclesiastics to maltreat those
marked to be their successors. It might have been simply a matter
of jealousy—"Bears, like the Turk, no brother near the throne."
Herod the Great killed three of his own sons. With bishops it may
have been the feeling that the man chosen was the wrong man,
bound to ruin their lifework.

Anyhow we had seen Cardinal Moran downgrading Archbishop
Kelly in Sydney, and Archbishop Kelly making life intolerable for
Archbishop Sheehan. In Melbourne I met an old friend, Archbishop
Simmons. He had left Sydney High School before I went there: but
in my first outdoor speaking time in Sydney, 1925–26, he was a curate
and used to attend my meetings at Newtown Bridge. Now, eighteen
years later, I met him as Coadjutor Archbishop with right of succession to Mannix. I never heard a complaint from him: but it would
have been hard to mistake the situation. He had apparently been
wished on Archbishop Mannix by Rome, as Archbishop Spellman
had been wished on Cardinal O'Connell in Boston. It doesn't seem
ever to pay.

Before the fall of France my wife and I found ourselves in Italy
and France a couple of times, and once made our way through Spain
to Lisbon and so by ship to New York. We had to wait the greater
part of a day in Irún. We spent the whole day wandering round
the town and returned to find that the three journalists who were on
the journey with us had remained the whole time in the railway station. I asked why. One of them said, "There was menace in the air."
I said, "Nonsense. The place was a lot gayer than Cardiff or Pittsburgh." "That," said the other man, "was on the surface." I asked
how deep below the surface he could see in the railway station. All
the way from Irún to Lisbon they were writing articles on Spain.
A little while after, the body of the one who had felt the menace
was found floating in the Bosporus. He had not trusted the Spanish
Nationalists, but he had assumed that Communists were fellow-
creatures.

One thing about Franco never reached our world. Whatever the
nature of his understanding with Hitler, there was no persecution

of Jews in Spain. Franco has Jewish blood both on his father's side and from his mother's family, the Bahamondes. And he would not agree to let the Germans take over Gibraltar and close the entry to the Mediterranean.

Once more I found myself in Lisbon: one way or another I spent a lot of time there, waiting for plane or ship to get me to America. I should have liked to visit Fátima but had been warned to stay within reach of a telephone message: they never knew when they might find a berth for me. I got to know a lot of people. At one time it seemed certain that Hitler would take over Portugal—Salazar made it quite clear that Portugal was too small to resist. He sent a great part of his Army away to the Azores to be out of the way. I used to go down to the wharf to see the soldiers embark, surrounded by delighted wives and lovers. It was the only time I ever saw women delighted to see their men go. At a point it seemed that a German invasion was about to happen. I was told that Salazar and his secretaries stayed on their knees all night saying the Rosary. Churchill had said, "If the Germans land, we will fight them on the beaches. . . . We will fight them with bottles"—and is supposed to have added, "It's all we have." Bottles or Rosaries, the Germans did not land in either country.

IV

With all my to-ing and fro-ing I spent most of the war in America. My wife and I avoided anything in the nature of propaganda—I remember after one of my talks a man rose in the audience and said, "You haven't even asked us for a destroyer." It would have been idiotic to go on talking as if the war were not happening. But we confined ourselves to relating our experiences.

My wife produced *This Burning Heat,* a book on the blitz as lived through by ordinary people known to her—Beatrice Warde, an American working in London for Lanston Monotype; Chesterton's secretary, Dorothy Collins; our daughter's school mistress; Caryll Houselander; members of the Grail; Shane Leslie; our London office manager, Edward Connor. The title came from St. Peter's first epistle —"Think not strange this burning heat which is to try you." In the Preface my wife wrote:

Theories abound as to the inevitably de-spiritualising effect of war. These documents show the *spiritual* effect of *this* war on a number of widely different people who are actually living through it. They suggest how under this especially searching trial men are asking questions almost as old as the human race. The philosopher in his study asks these questions, and the more comfortable his study the more negative his answers seem to be. The problem of evil is seen starker from a cushioned armchair than from the gridiron of St. Lawrence.

"Gridiron" indeed was not at all a bad figure for cities ablaze. But in so far as the saving of civilization was at issue in the war, Maisie Ward's principal contribution to its saving came in her biography of Gilbert Keith Chesterton. It is curious how at every crisis in the war Chesterton leaped to men's minds. It was, I think, after the fall of Norway, or perhaps Tobruk, that the London *Times* quoted from his *Ballad of the White Horse*

> I give you naught for your comfort
> Yea naught for your desire
> Save that the sky grows darker yet
> And the sea rises higher.

American Catholic opinion seemed to be hardened against America's entry into the war. The most persistent radio voice of that period was Father Coughlin's: he loathed England. His followers used to attend Catholic meetings, call upon the speaker to agree with Father Coughlin, break up the meeting if he didn't. One such group asked Maisie what she thought of Father Coughlin's attacks on the British Empire. She answered, "As a Catholic I never criticize a priest in public. As an Englishwoman I do not care two straws what Father Coughlin thinks of the Empire." The audience liked her answer.

A far more serious champion of America's staying out of the war was the Paulist Father Gillis. He was editor of *The Catholic World* and had a vast radio audience. I had met him on my first visit to America, sitting next to him at meals for two weeks in the Paulist house in New York. Not from him did I learn that he was in continuing pain from a skin disease on his body, caught while barnstorming on the mission. At the outbreak of the war he led a group of Catholics on a visit to England and the Continent. Catholics in England decided to give them a dinner. I, alas, was not there. Responding to the toast of their health Father Gillis gave a carefully prepared speech—his first transatlantic speech, I think—on all the shared heritage which made Americans and English true kinsmen. When he sat down, Hilaire Belloc rose and said all this talk of kinship was nonsense, he himself felt closer to Hottentots than to Americans.

I happened to be traveling back to America on the same ship as Father Gillis: we spent hours every day tramping round the deck as he told of his anger. I pointed out that Belloc must have been drunk—Father Gillis had told me how he had seen him take a bottle of wine from the table and put it into a capacious inner pocket of his greatcoat, and Belloc sober would never have done that. Anyhow Belloc was not an Englishman.

Father Gillis was not to be mollified. Belloc he could have put up with, if one of the Englishmen had answered him. On the contrary one of those who did speak added fuel to the fire by remarking that the play Lincoln had been watching when Booth shot him was *Our American Cousin*—a remark received with uproarious delight by Belloc.

I do not say that this episode was the reason for Father Gillis's campaign against America's entry into the war: it certainly added a continuing and growing violence to his attacks on Roosevelt and his wife as warmongers. I think this had become an obsession. I felt some of it on the night of Pearl Harbor. All America had heard the news. Father Gillis came on the radio that night, made no reference to the tragedy or all that must flow from it, gave the same sort of talk that he had been giving for so long.

Lecturing round America, mainly to Catholic audiences, I found the feeling that too many Englishmen were throwing away American friendship by a kind of nationalist arrogance. It seems certain that treatment of this sort turned Edmund Wilson into an enemy. I met Jesuits who had stayed in English Jesuit houses and been given the feeling that the American Society of Jesus was only a sort of Third Order, tertiaries, compared with the European real thing.

On one of my visits to England I called on the Ministry of Information to tell them of the harm I thought English Catholics were doing by this sort of thing. The man I met was clearly not listening. To test this I said to him, "I think variety is the spice of change, don't you?" "I do so agree with you," he said. I remember that visit to the ministry for a pleasant incident. While I was waiting to be admitted, two officials kept a man waiting forty-five minutes while they tried to make the sealing-wax machine work. In the end they gave up and used the stick of sealing wax and the matches which had been there all the time. Why do I mention this? It has no bearing on my theme, which is my own growth in understanding of the

Church. But perhaps it has. After all, the Church has a bureaucracy. You can learn a lot about any one bureaucracy by watching any other in action.

Coming down for breakfast at London's Basil Street Hotel I heard the staff and some of the guests talking of the atom bomb on Japan. In the afternoon papers I read of what had happened to Hiroshima and Nagasaki (where descendants of St. Francis Xavier's converts had preserved the Faith for centuries with no contact with the Church). I cannot remember my feelings then, or on the following days as details came through. I wish I could remember. As my mind cleared, my one dominant feeling was the wish that it had not happened.

Two or three years later Tom Murray, one of the members of America's Atomic Energy Commission, told me that he had felt bound in conscience to consult the Pope, Pius XII, about the morality of his position. If I understood him aright the Pope's answer was to the effect that America's having the bomb made it less likely that Russia would use it. In all the years since no other city has been atom-bombed by anybody, I suppose we should thank God that that particular blood is on no hands but ours.

One of the earliest to see that we were in a new world was Ronald Knox. He tore himself away from his translating of the Bible to write *God and the Atom*. His main point as I remember was that this unlocking of the immeasurable powers locked up in a point of matter occupying space so infinitesimal that it could not be seen by any microscope meant a world that man cannot cope with—unless he can learn to release some of the spiritual and moral energies locked up in the human mind, which occupies no space at all: after all it was the human mind which split the atom, not vice versa. What sign we have given of the release of those spiritual and moral energies I should find it hard to say. We have more or less mastered outer space, but our own depths mock us by their inaccessibility.

v

The war in Europe over, the authorities asked me to go to the British Zone of Germany and give lectures there. I answered that there was no point in going to any country as an agent of the occupying power, but that I should be happy to go at my own expense, representing no one but myself, if they would give me a visa. It took me nine months to get the visa—I have a feeling that all authorities everywhere feel dubious about a man who prefers to pay his own expenses.

I went first to Belgium, where I met a rather startling priest. He said, "I suppose you, like me, are a member of the Vatican Secret Service." When I said No, he wagged a knowing finger at me. I felt he was rather an advanced neurotic. Later he gave me what may have been an explanation—he claimed that when the Partisans in Belgium decided that a fellow-Belgian must die as a traitor, the final decision for or against execution was left to him. A post like that would have made me neurotic.

I went on to Holland and was horrified at the destruction our bombers had wrought, in Nijmegen especially. But that was as nothing compared with the smashing of Aachen, the first German town I came to (it was the Aix to which Browning's galloper brought the good news from Ghent). Cologne too was grim. There I met a woman whose husband had been tortured and killed by the Nazis. She was wholly without rancor against either the Nazis or the Allies, whose bombing of Cologne had been so thorough.

She had read some book or other of mine, and she introduced me to a group of leading Rhinelanders, mainly Catholics, including Herr Adenauer, who had been Mayor of Cologne, had been maltreated by the Nazis and imprisoned by the British, and who would be as powerful in Germany's remaking as De Gaulle was to be in France's. With this group I had a three-hour discussion. You would hardly guess on what—on what I had learned from the street corner of how God should be presented to an un-believing or half-believing world. Herr Adenauer seemed to give the whole force of his mind to the matter. I have never been so closely or determinedly questioned by anyone. He was a believing Catholic himself and I think he found my line interesting—I came away thinking that it would be marvelous to have him as head of government in England or America.

I lectured to a great number of audiences—German, British and mixed, in universities and halls. In the University of Cologne I was asked to lecture on Bernard Shaw—I was not expecting this, but I had read just about everything he had published and had my own views on him. There was one thing I told them about him that seemed new to them. In an article he had himself written in the London *Times* some time in 1917 he said how much he owed to Samuel Butler—all the Life-Force stuff especially. But in that second last year of World War I Germans had more pressing matters to bother about than where Bernard Shaw got his ideas.

All this mass of talking, two or three times a day, does not stay very clearly in my memory thirty years after. But there was a day in Paderborn which is still wholly vivid to me. I was taken to a home for small boys and girls blinded by our bombing. They had been taught to sing some English songs in my honor, God help me.

As in England while the war was on, so in Germany when the war was over, I heard no hate-talk, in fact got no hate-feel. One man asked me if I could send him telephone books from the Midland cities of England, he wanted to study the distribution of certain English family names.

I can no longer remember at what stage I myself became aware of the cremating of Jews by the Nazis—six million of them perhaps. The matter arose once on this visit. I met only one man of the type we regard as a typical German, practically a stage German, arrogance and all. He hectored me about the inhumanity of the British administrators of their zone. I stood half an hour of it, then said, "At least they don't cremate you."

Apart from that there was no discussion of the war. Nor did I at that time or for long after, either in Germany or anywhere else, hear any suggestion that the Pope had failed in his duty to speak out against Nazi brutalities. That Pius XI was against both Fascism and Nazism had been quite clear. I have already quoted his phrase about the concordat with Mussolini—"I would make a concordat with the devil if it were for the good of souls." He could have had no warmer feelings about the concordat with Hitler, negotiated under his supervision by Cardinal Pacelli.

Karl Adam had been fired, you may remember, by the Nazis from his chair at Tübingen for preaching on the Jewish contribution to Christianity. In 1933 Cardinal Faulhaber's publication of a book of his sermons, *Judaism, Christianity and Germanism,* caused the Hitler Youth to riot. In 1934 Rome placed Rosenberg's *Myth of Blood,* second only to *Mein Kampf* as Nazi scripture, on the Index. A year later we find Cardinal Pacelli, who was soon to be Pius XII, writing to Cardinal Schulte urging the German hierarchy to take St. Ambrose as their example—Ambrose, who, after the Emperor Theodosius had been guilty of a massacre in Salonika, stood in the doorway of Milan Cathedral and refused to allow the Emperor to enter until he should have done penance for the massacre: it was one of the great turning points of history.

When Hitler visited Rome just before the outbreak of war, the Pope left Rome and issued an encyclical letter condemning Racism. It seems he also issued instructions that priests and nuns must not be in the crowds as Hitler drove through. I heard, but cannot guarantee, a story that Mussolini instructed members of his own black-shirted toughs and their ladies, to dress as priests and nuns and lead the applause as Hitler passed.

That the Catholic Church could regard Nazism as anything but a mortal threat is unthinkable of course: unthinkable too that Nazism could allow the Church to survive unabsorbed. As the war came closer, the Nazi grip tightened, with regulations forbidding even such freedom as the concordat prescribed, and laws (on sterilization, for instance) which Catholics could but abominate. Pius XI issued a pastoral in condemnation—*Mit brennender Sorge*—with burning sorrow. It was smuggled into Germany and read in hundreds of Catholic pulpits. I was shown a captured Nazi document which spelled out that the Catholic Church was the one serious religious obstacle in Nazism's way.

What happened to the Church in Germany when the war broke out? What happened to Cardinal Pacelli's reminder of St. Ambrose and his defiance of the Emperor Theodosius? It is a melancholy story. Long afterwards we published a book about it by Gordon Zahn. We must take three elements into consideration.

The first is that when war is actually on, psyches are turned inside out: German victories were balm to men, even bishops, who remembered Germany's defeat twenty years before: and I have a feeling that Germans are more responsive to military bands than most people.

The second is the skilled psychological use of terror: the return of the headsman with axe or sword was very chilling. When I ask myself how I would have reacted, I am less disposed to condemn priests and bishops for not following the solitary example of Jägerstatter, who chose to be beheaded rather than fight for injustice: but I hope I would not have called him a traitor as some bishops did.

The third is that the issue was not a clear choice of darkness or light: Soviet Russia was the enemy that all Germans saw: I don't think what has happened since proves them clearly wrong in deciding to stay with the devil they knew and hope for the best. Hitler? Stalin? Take your choice.

Anyhow, in 1963 we read of a collective Act of Repentance made by the German hierarchy for what they should have done and failed to do in the Hitler time.

What of the recent Hochhuth attack on Pope Pius XII for not at least speaking out against the slaughter of Jews? Hochhuth himself seems to me an interesting study. The two great German crimes were the extermination of the Jews and the savagery against the Poles. So, the Nazis having slain Poles in their thousands, he writes a play accusing Winston Churchill of plotting the death of one Pole. The Nazis having slain six million Jews, he writes a play accusing Pius XII of not speaking out in condemnation.

But Hochhuth is not the point. The Pope is. I may be oversimplifying but the decisive question seems to be what effect he thought a protest by him would have had. He had urged the German bishops to take Ambrose as their model. Pius XII may or may not have been an Ambrose, Hitler quite certainly was no Theodosius. There is no evidence of his being stopped by condemnation: all the evidence is that condemnation maddened him further. In the face of that evidence, was the Pope likely to feel that protest by him would save a single Jew? Or might it not cause Hitler to order Mussolini to set about a similar extermination of the Jews of Italy? If the Pope decided that protest would cause more slaughter, it is hard to see what he is to be accused of.

But supposing a Catholic still feels that he failed his Lord, what is that Catholic's position as a Catholic? Alas, a sufficient number of popes and bishops and laymen have failed Christ often enough, as he knew they would. We may weep for him, we may weep for them, we may weep for ourselves. But he is still working in the world through his Church—as effectively as we, his unprofitable servants, will let him.

CHAPTER 18

THE CALM BEFORE THE STORM

We had been in and out of France right up to the German occupation, and began again the moment France was free. Like everyone
else we had been tickled by stories of Churchill's wit making General
de Gaulle look foolish. Two stories remain in my head. One tells of a
stormy scene in Downing Street, with De Gaulle striding out and
slamming the door behind him. A secretary said to Churchill, "The
General seemed angry." "Yes," said Churchill. "He told me that he
saw himself as the second Joan of Arc. I reminded him that we had to
burn the first." The other story is that Churchill said to De Gaulle:
"Si vous m'opposerez, je vous écraserai." Clare Luce told me that she
asked Churchill if he had actually said it. Churchill just smiled.

But all my outdoor experience told me that it was folly to madden
one's listeners, the satisfaction one gets at the moment from the neatness of the thrust invariably costs more than it was worth. I knew
De Gaulle would want to exact payment. And when the time came
he did. His blocking of Britain's application to be admitted to the
European Economic Community may have had other reasons. But
this one would have sufficed.

I

France, of course, had an untouched look compared with Germany.
We set about meeting old friends, like the Jesuit Père Huby, who
had introduced me before the war to that great scholar Père Lebreton, who gave me a proof copy of a work that was a genuine curiosity.
Père Rousselot before his death in World War I, had followed his *Intellectualisme de St. Thomas* with the *Problème de
l'amour au moyen age*. He had published an English edition of this
in Germany. Père Lebreton gave me the proof copy, corrected by the
author himself. It was destroyed when the first German fire-blitz on
London turned our office into a hole in the ground. Thirty-five years
after, all I can remember of the book is its brilliant development of

the idea that all human love draws its energy from God's love, however we may distort and pervert it.

Among new friends was the Jesuit Père de Lubac. We were the publishers of his *Drama of Atheist Humanism* and a study of Proudhon which we translated as *The Un-Marxian Socialist*. A friend had described him to me as the most intelligent French Catholic and one of the three most intelligent living Frenchmen! What I had read of his fitted well with that judgment, my meeting with him confirmed it. I had an extra reason for meeting him. Crossing to England, my son had met an American girl who was on her way to Paris and was interested in the Faith. He asked if I could introduce her to a French priest. I sent her a letter of introduction to Père de Lubac. She became a Catholic.

He himself was to have trouble with some of the Roman authorities. At one time he was removed from his Professorship of Theology in Lyons and forbidden to preach or write. The Archbishop of Lyons, Cardinal Gerlier, refused to appoint a successor, saying that as far as he was concerned Père de Lubac still held the chair. There was much theological stirring in France, with the Dominican Père Garrigou Lagrange as a pillar of conservatism. We had ourselves published a book by Père Sertillanges which, while not denying creation in time, held that it could not be proved from Genesis. All this could make interesting reading, right up to the publication by Pius XII of the encyclical *Divino Afflante* in 1943, which opened the door (cautiously as it seemed, but widely enough as it turned out) to a new era of Catholic Scripture scholarship.

A handful of phrases from the encyclical will show the liberating effect. "Being thoroughly prepared by the knowledge of the ancient languages and by the aids afforded by the art of criticism, let the Catholic exegete undertake the task of discovering and expounding the genuine meaning of the Sacred Books." "Discovering" is a strong word, with its assumption that there are meanings undiscovered.

"An interpreter must, without neglecting any light from recent research, endeavor to discover the peculiar character and circumstances of the sacred writer, the age in which he lived, the sources, written or oral to which he had recourse, and the forms of expression he employed."

"He must go back wholly in spirit to remote centuries of the East and with the aid of history, archeology, theology and other sciences, accurately determine what modes of writing the authors of that ancient period would be likely to use, and in fact did use." And all this was not simply a permission: "This part of his office cannot be neglected without serious detriment to Catholic exegesis."

In 1955 the secretary of the Pontifical Biblical Commission stated that Catholic exegetes were no longer bound by the decrees of the Commission issued from 1905 to 1915 in the wake of the Modernist troubles.

I pause upon the injunction to go back in "spirit to remote centuries." Modern scriptural scholarship has done marvels in this field, but all the same a modern man cannot actually become an ancient Israelite or Mesopotamian. Writing a small book on the first three chapters of Genesis, I became interested in the "orgy," practiced in the Near East, including Mesopotamia. I wondered if before the call from God Abraham had practiced it. From scholars I learned much about the orgy itself—one day in the year on which everyone was out of doors, and anyone could copulate with anyone, mistress with slave, for instance, only incest forbidden. I gathered that it was a wholly religious activity, celebrating the original chaos out of which the gods had produced the universe. But I wondered what it actually meant to the individual, for copulation has its own excitements and my experience as a Catholic told me that people can practice a religion without being "wholly religious." In particular I wondered whether there was any account of what it felt like the morning after—when husband and wife met and recalled seeing the other the day before, or what mistress might feel about slave. I asked a world-famous Comparative Religionist—he was not a Catholic, as it happens I do not know personally any Catholic expert in the field. He told me that there was no known evidence. But I left him a little gloomy because the question had never occurred to himself.

II

All this interested us and as publishers we kept reasonably abreast. But as ourselves we were more interested in the activity of Catholics among the workers and the poor. We had become more and more conscious of the gap between the mass of Catholics and the intellectuals: "the hungry sheep looked up and were not fed"—because the shepherds were talking to one another. Our particular interest was, as it had always been, in what happened to the mass of Catholics.

In those early postwar visits to France the most interesting thing we met was the Priest Worker movement. And no one fascinated us more than the first priest-worker we came to know personally, the young Jesuit Henri Perrin. When Germany held so much of France and was conscripting Frenchmen for work in Germany's factories, he had trained as a mechanic and in 1943 had gone to Germany as a volunteer, in order that the enslaved Frenchmen should not be priestless. We had published the book of his experiences, *Priest-Workman in Germany*, translated by our daughter Rosemary.

His first shock was to find the Catholic Church functioning in Germany! He found "a living, praying liturgy, a whole community reaching to God . . . a German soldier got into the place next to me, a big sergeant of thirty-five or so, who took up the dialogue Mass in a deep, firm voice. And I felt prayer become really tragic . . . we were sons of the same Father . . . I prayed desperately that Christendom might one day rise again."

German priests received him as a brother, had him say his Mass in their churches, at great risk from the Gestapo. After four months in the factory, the Gestapo did discover that he was a priest and he was imprisoned. In his cell he kept a diary written on scraps of wrapping paper or lavatory paper. As he expected he found that God meant nothing at all to most of the Christians he found either in the factory or the prison.

"Our job must be not so much to recall to them their duty as Christians but to awaken in them the desire to become Christians." (So, as I have shown, we had found in our street corner crowds: we had so to show them Christianity that they would see that there was a point in being Christians, to awaken an awareness of an emptiness in themselves that Christianity could fill.) Père Perrin continues, "Just as Christianising a pagan world has to be done progressively, by almost imperceptible degrees, so the paganisation of Christians has worked unnoticed like the discoloration and death of autumn leaves which slowly die and fall off the tree."

How he set about remaking the lost contact he tells in the book. He managed to get other prisoners to night prayers in his cell. One or other of them would say prayers he remembered in German, Italian, Polish, Czech, Hungarian, Dutch, French. They would make the sign of the cross and each in his own language say an Our Father and a Hail Mary. There were Russians among the prisoners, devoted to Stalin. They too came to join in the prayers and the final handclasp.

Even Mass he did arrange sometimes to say in the cell, with some asleep, one making use of the extremely primitive lavatory close by the makeshift altar.

The book is wholly realistic—about the sheer heroism, for instance, that it took to hold back and go up last and so get least of the soup which was almost all they had by way of food.

Reviewers found in Père Perrin's book an awareness of the Mystical Body *experienced*, and a hope that the experience might be for all men:

> Perhaps one day we should be able to live another liturgy, coming spontaneously from the heart of a priestly people gathered round their priest; with him in moving dialogue, with united actions, they could offer for the whole earth, expressed by a little bread and wine, to make of it the Body of Christ which purifies and sanctifies the world, a loving Mass in which priest and people grow into one, are fused more and more into Christ, their hearts wrung by the thought of those who neither can nor want to be there: a Mass which is a real mystery of unity, love and Redemption nourishing young men in the full flush of vitality. . . .

This he wrote in his cell, surrounded by the thieves, pimps, black marketeers who shared prison with him. And the man who wrote it was the Henri Perrin we met one day in Paris. He was alive with it. He asked his Jesuit superiors to let him return to his working among the workers and they consented. My wife lunched with him at a workers' restaurant. He was living with another Jesuit in an "airless hole," no drainage, no electricity, no running water. He had been fired from one job already, for inefficiency, he was told, but he thinks the bosses had discovered he was a priest. He was filled with hope in this new apostolate.

I have lingered on Père Perrin because of the end of his story. The next time my wife met him he was different. He had bought a café and with a number of friends was using it for various youth activities. The Mystical Body seemed to have moved to somewhere in the back of his mind. She stayed for his evening Mass and found his sermon simply ten minutes of kindly chat, none of the height and depth and breadth of Christ's mystery as he had lived it and preached it in prison.

I was not with her on this occasion but he had expressed so strong a wish to see me that I lunched with him the day after. I found that he wanted me to ask Dorothy Day to raise money for his restaurant.

He seemed stunned when I told him of the miserable poverty in which Dorothy lived and worked, with never enough money for her own breadline and that of the other Houses of Hospitality. He really had thought America so rich that anyone there could get money for anything.

He talked straight "party line," a kind of proletarian mystique as uttered by the Soviet. I was prepared to accept any evil report of the Capitalist world, but he would hear no evil of the Soviet. I begged him to examine the basis of his assumptions about Russia: from what I had heard myself from people who had been there I painted something of that picture of Stalin which Khrushchev would later give in such appalling detail. I didn't ask him to take my word for any of this, but at least to check on it. I pressed him for an answer as to what steps he had taken to verify his dream. Dream was the word. I felt I was talking to a somnambulist.

As I think back I ask myself if I am not exaggerating the difference in him: may it not have been only the difference between a man who shared my own spiritual vision and a man in whom it had died? But I am used enough to men who hold views that I don't: a change of view would not make the difference between vitality abounding and somnambulism in my impression of him, unless it made the difference in him.

Neither of us saw him again. He had asked to be released from the Jesuits, was accepted as a secular priest by the Archbishop of Sens and went to work on the construction of the Isère-Arc tunnel. We had his description of the ten to twelve hours he and the others worked every day, sleeping in overcrowded dormitories, with no means of drying clothes taken off wet at night and put on again damp next morning. He became the workers' secretary and led them to success in a strike. He remained close friends with the local priest and said his Mass every evening in the village church. A workman was killed and in his funeral sermon, Henri Perrin blamed the management. So he was fired: the workers struck to have him back and won.

Then the order came from Rome, all but breaking the back of the Priest Worker movement. He was one of some eighty priests (out of not much more than 100) who signed a manifesto refusing to obey —"to give up the struggle now would be to betray their proletarian state"—almost, they seemed to say, their proletarian vocation. Henri asked the Archbishop for six months' leave of absence. Then came

his death—the motorcycle he was riding had swerved. In his pocket
was a letter asking to be laicized, returned to the lay state. It had
been in his pocket a fortnight. He had not sent it. Would he have?
It is necessary to see what led up to Rome's decree.

III

It was while Henri Perrin was in Germany that the Priest Worker
movement came to life in France. The Mission de France had been
founded to train priests for those French bishops who felt that France
was no longer "eldest daughter of the Church" if she had ever been,
but as to a great mass of her people was as much in need of Chris-
tianization from the ground up as any of the countries to which she
was sending missionaries. Part of the training was six months' work
in a factory or on a farm, that the priests might have some awareness
of the life their flocks had to live.

The Abbé Godin saw the excellence of the Mission de France but
his experiences as Chaplain to the Young Christian Workers had
shown him that something at once wider and more specialized was
needed—wider in that it must include laity as well as priests, more
specialized in that for all its members the work must mean moving
into, giving themselves to, becoming and remaining part of, the
world they hoped to bring back to Christ. He and his priest friend
Yvan Daniel were asked by Cardinal Suhard to write a report on all
this. It was published under the title *France Pays de Mission?* The
Cardinal saw the point. In January 1944 at a solemn High Mass he
launched the Mission de Paris. That night the chimney of the room
in which the Abbé Godin was sleeping got blocked; fumes pouring
into the room killed him in his sleep.

The work went on. Three years later Maisie embodied the report
in a book which she called *France Pagan?* She visited Paris again and
again, meeting and growing into friendship with priests and families
who had given themselves to the mission in groups all over Paris.
Dominicans were in the work, and the vastly learned Père Chenu
told her of a retreat he had given to forty-eight leaders of groups in
Montreuil alone. Capuchins put up a wooden shack in which they
lived, from which they went out to their work in factories, in which
the homeless could spend the night.

Godin's work was being done by hundreds. But there was general
agreement that if any one individual priest was his successor it was

the Dominican Père Loew in Marseilles. Actually he had been a year or two ahead of Godin, for he had been working on the docks there since 1942. And he stood for a special element in the work which might have saved it from the tragedy of its closing. He held that priests should not go to live among the poor individually but as a small team, and that the team should not only work in the docks but run a parish.

As we first met them there were four of them—a secular, a Jesuit, two Dominicans. Two of them worked on the docks, two ran the parish: every so often they switched, the "dockers" running the parish, the parish men working on the docks. They lived on the ground floor of a large apartment house, their own apartment open day and night, a public telephone in their living room.

There is no possibility of telling the whole story here. Maisie translated his book, and wrote of her own experiences, in Marseilles as well as Paris, in *Unfinished Business*. I found the movement fascinating, but she was far more deeply in it than I.

We published a story, *9 Rue Notre Dame*, by the Abbé Pézéril, which showed a side effect of the Priest Worker movement. It is a study of an older priest, successful, content with his life, who makes acquaintance with a young priest-worker and ends by asking him to absolve him from sins he had not earlier been aware of—acrimony and negligence. And talking of this novel reminds me of the death-bed of a better-known novelist, Georges Bernanos. As I heard it he sent for a priest, asked the priest who came who he was; the answer was Monsignor So-and-So. The dying man refused his ministrations —he was a sinner and wanted no high ecclesiastics. So the Monsignor got hold of the Abbé Pézéril, told him Bernanos was dying but would have the Last Sacrament only from a priest who was nobody in particular. The Abbé Pézéril passed the test.

I move rapidly on to the tragedy. From the beginning the problem was to what extent the priest-workers should "join in the effort to change the shape of things, in the political, social, economic struggle." At the beginning the decision of the heads of the various groups involved was against (somewhat as our Catholic Evidence Guild had concentrated on Christ rather than on the Church's social teachings).

But in the nature of things priests doing the work grew more and more involved. Their education made them natural leaders; they became union officials; and, again in the nature of things as things then looked, they became Communists. Some of them were getting mar-

ried. Rome grew more and more worried. The Nuncio had long dis-
cussions with Cardinal Feltin. The Cardinal and other French
bishops went to Rome to save what they could of the movement. I
have not heard that either the Nuncio or his Roman superiors talked
to any priest-workers. Perhaps they did. Anyhow Rome acted—priests
who were to be workers must be carefully selected and trained, they
must not become union officials but must remain linked with the parish work: most crushing of all, they must not give more than three
hours a day to manual work—which meant good-bye to docks and
factories.

I have spoken of the manifesto refusing obedience, signed by
eighty-two of the priest-workers, who now called themselves Worker
Priests. Maisie read it on her journey to Marseilles to see Jacques
Loew. Like Abbé Daniel and others whom she had met in Paris, he
had seen it coming with the bishops standing by while priests of no
great priestliness were getting into the movement and twisting it
their way. Père Loew had been a pupil of the Scripture scholar Père
Lagrange, who had known what it was to be under Rome's scourge.
Like Lagrange, he obeyed. Priests might still do three hours' work a
day, so he established a brickworks in which he and the priests with
him might do their three hours: and the brickworks meant work for
the men of the parish. I have not paused to say how magnificently
the parish of St. Trophime functioned.

John XXIII dealt what looked like the final blow, abolishing even
the three hours. It was out of no want of love for the poor that Pope
John acted. The teaching on the rights of the working class in Leo
XIII's *Rerum Novarum*, and Pius XI's *Quadragesimo Anno*, Pius
XII's Pentecost address of 1941, John summed up and developed
in *Mater et Magistra*, seeing the question on a world plane.

It remained for Paul VI to embody all this, together with the Vatican II document on the Church in the Modern World, in a really
wonderful encyclical, *On the Development of Peoples*. His theme is
that in the effort of the democracies to end the appalling gaps between rich and poor in their own country, there were three elements
—direct and immediate help to the poor, a fairer division of the
wealth produced between what had too often been exploiters and
exploited, and government seeing that the proper balance was kept.
The Pope showed how all three must be applied *to the world as a
whole*. Barbara Ward says of the encyclical that it is the fruit of the
most accurate study of social phenomena, "it goes to the root of the

historical problem posed by colonialism and the post-colonial relationship between the wealthy nations and the poverty-stricken."

It is strange that even Catholics do not see the quality of Pope Paul. In a world where nothing seems to matter as much as what happens in bed, they judge him by their own view on contraception. But life is not lived in bed, and in the wider world he has done magnificently. There is the drawing together, for instance, of Catholic and Eastern Orthodox at which we shall be looking, and the giving of the ring he wore as Archbishop of Milan to the Archbishop of Canterbury. There is his remaking of the Pontifical Biblical Commission with twenty scholars. And there is the encyclical we have just been discussing.

Sitting close to the platform in Bombay when he was receiving high dignitaries of the government I was struck by the contrast between the deathly weariness on his face as each person moved away from him, and the almost-radiance as he welcomed the next comer. The encyclical is a marvel of compassion for the suffering poor, and of anger at avarice as "the most evident form of moral underdevelopment."

To return to the Priest Worker movement, which seemed to have been extinguished by Pope John. Pope Paul sent for Père Loew several times, listened carefully, questioned him, laid on him the obligation of seeing that he, the Pope, should be kept informed of all that he should know of this area of human life. In 1965 he allowed the French bishops to bring the movement back to life. There are now 700 priest-workers in France.

We last saw Jacques Loew at Cîteaux, where he and other priest-workers were on retreat. He is now at the École de la Foi in Fribourg training priests for the work.

IV

We have gone ahead of our story. At no point of course have I let chronology rule me; but overshooting the Vatican Council may seem to be carrying carefreeness about time rather far.

In fact one now sees the seventeen years between the ending of World War II and the summoning of Vatican II very much as a calm before a storm, so very calm a calm that we ought to have known that trouble was brewing. Of a vast Lay Congress in Rome I remember only two things—the delight I caused by limiting my own speech to forty minutes, and the feeling of the whole Congress that the ball was at our feet. Solid work was being done in so many areas. The occasional eruptions were all small-scale, Pius XII seemed to have everything competently in hand. Considering what the explosion was to be like when it came, it is hard to believe that a Jesuit paleontologist should have filled so much of the Catholic horizon.

The open-air speakers of the Catholic Evidence Guild in England used to mock themselves by singing a song to show that *aggiornamento* had not passed them by. We sang it to the tune of "The Vicar of Bray." One stanza began—

> Scholastic junk we do debunk
> The Summae of Aquinas
> We've read them both and given them
> A gamma triple minus.

But the stanza I have in mind ran—

> No more naïve, we don't believe
> In Adam and the garden
> We've read but do not understand
> The works of Père de Chardin.

Many a reader of Teilhard who would not dream of singing anything so frivolous might well have sighed over the last two lines. No writer of our time has ever secured so vast and rapturous a following of readers who would have found it hard to say, even to themselves, what he was saying. I myself was long kept from reading him by the incoherence of people to whom he had come as a new revelation. They had felt the impact but did not know what had hit them.

When the news flew around that *Le Phénomène humain* had been condemned by Rome, they felt their Faith rocking on its foundation. When it was made clear that all that had happened was an instruction that his books were not to be read in seminaries, they felt better but were not really mollified. It was almost as if Rome had ordered seminarians not to be told about the experience of Peter, James and John on the mount of Transfiguration. Yet given their own difficulty in putting the revelation into words they might not have been so sure that seminarians were quite ready for him.

In the end of course I had to read him. Reading *Le Phénomène humain* and *Le Milieu divin* I learned why this scientist writing on theology had fascinated people who had no habit of reading either science or theology. It was the vitality in him. So many writers on profundities seem to crawl across the page. Depths in the readers, depths so many of them had not known were there, responded to the vision of God and man with which Teilhard was ablaze. They had nothing in their minds to test the vision with, they knew they were shaken by it.

I knew that this response to Teilhard was possible because I myself responded like that to half of the *Phénomène humain*, the scientific half. In my day at Sydney University we had to do one year of one science: there was a gentlemen's agreement that if you took Geology you would not fail: in my final examinations we had to attempt "only seven questions"—"only" made me laugh, I did not know even what most of the questions meant. I had memorized answers to two questions, which I was told were sure to be set. One of them was. I answered that: it was on Paleontology. The other wasn't. I answered that too. The gentlemen's agreement was honored.

So that I read the scientific sections of the book utterly gripped, but having no knowledge of my own with which to question them. The theological sections I read with intense interest, but I had enough theological knowledge to question them again and again. Great numbers of readers know as little of theology as I of paleontology. Without seeing very clearly the shape of Teilhard's universe, they felt that there *was* a shape—a shape which brought those ancient enemies Religion and Science into happy wedlock, Science's consent to the union uttered (not exactly, of course) in the Preface by Julian Huxley, whose grandfather had thought up the word "agnostic."

Both books have their own superbness. *Le Phénomène* considers the evolution of the universe up to its present state, on to its goal, the Omega Point. Every element in creation is to have its full development—the material universe is not only the stage on which man is to perform as long as he needs it, but has a perfection of its own to attain and abide in: men's minds are to grow into means of communication with one another, into a oneness with one another, which we can barely conceive, yet not merged and depersonalized.

The continuing problem for mankind has been the balance between the rights of the individual (with a tendency towards anarchy) and the needs of society (with a tendency towards tyranny). At Omega Point there will be a maximum unity for the whole species combined with a maximum development in the personality of each man.

In *Le Milieu*, Teilhard finds Christ at the end of the road on which evolution is moving—Christ in fact is the fulfillment towards which the whole evolutionary process has moved from the beginning. The Second Coming will not be the nipping of evolution in the bud, it will come as evolution's full flowering. When? Millions of years hence is Teilhard's pessimistic "perhaps." All will depend on mankind's use of its powers, especially love, "the basic human energy, energy in its pure state," reaching its perfection in "a great love for Christ in the very act of loving the universe."

I have spoken of Léon Bloy's violence as a hurling of boiling lava off his racked chest. There is something comparable in Teilhard. His insights were too vast for one man to cope with, even a man with a richer theological equipment than his. Two gaps in his universe-picture I found myself insistently aware of. I can find no theology of sin in what I read of his, I have been unable to discover what he made of death. Sin and death add up to a considerable part of the human problem.

Naturally the magisterium had to consider not only the insights but the gaps and the relation of the whole of Teilhardism to revelation: it did not condemn, apart from the warning about seminaries. But plenty of individual theologians did. I was very much interested in Maritain's raging at Teilhard in *Le Paysan de la Garonne*. When I first knew Maritain his bête noire was that very original Catholic thinker Blondel. As the years rolled by he was able to sort out what he could value in Blondel from what he disliked. He met Teilhard's ideas too late for that second stage. I have a feeling that with twenty years to work in, he might well have made a remarkable synthesis of classical theology with Teilhard's insights—as Père de Lubac, deep in his eighties, is so valiantly trying to do.

So we come to Vatican II. One other book appeared on its threshold which made a different kind of difference. We published Hans Küng's *Council, Reform and Reunion*. I do not discuss it here, much has happened since. But in one way at least it was a portent. The Catholic University in Washington forbade the author to lecture in the university. The students effected a revolution by telling the world of the veto. Thus they not only insured vast sales for the book, whose publication might otherwise have caused no great stir, but served notice that authority can no longer count on getting away with it!

CHAPTER 19

THE CHURCH EXAMINES HER CONSCIENCE

At the beginning of Mass we—and the priest—confess that we have sinned exceedingly in our thoughts and in our words, in what we have done and in what we have failed to do. The Ecumenical Council called by John XXIII is best studied, I think, as the Church's public examination of her own conscience, principally under that last heading, what she has failed to do—an examination of her conscience followed perhaps by contrition, certainly by a firm purpose of amendment. Pope John was the first Pope in memory who could have conceived a Council so, largely because he had too rich a sense of humor not to see the defects in himself, and as a consequence the high probability of defects in his predecessors and their curias. Cardinal Griffin once told me that when he was informed that he was to be Archbishop of Westminster he had been in tears for a couple of hours. My guess is that when Cardinal Roncalli found that the Conclave had chosen him Pope, he laughed uncontrollably, thinking it as good a joke as had ever been played on the Church.

Looking here and there in the documents of Vatican II, we come upon phrases which do not sound as if they come from a penitent. The *Declaration on Religious Liberty*, for instance, uses the phrase which maddens so many, "one true Church," and says (14) "It is her duty to give utterance to, and authoritatively to teach, that Truth which is Christ himself, and to declare and confirm by her authority those principles of the moral law which have their origin in human nature itself." In other words the Church has not ceased and will not cease to do the work for which Christ founded her—teaching doctrine and morals, giving us Mass and sacraments.

But she is taking a long close look at herself all the same. "Holiness" is one of the famous Four Marks. But the *Dogmatic Constitution on the Church*, known from its opening words as *Lumen Gentium*, draws some distinctions: "Even now, on this earth, the Church is marked with a genuine though imperfect holiness" (48). Throughout, the Council's chosen phrase, by Pope John's special request, is "Pilgrim Church": with no disrespect to John Bunyan, the book of the Council Documents could also be called *The Pilgrim's Progress.* "The Church, embracing sinners in her bosom, is at the same time holy and always in need of being purified, incessantly pursues the path of penance and renewal" (8) (it was one of the Reformers who created the phrase "simul justus et peccator"). In the *Decree on Ecumenism* (4) we read, "all are led to examine their own faithfulness to Christ's will for the Church and wherever necessary undertake with vigor the task of renewal and reform." "The Church constantly moves forward toward the fullness of divine truth until the words of God reach their complete fulfillment in her" (*Dogmatic Constitution on Divine Revelation* 8).

A long close look at herself indeed: an even longer closer look at her performance, to see where it could be improved. Most of the bishops I met were amazed at the amount of improvement which has emerged, not as possible only but as essential. The daily running of the Church had too much routine in it, a kind of hardening, with not enough self-questioning, not a close enough study of the world whose conversion had been entrusted to her by her Founder. The Church was as always the Rock, but had come to look unattractively rock-ribbed.

When Pope John announced that there would be a General Council, Cardinal Tardini, one of the men who worked longest and most closely with Pius XII, is said to have seen it not only as dangerous but as pointless—the other Christian bodies in disarray, the Church's victory assured, why bother with a Council? That really was triumphalism. One wonders where he got the ivory for his tower.

The Council did not say in so many words that it was examining the Church's conscience, that is not the way of Councils. But in a dozen areas it set out what ought to be done, without any pretense that it was in fact being done. A dozen areas, I say. From the particular angle of the book I am writing, I select six such areas—her own Structure; Liturgy; Scripture; her relation to Other Churches; her obligation to the World as World; the Jews. These are the areas in which my own experience of the Church, as recorded in this book, had shown most need for rethinking in depth. The Council was concerned not with Trinity and Incarnation, not with the World to Come, but with the demands which life on the road makes on the Pilgrim Church.

I

Structure. The Council made it quite clear that the Church had become too centralized. A man I know remarked that Pius XII had only one fault—he thought bishops didn't matter. How else, he went on, quoting W. S. Gilbert, can we explain the appointment of "So-and-so and Whats-his-name and likewise You-know-who?" Certainly one got the impression that, as all decisions were made in Rome, the personality of the man on the spot did not matter enormously. I remember the stir caused in Australia by the decision of the Apostolic Delegate, Archbishop Panico, not only to attend meetings of the hierarchy (which was new) but to preside over them (which was startling). He got away with it too, save for Archbishop Mannix, who refused to attend meetings thus presided over. When I was in Australia in 1944 I was told by a Labour Party Cabinet Minister, Arthur Calwell, that Anthony Eden, Britain's Foreign Secretary, had told Rome how happy Britain would be if Mannix were made a Cardinal. He was not, of course. I am not suggesting, or even hinting, that he should have been: I merely note that his kind of independence was out of favor in Rome at that time.

Rumors of course can exaggerate. That I heard of bishops, successors of the Apostles, treated as delinquent office boys by quite minor curial officials in Rome, is no proof that such things actually happened. But the frequency of the rumors suggests that diocesan bishops mattered a great deal less than the Curia, the Pope's cabinet. This, I imagine, was behind the Council's determination to press for a declaration of collegiality—making it clear that bishops were not the Pope's representatives, but his colleagues (which we of the Evidence Guild had been teaching for forty years).

The establishment of an Episcopal Synod—composed of bishops representing national hierarchies—to meet at regular intervals in Rome to effect collaboration with the Pope was something wholly new. It was new in providing a context for the bishops to play their part in the conduct of the Church's life, but new also as an admission that the nations who combined to make the Church's catholicity each had their distinctive contribution to make to the fullness of the Church as Christ's. The Council said what no Council had yet said—"each nation develops the ability to express Christ's message in its own way" (*The Church in the World* 44).

It felt too, that the specific differences thus recognized between Catholics of different national cultures would best be met by leaving ways of Catholic life to grow naturally under the guidance of national hierarchies in matters where the revelation of Christ is not directly involved. There have been too many instances in which national differences were treated as things to be crushed out. The Australian aboriginal, to take an example close to my own awareness, has a culture of his own which could quite literally enrich catholicity: so far no use has been made of it: the few aboriginals who have tried for the priesthood have not gone through—the effort to reshape their minds and speech into Latin did not help.

But there was one element in the Church's structure which was far more important even than the downgrading of bishops and ignoring of national differences, namely the submergence of the laity. In the long run their emergence in the Council documents may outweigh all other changes the Council has made.

Nineteen centuries after Christ the majority of the human race—"two thousand million human beings" by the Council's count—has not been taught Christ's Gospel. The Church, Matthew tells us, was founded to teach and baptize all nations, to go into all the world and preach the Gospel to every human creature, as we read in Mark. It is sobering to realize that the Church has not only not done what Christ founded it to do, it has not even approached doing it. Books could be written saying why.

But one fact stares us in the face. For so vast a work as the winning of the whole world to Christ, the whole of the Church's resources should have been mobilized, and they have not been. There are, for instance, scores of thousands of the parish clergy, not very much consulted through the ages, not as such represented at Vatican II. But what I have especially in mind are the thousands of millions of laymen and laywomen. It is not only that they have not been used in the spreading of the Faith to the world: they have not played their part in the development of the Church's own understanding of Revelation. Christ's revelation grows first of all by being lived: the lived experience passes into the Church's conscious mind and thence into the Church's utterance. The laity have lived it, quantitatively at least, beyond their leaders, but qualitatively in their own way too, since they have had to apply it to a far greater variety of life, live it under a far greater variety of strains. And there has been no way in which the Church could draw on this ocean of experience and be the richer for it—no way in which the laity could be consulted in matters of doctrine—Newman's view that it should had Pius IX weeping.

The Council says in so many words that the Church is not Pope and hierarchy with nuns added for variety: it is the whole body of Catholics. Christ is acting through all. "The faithful join in the offering of the Mass by virtue of their royal priesthood" (*The Church* 10). "The faithful offer the Immaculate Victim not only through the hands of the priest but also with him" (*Liturgy* 48).

It says that the Church's saving work must be done by the laity as well as clergy—in other words the laity are part of the apostolate. Consider two things said in the *Dogmatic Constitution on the Church.* "The laity are made sharers in the priestly, prophetic and kingly functions of Christ" (31). "Through baptism and confirmation all are commissioned to a participation in the saving mission of the Church . . . the laity are called in a special way to make the Church present and operative in those places and circumstances where only through them can she become the salt of the earth" (32). Which is one special way of saying, "the head cannot say to the feet, I have no need of you" (1 Corinthians 12:21), which the visible head seemed to have got into the way of thinking.

I have said that the emergence of the laity may outweigh all the other Council changes. Why "may"? Because the emergence may not get beyond the drawing board, not be a real emergence at all. For real emergence there must not only be a change in the clergy but a change in the laity. I have known priests who are far more afraid of the laity than of the Communists. What will happen about that I cannot even prophesy—I have already quoted the Cardinal of Lima's statement that we cannot have an apostolic laity unless we have an apostolic clergy. But I know something about the laity. The Council was not admitting them to a privilege, it was calling them to vast labor. Everybody likes privilege, but who likes labor? To do what the Council desiderates, the laity must study Christ's revelation, so that it grows in them and they in it. And this not only have the laity not done, but the Church has shown precious little desire that they should. To enter the apostolate untrained, unequipped, is to ask to be cut to pieces.

But that kind of study of the Faith, plus the development of the power to communicate to others what has been studied, would require a total change in our habits, practically a remaking. It cannot be done in spare moments—when we happen, say, to feel in the mood for a little "apostling." It will eat into the time we now give to our work, to our play, to our love-making, worst of all to our leisure.

Will the laity do it? There is not a lot of evidence. We have seen an incredible willingness for sacrifice in the Catholic Worker movement, a notable willingness for study in the Catholic Evidence Guild, a generosity in Peace Corps workers in poorer countries. But the percentage of laity actually involved is tiny. If it stays that way the emergence will not have got far beyond the documents. The involved ones are those who have *seen* the needs. The majority have not seen them—because they have not looked very hard. For the forty years since I read them I have been haunted by Jean-Paul Richter's words—"If we don't use our eyes to see with, we shall use them to weep with." On this matter the Council has used its eyes to see with.

II

Liturgy. The first document the Council had ready for publication was on the Liturgy, the public worship of the Church, the hymn of two worlds interpenetrating, one life throughout. And this was not mere chance. The Mass is the one place where we regularly meet God not as individuals (which we can do anywhere, anywhen) but *as his people.* Unless this meeting is right nothing else in Catholic life will be; unless it is real and vital, everything else in our Catholic life will be thin, impoverished. We had always known that the Mass is at the center of our Catholic life: but the Council is saying that too many of us were off center. The changes in the ritual had as their aim to center us aright. And there can be something wrenching in being suddenly and violently re-centered. I once compared it to having one's stroke at tennis corrected by an expert. At first the change is sheer misery. The old stroke was not very effective but it came naturally, so to speak. With the new one we cannot get the ball over the net or even hit it. But once we have made it our own, tennis becomes a new game. This or something like it was what Pope Paul had in mind when, at one of his weekly audiences, he spoke of a layman who had told him that he was happy because *for the first time in his life* "he had participated in the Sacrifice of the Mass to the full spiritual measure."

What was the lack of full spiritual measure that Council and Pope had in mind to correct? Two things especially.

(1) For many Catholics Mass had been a time for being alone with

God: the changes made them feel that the congregation was crowding in on that prized intimacy. This was all very spiritual but it missed the point of the Mass. The prayer of contemplation and the offering of sacrifice are different approaches to God. The Council said so sharply: "liturgical services are not private functions." At Mass, as we have just noted, we meet God as his people. We go to Mass *in order to* join with others in an action we and they are performing together. *Together* is the point.

(2) This action-with-others is not simply praying together or singing together, it is doing together. It is the offering to God of Christ once and for all slain on Calvary, now forever living. The Mass is Calvary as Christ in heaven continually offers it to his Father. That of course every instructed Catholic knew. But we had not been reminded often enough that we ourselves were taking part in the actual offering—not simply watching the priest make the offering but making it with him. It was actually there in the old Mass, but it was easy to miss. When the priest turned to us and said, "Orate fratres," "Pray, brethren," he usually turned back to the altar to say what he was asking us to pray *for*—"that my sacrifice and yours may be acceptable to God the almighty Father." So the sacrifice *was* ours as well as his.

But, I repeat, it was easy to miss. The Council leaves us no excuse for missing it. Let us look at it again. "The faithful offer the Immaculate Victim not only through the hands of the priest but with him" (*Liturgy* 48). Even that does not say the key word: for that we turn to the *Dogmatic Constitution on the Church* (10)—"The Faithful join in the offering of the Eucharist by virtue of their royal priesthood."

My mind goes back to the twenties. That very great, very Irish, spiritual master, the Holy Ghost father Edward Leen, wrote an article on the Priesthood of the Laity. The Irish bishops were so shocked that all copies of the magazine were recalled, and the author had to make a public apology. A few years later we published his *Progress Through Mental Prayer*. We were thought reckless to publish the work of such a firebrand. I imagine none of the bishops who condemned his article lived long enough to see the Council clear his name, nor did he.

The Council refers to the Mass as our share in, our foretaste of, the Liturgy being celebrated by Christ in heaven, as we find it in the Epistle to the Hebrews, and in Revelation. Christ's redeeming sacrifice—Death, Resurrection, Ascension—was complete. But it still has to be applied to each individual human being. That is why Hebrews tells us that he entered heaven to appear in the presence of God on our behalf (9:24). The Epistle had already told us that "His priestly office is unchanging . . . He is living on to make intercession for us." Because Christ wills it so, his continuing intercession breaks through to our altars. Christ is doing this at the altar, the priest is doing it with him. And we are doing it too. By baptism we are cells in the Body of Christ who is making the offering, of Christ who is being offered: we cannot help being part of the action of the Mass. We can only behave as if we were not.

Compared with the immensity of what is being done—by ourselves —at the Mass, questions of Latin or vernacular, silence or dialogue, are secondary. Which does not mean that they are unimportant. And the Council forces us to do something about the meaning of Ritual. Since the Mass is our action-with-others, there must be an accepted order—we cannot be acting together separately. The ritual cannot be formed by individuals—pastor, or more likely curate—to their own taste or fancy. The Council laid it down that even a priest may not "add, remove or change anything in the liturgy on his own authority."

But the Council would surely have startled some of its predecessors when it said, "Even in the Liturgy the Church has no wish to impose a rigid uniformity in matters which do not involve the faith or the good of the whole community" (37). "Even in the Liturgy"—that is quite a phrase! The statement goes on, "Rather she respects and fosters the spiritual adornments and gifts of the various races and peoples." "Elements of initiation rites, found among primitive peoples, may be capable of adaptation to Christian ritual" (65). A lot of Roman officials must have turned in their graves at this—especially some of those who insisted on men's heads being bare at Mass. Missionaries had pointed out that there were countries in which it was a degradation for a man to appear in public without hat or turban: they pleaded that men converted to the Church should be allowed to keep their heads covered at Mass. Twice Rome refused, at last agreed that they might keep their turbans *but must remove them at the elevation!* It is hard to believe in the sanity of the men who made these decisions, the last especially.

A liturgy must express what the worshipers are thinking and feeling, or it is lifeless. If the thinking and feeling change, then to stay alive, the liturgy must change too. This also the Council saw. Yesterday's rituals may not be right for today. Still more: rituals must take account of national differences. "Where we of the West bend the knee, the Japanese bow; the kissing of the Missal at the Gospel says nothing at all to the Japanese, who are not a kissing people." (I am quoting myself, not the Council.) In the same article I went on, "Our private prayer is the approach to God of the individual self which each of us uniquely is: it changes as we change, from one moment to the next perhaps. Liturgy is the corporate approach of men to God (the angels doubtless have their own), and it too will change as men change. It will not change week by week of course. But a liturgy can come to be seriously out of contact with those who must use it." "Out of contact" the Council saw as our position. It made changes.

They have not suited everybody. I know people to whom some of them are detestable—especially the prayers spoken by the congregation in the vernacular. I make two comments. First, to me it seems splendid that we are all saying some of the greatest of the Church's prayers aloud, together, in English. For that alone I should feel with the man Pope Paul quoted as feeling "that for the first time he had participated in the Sacrifice of the Mass to the full spiritual measure."

For my second comment, I find myself quoting Pope Paul again. Ideally, of course, we should be gripped by what is happening at Mass. But the mind *will* wander. The Pope might have been talking of me when he said: "Previously our presence was sufficient; now attention is demanded and action. Previously one could doze, but no longer."

III

Scripture. In the encyclical *Humani Generis* Pius XII had said, "Without Biblical theology, dogmatic theology becomes sterile." Surely that is the most surprising thing a Pope has said in this century. In the *Dogmatic Constitution on Divine Revelation* (24), the Council wrote its own endorsement of this: "The study of the sacred writings is the soul of sacred theology." To match these two statements you would almost have to go back to St. Jerome's "Ignorance of Scripture is ignorance of Christ." Certainly in recent centuries the Church, as most of us met it, did nothing to remind us that if we were not studying Scripture we were missing theology's soul, leaving theology sterile, remaining in ignorance of Christ. Pius XI did remind us of Jerome's words and did attach an indulgence to a quarter-hour of Scripture reading. That was something new and good: but it seems a tiny inducement to urge us away from sterility. "Sterility" indeed was not so much as hinted. (I remember telling my Hyde Park crowd about the indulgence—"Indulgences are not in Scripture," they said.)

Speaking for the committed laity, I do not exaggerate when I say that we saw theology as all-sufficient, Scripture as a quarry from which we could dig out supporting texts. That they would "support" we took for granted. There was an infallible Church, there was inspired Scripture. We had no sense of rivalry between them. But I think few of us saw that we were in the presence of two energizings of one same Word and the Spirit he sent. The Word of God was conceived in the womb of Mary by the power of the Holy Spirit: by the power of the same Spirit the Word of God was conceived in the minds of Scripture's writers. So our document can say that the Church venerates the Scriptures just as she venerates the body of the Lord, since from the table of both she reserves and offers to the faithful the bread of life!

It does not say, as some hasty readers seem to think, that the two conceivings are quite the same—one cannot meet Christ, body, blood, soul and divinity in the Scriptures as the apostles met him in Palestine, or as we receive him eucharistically. Christ said, "Unless you shall eat the flesh of the Son of Man and drink his blood you shall not have life in you." We hear nothing quite like that from him about Scripture: he quotes the Old Testament often, tells Pharisees to read it as giving testimony of him, but gives us no command to read it. None the less, though the conceivings are different and the receivings, they are of the same Word.

Not having sufficiently meditated on this, we did not see what positive gain Scripture held for us. The Council leaves us in no doubt. The Church is infallible, but also, "An infallible teaching flows from Scripture." Sacrament and Scripture both nourish, we should see to it that we are nourished by both. Doctrine and Scripture are not two different arrangements of the same material. They are two approaches from different angles to the same reality. Scripture contains elements which the teaching Church has not yet formulated doctrinally; and doctrine has elements not explicit in Scripture.

Some of Scripture's books may strike us as so far beyond the human level that we feel the Holy Spirit must have inspired the writers, some are so matter-of-fact that we cannot imagine what the

Holy Spirit could have contributed. But in all of them, whatever our aware reaction, God abides: and with God abiding in them the reader can make his own contact. Every reader, I imagine, knows what it is to come upon phrases which touch a nerve in himself.

But that raises the question, what reason is there, apart from our own subjective reaction, for thinking God inspired the books of Scripture? The New Testament means most to us. Christians of any level of orthodoxy are agreed that it is divinely inspired. Yet the New Testament does not say so, indeed it says nothing of itself at all, shows no awareness of itself as Scripture or even as a book. Except for Epistles by the same author, no book of the New Testament refers explicitly to another, except 2 Peter, which contains both a tribute and a warning about one particular letter of Paul (it doesn't actually say which) and "all his letters." "There are passages in them difficult to understand; and these, like the rest of Scripture, are twisted into a wrong sense by ignorant and restless minds to their own undoing."

For Catholics it is the Church that guarantees the New Testament. We accept its books as inspired on the word of the Church—the Word in his Church giving testimony to the Word in his Scripture. But men who do not accept the Church's authority, do accept Scripture. Why? That men agree in accepting the Bible is wonderful. But what do they think it *is*, what do they accept it *as?* That question will have to be faced if Ecumenism is to make any progress. Scripture's value, Scripture's authority, are wrapped up in the answer.

IV

The Church and the Other Churches. In the *Decree on Ecumenism,* and indeed throughout, the Council draws a line between the Eastern Orthodox Churches and those born of the Reformation. I am told that the Church has never officially declared the Orthodox Churches as in heresy or even in schism. How does she see them? Unity has been fractured, so to speak, and must be restored. For the fracture, says the decree, "both sides were to blame." A letter Pope Paul wrote to Athenagoras, Patriarch of Constantinople, says that the fracture took place in 1054, when the Roman Legate Cardinal Humbert and the Greek Patriarch Michael Cerularius each excommunicated the other—thus effectively rupturing "the full communion of faith, fraternal accord, sacramental life," which had existed for the Church's first thousand years, roughly half the Church's life.

The Council makes no criticism whatever of the Orthodox Churches. There are doctrinal differences—on the *filioque*, for instance, the procession of the Holy Spirit from the Father *and the Son.* One rubs one's eyes at the Council's mildness about these divisions. Mildness unparalleled? Not often paralleled, certainly. "It is hardly surprising if one tradition has come nearer than the other to the exact appreciation of certain aspects of a revealed mystery or has explained them in a different manner. These various theological formulations are often to be considered as complementary rather than competing" (17).

Upon discipline and liturgy the Council affirms the right of the Orthodox Churches to govern themselves: "Although this has not always been honored, the strict observance of this traditional principle is among the prerequisites for any restoration of unity" (16).

Views like these were not in the minds of Michael Cerularius and Cardinal Humbert nine hundred years before—one wonders which of them would have been more horrified. In synchronized ceremonies in Rome and Constantinople, Pope Paul and Patriarch Athenagoras withdrew the nine-hundred-year-old excommunications. The two leaders met in Jerusalem and read aloud alternate verses from St. John's account of the Last Supper.

What is needed for the restoration of the fractured unity? The Council speaks of "the removal of the dividing wall, that there may be one dwelling." Clearly it would take more than the removal of a wall to reunite the separated Churches of the West with the See of Rome. In his Christmas Allocution of 1958 Pope John spoke of the other Christian Churches as "bearing the name of Christ on their forehead." In taking that as the key to its own relations with the other Churches, welcoming observers from all of them, speaking of "the Holy Spirit at work in them" and "their participation in the mystery of Redemption," Vatican II was very definitely examining the conscience of Vatican I. For at the First Vatican Council there had been only one real scene, and it was on this very point, as Abbot Cuthbert Butler tells in his history of the Council.

Archbishop Strossmayer, speaking on the Proem to the Constitution *De Fide Catholicā*, had criticized its attribution of all the errors of the day—rationalism, pantheism, materialism, atheism—to Protestantism: but they all started before Protestantism. He mentioned that there were many serious Protestant scholars who could help us in opposing them and said he would like to see Guizot's refutation of

THE CHURCH EXAMINES HER CONSCIENCE 291

Renan in the hands of all. "I believe that there are in Germany, England, America, a great crowd of Protestants who love Our Lord Jesus Christ and deserve to have applied to them the words of St. Augustine 'They err indeed, but in good faith.'"

At this there were protesting murmurs. And the President, Cardinal de Angelis, said: "I pray you to refrain from words that cause scandal to some Fathers."

The Archbishop would not stop and the murmurs swelled—"He is Lucifer, anathema, anathema." He was finally silenced. What proportion of the bishops joined in the protest against the suggestion that Protestants might be Christians, there is no way of saying. The unfriendly correspondent of the London *Times* thought perhaps 200 (out of under a thousand). Anyhow the words attributing the errors of the day to Protestantism were withdrawn from the Proem.

Archbishop Strossmayer would have found a very different atmosphere in Vatican II. The statement on *The Church* (2) ended any idea which might still linger in Catholic minds that salvation is only for those who are visible members of the Visible Church. In *Ecumenism* we find something wholly new in papal and conciliar documents. In a speech I made in Sydney, some time before the Council had issued its *Decree on Ecumenism*, I had said that the union of hearts for which Pope John was appealing did not mean that we must be nice to the other Christian bodies since there was no way of getting rid of them. And I quoted the American Jew George Sokolsky's attack on Tolerance—"If a Christian said to me, 'I have decided to tolerate you, come to dinner,' do you think I'd go? I don't want to be tolerated, I want to be respected for my difference." I related this to ourselves and the Protestant Churches. We must realize their positive function in Our Lord's service: since for all sorts of reasons, good and bad, there are millions who are suspicious of the Catholic Church and will not accept anything from her, even Christ, it is splendid that he is being brought to them by Churches they *will* listen to. But Vatican II went further: "Whatever is wrought by the grace of the Holy Spirit in the hearts of our separated brethren can contribute to our own spiritual up-building" (*Ecumenism* 4). I doubt if anything the Council said was more revolutionary than that. Yet it hardly stirred a ripple.

What then is the present state of Ecumenism? In *Mystici Corporis Christi* Pius XII had spoken of the other Christian bodies as "related to" the Mystical Body of Christ but not, *reapse*, members. *Reapse* is a rare Latin word, probably a form of *re ipsa,* meaning "in very fact" or perhaps "in the full sense." Whatever its exact meaning here, it modifies the flat negative. Vatican II did not find clarification easy. "Men who believe in Christ and have been properly baptised are brought into a certain, though imperfect, communion with the Catholic Church" (*Ecumenism* 3). So far we have a repetition of Pius XII. But the decree introduces a new element: "All those justified by faith through Baptism are incorporated into Christ." Is the Council drawing a distinction between these other Churches (which are "related" to the Mystical Body) and those who belong to them (who may be members)? Yet the Council sees the Holy Spirit at work in the Churches, and sees their significance in the mystery of Salvation.

I think we may expect a further statement, but it will not be easy to compose. After all there are hundreds of Protestant sects, and some of them are very strange indeed, hardly recognizable as Christian. Even within any one Church there are enormous differences, with a total acceptance of Trinity and Incarnation at one end, and a total rejection at the other, and daggers drawn at both. I can imagine the uproar if the Church issued lists of acceptable Protestantisms and unacceptable. On the other hand a blanket "anything goes" would leave revelation shattered.

There was indeed a honeymoon period while Pope John lived, the union of hearts growing visibly, the disunion of minds not raising its troubled head. But the disunion was real and vital—each group holding what they did because they believed Christ wanted them to hold it: this was no matter for the give and take of diplomacy, but for each plumbing its own doctrines to the depths. Doctrines, I say. But what of morals? Abortion was not in John's time a burning issue as it is now. But contraception was. Cardinal Suenens told me that an Anglican archbishop had told him that he saw no possibility of agreement while Rome maintained its teaching on that!

In fact reunion is not simply a matter of a handful of differences to be ironed out. As we now see the Reformation breach need never have happened. It was not in the nature of things and ineluctable, but only in the sinfulness of men on both sides and the perversity of things. But anguish produced the revolt and the centuries established it. By Pope John, Catholics and Protestants have been brought closer than they have ever been, meeting for the first time as brothers in Christ. And they discover that four centuries of division had as a result that Catholics and Protestants—I mean typical Protestants, offspring of the Reformation—differ in the very depths of their personalities. A man who understands the Faith, accepts it and practices it, is almost living on a different planet from one who doesn't: the things he takes for granted are different, his mental habits are different, his spontaneous reactions are different, his universe is different.

There is his acceptance of authority, for instance, which to a Protestant looks like intellectual suicide but to himself seems the only possible condition of intellectual freedom. There is the Mass, which to a Protestant looks like a denial of Calvary, to himself is an assertion of Calvary's continuing effectiveness. There is Christ's mother: that we should ask her to care for us, pray for us, seems to flow naturally from her Son's redeeming work, to Protestants it seems a plain denial of it. Point by point answering is not enough. We can clear away errors which distort the reality of our belief, but the reality thus clarified may be not much easier for others to accept than the errors they used to think we held. It is no exaggeration to say that they and we inhabit a different mental universe—if only because we see as our fellow-citizens, so to speak, all men from the beginning of the human race who have not refused God. It is folly to think that all we need is to find the right formula.

So, once again, where is Ecumenism now? There is a new amiability in all save the extremists, born perhaps of our seeing more of each other and working together on common interests: born more remotely perhaps of each side's having seen the face of brute totalitarianism, so much uglier than either of us ever thought the other's face was.

But, short of amiability, there is definitely a new and improved situation. My guess is that there was a long period in which if the Pope could have abolished all the Protestant bodies by a stroke of the pen, he would have made that stroke and had a Te Deum sung in St. Peter's. We really did think—up till how recently? up till Cardinal Tardini perhaps?—that the Protestant Churches were keeping their members out of the Catholic Church: we now know that they are keeping vast numbers either out of total irreligion, or out of strange occultisms and diabolisms which would also be irreligious. I think Vatican II would have been as alarmed as Vatican I would have rejoiced, if the other Christian Churches were to vanish from the scene. I cannot speak for them, but I feel few intelligent Protestants would want to see the Catholic Church go. Belief in God and his Christ is already too scarce, and getting scarcer.

The upshot is that we all think in a pallid way that re-union would be good. But pallor will conquer nothing. We must ache at not having the oneness Christ wants of us.

v

The Church and the World as World. In the *Pastoral Constitution on the Church in the Modern World* (with its opening words *Gaudium et Spes*—Joy and hope), I wonder how many noticed the Council's cool assumption that the shaping of our world is part of our duty to God, of our duty as Christians. "Christ's redemptive work . . . involves also the renewal of the whole temporal order . . . the Church's mission is to penetrate and perfect the temporal sphere with the spirit of the Gospel" (*Laity* 5). "God's plan for the world is that men should work together to restore the temporal sphere of things and develop it unceasingly" (*Laity* 7).

In speaking like this the Council may or may not have been examining its conscience: it was certainly examining ours. We may have felt it our duty as citizens to work for the reform of the social and economic order: but our duty as citizens never weighed heavily on our conscience. But if it is part of our duty as Christians, we shall have to answer to Christ about it. How conscious have we been that it is an essential part of the Church's mission to reform the temporal sphere? How conscious of it has the Church made us? How conscious of it indeed has the Church herself been?

The Council notes as tragic the fact of "man painfully searching for a better world, not working with equal zeal for the betterment of his own spirit." It is indeed tragic: but among Catholics there has often been the contrary unbalance, a real effort for personal holiness, but no working for a better world. We have not been at the head of the fight for civil rights.

In plain truth the world as a danger to man's soul has occupied more of the Church's mind than the world as entrusted to man by God for the development of its possibilities, especially as they concern the life of men in it. The suffering of individuals the Church has relieved as no other group in history has—hospitals, orphanages, houses for the aged, homes for the insane: it is close to the literal truth to say that all of these are practically her own invention.

But an ideal human society here on earth *as a goal to be worked for*—that has not been through the ages a notable part of her message. The nineteenth century was close to its end before we had Leo XIII's encyclical on the Condition of the Working Classes: not so long before that we had Rome condemning "the right to work"! Pius XI and Pius XII and John and Paul have continued Leo's initiative splendidly. But that sort of duty to the world has not yet become part of the Catholic outlook on life. Even in those who take their faith in full seriousness, the concentration on their own growth in Christ has not been balanced by a concern for mankind as a whole.

Unbalance always tends to its opposite. There has been an astonishing growth among Christians of secularism—the exclusion from consideration of any world but this—and it has affected Catholics. Towards the end of the Council I tried to analyze it:

> Men who would not have thought of themselves as atheist were using their minds less and less on God: a kind of reverence for God remained, while to the word God less and less meaning was attached. But for a God not comprehended what function could there be? The notion of God as caring, intervening, commanding, judging, grew less and less till it was no longer there. From God inactive to God dead was an easy step. It did not amount to rejection, more like the taking off of a garment not needed in the climate in which we now are.
>
> Some of our best known clerical and academic spokesmen have given up any hope of building men's relation to God—and so to one another—into the texture of life. At best they hope it will survive on the margin of religion's real task, which they see as the perfecting of man's social condition here. And in many there is an actual turning away from divine revelation not only as marginal to that task but as an active distraction from it.

So I analyzed the situation then. I have seen it more clearly since, and I have noticed what I had not then noticed—that most Christian writing along these lines has the same root weakness as Marx's—the clutching, evading human self is left out of the problem. One hears all the time that man has reached maturity. When I first read Bonhoeffer's statement that man has come of age I wrote, "What a coming of age party man had—millions dead in Hitler's gas-chambers, ten thousand Polish officers murdered in Katyn Wood, hundreds of thousands destroyed in a couple of flashes at Hiroshima and Nagasaki." The Council was more realistic: "The whole human family has

reached an hour of supreme crisis in its advance towards maturity"
(*Church in the Modern World* 77).

Indeed realism is the atmosphere of this whole document. "Man
is the source, the center and the purpose of all economic and social
life" (63). This centrality of man the Council applies to two
matters particularly—poverty and marriage.

We are reminded of a "saying of the Fathers"—"Feed the man
dying of hunger because if you have not fed him, you have killed
him." All individuals must undertake a genuine sharing of their
goods, so must all nations. There may be various arrangements of
property but always on the understanding that "God intended the
earth and all that it contains for the use of every human being, the
use of every people" (19).

It is interesting that marriage should be treated in this particular
document—we remember that the author of Genesis proceeds
straight from the description of man's breaking away from the law of
God to sex and marriage, as though the evil results are seen most
unmistakably in that area of life. The Council places conjugal love
alongside procreation as the two primary ways in which marriage
serves man. It was unable to deal with birth control because Pope
Paul had announced his own decision to issue a statement upon it.
But it says one thing which in the event the Pope did not follow up.
Parents have a personal responsibility to "take into account both their
own welfare and the welfare of their children, those already born and
those who may be foreseen . . . they will reckon with both the material and spiritual condition of the times as well as their state in
life"—we remembered how Jeremiah, the Old Testament's one
celibate, exercised this "responsibility" by deciding the world was
too awful to bring children into!

But where the Council shows its realism most notably is in its examination not only of what the Church has to offer the world but of
what the Church must learn from the world.

It had almost become a cliché at Catholic meetings that the
Church had the answers to the world's problems if only the world
would listen. As against this the Council states the obvious—"The
Church has not always at her disposal the solution to particular
problems" (33). There are all sorts of elements involved on which
the Church has no revelation from Christ, for which men must find
their own solutions. Yet revelation can cast light on the whole

human situation: and because of it the Church "can contribute towards making the family of man and its history *more human*."

That I found notable. But what comes next verges on the astounding—what the world has to offer the Church. It is what we of the
street corner had been feeling towards forty years earlier, particularly
in the matter of heretic-burning—that religion and civilization have
their own different rhythms of progress. "What are called the exact
sciences sharpen critical judgment to a very fine edge. Recent
psychological research explains human activity more profoundly. Historical studies make a signal contribution towards bringing men to
see things in their changeable and evolutionary aspects" (54). All
this the magisterium must study, both as it affects the human situation to which Christ's revelation must be applied and as it affects
themselves—not only in their applying it, but in their understanding
of it. Every new truth established about creation tells us more about
the Creator. On the other hand civilization makes no steady and continuous advance: there can be progress, there can be regress: not
every new idea proposed is good. To all this the Church must bring
her own understanding.

Dr. McAfee Brown notes the striking contrast between this document and Pius IX's *Syllabus Errorum*, written a century earlier. On
so many points the Council was examining Pius IX's conscience.

VI

The Jews. Of our outdoor questioners I liked especially the Jews.
We always understood what they were saying. More to the point for
us, they always understood what we were saying. On the Trinity,
for instance, though we could not persuade them to accept it, we persuaded any number of them to agree that we were monotheists. Two
of them stand out.

Paul Winter was from Czechoslovakia. His family had been
murdered by the Nazis. He was a considerable Scripture scholar and
heckled us closely; but I often drew on his knowledge. He had a great
personal love for Jesus and wrote a closely argued book on his trial.
At lunch one day he gave it as his experience that however friendly
Christians might be they had a deep instinctive dislike for Jews. I
said, "I haven't." He looked at me for a long half-minute, then said,
"I believe that's true."

Edward Siderman was not a scholar but had as clear a mind as is

good for anyone. He heckled us for forty years, beginning as an agnostic: he admitted that we got him back to the synagogue. He had
years of close argument with the Dominican Father Vincent McNabb.
At Father Vincent's death, Siderman wrote a small book, reproducing
the friar's words with remarkable accuracy. He asked me to write an
Introduction. In it I said, "I think the heckler loved the friar, I know
the friar loved the heckler." Twenty years later, when he was dying,
he was visited in hospital by another Dominican, who told us that
they talked religion for an hour: there was no question of his becoming a Catholic, but, "I could feel God in the room." I had the same
feeling, as it happens, when I was present at a Jewish service in a
funeral parlor: I came away feeling that it would be wonderful if we
could have the Jewish awareness of God's majesty.

Naturally Jews questioned me about the maltreatment of Israel by
Christians. As with the Inquisition I had to get my own mind clear
about it, then discuss it from the platform with men to whom it
mattered so anguishingly. I summarize what in forty years I found to
say.

Treating Jews cruelly is not an exclusively Christian habit. The Old
Testament is filled with examples of what Gentile nations did to
them. Three times they were expelled from pagan Rome. Though on
the whole they flourished in Moslem Spain, yet we find that in 1066
four thousand of them were massacred in Granada; and in the middle of the following century they might almost have been wiped out
if great numbers had not fled for refuge to the Christian part of
Spain. It was not love for the crucified Christ that caused Hitler to
send millions of them to the gas chamber, or that lies behind the
Soviet persecution of which Jews are even now complaining.

Which does not mean that Christian nations have not maltreated
Jews. Spain itself expelled them in 1492. Several of the Crusades began with massacres of Jews before the Crusaders ever left Europe. In
the twelfth century and again in the thirteenth, French kings decided on their expulsion. Edward I drove them from England in 1290,
and they only began to come back in very small numbers centuries
afterwards. And short of expulsion, there were all sorts of restrictive
laws as to occupation, residence and even dress in most Catholic
countries. In a general way, popes were kinder to them than their
subjects tended to be; but the whole story of Jewish and Christian
relations is a bleak one.

Father Abbott, S.J., in the Documents of Vatican II notes that the

Fourth Lateran Council—held in 1215, the year of Magna Charta—decreed that Jews must be prevented from charging Christian borrowers too high a rate of interest; baptized Jews must not observe Jewish customs; Jews must stay indoors during Easter Week, must pay tithes to the Church plus an annual tax (at Easter), must wear a distinctive dress from their twelfth year; and a Christian prince giving office to a Jew incurred excommunication.

Why should there be this recurrent tendency to maltreat Jews? One simple explanation is that whenever things are going wrong and a scapegoat is needed, they are available—for they are a minority, they are recognizable, and their high intelligence causes them to be successful and therefore envied. One can think of scores of examples of persecution which this kind of explanation would seem to fit—as when the Black Death was wiping out millions (including Jews of course) and the rumor spread that the cause of the disease was that the Jews were everywhere poisoning the wells. As I say, when any sort of national psychosis exists, the Jews seem to be marked for victimhood whatever the nation. Yet it remains that Christians could be stirred to action against them only too readily.

A rumor would spread that the Jews were using the blood of murdered Christians in their Passover ritual, and Christian knives would be drawn. Popes would issue indignant denials of the accusation, but it persisted. The part Jews had played in Our Lord's crucifixion has been flung against them ever since, and arouses anything from mild dislike to the sort of loathing Luther had. The charge of deicide, God-slaying, was available for anyone who wanted to stir hatred, even in a world in which only a minority believed in Christ's Godhead. The news that Vatican II meant to make an official denial of the charge caused a good deal of excitement.

What *was* the part of the Jewish people in Christ's death? On the face of it, one would say it would be impossible to imagine any crime committed nineteen hundred years ago for which the descendants of the criminal still merited massacre. Even if every member of the race had been involved in the original crime, seventy generations seems a long while for guilt to persist. But what reason is there to think that the whole of the Jewish nation was involved in the handing over of Christ to the Roman officials who had him crucified?

The idea is quite monstrous. In the first place, we remember that in Christ's time there were more Jews living outside Palestine than inside: they were scattered throughout the Gentile world, they were to be found in the Roman Empire, in Persia, in India. So the majority of Jews living at the time knew nothing of the crime. What of the Jews in Palestine? Those who were not in the city of Jerusalem on the Friday did not even know it had happened till afterwards.

We know there was a hard core of "scribes and Pharisees" who followed Our Lord around, and were continually in argument with him and very early determined on his death. But of their numbers we have no notion. The Sanhedrin, which finally handed him over to Pilate, had seventy members: we know that some of these, like Nicodemus and Joseph of Arimathea, were on his side. We must not be misled by thinking of the Sanhedrin as the governing body and therefore entitled to speak for the Jewish people: they were Sadducee in majority, collaborators with the Roman conqueror, and the High Priests were Roman appointees. The High Priest of the moment, Caiaphas, actually gave as a reason for destroying Christ that his raising to life of a dead man so close to Jerusalem might upset the Romans and cost the High Priests their positions.

What did the great mass of the people of Jerusalem think about Christ? We have two pieces of evidence: on the one hand, his enemies did not dare to have him arrested in the daytime for fear of the populace; and on the other, the morning of his death found a crowd gathered round Pilate's judgment seat, clamoring for his crucifixion. It is quite fantastic what has been built upon that crowd. We do not know who they were or what their number: they give a certain air of having been brought there to shout against Christ. But for the rest we know nothing of them. Yet their cry, "His blood be on our heads and on our children's heads," has been treated by Christians through the ages as a solemn pronouncement of the Jewish race, justifying the slaughter of any Jew anywhere.

We do know something about the numbers of those Jews of the time who accepted Our Lord—there were a hundred and twenty in the Upper Room when the Holy Ghost came upon them; St. Paul tells us that after his Resurrection, Christ appeared to five hundred of them at one time. Have we any solid ground for believing that his enemies numbered more?

When I learned that Vatican II was to issue a document on the whole matter of the Church and the Jews, and specifically on the charge of deicide, God-murder, I was filled with happy anticipation. The happiness did not survive the document.

The *Declaration on the Relationship of the Church to Non-*

Christian Religions begins with a word each on Hinduism, Buddhism and Islam. It speaks of what is "true and holy" in these religions, the spiritual and moral qualities found in them, the values in their society and culture.

A *peritus* who was at the Council because of his knowledge of Arabic and the Arab peoples, told me that the Mohammedans took no interest whatever in what the Council had to say about themselves but were passionately concerned lest the Jews be cleared of the charge of deicide!

Of Judaism the document tells what the Old Testament means for Christians, and tells of the racial origin of Jesus and Mary and the Apostles. But there is no word of Catholic maltreatment of the Jews through the centuries. On the matter of Jewish guilt for Christ's death, the plain statement that "the Jewish people is not guilty of deicide" was struck out before the vote was taken: we may assume this pleased the Arabs. The Declaration says only, "What happened in his passion cannot be blamed on all the Jews then living without distinction, nor upon the Jews of today." That is all—not a word of what has been set out above to show how monstrous it was that the accusation should ever have been made at all. I do not know what Jews feel about it. I blush for it.

The Declaration goes on to say that "the Jews should not be presented as repudiated or cursed by God, as if such views followed from Holy Scripture." When this statement was put to the vote, 1,821 bishops voted for it, 245 against—at least a smaller proportion than of those at Vatican I who objected to Archbishop Strossmayer's saying a good word for Protestants!

The figures I have just given I found in Father Abbott's splendid edition of the Council Documents. On the question we are discussing, he mentions that the Council makes no reference to a statement of the Catechism of the Council of Trent for Parish Priests published by order of Pope Pius IV. It says: "The guilt for Christ's death seems more enormous in us than in the Jews, since according to Paul, 'If they had known it, they would never have crucified the Lord of Glory,' while we, professing to know him, yet denying him by our sins, seem in some sense to be laying violent hands on him." Certainly I had been taught all my Catholic life that we had all, by our sins, had our share of guilt for his crucifixion.

As I read the Council documents I am full of admiration. Some may find other topics they would have wished the Council to discuss, so indeed would I. But surely they and I can agree that what they have said is immeasurably worth saying. To one who has done some reading in earlier Councils, this one is unique. Nor have I any feeling that, with the Council dispersed, there is a lack of eagerness to put its decrees into effect. Men grown old in other ways of seeing their Church cannot be simply forced into new, they are entitled to be convinced. And some of those who attack them are not very convincing. In all its history the Church has never changed so much so quickly.

My questioning is of a different sort, whether the Council itself was not too late. I am back to the bus for Bootle which I might have missed that wartime Christmas Eve, and the memory of a lot of buses the Church might have caught through the centuries. The changes decreed in the Church's structure, for instance, were vastly valuable: it would have been a solidly constructed building. The trouble was that too many of the tenants had already moved out.

I have already mentioned the difference both Trent and *Rerum Novarum* would have made if they had come before Luther, before Marx, instead of after. I remember vividly the days before the vote on the *Declaration on Religious Liberty*. We were in Rome at the time, and every day we met the declaration's sole begetter, Father John Courtney Murray. From day to day his hopes shot up and down like a temperature chart. Towards the end he was close to despair. The Controlling Committee, strictly applying the rules, decided that the vote must be postponed. His bliss was something to see when Pope Paul overruled the committee and the vote was taken. I felt it would have been cruel even to whisper my feeling that the declaration would have been earthshaking if only it had come when Catholics anywhere had power to persecute: as it was, who cared? I was speaking shortly after in Hyde Park and had to listen to hecklers mocking the Church for deciding that religious persecution was wrong—in a day when not only had she no power to inflict it but she herself was already suffering it behind the Iron Curtain.

I pause upon Father Murray. Whenever I went to Washington we used to lunch together at the Mayflower. I wonder what the Pilgrim Fathers would have thought of the pair of us. He had been forbidden to write his theories on the ideal Church-State relation. I suggested that he might write not on the ideal, but on what the relation should be *given the existent religious pluralism of the United States.* The resultant book, *We Hold These Truths*, went deeply both into the Faith and into the American Constitution. It was no mere theorizing. I call this present book *The Church and I*. His own book might have been called *America and I*. It was a great personal triumph. At Vatican II the *Declaration on Religious Liberty* was a great personal triumph, too. Not many men have scored two such. But he told me that on his return from Rome his Jesuit students regarded him, and treated him, as "old hat." And this was symbolic of what the whole Council meant to great numbers—it too was already "old hat."

Does this mean I thought that the Council was a waste of effort, that I saw no hope for the Church? Actually it meant only that I was applying human measures, knowing perfectly well that the Church lives by another rhythm than the human. All our calculations can be shattered by the action of the Spirit. We have the prayer, "Send forth thy Spirit and our hearts shall be created, and thou shalt renew the face of the earth." In other words, the Spirit renews the earth by renewing men's hearts. And I see the Council as a renewing of hearts almost without parallel.

But it would be foolish to pretend that just now the situation of the Church looks full of statable, testable hope.

CHAPTER 20

PRESENT DISCONTENTS

I had just listened to a notable warning on the difficulties facing the Church by Archbishop Dwyer of Portland, Oregon. On our way to lunch after his talk we had this conversation:

I: Do you think things are getting worse or better?

Archbishop: I don't see many grounds for hope.

I: Neither do I. My hope is in the Lord.

Archbishop: So is mine. But the Lord hasn't left himself many options, has he?

Earlier in that year I had a conversation with the Benedictine Bishop Butler in London to very much the same effect. And so it went back over the years to the Council itself. I found an excuse to take myself to Rome during each of its sessions, celebrated the Golden Jubilee of my first Communion at the Council Mass in St. Peter's. At dinner tables and street corner cafés I heard inside stories far more interesting than anything that actually happened. I wouldn't have missed any of it, enjoyed most of it, but not often did I come away cheerful. From end to end of the Council I met no optimism, just the feeling that in the long run the Church would come through, a trust in the Lord which had more than an edge of bleakness.

But the Council's documents were not bleak. They make no reference to the vast numbers of Catholics already fallen away, at least from Mass and the sacraments. The sexual revolution was already far advanced, already eating into Catholic life, but it is not mentioned. The explosion within the Church in its full violence only happened when the Council was near its end, but the signs of its coming were there, were everywhere in fact save in the Council's documents.

Apparently the bishops had decided not to diagnose the Church's ills but to write prescriptions for their healing. To change the metaphor, the documents were blueprints of a new and desirable structure. You do not draw warnings in blueprints. But of course blueprints do not build: you cannot live in them.

I

The rebuilding is going on, too slowly for some, too fast for some. What is the state of Catholic life? The answer would be different for different places, but in the Western world the differences would be only in the proportion of the elements making for uncertainty, unrest, discontent. The elements themselves would be the same all over, and in any proportion they devitalize.

The only vitality observable seems to go into attacks on the "institutional Church," or on doctrines long held. Dimming is the word. God is in a cloud not of his own infinity but of man's diminished interest. Christ is in eclipse. I cannot remember when I last heard a sermon on him.

Silence wraps the unnumbered millions of the dead—hell and purgatory tacitly assumed non-existent; heaven, Christ's mother and the saints, the resurrection of the body not much referred to, felt as embarrassments, all of them.

The Church itself has been turned from a teacher into a question mark. These last dozen years there seems to be no assertion or denial that Catholics in good standing do not hold themselves free to make: so that one is left wondering what is the point or even the meaning of membership of the Church. There is a crisis in the mind, a crisis of authority, a crisis of belief. I look back so short a time to the high euphoria of Pius XII's reign. In the Beaux Arts in Brussels, in the fifties (I think), François Mauriac and Graham Greene discussed the future of Christian civilization. I had gone to the meeting wondering if these two rays of sunshine might find anything good to say. In fact they were full of hope. I think they would not see so much that is hopeful now.

But already in that summer of high euphoria there was a dimming of awareness of Christ Our Lord. I approach this matter with a certain shrinking not only because it is gloom-making in itself but because I have written of it so often that my every instinct tells me to shut up about it. It is one topic on which I am sick of reading myself. But the condition of Catholic life cannot be discussed without it.

I lectured on it for the first time in Madras two or three years ago. A Madras paper called it Sheed's disease, not because I suffered from it, but because I had isolated and analyzed it—as it might be

Parkinson's. The disease was this—that Christians who would have been horrified to have their devotion to Jesus questioned did not in fact find him very interesting.

For years before that I had seen that his life on earth was known only sketchily, even by daily communicants! I was once at a dinner party on Long Island with a dozen or so Catholics. One of them, a world-famous tenor, expounded his view that Judas had wanted Christ arrested simply in order to force him to exert his power and overcome his enemies in one stroke: he was not really a traitor at all—he was mistaken in his method, but his motive was good. I mentioned that St. John, who knew Judas, had said that he was a thief (John 12:6). Neither the world-famous tenor, nor anybody else present, knew that John had said this. More recently, I saw no comment by any reviewer of the wildly successful musical *Jesus Christ Superstar*, that St. John's view of Judas had been omitted: to say nothing of the contrast between Superstar's showing of Judas as saying to the High Priests that money did not concern him and Matthew's statement that he asked the High Priests how much they would pay him. In a dozen areas of the English-speaking world I had presented listeners with an elementary examination on the Gospel Jesus—ten or twelve questions whose answers lie on the very surface of the Gospels: the audience answered in their own minds and marked their own mental papers as I gave the Gospel answers. An evening in Dublin stays in my mind. I had given the test, 3,000 people looked glum: thanking me at the end of the evening, the chairman began, "I have just failed a test": 3,000 people relaxed—ah well, if Monsignor didn't know the answers why should they worry?

Only slowly it dawned on me that there was a real fading of their Redeemer into the background of Catholic minds. There was a Catholic way of life, Catholic sacraments, Catholic folkways, Catholic sensibilities (in Mauriac's phrase), a Catholic slant (which a Jesuit assured me his school gave the boys). But Our Lord was less and less seen as the life-giving source of it all.

It took me even longer to realize that there was a dimming of the supernatural as a whole. I never heard a sermon, for instance, on Sanctifying Grace (when I joined the Guild all I knew about Grace was that it was something to die in a state of, but I soon discovered that we could not teach the Faith to our crowds without it). Looking back, I cannot remember a sermon on Christ's relation to his Father. But then I never heard a sermon on the Blessed Trinity—which was finding its only resting place at the end of prayers: and this while non-captive audiences outdoors were gripped by the doctrine of the Trinity as by nothing else we gave them. I had fallen into the way of quoting to Catholic groups the Japanese convert who said, "Honorable Father very nice, honorable Son very nice, honorable Bird very difficult." There would always be a smile from the audience, but no embarrassment about their own inability to say anything more luminous about the One to whom the Son of God committed the world he redeemed.

There was the same sort of pulpit ignoring of Heaven, the goal to which we are all meant to be moving. When the Jesuits at Sixteenth Street in New York asked me to preach at the eleven o'clock Mass I seized on the opportunity to give a sermon on Heaven, so that I should not die without ever having heard one. Three other times I had been invited to preach—at the University of Chicago with a Baptist minister in charge; at the Presbyterian church in East Brunswick, New Jersey; and at the Catholic church of St. Augustine in Larchmont. In all three I talked on the Trinity, as being a doctrine held by all three religions. The Chicago reaction was surprising. Many of the congregation surged up to me at the end of the service: they thought it was a wonderful doctrine and that I had created it. When I told them that the Baptist Church already believed it, they lost interest.

To return to ourselves. I do not mean that any of the great dogmas were denied. It just did not occur to anyone that they mattered. All that mattered was the Catholic slant—which was called the Faith! And it was not only that this was felt to be all that the laity needed. Owing to the journeying life I live, I have read more statements than most people by priests who have left the Church. I cannot remember one in which Our Lord is discussed. Yet he *must* have been at the center of their life as priests, at least when they entered on it.

II

It was within this devitalized Catholicism that the explosion happened. There had been rumblings well in advance, including the revival of questionings which had gone underground when the first Modernists were crushed at the beginning of the century. The great scholars were bringing their great scholarship to bear on them; the smaller scholars were understanding as much as they could of the greater, and could not wait to spring their surprises on a Catholic public which knew precious little about any of it. Suddenly we had the explosion, with no teaching on Faith or morals one did not hear denied by a priest.

The detonator was the Council, not in itself but as reported in the newspapers. We got the impression of a hierarchy split right down the middle, of strings being pulled and deals slipped over in the sort of smoke-filled rooms we had associated with politics. As Bishop Wright phrased it, we were shown it as a struggle between the goodies and the baddies—with Cardinal Ottaviani the baddest of the baddies. And Church dogmas had been hard enough to accept, even when Catholics felt that they came from a united magisterium, guaranteed by the Holy Spirit.

There really was a crisis of authority, which for large numbers became a crisis of belief. The outsider looking in could not be blamed if he saw the Church as ungovernable sheep ignoring unnerved shepherds. A shepherd of untroubled nerve like Cardinal McIntyre of Los Angeles became a national figure.

No, the outsider could not be blamed for seeing the Church so, but he would be missing one element which might in the end be decisive—I mean the Catholic who may or may not be troubled in mind but is unshaken in his conviction that he is in Christ's Church.

In *God and Mammon* François Mauriac describes himself: "I belong to the race of people who, born in Catholicism realise in earliest manhood that they will never escape from it, never leave it. They were within it, they are within it, and they will be within it for ever and ever." Hilaire Belloc was of that race, I think. I too, come to that. There are millions of us, and not only those who were born to it: the Faith can "take" at any age or stage.

What did the changes mean to Catholics of that sort of radical belonging? It would depend, to some extent, on the degree of their understanding of the Church. And by many the intellect had not been much used. But this does not mean that their Catholicism was only routine, their Faith only a surface coating. To come back to Ross Hoffman's phrase that the Faith is not a thesis to be demonstrated but a reality to be recognized, they had recognized it, it was living in them; which means that Jesus was. The eating is not the only proof of the pudding: but no one should be despised for finding it sufficient proof.

The committed Catholic, if he had used his mind on the Church, used his mind on the changes also. He liked some, disliked some but was not profoundly distressed. Those who had not done much thinking might well have found some of the changes unpleasantly disruptive of some settled illusions. Two such illusions were in the atmosphere many a pre-John Catholic breathed—that the clergy were by vocation guarded from sex's temptations; and that whatever came out of Rome was clothed in the Pope's (in fact rather rigidly defined, rarely exercised) infallibility.

No Catholic surely ever heard either illusion preached. They seem to have been there by osmosis. But our leaders knew they were there and did nothing to correct them—on the ground, I suppose, that they did no harm. Harm they did in plenty, not only when they were exploded in these recent years, but even before the explosion. Holding what is not true is always harmful. And these illusions blocked the way to the understanding of sex—especially of the sheer strength celibacy calls for—and the understanding of the papacy—with the Pope's role as guardian and teacher of revelation not grasped at all, only uttered in the mouth. As it happened, when the explosion came, it was at those two points that it was earliest violent—priests marrying, priests attacking the Pope either as too conservative or not conservative enough—in France The Trumpeters of Jericho wanted Pope Paul deposed for liberalism. So uncounted thousands simply dropped out. But the Catholics who remain have got their troubles into perspective, and in the new perspective are more firmly *in* the Church than ever, though not necessarily happy about everything.

III

This talk of "committed," "radically belonging" Catholics is oversimplified of course. The plain fact is that there are profoundly disturbed, deeply unhappy Catholics, who have not left the Church. For many of them the especial trouble lies in the Church's position on sex.

To hear dogmas denied was upsetting to Catholics who had never thought of questioning them. But for those who had known them mainly as formulas, not as seen realities by which they were living, the denial meant no great rending or tearing. The dogmas were not part of their lived life, the sex revolution was a different matter. They knew about sex, they wondered if Pope and bishops did. The conflicts about sex affected them emotionally as dogmatic arguments never could.

They felt that their experience had entitled them to take sides—

on the question of priestly celibacy, for instance. But that was as nothing to the question of contraception. I have already discussed this both as a problem in itself and as the Pope treated it in his encyclical. Here I am concerned with it only as it affects the question of authority and obedience, in fact of unity. A great number of Catholics have made up their minds that the Pope was wrong. Never has an encyclical been refused so categorically by so many practicing Catholics.

The refusal had two elements in it—the conviction that this particular decision was wrong; the question whether moral teaching was the Church's business. People gathered that the encyclical was not an infallible pronouncement. But it was the first encyclical ever issued on which not only would every Catholic be certain to have an opinion of his own, but on which there was solid reason to believe that the majority opinion might be hostile. It might therefore have saved trouble if it had been accompanied by a full explanation of the Church's claim to teach—making clear when her teaching is infallible, and what authority it has when it is not. There was no such explanation. The result has been that an encyclical which was meant to decide a single question of morals has left many Catholics feeling that the Church cannot decide *any* question of morals.

This matter, so much vaster than the question of contraception, cannot be left as it is. Authority must speak a clarifying word. And how will it be listened to? "The moral law is a set of taboos belonging to the pre-Darwin, pre-Freud, pre-Einstein, pre-Hiroshima age." That is the secular orthodoxy of the moment. When we meet it, we should not rush into a discussion of Darwin, Freud, Einstein or even Hiroshima. The key phrase is Moral Law. For the challenge is directed against a view of the moral law which the Church does not hold, and which has no bearing whatever on the one she does hold. It assumes that the moral law is a set of practical rules which men have worked out for themselves over the ages—rules which got themselves linked up with religion, grew ossified and are wholly irrelevant to the very new world in which we now live: so that it is high time men made themselves another set.

But man cannot make the fundamental laws of right and wrong for himself, for the almost unbearably simple reason that he did not make himself. As to how anything whatsoever should be handled, *if* the maker of the thing has spoken, then his must be the final word. The thing must be handled his way, because that is the way

he made it to work. If man had made himself, then he would reasonably decide how best to handle himself. But God made man; upon
how men should handle themselves morally, he has in fact spoken.
That is what the moral law is.

If men do not know the rules their Maker has given, then they
must do their best by trial and error—trying a particular line of conduct, seeing how it works, modifying it, scrapping it altogether perhaps. But trial and error have one fatal defect as a method of deciding
what is morally right for men: the decisive trial takes place after
death, where they cannot see it. This life on earth is only the first
stage. Everything depends on the state in which we enter the second.
Christ has said it with almost unbearable clarity: it is better to enter
the next life blinded or maimed or crippled through obedience to
God's law, than be cast, sound in body, into the fire that does not
die. He said this, we remind ourselves, in special reference to one
whose eye had caused him to look at a woman and lust for her.

And there is another here-and-now drawback about the method
of trial and error—namely that the laws of morality *are* laws. Purity
and honesty and the worship of God are as much laws as the laws
of diet. They operate whether we know them or not; defective conduct in their regard will damage men as certainly as defective diet.
In the bodily order God has not taught us the laws; men have moved
towards knowledge as best they can with endless trial and endless
error. But in the moral order God *has* taught us the laws—the results
of damage to the soul being so much vaster. Christ lists for us sins
which "defile a man" (Matthew 15:18), heading the list with evil
thoughts, murder, fornication and adultery and proceeding through
the Commandments. Changing situations may raise problems as to
how the laws are to be applied. Freud, for instance, has led to a
new examination of the degree of responsibility in those who disobey
them. All this demands discussion, but only when the basic question
has been clarified.

Clarification is not easy. The reality of God is growing steadily
dimmer in men's minds, the concept of the laws of morality as
Maker's Instructions for the running of our own selves seems to have
vanished altogether. Even if at odd moments conscience troubles people about what they are doing, words like "taboo" have reduced the
authority of conscience so that it cannot stand up to the pressure
of strong temptations.

The result—as I am weary of saying and my hearers of hearing—

is that masses of people simply have no moral standards. By this I do not mean that they are living in a riot of immorality. Most of them have not the constitution for it, they would be dead in a week if they tried. What I am saying is that they have no moral *standards*: when they are tempted to some sin they feel they *can* manage they have no principle to test its rightness or wrongness. In the long run they can only follow their own inclination.

Neither in this nor in any other field is inclination likely to produce right conduct. Does it, by chance, produce happiness? All the evidence says that it does not. The sin gets a stronger and stronger grip, the compulsion always harder to resist, the pleasure smaller and smaller. The moral muscles get flabby from want of exercise, there being no exercise in following inclination: and in flabby muscles there is neither health nor happiness. To tone them calls for effort. But unless men see reason to make the effort, they will not make it.

In the known Law of God there is reason to make the effort. Christ told his Apostles to teach all nations to the end of time to observe all things that he had commanded them: and they had from him a divine commission to "bind and loose," a phrase of the rabbis for declaring what was forbidden and what was permitted. As a Christian one cannot handle oneself as though Christ had not spoken.

Meanwhile, whatever may be decided on the question of principle, we have the fact—that a very considerable percentage of young Catholic men and women, the parents of the next Catholic generation, are practicing birth control. How Catholic is that generation likely to be? As we have noted, the encyclical does not actually say that those who contraceive must not receive the Sacraments. If they cannot, there seems small chance of their bringing up their children to receive them.

IV

We have been talking of Catholics who are upset at finding illusions shattered, illusions which they would not have had if their minds had been healthily in action: to adapt an old phrase, reality makes a bloody entry. We have been considering Catholics who are wondering what right the Church has to teach them morals. But there are Catholics in plenty who are criticizing the Church not from unhappiness over a lost euphoria, or from a desire to make their own moralities, but from a clearly statable view of what they think it should be doing and isn't. Their complaint is that the Church's rulers, even the best of them, live in an unreal world, with the healing of Christ not applied to the real world's real needs.

Pius XII, they say, was writing on the Mystical Body and on the Liturgy, with not a word on the millions of Jews Hitler was slaughtering. Paul VI was bothered about Contraception and Clerical Celibacy and his own authority, while thousands were being slaughtered in Vietnam. And it is not only at the top that they find this ignoring of reality—almost everywhere the poor are being exploited, almost everywhere they see the rich honored by the Church, sought after by the Church, as they never were by Jesus.

I am stating the case as put by the critics. For myself I should be prepared to defend both Popes: but my concern here is not with this or that detail but with the larger question of whether the Church should be *primarily* concerned with the cleansing and perfecting of this world. That is a question on which every Catholic is forced to use his mind.

The difficulty is that we have so little practice in using the mind— most of our decisions are made by feelings, imagination, wishes, prejudices. The air is filled with the clamor of extremists, the avant-garde who attack, and what we may call the derrière-ditch who defend. And the manner in which the discussion is conducted does not help. In a general way, the last-ditch men rage and the avant-garde sneer. I know, because I have been raged at and sneered at. My book *Is It the Same Church?* was called a nightmare by a critic on the left; a rightist said it was only the second book he had burned in his life; for my consolation a more central reviewer praised it as "rich in theological butterfat" (he lived in a dairying district). And two reviewers expressed pleased surprise at finding that I did not seem to be angry with anyone.

What is strange is that extreme right and extreme left have no desire to talk with each other. In one week I gave a lecture to the *Wanderer Forum* (definitely rightist people) and published an article in the *National Catholic Reporter* (then very much to the left). I was attacked by partisans of each for giving my views to the other. I explained that I am prepared to talk to anyone who will listen to me, but see more point in talking to those who differ. I suggested that it might be a good idea if the two editorial boards would lunch together at regular intervals. Everyone assumed that I was joking.

One meets the sneer everywhere. A priest, leading the struggle against the Vietnam war, described Dorothy Day's work for the poor as "putting a Band-Aid on a cancerous world"—all because only the revolution matters and relieving human misery tends to postpone the revolution. Another flipped aside contraception, abortion and infallibility as "Mickey Mouse questions," because they did not seem important to him. "Abortion" comes strangely here. I wonder how Mickey Mouse would cartoon the million infant Americans slain in the womb in the Eastern United States alone during legalized abortion's first year—Vietnam's slaughter does not match that.

So in our effort to use our minds on the issue of this-worldliness and other-worldliness we are not much helped by the most articulate partisans. And there is a difficulty within ourselves: this world is so very evidently present, catching our attention through every bodily sense and appetite: the next world *seems* so very next! One result is that between the views in conflict those who maintain the great spiritual realities—Trinity and Incarnation, Redemption and Eternal Life—get no assistance from our day-to-day experience of living.

No one who remains in the Church will deny the primacy of God, for instance. But God does *not* demand our attention, and even when (briefly, too often) he gets it he does not "display" his attributes in any very eye-catching, appetite-catching, way. I may be wrong in thinking it is through sheer boredom with God that many of our leading writers and speakers have given themselves heart and soul to social issues as if nothing else existed. At any rate, I am not wrong in thinking that it takes less mental effort to hold an audience on the world's agonies than on eternity's promises: it takes a vast mental effort to see, and an effort still vaster to make an audience see, that the healing of the world's agonies depends on man's response to God's revelation.

Since not a sufficient number of the people we read or hear will make the effort for us, we must make it for ourselves. Our effective membership of the Church depends on our idea of what the Church exists to do. And the final authority on that is the Jesus who brought it into existence. We must find out what he had in mind for it.

What, for instance, did he actually do for the poor? He only says it once—"Tell John the Baptist that the poor have the Gospel preached to them." If anyone thinks this is just the old pie-in-the-sky stuff, he is a long way both from the mind of Jesus and from the elements of the human situation. About Jesus and about man he is an unsophisticate.

PART TWO

REFLECTION ON EXPERIENCE

Part One is a recording of remembered experience, what I saw not how I judged it, photography not commentary. No one can turn himself into a camera, of course, but at least I have invented nothing and evaded nothing.

Part Two is more of the computer kind. Life has fed these experiences into me, what do they all add up to? How do I see the Church itself?

An increasing number of Catholics find the Church as they meet it a trial to their Faith: it is no trial to mine. I know more than most about its day-in-day-out reality, yet not only can I not imagine myself outside it, I delight in being in it.

No one reading Part One, I think, will regard me as starry-eyed. Here is Part Two.

CHAPTER 21

THE JESUS REVOLUTION

I

When, a few years ago, the Church established the Feast of Christ the Worker, there were those who felt that it was at last taking a cautious step in the direction of its Founder's word that a rich man could get into the Kingdom of Heaven less easily than a camel through the eye of a needle. Jesus, they felt, had been a proletarian revolutionary, whereas the Church had linked itself with the rich, the Establishment. To those who saw it so, that first step was so very cautious as to be a mockery, the Church was still bothering with the world to come and ignoring the agonies of the world in which men actually are. At the turn of the century, Joe Hills had put the Christian answer to the starving savagely into his "Pie in the Sky" song. More and more Catholics were coming to feel that Joe Hills, not the Church, was speaking for Christ; and they noted that the Establishment executed Joe as an earlier Establishment had executed Jesus.

Now, it is true that Jesus attacked the rich. But it was not for their exploitation of the poor that he attacked them: it was precisely for thinking only of this world and ignoring the next—"laying up treasures on earth where moth and rust consume, instead of in heaven" (Matthew 6:19–20). There was a rich man complacent in his wealth: but God said to him, "Fool! This night your soul is required of you. And the things you have prepared, whose will they be?" (Luke 12:20). The Old Testament speaks of the fool who says in his heart there is no God. Jesus reserves the word for the man who forgets that he must die. I can find no hint of Jesus as a proletarian revolutionary. His criticism of the rich is always for the harm their wealth does to themselves. "Delight in riches chokes God's word in them so that it proves unfruitful" (Matthew 13:22)—in other words, wealth sterilizes. In the parable of Dives and Lazarus, the rich man had not exploited Lazarus, simply been heartless about him, gorged while he starved: what he was punished for was giving himself totally

to this world's pleasures. To ignore the suffering of the needy is the
way of damnation.

We hear from Jesus no condemnation of the social-economic
structure, any more than of the Roman domination of the Jewish
homeland: he did not lead any Palestine Liberation Front—there
was one but he never mentions it. Into our heads floats perhaps, "He
put down the mighty from their thrones, and exalted those of low degree" (Luke 1:52), but that was his mother speaking, not himself.
Peter did indeed tell the Jewish crowd that "Jesus had healed all who
were oppressed"—but oppressed by what or whom? "By the devil"
(Acts 10:38). Exploitation and conquest were symptoms of a deeper
disease, a disease in the depths of men's very selves. To the healing
of that Jesus gave himself wholly. Those other evils could not be
healed till the self was.

It was the same with his immediate followers. Only in the Epistle
of James (5:4) do we meet "Laborers mowed your fields and you
cheated them . . . the cries of the reapers have reached the ears of
the Lord of the world." James too had clearly meditated on Jesus's
words about rust and moth, "Your riches have rotted and your gar-
ments are moth-eaten. Your gold and silver have rusted and their
rust will eat your flesh like fire" (James 5:2–3).

But James was an exception. Paul and the rest concentrate as Jesus
did on the harm wealth does to the wealthy. "Those who desire to
be rich fall into many senseless and hurtful desires that plunge men
into destruction. For the love of money is the root of all evils" (1
Timothy 6:9–10).

The root was what concerned Jesus and his earliest Church. Render unto Caesar the things that are Caesar's is a sound rule *provided*
you render unto God the things that are God's. Without that, all the
political reformer can do is substitute new Caesars for the old. So
with slavery. It was age-old and universal, but we never hear Jesus
mention it. And we find Paul taking it for granted, sending his new
convert, the runaway slave Onesimus, back to his owner Philemon,
an earlier convert. One feels that he tells slaves to obey their masters
very much as he tells wives to obey their husbands—because that was
how each should behave, things being as they were. But husbands
must love their wives as themselves, Philemon must treat Onesimus
"as a beloved brother, not only in the flesh, but in the Lord." For a
mightier work had already begun on which all other healings de-

pended—in family life, in the life of society as a whole: only in Christ was there "neither slave nor freeman, neither male nor female."

The Roman tyranny over his own people, the exploitation within Judaism of poor by rich—these evils were rooted in the hearts and minds of men. He went to their root. He brought a revelation—that is an unveiling—of God. In that unveiled God men could see life unveiled, could see man himself unveiled, and could set about living by reality thus seen. That in essence was the Jesus Revolution.

For the first time God was shown, as prophets and kings had never seen him, in his own innermost life—an infinite unity that was not solitude, three selves in a community that was unflawed oneness: the Chosen People had known that God loved them, now at last they could say God *is* love. They had come to an awareness that death was not the end: only now could they know of the nature of life after death, and its splendor, with men seeing God face to face and brought to maturity in the seeing.

Men aflame with indignation over the cruelties and injustices all around us might rage against this talk of God unveiled and splendor after death as unbearably remote, utterly callous, theologizing while men are in agony. But if they do, it is against Jesus they are raging, it is Jesus they find callous and remote, Jesus they accuse of theologizing—Jesus who saw love of God as the only sure ground of love of men, and love of men as the ground rule for human living. Tyranny and exploitation are a failure in that: they cannot be cured if it is not.

He knew the hearts of men, knew how instinctively and gluttonously we love ourselves. Reforming political and social structures without healing the individual selves—that indeed is putting a Band-Aid on a cancerous world. The Band-Aid is good and must be used— I mean that we must work for social and political structures that will keep human selfishness more effectually in check; but unless some way is found of working on the cancer itself the new structures will still be cancerous. We must heal individual suffering, as Jesus continually did. But healing the body does not of itself heal the heart: after curing the paralyzed man at the pool by the sheep gate, he told him, "Sin no more or some worse thing will happen to you."

Jesus could be moved to instant compassion by men's suffering. But the cancer in the human heart was what he had come to cure. And the first step in the cure was to *see* reality—God, man, life—as it actually is: "the truth will make you free." But the world he showed men was so new, they could not be quickly at home in it. Its two key

rules were to love God with every fiber of their being, to love other
men as they loved themselves. About their observance of the first
they might have deceived themselves without much difficulty: but
the second poses direct challenges to self every hour of every day. To
see it as a law of the real world is only a beginning: we still need the
strength to live by it.

And it was to give us the gifts of truth and life and union with
God that he came: that men might receive them till the end of time
he entrusted them to his Church. It was to teach about time and
eternity, it was to baptize—baptism being the way of rebirth, birth
into Christ's own life, it was to give men his flesh and blood for the
food of that life in them. This is the Church's primary function as it
was his.

If one sees no value in revealed truth or sacrament and has no belief in life after death, then the Church and its Founder must equally
be dismissed as distracting men from the world's real needs. But in
fact Christ and his Church have brought more healing to the world's
evils than any other agency whatever—precisely because he founded
it to work directly on the cancer. In the beginning the new Church
no more attacked conquest or exploitation than did its Founder.
Three hundred years later, we find Augustine saying that a great
empire was a great robbery: a century or so after that only the Christian bishops defended what we now call civil rights against the new
barbarian rulers; in another century or so the monks were saving
what could be saved of Europe's civilization. But the Church's teaching that in Christ there was no distinction of race or sex or social
condition but all one in Christ was at work from the beginning: Paul
could call upon Philemon to treat Onesimus as a beloved brother.
Cicero had spoken of religious rites which could be desecrated by
the presence of slaves. In Christ's Church no such idea was possible:
by 217 a slave had risen to be Pope, the great Callistus.

So Jesus gave no blueprint for an ideal political order, not even a
thumbnail sketch, not so much as a hint of the shape such an order
might take: only that whoever had to run it must be the servant of
all the rest. He had not come to do things for men that they could
do, or learn to do, for themselves. They must still work out their own
social structures, more or less intelligently, more or less idealistically,
with perfection highly improbable. Utopia, we constantly remind
ourselves, is Greek for Nowhere. "The best laid schemes of mice and
men," says Robert Burns, "gang aft agley," which is a Scottish way of

saying they tend to go haywire. There may be defects of intelligence in the planning. There will certainly be defects of idealism in the functioning—a clutching at personal satisfaction, an evasion of troubling duty. The clutching, evading self is the cancer at the center of all human effort.

It is a truism that no skill in cookery can make a good omelet out of bad eggs. That no skill in sociology can make a good society out of bad men is equally true, but too often ignored to be a truism. It is a mark of their unsophistication that hardly any of the great system-makers seem to have given a thought to it.

Marx, as we have seen, assumed that when the Classless Society arrived men would be as incapable of acting anti-socially as bees in a beehive. But as some humorist (Voltaire, likely enough) has noted, the first bee did not eat forbidden honey: no bee is slothful, no bee is self-important. And it is a very rare man who has no tinge of either: most of us are heavily stained with both—to say nothing of anger, envy, lust and gluttony. It was of the essence of Christ's wisdom that he never forgot it. The whole of his effort was for the healing of the individual self; his concentration upon that was at the very heart of his practicality. He came, he said, to bring men two gifts—truth (John 18:37) and life (John 10:10)—truth that they might see the reality of God and themselves, life that they might live at the level of seen reality. It was to bring these two gifts that he had come into the world: through his Church he will give them to men till the world ends (Matthew 28:18–20). If we do not see them as he saw them we shall make no sense of him or of the Church.

II

The healing of the human disease of self involved Christ's dying. We must bring the whole power of our minds to bear upon Why? It calls for no effort to accept Christ's redeeming sacrifice *as a doctrine*, a document to be kept in the mind's files, not denied but not much thought about, not taken out for close study. Accepted like that there is no light in it for us, no nourishment. We ought to see it as a fact of life, part of the reality in which we do our daily living, like food and sunlight and the probability of sin and the certainty of death. But to see it so calls for a degree of mental effort that not all of us make.

Paul said that if Christ did not rise, we are the most miserable of men (1 Corinthians 15:19). Have we any feeling of what that misery might be? When did we last ask ourselves what actual difference Christ's death and Resurrection make to us? In the answer to that lies the meaning of our Christianity. But there are two principal difficulties in the way, not only of our seeing the answer but even of our thinking the question worth asking.

The first difficulty is that it involves elements—a fallen race, for instance, redemptive suffering, God intervening—for which we have lost the aptitude: life as we share it with our neighbors has its own values and relevances, and these are not among them. It is horribly difficult to convince ourselves that they matter, so remote do they seem, so thin and hard to take hold of: most of us can't state them to our unbelieving friends, or even to ourselves. The second of these difficulties can be stated in one word, Adam. Let us look at him first.

There has come to be a way of so stating the doctrine of the Redemption that what happened in the Garden of Eden was practically the whole story, with what happened at Calvary providing the happy ending. We have just heard Paul say what our state would have been if Christ had not risen: there have been theologians who give the impression that if Adam had not fallen they themselves would be the most miserable of men: that if the Fall fell nothing could stand!

But if any of my readers, stung by my opening remarks, should decide to go profoundly into the doctrine of the Redemption, I would urge him not to begin with Adam. He would probably have learned at school that Catholics are not bound to believe that the earth was created in six days six thousand years ago. But the scientists would also make it hard for him to believe that the whole human race is descended from one couple, harder that mankind began in a paradisal state. He might get so bogged down in Adam and the scientists that he would never reach Jesus at all.

And it is not only the scientists who would bother him. He would discover that after the opening chapters of Genesis the Old Testament barely mentions Adam, and that the Gospels never mention him at all. Paul, in Romans and in 1 Corinthians, is the first we find linking up Christ's redeeming sacrifice with Adam's sin: "A man brought us death, and a man should bring us resurrection from the dead; just as all have died in Adam, so with Christ all will be brought to life" (1 Corinthians 15:21–22). Thus Paul saw Jesus as the Second Adam. But we never hear the Second Adam, nor anyone else in the New Testament but Paul, mention the First. I do not mean that Paul thought it all up for himself, leaving us stuck with it. To the Romans, whom he had not visited, as to the Corinthians, whom he had, he writes of it as something already known, not requiring any special argument. But at least it is clear that by Christ and the early Church the Genesis story was not seen as so essential to the understanding of the Redemption as it has often been made to seem. If we do it in the reverse order, seeing in depth what Christ and the Church tell of redemption, then come to Adam and the sin at the race's origin we shall find the insights of Genesis and Paul truly light-bearing.

The essential of what his dying and rising meant to us and all men can be stated without reference to Genesis. It lies in two clear facts: (1) However man got that way, something is wrong with him: in the best of us there is a muddied mixture of weaknesses and strengths, vices and virtues: the thrust of self mars the relation in which we should all stand to God and our fellow-men; (2) Jesus was different. Redemption means that we are lifted out of the kind of men we are, into the possibility of being the kind of man Christ was: his life principle becomes ours.

Christ lived, suffered, died, to save his people from their sins (Matthew 1:21). If this is simply "believed," filed away in the mind and never adverted to, then it is not alive in us. It does not enter into our decisions and actions. The mind gets no light from it, the will draws no strength from it. Beliefs we don't live by tend to die. If this one needs to be brought to life in us, we must give our whole mind to it. And that means thinking hard about sin, and about mankind, and about redemptive suffering. That all this lies outside our normal way of thinking means not that it is unreal but that we have let go some of our own reality.

Jesus was "the Lamb of God who takes away the sin of the world," said the Baptist. Between men and God stood sin, separating them: at-one-ment was needed (we conceal its meaning, pronouncing it a-tone-ment). Reduced to its simplest terms, Redemption was something Jesus did about sin. So what is sin?

Just as our pronunciation of the word "atonement" conceals its meaning, so the word "redeem"—literally to "buy back"—has actually misled men as to what Christ did about sin. Sin is not the equivalent of money unpaid, but disobedience, ingratitude, perversion in the will, refusal of love. As such it is evil in itself, and evil in its effects—

"The man who commits sin violates order, sin is of its nature disorder" (1 John 3:4).

Each of us commits his own sins, but there is something generic or racial about sin, a root of sin that no one of us is without, what I have called (in *What Difference Does Jesus Make?*) "a *solidarity in sin which is a parody of men's solidarity in nature, the whole race involved in the wreck of things.*" We are not much given to taking account of the human race—all men that ever have existed or ever will exist. It is too big, too scattered through space and time, to strike us as one: we have never seen it, naturally; we have not experienced it; we are not really aware of it. But it would be strange if God, to whom no man is absent, no man more immediately present than any other, in whose image every man is made, for whom no idea is too big, did not see the human race as one single reality. It was the race that Jesus died to redeem, it is as members of the race that each one of us gains or refuses salvation.

Whatever we think of men's solidarity in sin, nothing tempts us to deny their solidarity in nature. From the moment men appear on our planet we never come across anything they say, or do, or make, without realizing their kinship with us. And this applies to their sins as to everything else: about any sinner, any time, any place, we can feel what Jeremy Taylor (or somebody) felt about the criminal he saw being led to execution—"There but for the grace of God go I." Sin has always been a failure in loving, a refusal of love, self-interest having its way not only against God but against what we owe one another.

Christ's life and death were a direct confrontation of sin along sin's whole line. As against disobedience, he was obedient even unto death; as against perversion in the will he placed his "not my will but thine," at the cost of an agony of which he all but died in Gethsemane; as against refusal of love to the end he loved men, asking God to forgive his torturers, loved God, into whose hands he commended his spirit. In him there was no refusal, all that lay between man and God was annihilated.

In him. How did the effect reach the rest of us?

III

In the man Christ Jesus the union of humanity with God was complete. His passion and death had done something not only for the

human race but for himself. "Though he was Son, he learned obedience by the things he suffered; and being made perfect . . ." So we
read in Hebrews 5:8-9.

We should have to be deep sunk in a pious coma not to be startled
by that *being made perfect.* We have met the verb before—"Jesus
knowing that all was now *finished,* said to *fulfil* the scripture, 'I
thirst' . . . And he said 'It is finished' and bowed his head and gave
up his spirit." "Perfect," "finished," "fulfil"—all are the same verb in
Greek. And now, in the phrase "being made perfect," we have it
again, this time applied to himself. Not only his work had attained
completeness but himself too.

If we see God's becoming man only as a theological diagram, then
the notion that there was still obedience for Jesus to learn, perfection
to attain, may come as a shock. But we must never let the diagram
take control. What a Godman can do we learn only from seeing what
Jesus did in fact do. Read what Luke tells us of Jesus at twelve: "He
went down to Nazareth with his parents and was obedient to them
. . . and he grew in wisdom." At the end of his life he "grew" in obedience too. How could one who had never disobeyed learn obedience?
Precisely by suffering—"obedience unto death, even to the death of
the cross." The actual suffering and dying, for which he had always
been willing, did not make him more obedient, but gave a new dimension to his obedience.

It is worth pausing a moment on this. Jesus had said, "Greater
love has no man than that he lay down his life for his friend." But
Paul, surely with those words in mind, said, "If I deliver my body to
be burned, but have not love, I gain nothing" (1 Corinthians 13:3).
Dying is not a substitute for love or obedience: but the love and
obedience for which a man dies gain a last edge of perfection in his
dying, an experienced depth not statable in words.

But it was not for his own perfecting that Jesus died. He died
for mankind. A few months earlier he had said, "I lay down my life
for my flock" (John 10:15). At the Last Supper he had said, "This
is my blood of the new covenant, which is poured out for many for
the forgiveness of sins" (Matthew 26:28). That "many" must not
mislead us: in Jewish usage it could quite normally mean "all." And
so it was here. He died "for all" (1 Timothy 2:6).

And "all" really means all. The utopias in books—Plato's Republic,
More's Utopia, Campanella's City of the Sun, William Morris's
Nowhere, Samuel Butler's Erewhon, Karl Marx's Classless Society—

all begin when they begin, so to speak; they have no place for the dead who went before. But all men that have ever been are associated with Christ's passion and death, only their own refusal can exclude them from his Kingdom. Faith may accept this, though our imagination finds it hard to cope with. But for our intellect the question remains—What connection can there be between Christ's sufferings and our healing?

That Jesus died is no virtue in us. Nor is it any guilt in us that our ancestors sinned. No one will be lost simply because he is born into a sinful race. No one will be saved simply because God's Son died to save all men. Redemption, in Francis Thompson's phrase, is not a machinery to

> Pack and label men for God
> And save them by the barrel load

any more than the race's sinfulness packs and labels men for hell and damns them by the barrel load. Before Christ as after, each man's future depends on the choices he himself makes. "I have set before you life and death, therefore choose life" (Deuteronomy 30:19). That was true when Moses said it a dozen centuries before Christ. It is still true. No man would attain to eternal life if Christ had not died. But no man will attain it solely because he died. We must work out our own salvation: what Jesus did was to change the conditions in which we must work it out. And the essence of the change lay in the new relation of mankind with God—from servants they were to be sons. Earlier we summed up redemption in a single phrase—we are lifted out of the kind of men we are into the possibility of being the kind of man Christ was: better, from the kind of men we are by birth we must be re-born into the kind of man Jesus became by his obedience unto death.

IV

The key word is re-birth. We find it in the account John gives of the conversation Jesus had with Nicodemus (3:5)—"unless one be born again of water and the Spirit he cannot enter the Kingdom of God." "*Do not marvel,*" Our Lord told Nicodemus. Those three words should warn us that something of great importance is coming. Too many Christians ignore the warning, do not take rebirth seriously enough to marvel, or even to look at the words. They are stunning words. Merely by being born into the human race, we *cannot* enter the Kingdom of God. As once-born we are incapable of salvation. We must be re-born.

For the birth was into Christ. Once more our pronunciation conceals a meaning. "Christened" means "Chrīst-ened" and we say it as "crissened," and think of it only as the way a child gets its individual name. We should not go to a baptism as lightly as we do if we heard ourselves saying "Chrīst-ening." Paul told the Galatians (3:27), "As many of you as were baptised into Christ have put on Christ": he had just said, "In Christ Jesus you are all sons of God"—as Jesus was. Observe the phrase "*in* Christ Jesus." It occurs fifty times in these first books of the first Christians.

Jesus did not simply bring splendid new truths about God and man, different new rules about loving your enemies and doing good to those who hate you. The Christian life was not simply to be an effort to live by the truths and the rules. There is a new birth *into Christ:* Christ himself—not his memory, not his example, not his words, but himself—lives in us here and now, to the limit of our willingness to let him.

From boyhood I had carried in my head Wordsworth's lines:

> I've measured it from side to side:
> 'Tis three feet long, and two feet wide.

I had almost forgotten that he was describing a child's grave, so aptly the three-by-two served as a measure to which we so easily reduce the great business of living. We know about vast realities, Trinity and Incarnation and Redemption and Heaven and Hell, we might die rather than deny them; but we all too readily leave them out of the three-by-two, the scaled-down world in which we live our daily life. We can have our personal life of Mass and Communion on the periphery of the three-by-two, without giving any real thought to these mightier realities.

> Our nature is subdued
> To what it works in, like the dyer's hand.

Our nature works in, lives in, the three-by-two, and cannot help being affected by its thought-styles. There is not as much difference as we might hope between the unbeliever who denies Christ's revelation and the believer who never gives his mind to it.

To Christians, thus blandly living along with their world, it can only be a shock if they bring their minds to bear on rebirth into Christ, on Christ living in them here and now, as facts about themselves, facts of the utmost practicality, the very foundation realities of their lives as Christened.

We are of course under no compulsion to think about them. After all Gandhi never mentions them, and in the three-by-two there is no doubt whatever that he was a better Christian than any of us. I'm sorry about Gandhi, but Jesus was a Christian too, to say nothing of Paul and Peter and John. They thought about them. And so shall you and I.

v

Rebirth into Christ, Christ living in you and me *here and now*—life with Christ in God—that is the teaching of Christ, the Christianity of the New Testament. Unbelievers, of course, dismiss it as meaningless. What do we make of it, you and I? We don't think it meaningless, of course: we do not thus flip aside the teaching of Jesus himself, of Peter and Paul and John. But has it any meaning *for us*, any meaning that we feel any urge to unveil? Do we ever give it a thought? We regard it perhaps as the stuff of theology (to which we do not aspire), as edification for the pious (among whom we should blush to be numbered). But rebirth and Christ's indwelling are only stuff for theology (and piety) because they are the stuff of reality. They go to the identity of every mother's son of us.

Christ had not come slumming, then returned where he belonged, leaving men in the insufficiency in which they were born, with no future but to pile up another debt. He offered men real incorporation with himself: it is as reborn *in him*, members *of him*, that we receive what he won for our race on Calvary. "You have been born anew, not of perishable semen but of imperishable, by the word [logos] of the living God." So said Peter in his First Epistle (1:23). We are saved "by the washing of re-birth and renewal in the Holy Spirit," so Paul told Titus.

Birth means entry into life. Rebirth means entry into another life —not replacing the first, but to be lived here along with the first, our main business on earth being to bring them into harmony. It is the whole point of our Christianness, our Christ-enedness. Paul struggles to make clear the incredible thing he is saying. "Baptised in

Christ we have put on Christ" (Galatians 3:27); "If anyone is in Christ he is a new creation" (2 Corinthians 5:17). "Put on the new nature created after the likeness of God" (Ephesians 4:24). In his Second Epistle Peter takes the idea as far as it will go: "We are to be made partakers of the divine nature." It is an astonishing phrase. But at the Last Supper Jesus had said, "I am in my Father, and you in me, and I in you." That is the formula of our redemption.

I make no apology for lingering on these phrases because Paul and Peter and John and Jesus are talking about you and me. It would be eccentric not to listen.

CHAPTER 22

THE CHURCH CHRIST FOUNDED

Dying on Calvary, Jesus said, "It is finished." Something was completed. But something was beginning too, and the something that was beginning was not the paradisal enjoyment by men, either by all men or by an elect, of what he had won for them by his sacrifice —rebirth in him, the Trinity indwelling them. What was beginning had in it vast labor and anguish and the possibility of failure for men, and with work still for Christ himself to do.

At the right hand of his Father in heaven, Christ's priesthood continues as intercession for us (Hebrews 7:25); and in the days between his Resurrection and his Ascension he made final preparations for the continuance of his work on earth. The Holy Spirit would come upon his Apostles, and in his power they were to be Christ's witnesses to the end of the earth (Acts 1). They were to *teach* whatsoever he had commanded them: they were to *baptize*, that men might be reborn into a new life in him. And *he himself would be with them* until time should end.

Christ was not simply establishing an organization from which men might receive these his gifts of truth and life and union with himself by way of doctrine and sacrament, a sort of service station to which they might go for refill or repair. His Church was to be an organism into which we are built that we may live in the full stream of Christ's life. Paul worked this out in terms of a body and its cells. Jesus himself spoke of himself as the Vine and of us as its branches (John 15). Pause a moment upon this. A vine does not decide to have branches, as a business might; not only is there one life flowing in vine and branches, but the vine needs the branches—no branches, no grapes.

I

That in general is how Jesus saw his Church. But just as to know Christ we not only luxuriate in his Godhead but study his humanity, and just as to know redeemed man we must study not only redemption but men, so to know the Church we must study not only Jesus's plan for it, but what in concrete fact it is—as history shows it, as we ourselves experience it. For long enough this study was left to the historians and the sociologists. It goes with the explosion touched off by Pope John that the ordinary Catholic has had it forced on him. Faith comes by hearing, and today many Catholic eardrums seem to have been shattered. One wonders if in heaven Pope John is saying to all and sundry, "I didn't know it was loaded."

The Catholic who comes to it unprepared is troubled to find that the Church does not always look much like his idea of Christ. The heavenly Jerusalem seems such a very earthly—indeed earthy— Jerusalem. It is hard, says Jesus, for a rich man to enter the Kingdom of God; equally it is hard for a rich Church to look like the Kingdom of God. At one time or another the citizens of the Kingdom have practiced every abomination; and not the citizens only but the successors of St. Peter. A study of the Church really can be shattering, but those who do not make the study are doomed, first to an incomprehension of what was in Christ's mind, and second, as a consequence, to a real confusion in their own faith.

From any angle Christ was taking a vast risk, asking for trouble, when he chose to entrust so much to men—considering what men are. To understand the Church we must consider men. It is not enough to examine an architect's plans, we must take account of the building material he is to use. *How was Christ to build an ideal Church out of people like us?*

As a union of matter and spirit—a marriage of two incompatibles if ever there was one—man is unique. Man, as I wrote in *Theology and Sanity*, is the cockpit of a battle, body rebelling against spirit, imagination playing the devil with intellect, passions storming will. The mediaeval stories of men wearing their heads under their arms were not unjustly felt to be pretty startling. But we ourselves, with our intellects so often under our imaginations, our will so often under our passions, are more startling still. The only reason we are not startled is that we are more sensitive to the shape, and therefore to any misshapenness, of body than of spirit. We are the only beings who can either choose or refuse God, can half-choose and half-refuse, can choose and refuse and choose again—and who knows what the issue will be?

As Jesus works in it the Church is an essential support of the Faith, but as its members serve him well or ill it can be a trial to the faith

—uninstructed faith, that is. This uninstruction sounds in the cry we hear against the Institutional Church—Catholics wondering if they ought to remain in the Church they find so corrupt. Think of Institutional Israel, the Chosen People. The prophets tell of gross and abominable wickedness in the highest places: but if all the holy men and women had shaken Israel's dust off their feet, there would have been no Israel left to preserve the treasures God had entrusted to it for mankind's use, no Israel to produce Mary and Joseph and Jesus and Peter and John and Paul, nor men like Gamaliel (at whose feet Paul had sat) and Rabbi Akiba, who in this world did not accept Christ Our Lord.

In fact it never occurred to the prophets to shake Israel's dust from their feet, as it does not occur to me to shake Rome's (at its worst no dustier) from mine. They would have seen that as moving away from God, whose People Israel was: they must cling closer to God and condemn the evils which hindered his purpose. So with the Church. Nothing that its highest officials could do or say would make me think of leaving it. I was not baptized into the Pope, I do not receive the Curia sacramentally. To leave because of them—even if they were worse than their worst enemy thinks them—would be to give them an importance that is not theirs, and to have missed the meaning of my membership of the Church and Christ's headship of it and of me.

For the entrusting of his gifts to the Apostles meant that he chose to bring healing to the world through men who themselves need it: we are helped in the saving of our souls by men who are under no guarantee that they will save their own. By baptism all of us, priests and laity, are born again, Christ's life is in us, the Holy Spirit is indwelling in us as in Christ, we are nourished by Christ himself eucharistically. What is the life doing in us?

It is leavening the lump, the clutching, evading lump that by our first birth we all are. Man's healing is not a single process, complete in one act. The leavening of the lump is a lifetime's labor. The elements in us that the leaven has not reached can play the devil with our best intentions, the leavened elements can come unleavened and contribute to the mess we spend so much time making of our lives.

That is the plain fact about all of us, popes like the rest. We are on the way to the goal, which is heaven. Jesus walks it with us, but not *for* us. It must be our own walking. The life in us is Christ's but *we* must live it. Living it, we grow in it. Jesus learned obedience by the things he suffered (Hebrews 5:8), and so grew to his completeness. We need a lot more bringing to completeness than he did, futility lies in wait for the best of us as never for him.

In the full knowledge of all the ways of man's inadequacy Jesus entrusted to men the conveying of his gifts of truth and life and oneness with himself. Aristotle thought slaves were tools, differing only from a carpenter's by happening to be alive. Christ did not thus make tools either of his Apostles or their successors. He did not search for an elite, but took the men he found to hand. There was Peter, constantly getting himself into situations in which his courage would not sustain him; there were James and John going behind the backs of the others to ask Jesus for the highest places in his Kingdom. Coming down from the Mount of Transfiguration with these three, he cried out to the rest, "O faithless and perverse generation, how long am I to bear with you?" So soon after, he was entrusting his gifts of truth and life to them, promising to be with them till the end of time. So his Church has remained, not an elite but a cross section of the human race. At every stage we feel the same cry must be on his lips, "How long can I bear with you?"—unless, in his ultimate learning of obedience, impatience left him for ever.

It is worth our while to take a longer look at the Church as it came new from his hands.

II

Listen to Paul writing of sins to be avoided—drunkenness, violence, brawling, love of money (1 Timothy 3:3). Very proper, you think. All Christians should avoid them. But Paul was not writing about "all Christians," he was writing about "bishops." He goes on to deacons—they must not be double tongued, not heavy drinkers, not greedy for gain. For deaconesses one is fainly relieved to find him making no mention of drunkenness: but he does find it necessary to say they must not be slanderers. Needless to say this is not to be taken as a portrait of the first officials of the new Church, but only as a listing of faults already to be found among them. Then, as now, and in every age between, the clergy had to contend in themselves with faults which it is their duty to help the rest of us to overcome.

Thus early, indeed, the mass of Christians were uncannily like ourselves. Paul finds among the Corinthians "quarrelling, jealousy, anger, selfishness, slander, gossip, conceit" (2 Corinthians 12:20). He might be describing church choirs one has known. All the Epistles warn of vices to be checked. It is profitable—yes, I mean profitable—to read through some of the longer lists—1 Corinthians 6:9–10, 2 Corinthians 12:20; Galatians 5:19–21; Colossians 3:5.

As we pass from Gospels to Epistles, two vices surprise us by the frequency of their mention—lust, of which Jesus says little, drunkenness, which he barely mentions: Paul, of course, was writing for Gentiles. Sexual sins seem to have been all over the new Church—fornications ("by which a man sins against his own body, which is the temple of the Holy Spirit" [1 Corinthians 6:18–19]), adultery, sodomy, "things done in secret of which it would be a shame to speak." Drunkenness was as prevalent as lust: as we have seen, Paul finds it a peril to priests and deacons; the older women must be warned against becoming "slaves to drink" (Titus 2:3); incredibly, there was drunkenness even at the meal which preceded the Eucharist (1 Corinthians 11:21).

Lust and drunkenness are sins of individuals. What startles us more are the evils which rend whole communities. We meet these again and again in the epistles. Clearly class distinctions had not vanished: "Do not be haughty but associate with the lowly" (Romans 12:16). John tells of rich Christians "who close their heart against a brother in need" (1 John 3:17); James, of obsequiousness shown to them at Christian meetings; Paul, of rich Christians who bring their own food to the pre-Eucharistic meal "to the contempt of the Church of God and the humiliation of those who have nothing" (1 Corinthians 11:22). But on both sides of the class barrier, in have-nots as in haves, is the thrusting self.

We read of anger and strife, quarreling and dissension. Some of it arose from honest difference of opinion, notably about the old Jewish ritual and dietary laws—how far were they binding upon Gentile converts? Upon Christians who had been Jews? But within twenty years of Calvary there have appeared doctrinal divisions, with lying teachers "creating dissensions and difficulties in opposition to the doctrine you have been taught" (Romans 16:17), "perverting the Gospel of Christ" (Galatians 1:7). "Senseless Galatians," Paul cries, "who has bewitched you?" (Galatians 3). He sees such teachers as "puffed up with conceit, knowing nothing, having a morbid craving for controversy and for disputes" (1 Timothy 6:4). Nor was all this mere emptiness and folly: the talk of these men "will lead more and more people into ungodliness, eating its way like gangrene" (2 Timothy 2:16–17).

Jesus had described the worst of the Scribes and Pharisees with their craving for adulation and their love of money (Matthew 23). For the same type among Christians, with a greater concentration of invective, read 2 Timothy 3:2–5: "Lovers of self, lovers of money, proud, arrogant, abusive . . . Slanderers, profligates . . . treacherous, swollen with conceit, lovers of pleasure rather than lovers of God, holding the form of religion but denying the power of it." And note the climax: "They make their way into households and capture weak women." In other words, Dickens's Mr. Stiggins was on the scene very early. And not only he. Sinclair Lewis's Elmer Gantry was there as well. "In their greed," says Peter, "they will exploit you with false words . . . because of them the way of truth will be reviled. . . . They have eyes full of adultery, insatiable for sin . . . hearts trained in greed" (2 Peter 2:14).

What all this adds up to is that the Christians of the first thirty years were as mixed a lot as we have been in all generations since. Holiness was not made by Jesus a qualification for membership, rather the reverse—the just are in less urgent need than sinners. At any given moment the Church seems to be made up of people on the road to heaven, people on the road to hell, and people going nowhere in particular. So it was in the beginning. So Jesus knew it would be.

III

The early Christians were a mixed lot. There were Ananias and his wife, Sapphira, who for love of money lied to the Holy Spirit, Aquila and his wife, Priscilla, who risked their necks for Paul's life (Romans 16:3–4). So the Church has been ever since, not an elite, but a cross section of mankind at its best and worst, with the "crossness" showing at every level, so that not only those outside are often shocked at it, but even its own members can find it a trial to their faith.

We remember the perfect aptness to our age of Matthew Arnold's description of his own—

> Wandering between two worlds, one dead,
> The other powerless to be born.

We may have forgotten his equally notable comment that whereas
other religions seem to attract their own special type, the Catholic
Church suggests "all the pell-mell of the men and women of Shakespeare's plays." What spiritual leader in his senses would choose to
entrust the carrying on of all he had lived and died for to "the men
and women of Shakespeare's plays"? Jesus did precisely that. Had
the Church simply been so many millions who accept him as their
Savior and try to live by his teachings, there would have been no
problem. That they should be a pretty mixed bunch would be in
the nature of the case! But he had a teaching, redeeming, sanctifying
work still to do in the world and he chose to do it through this pell-
mell of Shakespearean characters, branches of a vine that is himself.

Before he died on the Cross he had said, "It is finished." What,
then, was there still to do? We cannot see the answer to that unless
we grasp what it was that was accomplished. We have looked at that,
let us take one more look at ourselves.

In most of us there is a gap between reality as we accept it mentally, and the pared-down section of it, what I have called the three-
by-two in which we actually live our daily lives—family and friends
and enemies, our job, the people we work with or for, financial pressures, pleasures and pains, the up and down of emotions and appetites. In any life money and sex are hard to keep in order; in the
three-by-two they inevitably get out of proportion for lack of anything of their own intensity to balance against them.

Cows, we have noted, seem to have no interest beyond the patch
of grass under their noses. We can let ourselves relapse into a similar
sub-nasalism. This could mean not letting Jesus take our minds off
our own particular patch of grass, testing whatever he tells us by the
measure of the three-by-two. For the three-by-two has its own way
of life. Roughly it is based upon keeping up, socially and intellectually and morally, with the Joneses—a general name for the people
who set the standards and the values, whose approval we want to
win, of whose raised eyebrows or amused smile we live in fear.

In our three-by-two the Joneses are very secular indeed, only the
three-by-two matters, namely the universe that can be reached by
our bodily senses and the instruments which extend their reach. As
much of this as can be directly seen to affect their daily lives is their
patch of grass. Why man exists, why anything exists, what follows
death—with questions so towering they do not concern themselves.
In this area keeping up with the Joneses means staying down with

them. Even if we ourselves believe in God, we don't talk about him to the Joneses, there is something daunting about the eyebrows they would raise.

Into the three-by-two Jesus cannot be fitted: he overlaps it on every side. The parts our Joneses remember of the Sermon on the Mount they approve (not, of course, its five mentions of hell, they had not noticed those). They approve too of his command to love our neighbor as ourself (making their sensible allowance for the element of exaggeration in it!). De-mythologizing they are all for, stripping away the myths—a myth for the Joneses being any word or action attributed to him in the Gospels which the Joneses would not say or do. And Peter's phrase about Jesus "sitting now at the right hand of God, annihilating death to make us heirs of life" would sound to them like mere gibbering, every word of it. You ought to try it on your own Joneses some time.

In the light of all this we should consider what cleansing our minds need, what de-Jonesefying.

IV

Anyone who finds the Church on earth so imperfect as to be no longer tolerable should ask himself solidly, somberly, "How is a perfect society to be built up of people like me?" If he sees no difficulty in that then either he is a person of unique perfection, or he does not know himself very well. Even what we think of as the average decent Christian (you perhaps? me perhaps?) cannot be half-witted enough to think of himself as ideal building material for a perfect social order. And Jesus did not, very definitely did not, build his Church of average decent Christians. As we have just seen, among the early Christians almost every fault people complain of in the Church of history and the Church of now was already in full bloom.

Jesus and his Church cannot be understood at all unless we realize that it was his choice to unite men to himself, and continue his redemptive work, *through humanity*—not through some triply refined essence of man, but through the humanity that actually exists. He took what he found, he still takes what he finds. As I said in *Theology and Sanity*, there is a thoroughgoing democracy about salvation. Most of the Kingdom's citizens get in as babies and you cannot test babies as to their moral fitness for baptism. Nor for those who enter later is there any intelligence test or character test. I remember telling a woman who hesitated to join the Church because she was an alcoholic, that alcoholics are far better off inside the Church than outside. By the same reasoning, in a long correspondence, I persuaded a nymphomaniac to remain in the Church.

To continue my raid on *Theology and Sanity*—there are "spiritual" types who find the idea revolting that Christ should be sanctifying them in and through the ragtag and bobtail that in so many times and places the Church looks like: but this is to mistake refinement for spirituality. The hot smell of humanity is too strong for them. They would have their own direct relation with God, high above the muddied turbulence of humanity; or they would choose for companions on their spiritual pilgrimage the sorts of men and women they feel that God would choose. But this is folly. It is as though the man whom Jesus healed by the touch of his spittle had said— "Please, Lord, not spittle—so vulgar, so unhygienic." One must not be thus delicate about the gifts of God. But then one meets Christians who find Jesus himself too earthy for them—their salvation must set him quite a problem. Jesus anyhow had not their contempt for humanity: he chose to redeem mankind, not from above, but from within. He identified himself with men in man's fallenness: now he calls sin-damaged men to identification with himself in all his own suffering-won completeness.

So there were two incarnations—his own and his Church's. As Dawson puts it—"A religion must become incarnate in human culture, and clothe itself in social institutions and ways of apprehending reality if it is to exert a permanent influence on human life and behaviour."

Either way—choosing to be man, choosing to work on through men —Christ is true to the logic of his choice: and each choice sets the same sort of puzzle. Seeing him bleeding, thirsting, dying, the onlooker can feel only that he is a man with the limitations of a man. Seeing him raise others from the dead, seeing himself raised from the dead, how resist his claim to divinity? So with the Church: in the area Christ has guaranteed—the teaching of revealed truth, the promulgation of the moral law, the giving of life through the sacraments, the union with Christ's heavenly intercession in the Mass— it passes the human measure; in the running of its public life by its officials, in the living by us its members of our daily lives, it can startle and shock. If we are ever shocked to the point of no return by its officials, we should take another solid, somber look at ourselves: the same Christ who bears with us has to bear with them.

This is the logic of his choice. The Church's members, the Church's officials do not cease to be men, each of us with his own salvation to be worked out in fear and trembling. Paul told the Galatians (4:19), "I am in travail over you, until I can see Christ's image formed in you"—so that the Christian prays, "Make me less like myself, less unlike you." The same Paul said of himself that he castigated his body lest he who had converted others should himself be cast away.

Why did Christ decide on a choice so improbable? What must he think of it now? If he still cries, "How long shall I bear with you?" at least we can answer, "Dear Lord, you brought it on yourself."

v

What then of the Church's claim that she is not only one and Catholic and apostolic, but holy?

The holiness of the Church is not the holiness of her human members, but of Christ, whose body she is. Every one of us, inlived by him, has a source of holiness available for the taking. As I have told hundreds of audiences, the holiness of the Church is not the sum total of the holiness of all who belong to her, any more than the wetness of the rain is measured by the wetness of all who have gone out into it. If millions get wet, the rain is no wetter: if everyone stays indoors, the rain is no less wet. The Church is holy because it is Christ living on in the world. Its holiness therefore is a constant, neither increased nor diminished by our response.

Every man must make his own. The saints have responded totally, they have exposed themselves to the force of the rain, so to speak, and in their countless thousands they stand as proof to you and me that in the Church holiness is to be had for the willing. In regard to every saint we can say—there, but for resistance to the grace of God, go I.

Even in the eyes of the onlooker the Church is to be judged not by the sinners, not even by the average, but by the saints. That may seem like loading the dice, but it is not. In my early days in the Guild I was proud of an analogy I had thought up. A medicine, I said, is to be judged by those who take it, not by those who throw it down the sink: the Church is to be judged by those who know its teachings, obey its laws, receive its sacraments. The saints have done all these things with all their heart: those of us who have done them partially or not at all are less useful as evidence of their value. As I say, I was proud of this. Then in an unpublished letter of Newman's, which I was reading in the Birmingham Oratory archives, I found my own beautiful analogy, differing only by "out of the window" instead of "down the sink." I remembered what the fourth-century convert Victorinus had said: "Pereant qui ante nos nostra dixerunt"—the devil take those who said our best things before we did.

I should like to go on and on about the saints. The *Imitation of Christ* is a spiritual masterpiece, but it is a small thing compared with the Imitation of Christ that the saints of all the ages have collaborated in producing. "The portrait of a saint," says Clare Luce in *Saints for Now*, "is only a fragment of a great and still uncompleted mosaic, the portrait of Jesus."

Theologians talk of the deposit of Faith; there is this deposit of holiness also for us to draw on. However ill one lives the Catholic life oneself one has the awareness of holiness there. I remember a conversation between Christopher Dawson and Edward Watkin. They were discussing some of the grimmer facts of the Church's history. It was a scarifying experience. After a silence Dawson said, "But there's something there."

Belloc wrote in *Essays of a Catholic*: ". . . Even in these our earthly miseries we always hear the distant something of an eternal music and smell a native air. . . . Within that household the human spirit has roof and hearth." I cannot write like Belloc. I can but say again that the Church has given me truth and life and the possibility of union with Our Lord to the limit of my willingness to accept.

And at a simpler level it has given me my fellow-Catholics. As I began this book a thing I heard Chesterton say, "We're all in the same boat and we're all seasick," struck me as a good text for an account of life on Peter's boat. By now I'm not so sure. Writing the book has done something to me! There is plenty of health around us on board. In fact I find the run of my shipmates takes a lot of living up to.

And the Church never loses its power to surprise. It may be a small shock like that experienced by a man who, kneeling in the confessional in a town he had never visited before, heard the priest's voice saying, "Remember God loves you and I love you." It may be on a grander scale. I once visited a priest in hospital who was all but wholly paralyzed, needing even to be fed by others, in continual pain: to hear him speak I had to put my ear close to his mouth: I learned that every week forty or fifty priests came to confession to him. Newman was right—"This *is* a religion."

CHAPTER 23

THE CHURCH AS WE MEET IT

There has been sufficient Catholic worldliness and heartlessness and sheer wickedness at very high levels to make honest men, drawn to the Church, hesitate about joining it. Where, they ask, does Christ come in? Is it a mere juggle of words to say that the Church of Torquemada and Catherine de Médicis and Alexander VI and Cardinal Wolsey is Christ's?

I

It is no juggle of words. Joining the Church, in adult life or in infancy, we are joining Christ—really joining him as my heart and lungs are joined to me, so that I can live with his life to the limit of my willingness. Similarly joined to him are millions upon millions of others. To them too, we are joined. Some of them are immeasurably better than our own mediocre selves; some seem immeasurably worse—though who can tell? The possibilities of spectacular wickedness that came their way have not come ours. They and we make up the Body which Christ has linked to himself, made his own, lives in. Why has he given himself a Body of this sort? In order that through it he may continue to give to the world his healing, saving gifts of truth and life.

Like us these others are free to make their own response to his life-giving energies, accepting wholly, or with reservations, or not at all. They are not compelled to be good or industrious; they can choose sin or mere sloth: so can we. As members of Christ, great spiritual powers are theirs, and ours, for the taking: but no one is forced to take them.

In so far as any of us fail to unite our will and our actions totally with his, the work he would be doing through his Body is hampered. People—starving for lack of food he wants them to have, food of truth and law and sacrament—are left in their starvation. In so far as any one of us behaves badly, Christ's Body is defiled in the sight of men. Yet it is still his Body: and all the vitality is still in it.

The trouble is that the world, looking at the Church, does not see Christ, it sees only us. We—popes, bishops, princes, presidents, priests, nuns, you, I—are the face he presents to the world, and it does not always attract. A non-Catholic need not be a bigot to dislike the Church and fear it. It may happen that men see the Church as ugly because their own standard of beauty is wrong: like Our Lord she is hated often enough for what is right and true in her. But there are failures too. Men studying the ill actions of some of the popes judge Christ's Church by them and find it repulsive. But most men know little of dead popes: they judge Christ's Church by the Catholics they meet. If that thought doesn't scare you, you are hard to scare.

Christ chose thus to trust his work to men who would do it ill or well, but never perfectly, chose to trust *himself* to men, who would show him ill or well, marvelously well some of us, horrifyingly ill some of us. He knew that there would be failures, yet he chose this way. From the top down, the members of the Church are themselves, with their own weaknesses of vision and will to cope with. The mind of Christ is there for them, but the union of theirs with his may be less than perfect. When Christ told the Apostles that he must suffer and die, Peter protested—protested in the goodness of his heart maybe but, as on the Mount of Transfiguration, "not knowing what he was saying." Victory by suffering he could not grasp: there must be a better way. And Christ said, "Get thee behind me, Satan." In *The Catholic Center* Edward Watkin draws the lesson, "Only when 'Thou art Peter' and 'Get thee behind me, Satan' are alike borne in mind can we understand Church history. They are its double key, the former to its divine, the later to its human aspect."

If it is, as many an honest critic feels it to be, monstrous to associate the Church of Rome with Christ, the monstrousness is his. For he made the association. And it is a genuine association—men are in the Church, true enough; but so is he. The Church has a human element—large, visible, colorful; but a human-divine element too. Certain things Christ guarantees—the truth will always be taught, the sacraments will always give the life of sanctifying grace, the Mass will always present him, once slain now triumphant over death, to his heavenly Father in order that men individually may receive what he won for the race of men on Calvary.

To us, who see the Church from the inside, those things that he has guaranteed are vast, and most surely there. The failures, total

or partial, of the men to whom he has entrusted the dispensing of
these gifts are secondary. Even when, in a given time and place, the
failures appall, they are still secondary. The Church has had such
a long time, such an immense area, for scandals to happen in: it
is hard for the man outside to realize that this is not the whole story,
not even the main part of the story. They have never met Christ
in the Church. We have, even the worst of us. Everyone should read
The Vision of Piers Plowman. Langland sees horrors enough. He can
write, "God amend the Pope who pillages Holy Church." He can
write, not very hopefully, "May Christ in his kindness save the cardinals and prelates." But his own ideal is: "To live a lowly life in the
lore of Holy Church."

With the way in which the Church has carried out Christ's commission, libraries are filled, on two great matters especially—how she
has taught his truth, what she has done with his command of love.

As a test question on the Church's service of love, we have already
looked at the Inquisition, where his love seems to us so hard to find,
though the men who were responsible for it were sure they were serving it. The successors of these men know that love of God can co-
exist with error about some point of his revelation, and that men
who love God must not be condemned for being mistaken about
some element in his revelation. But neither must men who loved God
be condemned for not knowing what their successors would one day
know about men. Christ made willingness to die the proof of love,
and this proof men on both sides were willing to give. May we be
as willing. When a peasant came up to throw a stick of wood on
the pile on which the Bohemian John Hus was to be burned, Hus
said, "O Sancta simplicitas." I should like to be sure of dying in such
perfect charity.

II

Theologians and the Magisterium

What of the Church's service of truth? Upon that the Inquisition
gives us challenge, with one Pope forbidding torture and one impos-
ing it. We are in the presence of the distinction drawn in Chapter
4 between the daily running of the Church and direct teaching.

In 865 Nicholas I had sent his Responsa to Boris, Khan of the
Bulgarians, recently converted to Christianity. He covered a good deal

of ground, mainly sacramental. His statement about neither divine law nor human permitting judicial torture refers to thieves, not heretics—he had already said that no one must be forced to become a Christian, since what is not of the will is of no value.

Innocent IV's bull *Ad extirpanda* (1251) was the act of an administrator coping with a peril actually there and urgent. The administrator naturally concentrates on the situation he has to cope with rather than on fundamental principles. Innocent did not say that his decision for torture grew out of the revelation of Christ. It seemed to him plain common sense. Did he notice the irony? It was in a letter to the Bulgarians that Nicholas forbade torture, to meet a heresy from Bulgaria that Innocent decided to use it.

Practical legislation can never have the weight of direct teaching. We do not equate Innocent's bull with the Responsa of Nicholas which are a careful weighing of principles. And Vatican II's Declaration on Religious Liberty carries overwhelming authority, with 2,000 bishops weighing every word.

What Christ founded his Church for was to bring his gifts of truth and life and union with himself and so with his Father *and* with one another, to all the peoples of the world till the end of time. It was to be the union of men with God in Christ. As Christ looks at it now, how must he compare what it has done after 1,900 years with what he commissioned it to do? The vast majority of the human race—two thousand million, according to Vatican II—know nothing of him. But this means that they are starved of food Christ came that they might have. The value we ourselves attach to the food may be measured by how much their starvation means to us. We give no impression of seeing it as a continuing evil somehow to be overcome.

Part of the overcoming would involve seeing why the commission he gave his Church has been carried out with such very moderate success. We have already discussed one reason—the failure to mobilize all the Church's resources, the millions of the laity not used to reach the innumerable millions with whom, as the Council mentioned, they alone are in touch.

But even if they had been used to the limit, there would remain the deeper reason that Christendom cannot speak with one voice on a single point of what Christ brought to the world. Whatever else one may feel about the value of the Reformation Luther began, it means that the world to be won is offered a dozen different Christs and variants beyond counting of his teaching. Till recently one Christian body at least, the largest, could give one teaching through all its teachers. It cannot at this present moment.

Teaching does not mean repeating without error whatever Christ is reported in the Gospels as having said and done. He did not give the Apostles his truth embalmed to be handed on embalmed. It was meant to live in men, and grow in them. Primarily it grows by being lived—prayed; obeyed, disobeyed; doubted, accepted; rejoiced in, suffered in. It becomes an organic element in the people who live it.

This living of the truth is the primary way of its growth. Exploring is another. The human mind cannot simply be given a mass of truth to be held unexamined. It tends to sort out elements in the doctrines and find their bearing on one another. New interpretations are suggested, offered, quarreled about. New situations arise, new civilizations indeed, to which it must be applied, in which it must be lived. Philosophy, psychology, archaeology, the natural sciences are making their own separate exploration of man and his world, shedding light which in its first shedding can seem more like darkness, forcing the Christian to reconsider what he has assumed revelation to be saying.

At the heart of the growing process is the problem of language. What the Church comes to see must be uttered, stated in words. Otherwise it cannot be communicated. The realities thus communicated may and should vibrate to the depth of our being, but we cannot communicate solely by vibrations. *Cor ad cor loquitur* indeed, heart speaks to heart, but not only by heartbeats. "I would rather speak five words with my mind in order to instruct others," says St. Paul (1 Corinthians 14:18–19), "than ten thousand words in a tongue" ("speaking in a tongue" was one way of vibrating!).

So statements are necessary, but necessarily inadequate. There must always be mystery. We cannot know God as he knows himself, cannot even know ourselves as he knows us. The ultimate realities are unutterable. Yet God has uttered them. Utterance which brought them to birth in men's minds must operate in their growing.

Words can be light-bearing. But there is a danger in them. Men can grow too much attached to forms of words, seeing them as absolutes. A phrase apt to one culture might be pointless in another. "If Paul had gone East instead of West," I wrote towards the end of the Council, "our theology would have been phrased differently. If Augustine had drawn on Sankara instead of Plato, if Aquinas had 'baptised' Lao Tse instead of Aristotle, we should almost certainly have had today's avant garde bewailing the Asian stranglehold and clamoring for the Greeks. As it is, some theologian yet unborn may marry Christian theology to Asian thought forms, to the horror of his more conservative contemporaries."

The *living* of the revelation is by everybody. The *intellectual exploration* is largely for scholars—theologians in particular. As someone has said, they are the antennae with which the Church "feels" modern life and modern thought, drawing on the researches of Scripture specialists, linguists and philologists, comparative religionists, scientists of every sort. New interpretations swarm in vast quantity, of varying worth. "God's desire to be known by us," as I said in *God and the Human Condition*, "has at all times to cope with the marvelous ingenuity of the questing, discovering, uttering mind of man."

How is all this—the daily experience of Christians, the discoveries and theorizings of the learned in their bewildering multifariousness —to be tested against Christ's original revelation? How is it to be shaped teachably and conveyed to the millions of unspecialized men and women?

God, having given the revelation, did not simply leave it to take its chance. It is the function of the Church—Christ living on in it— to guard the integrity of the revelation and shape it teachably. With so many minds actively at work, changes are forever being proposed, some good, some bad, some enriching, some damaging. There must be a voice to say Yes or No or Wait. Otherwise there is no revelation, only a chaos. Authority is necessary not for itself but for the treasures it guards. And Vatican II makes it clear that the work to be done will be even vaster than we knew. For it has said that the differing theological formulations of the Eastern Orthodox Church are "complementary" to our own: these too are to be drawn upon for our enriching; and it has placed a new value for the understanding of revelation in the discoveries made in fields not directly religious, on the principle that every new truth learned about creation sheds light on the Creator.

How well has the teaching Church, the magisterium, carried out its double function of guarding the treasure and dispensing it? Guarding involves not only *censorship*, watching against adulteration by falsehood, but also *stimulating*, encouraging the forces of life and of growth in it. There is not much doubt that over the centuries the censoring has been done with more zeal than the stimulating. Authority can only too easily cross the line into authoritarianism. The law of charity is harder for officials to live up to than for the rest of us, even in normal times. In panic times—as at the Albigensian thrust and the Reformation earthquake—charity has a tough time. Rigidity, excusable perhaps in the crisis, becomes a habit which survives the crisis, to the peril of love, which is at revelation's heart. There is pleasure in the exercise of authority which only high sanctity can resist. Rigidity can come close to rigor mortis.

Meanwhile the theologians are continually at work, to the irritation often enough of the magisterium. If the danger of the official is rigidity, the danger of the theologian is self-confidence. There is no love so blind as that of the scholar for his discovery, *because it is his*. Copernicus, for instance, knew that one of the fourth-century Greeks had seen the possibility that the sun is in the center and the earth rotating—but he left this piece of knowledge out of the final statement of his theory.

So the theologian finds himself raging against the officials who do not love his baby as he loves it himself. Indeed his confidence in his conclusion leaves no place for past or future decisions of the magisterium, only in freedom from which does he see any hope. But, after all, Protestants have every conceivable freedom and they are hardly setting the world on fire. Like ourselves, they are speaking to fewer and fewer. Theologians are not necessarily right, or even necessarily bright. Today a theologian is anyone who calls himself one. I wonder at the nerve of some of them. But in a general way the theologian *is* abler intellectually than the official, and he can point to occasions where the officials have no reason to be proud of their performance. There is not only the Galileo case. Some of the statements on the Eucharist that Berengarius was called upon to sign in the eleventh century are pretty startling, good as the final one was. Certainly some of his rigidly orthodox opponents had stranger ideas than his own. And with all their special skills the theologians can differ from one another as violently as from the magisterium. Without the teaching Church, the whole sky would be filled with brilliant bits and pieces, and the mass of ordinary men would remain untaught.

But it was to the mass of ordinary men that Christ brought his healing, his redeeming, his light and life giving. Certainly an individual theologian treated unreasonably by authority (we talked of that in Chapter 13) stirs one to genuine sympathy. But his individual maltreatment bears no proportion at all to the vast majority of the human race going on living and dying without the bread of life. Any theologian who does not feel it so has forgotten his own shepherdship. Karl Rahner talks of the Church's being reduced to a tiny handful. This would mean not only a few million more added to the millions upon millions already lacking the food our Lord meant them to have, in darkness for want of the light. It would mean also a reduction almost to vanishing point of the Church's power to relieve their destitution.

In the face of so vast a destitution the theologian passes his life. If theology is no more to him than an intellectual game at which he happens to be skillful, it causes him no suffering. But on one for whom God and man are realities, it must weigh heavily—to the point of anguish even, certainly to the draining of the energies of heart and mind for its relief. There is no way in which energies could be more creatively drained.

The theologian is necessary, the magisterium even more so. If only each could see the other's difficulties, neither making a grievance of the other's failure to be perfect, each seeing the limitations in his own vision, each continually conscious that there is no map of the Infinite, that even of the finite there are dimensions beyond the range of men's vision! As Dorothy Donnelly says in *The Bone and the Star*, "the universe is more like a song to be listened to than a code to be deciphered." The decipherers should listen to the listeners, and the magisterium to both.

A dream, you think. Maybe. In cold reality, anyhow, the problem at this moment is that the magisterium has to find a way of protecting and channeling revelation which will rebuild the diminished confidence not only of theologians but of the people of God for whose service both magisterium and theologians exist. Anyone who thinks this problem easy has not understood it.

CHAPTER 24

ON BEING A CATHOLIC

I

We cannot be content to wonder why Christ chose to entrust to men, and such men, the gifts of Truth and Life by which we are to walk the Way which is himself, and leave it at that. We must look long and hard at the gifts. They are ours for the taking. But do we see any point in taking them? Truth, for instance. Men had died for it. What were they dying for? Would we ourselves think it worth dying for?

I have urged, ad nauseam, I fear, the intense practicality of the question, What is life all about? If a man does not know why he is here or where he is supposed to be going, then he can only play his life by ear. The obviousness of this seems fairly to glare at me. Yet people look at me as if insisting upon it were some odd obsession of my own. Certainly I never hear anyone else ask it: even the existentialists I know are not sufficiently interested in existence to ask what accounts for it.

If having heard the question, a man says he does not care why he's here or what follows death, one's temptation is to say, "Neither does a cow." The temptation must be resisted. If he really doesn't care what life means, it's his privilege—a very stunting privilege, blocking maturity, but definitely his. It is not a crime to be mentally retarded.

But there is another reason for leaving the cow out of the conversation—namely that a man does not always mean what he says. Long ago in Sydney I said something (I've forgotten what) that maddened a Communist. To soothe him a friend said, "Don't take it so seriously. Sheed didn't mean what he said." The Communist answered, "Sheed doesn't even mean what he thinks." However, about me, it is a fairly common human condition not to mean in depth what one thinks one thinks.

The college student who sings, and smiles as he sings,

Why was I born so beautiful?
Why was I born at all?

is not, of course, actually asking either question. If one pressed him on the second, he might shrug away the question as no concern of his. But the shrug may not be the last word, so to speak. There might well be a need—half felt or barely felt, but there—for something better than the surface of things: the widespread interest in astrology, in the occult, in demonism, must mean something like that. H. G. Wells's street arab is not the only one "in love with unimaginable goddesses"—and these are not always, or only, the lovely ladies of Mohammed's Paradise. A shallow man is not a man without depth but one who has lost contact with his depth; what exile could be gloomier? Even the Joneses—the ones we try to keep up with—can have rare moments in which they know torment from the loss of contact, and feel out towards what they have lost.

The fads of the day, like the philosophies of the day, are all efforts to fill the gaps left by the fading out of Christ's revelation. The fading may mean revelation totally rejected; it may mean its shadowy survival in consecrated phrases with no vital equivalents, words from which the blood has been siphoned out. Either way the man is in peril of living towards nothing in particular, a half-hope. In *God and Mammon* François Mauriac writes: "What stands out most vividly for me in the colossal and putrescent work of Proust is the image of a gaping hole, the sensation of infinite absence, and it is this chasm and emptiness—the absence of God in fact—which strikes me most about mankind according to Proust."

Proust apart, putrescence apart, it is not a bad picture of mankind today—"a gaping hole," "chasm and emptiness," God not necessarily denied but not adverted to. According to the amount of vitality still left in each individual, this may mean sheer despair, or apathy, or even a low-level contentment with things as they are. A universe ultimately meaningless can be mapped by science, its meaninglessness rationalized as philosophy. Science, philosophy, ideology are three ways of playing life by ear: for neither the philosopher nor the political reformer even pretends to know why the universe exists or where the road of life leads, and the scientist actually builds his system out of not knowing.

Christ, and only he, throws light upon life's whole meaning. But a Christian can settle into a routine—of truths not denied, sins repented, Mass attended, sacraments frequented—without a thought of life's whole meaning, or of the luxury of living in the light. The pious coma in which we tend to read or hear Scripture can spread its protective cover over the whole of our life in Christ. Yet every so often down in the piety something stirs. No grace could be more actual than the stirring. It would be a shame merely to wait till it passes off.

When Jesus told Pilate that he had come into the world to bear witness to the truth, Pilate said, "What is truth?" Jesus might well have given his favorite enigmatic answer, "Thou hast said it"—a way of saying that the words of the question contained the words of the answer. What is truth? Truth is what is. Is-ness is all.

But of course Pilate was not asking for a philosophical answer, or indeed any answer. His "What is truth?" was not a question. It was a contemptuous dismissal of the subject, equivalent to "Pouf! Is that all?" In every age this has been the reaction of the practical man. In our own it has been set up as a principle, under the name of relevance. For numbers of religion's most articulate spokesmen what matters about truth is not its trueness but its relevance, which means "What's in it for men?" By that test, they find, God does not measure up very clearly.

Well, what *is* there in God for men? For Jesus the universe exists because God willed it into being. Does that make any practical difference? Consider the alternative. If no mind or will is at its origin, then the only answer to why the universe is here lies in a one-word variant of the old drinking song—It's here because it's here because it's here . . . The song can end only in a hiccup. The man who wrote it had no notion that a time would come when masses of Christians in all sobriety could give no better account of their origins. A hiccup would have to be the last word on man and universe alike. What could be less relevant than that?

For Jesus—not only accepting Genesis but giving it new value by quoting the words at the end of Chapter 2 as God's—God is at our *origin*, so that men are not merely accidents that happened to happen. And he shows us God as our *goal*—men are to reach the fullness of their maturity in fullness of union with him. This life, I need hardly remind you, is a road, not a dwelling place: we are all going, not staying. The believer knows why he is on the road and where it leads: nobody else even pretends to. But to be on any road, and not know how one came to be on it, or where one is supposed to be going— that precisely is to be lost.

This is the lostness which we hear in the cry of the present generation for "identity," which has edged ahead of "relevance" as today's hit word. It is a genuine cry, a sure sign of the felt emptiness which is the other face of lostness. Yet in itself, while it utters the emptiness, it does nothing to fill it. The cry for identity can be only a kind of baying the moon, and what good does a dog ever get from that? If no mind meant the universe, a meaninglessness wraps all: whatever meaning men choose to allot themselves is only a transient flickering: if this or that individual does find something he can call his identity, he won't have it long: darkness awaits him—if no mind meant the universe.

For myself, accepting Christ as teacher, I know who I am, what I am, why I am. I know my relation to God and to Christ, to other men therefore. I know what life is about, where I am supposed to be going and how to get there. I know the shape and texture of reality. If "identity" is something over and above all this, I am not conscious of missing it.

Seeing reality thus does not make life all cozy and comfortable, with every question happily answered, the will happily at peace. The clutching, evading self still has to be coped with. Sin loses none of its attractions, duty none of its bleakness. Life is still a battle. But in any battle, to know what the fighting is about and what victory means, is an immeasurable advantage—indeed immeasurably relevant (if a believer may make bold to use the word).

This is the situation (the *Sitz im Leben*, if I may wax even bolder) of everyone who accepts Jesus *as teacher*. Why do I emphasize those two words? Because there are Christians who de-emphasize them to their own loss. In their depth, so they feel, they respond to Christ in his depth: the words in which teachings are uttered belong, so they feel, only to the surface. To such people Christ is an inspiration, an atmosphere, but not a teacher. We shall look more closely at them.

By faith the old type of fundamentalist meant that he accepted Christ as his personal Savior. He was sure that nothing else really mattered: he was saved. (I have quoted one of them who said to me, "I couldn't go to hell if I tried.") Discussion of Christ's Divinity, Father, Son and Holy Spirit, Sacraments—he brushed all that aside as mere theology (and what, he implied, could be merer than theology?). That, you may feel, narrows Christ's relevance pretty considerably.

But it is not the end of narrowing. Today there are those who find any formulation in words—even "personal savior"—an offense to the liberty of the Christian man. Christ is to be "felt," vibrated to,

but not actually listened to—save as particular sayings of his strike a
chord in them. The chord is what matters. In tune with him they
make their own religious and moral decisions, aware of no need for
his revelation. But the glory of the Christian, as Paul said in his first
letter to the Corinthians (2:16), is to have "the *mind* of Christ"—
in Greek the *nous*—that in him which did the knowing. To have his
mind is to be living mentally in his world, seeing the same universe
that he saw.

For there really is a shape of Reality, a map of Reality, and we can
know it only by Christ's telling. However much in tune with him a
man may feel, without Christ's words he cannot know Christ's
world. The words are only a beginning of light, but an indispensable beginning: words are not only conventional symbols, they have
energies of their own, they can deepen feeling and clarify thought.
We grow in our understanding of them, but we do not grow out of
them, rather we grow *with* them into the mind of Christ.

Without them the Christian is left to make his own guesses about
what God had in mind in bringing men into existence and what is
his design for them. A man may be positively vibrant with Christ,
certain that what he feels must be what Christ felt. But like everyone
else he needs to know what Christ *knew*: feeling attuned is no substitute for being informed.

Knowing what Christ has revealed about God and man, about life
and death, he will be living in the light. And he will be saved from
the danger of becoming his own Christ, saved too from the danger
(against which Paul warned all Christians) of "being conformed to
the fashion of this world," living in the mental atmosphere of the
age, with perhaps a tincture of Christ to add a comforting illusion of spiritual quality. To quote myself, he may be wearing Christ
as a flower in the buttonhole of the same kind of suit that everyone
else is wearing. So may anyone who is not constantly growing into
the thoughts of Christ.

The Christian must be prepared to look odd, to be thought eccentric. He has necessarily to be out of step with a generation going
nowhere in particular. He must be prepared for loneliness. Outside
the Churches he will not find any, even inside them he will not find
many, who have wholly accepted, for example, Jesus's teachings on
the relation of life on earth to life after death. Having given up the
heaven of harps and hosannas, too many have switched their minds

off the next life altogether—not actually holding it to be a fable, only acting as if it were.

A man who, having given his best mind to what follows death, is unable to accept survival is, as I think, in error, but honorably. Whereas to believe in it yet give no thought to it is to be, if not half-witted, at least only half alive mentally. What follows death ought to be a primary concern, if only because we shall be such a long time dead.

The difficulty of course lies in realization. In a moment of vision Mohammed saw this life as no more than the beat of a gnat's wing in comparison with eternity: the power of his realization has affected the lives of hundreds of millions ever since. How much does the same truth, which we too are by way of accepting, affect even our own life, yours and mine?

With the force of a gnat's wingbeat, perhaps. We tend to react, not according to the mightiness of the reality but to the immediate pressure of things. Now is so inescapably now. Here is so damnably here—or gloriously maybe, anyhow here, not in some future else-where. But maturity lies in a judgment not overwhelmed by the present fact.

II

We have talked before about the vastness of the universe Jesus has laid open to us, about how we would not actually deny any of it yet tend all the same to leave infinity and eternity out of account in our daily living. The result is that for practical purposes we find our-selves confined to the same scaled-down three-by-two world, the world immediately under our noses, as our neighbors.

We have talked too about "the Joneses," the lordly ones whom the rest try to keep up with, whose tastes and opinions set the standards, whose disapproval is at all costs to be avoided. In Chesterton's phrase "when you fall out of the Ark you fall into the fashion"—the Joneses *are* the fashion, "the fashion of this world" to which Paul warns us "not to be conformed." They may indeed be regarded generally as the "persons" of whom Jesus tells us that "God is no respecter."

The Catholic hardly realizes how much respect he himself accords them. He avoids talking about heaven and hell in their hearing, be-cause they would regard Christ's teaching on the next life as gro-tesque. What we may not realize is that his teaching on our life here below would seem to them rather more grotesque than the heaven of harps and hosannas, the phantasmagoria of demons and pitchforks, in which they think we believe.

For we cannot long study the New Testament without realizing that the first Christians saw themselves as having two births into two lives, each life with its own distinct death. To the Joneses what could be more grotesque? But it came fresh from the lips of Jesus himself. Unless one grasps what he said about all this, we simply do not know the elementary facts about ourselves as Christians.

Two lives? There is the life all men have, and the death all men must die. But Paul speaks of another life, not following our earthly life, but to be entered on here and lived parallel with the first. This other life can have its own death, though it is not meant to: "The wages of sin is death," says Paul. In the liveliness of the first life, the sinner may be quite unaware of what has died in him, even if he has heard of the second life: he may be feeling very lively indeed, in a euphoria that could be lethal.

The truth that the second birth was the whole point of Jesus's coming is especially vivid in John. But Christians, we have noted, did not have to wait till John told of Christ's conversation with Nicodemus—a typical "Jones," though he grew magnificently out of it—before they could know why the Church had from the beginning set such store by baptism. Thirty years before the Fourth Gospel, Paul, who had himself been baptized (by Ananias, *not* Sapphira's husband), wrote to Titus (3:5) of salvation "by the washing of re-birth and renewal in the Holy Spirit, which he poured out upon us richly through Jesus Christ our Saviour."

We were born as members of the human race, we have been re-born as members of Christ. When he says, "I am come that they may have life and have it more abundantly," he is not promising longevity, but a different reality of life. And this new life is not something he gives us, as our parents gave us theirs. "I *am* the life," he said at the Last Supper. If he had said, "I have the life," we might have replied, "Please give it to us." But he *is* the life. We can only ask him to live in us.

If only the second life had annihilated or eliminated the first! The trouble is that we have both, with the problem of building them into one. No other integration is so maddeningly difficult.

We have been reborn, reborn into Christ, Christ living in us, we living in him—as a vine lives in its branches and the branches are alive with the vine's life, as a body lives in its cells and the cells are alive with the body's life. This is not a lot of theological rhapsodizing, but plain down-to-earth fact, and of the highest practicality. It is a precise statement of what it is to be a Christian.

Precise—but too precise, you may think, wrapped up too tight, needing to be unwrapped. Why, you continue, warming to your theme, can't we have a plain uncomplicated statement, not needing unwrapping? Religion should be simple. But why, I ask mildly, *should* religion be simple? Only, I suppose, because it would be simpler that way! It would spare us "the insupportable fatigue of thought." There is a general notion that religion is love, and thinking dims loving: a mindless love is a poor thing to offer to God and his Christ —a poor thing even to offer a wife. So we give our minds to the unwrapping.

Birth is entry into life. The rebirth that Christ insists on as necessary for salvation, is entry into a second life, and the key to this second life is that we are indwelt by the Blessed Trinity, as Christ was. Each life has the powers of action proper to it. By birth we have the powers that go with being men—knowledge, love and a host of others; by rebirth we have the powers that go with being indwelt men—Faith, Hope, Charity and a host of others. We speak of Nature—what we are born to—and Grace—a free gift of God over and above. Theologians call this latter "supernatural life," since it carries with it powers to do what by nature we could not. But Faith and Hope and Charity are natural powers of *indwelt* men.

By Faith our intellect has the power of holding for true what God has revealed, not because we can prove it for ourselves but solely because God has revealed it. Hope has three elements—desire in the will for eternal union with God, the knowledge that it is difficult, the certainty that it is possible. Charity is love—love of God and love of our neighbor because God loves him. Charity is from a Greek word meaning love, and it is becoming normal now to speak of Faith, Hope and Love. We see why. For the modern world "charity" has come to mean help for the poor, given often enough without heart and poisoned by condescension. It is the coldest word in the language. The trouble is that the word "love" has been debased too: as I have noted any casual bodily union is called "making love," whereas it should be called "making lust." "Lust" is one four-letter word that seems to have died, "love" has taken over lust's territory. So I am staying with charity.

For one of the richest pieces of writing—not only in all Scripture but in all literature—read what Paul has to say of these three virtues in the thirteenth chapter of his First Epistle to the Corinthians with its wonderful contrast of life on earth and life in heaven: "Now we see as in a mirror dimly, but then face to face. Now I know in part, then I shall know [God] fully even as I am known. Meanwhile faith, hope and charity abide: but the greatest of these is charity." "Make charity your aim," the next chapter begins.

This new life is so real a transformation of the soul that the indwelt man can be, as Paul says, "a new creature in Christ" (2 Corinthians 5:17). Yet it remains the same soul, with the same intellect and will, not destroyed in order to be replaced by some new equipment but interpenetrated, elevated to a new level of life and power. Grace does not destroy nature but is built into it. The intellect has the new power of faith, the will the new powers of hope and charity. An analogy may help. The wire in an electric light bulb, connected with the battery, is luminous: looking at it we seem to see only light and no wire. A man seeing it for the first time might assume that the wire had gone and the light taken its place. In fact it is the same wire, but luminous. The soul of the indwelt man is luminous with the new life, but it does not cease to be the same soul.

After all, this is something of a shock to come to the individual Christian. Luminous, we say? You? Me? Watch us coming out of Mass. We do not look as if we had just joined with Christ in offering Calvary to his heavenly Father. We accept the dizzying realities of the Faith, and are not dizzy.

Consider the first practicing Catholic one meets, oneself would do. He is born into the life of Christ, indwelt by the Trinity, nourished by the Eucharist; he does not look, or even feel, reborn, or indwelt, or eucharistically nourished. Yet all these things he is. The Holy Spirit is at work in him. By Faith and Hope and Charity he has new powers to accept and love God and look forward to eternal union with him; by Prudence and Justice and Temperance and Fortitude he has new powers to handle himself and deal with others as God would have him. Why then does he sin? I have mentioned earlier the questioner who, over a space of forty years, challenged me with, "If I really believed what Catholics say they believe I wouldn't sin. But Catholics do sin. Therefore they don't really believe." How do we answer him? More important, how do we answer ourselves? He was once worrying my wife with the question, "If you believe all you say, why do you sin?" Four times she tried with reasonable patience to discuss the weakness in the will. But the fifth time he asked, "But why do you sin?" She exploded: "Because we damned well choose to." He did not try a sixth time.

The new life in us, the life of Grace, does not give us a new nature. Obviously it does not replace our body with a new body—if a man has a craving for alcohol before baptism, baptism will not remove it. He may emerge from his baptism craving for a drink as never before. Less obviously, but obviously enough all the same, it does not replace our soul with a new soul. Grace has to work in the nature it finds (very much as Christ had to build his Church on the men he found). Paul says that we (himself included) carry our treasure of truth and life and union with Christ "in earthen vessels." The vessels of course are ourselves, very fragile, easily cracked. Grace is a kind of supernature with its own powers of action, but it does not supersede nature. It interpenetrates the nature we have but does not of itself remove its defects. To return to the electric light illustration: if the mechanism is defective, switching on the electric power does not mend it. Increasing the power does not mend it. The mending of the mechanism is a separate matter.

A Catholic who, by the new life into which he has been reborn, has the virtue of Hope may still feel himself close to despair; he has the virtue of Charity, yet may act cruelly; he has the virtue of Justice, yet may cheat his employees. It is not enough to flip the problem aside with a casual "After all, we're only human." We're *not* "only human," we are Christ-ened. We dare not flip the problem aside, it goes to the whole meaning of life here and hereafter.

Look more closely at the powers of action above our nature which we receive with the new life. Theologians call them "habits," and there is light for us in seeing them so. A natural habit—good or bad—is acquired by a constant repetition of certain actions. Drinking too much, for instance, athletic or musical skills, cursing. Supernatural habits, faith and the rest, are not acquired in the same way by actions constantly repeated. They are given in one act by God. But they are habits as truly as the others—real modifications or developments of our nature giving us powers to act in special ways.

So, having two lives, we are in the difficult position of having two sets of habits. With Sanctifying Grace a naturally pessimistic man gets the virtue of Hope—without losing his tendency to pessimism. A naturally lustful man gets the virtue of Temperance, and lust continues to solicit him (as it solicited St. Augustine to the end of his life).

There is no contradiction. Grace gives us power to act virtuously for the love of God. But it does not of itself remove our natural tendency to act sinfully for the gratification of self. So that there is a war within us—two sets of habits in conflict, now one victorious, now the other. Every man's problem is to bring his natural habits and his supernatural habits into harmony. It is rather like a great musician playing on a defective piano. He cannot stop the discords and disharmonies solely by working harder at his music, someone must tune the piano. In the matter of sin our self is the defective piano and only our self can tune it.

The struggle might be lifelong. But we have to face it, all of us, from the highest to the lowest. If you think popes are spared it, you don't know Scripture, you don't know Theology, and you don't know History.

We have been considering the sex appetite as a specimen of a whole tangle of appetites which drag the self so many ways at once. Sexual sins are not the worst sins. Pride, treachery, cruelty are worse. But none of these create in the vast majority so urgent and continuous a craving as sexual sins: examining them we arrive at a clearer understanding of all sins, of sinfulness in fact. And sinfulness we must never overlook—as an abiding reality in ourselves: what Chesterton calls "the permanent possibility of selfishness that comes from having a self." If we think we are without sin we deceive ourselves, says St. John in his First Epistle. Belloc phrased it more colorfully: "My soul is soaked in a healthy conviction that sin has rendered us all more or less ugly in the sight of God. . . . Man has a worm in his heart."

Jesus begins the list of actions that defile men and women, i.e., make them dirty, with murder, fornication and adultery (Matthew 15). But the sin we find him attacking most often is love of money. There are those today who think legalism the only sin Jesus bothered about. But condemning the legalism of the scribes, he found their "extortion and rapacity" worse (Matthew 23:25). "They devour widows' houses, they shall receive the greater damnation" (Matthew 23:14). We have heard Paul calling love of money a "root of all evil": it led to the first sin recorded as committed by Christians (the money-love of Ananias and Sapphira).

Sins differ of course in gravity, but all are in fact ways of asserting the self, ways of refusal of love either to God or to one's neighbor. It may be by clutching at what it wants, it may be by evasion of what it dislikes, but always it is asserting itself as against reality, the self making its own will its law. As to the kind of men we are the will is decisive. There is something almost sardonic in Augustine's telling us that to be virtuous we have only to will it. Only!

The clutching and the evading express themselves as habits, we are born with them, we grow into them. As habits they are to be overcome, ultimately rooted out, only by the efforts we make against them—forcing ourselves not to do the thing we are craving to do, forcing ourselves to do the things we shrink from. Prayers and sacraments are no substitute for the effort, the agony perhaps.

Does the life in Christ into which we are reborn do nothing to help us in our individual war with temptation? It helps vastly if we will let it. Though grace does not make sin less attractive, it makes victory over sin possible: but *we* have to gain the victory. To begin with, Our Lord shows us the meaning of life as a whole. If we give our minds to that, we are living mentally in the real world, not only in the fragment of it under our noses. If we are not thus living in the real world, it is hard to see why its laws are what Christ says they are: under pressure of temptation, it is hard to live by laws whose *why* we simply can't see.

Even seeing reality as it is, we can sin. We can fool ourselves about our motives—like the man we have already mentioned who convinces himself that he uses bodily union for the enrichment of his wife's personality. But with no such auto-foolery, even with the situation seen in all clarity, one might still decide to grab the pleasure and damn the consequences: though that very phrase carries the admission that the consequences might indeed damn.

In other words, the understanding of what is involved is not a sufficient protection. The reborn life is a real life, the powers it carries with it—faith and hope and charity, justice, purity and the rest—are real powers of action, but we must strengthen them by habitual action if they are to work for us against the bad habits we have by nature. In either life, bad habits have to be worked against, good habits practiced hard—with the body powerfully gripped and continually stirred by the bad habits, and the supernatural habits not seeming to promise any comparable pleasures.

But the reborn life *is* a genuine life. If only the Christian lives it as fully as he can manage, using his mind on the truths, nourished by the sacraments, making full use of the healing discipline of the confessional, he will find the habits proper to it gathering their own strength. Above all he will find himself seeing Christ Our Lord closer and clearer. For that is the essence of it—the life is not something Christ gives us, it is Christ living in us. He *is* the life. "To live is Christ," says Paul. And again, "I live, now not I, but Christ lives in me."

Mysterious. Unspeakably. But for our own well-being we must try to speak it, at least to ourselves.

III

If you find my talking so much of the new life in Christ wearisome, if you wonder whether it is relevant to the hard realities of life as we have to live it, don't blame me. Our rebirth in Christ is the heart of the difference Jesus makes. Not knowing it, we cannot understand him or ourself: without it we can only play about on the surface of civil rights, with Jesus not as a life-principle, but only as a banner to be waved, a slogan to be shouted. It is in the Fourth Gospel that we actually hear him say to the Apostles at the Last Supper, "I am the Life." But that idea did not begin with the Fourth Gospel. A generation earlier, in Acts and Epistles, we find it dominating the thinking of the men Jesus himself had formed.

So early they saw the second life paralleling the shape and rhythm of the first. We have at its beginning baptism—as someone has said the Acts are fairly swimming in baptism. James (5:14) tells us of its earthly end, with the officials of the Church "praying over the sick man and anointing him with oil." And for the new life's daily bread we have the body and blood of the Lord.

The trouble about sacraments is that the whole atmosphere of our world makes it hard to feel their reality. It is not only the non-Catholic who asks how pouring water on the head can make an eternal difference to the soul. How can if affect the soul at all? We may find ourselves rather wondering. We point out, of course, that baptism is not only an on-pouring of water but an in-pouring of the Holy Spirit. Our questioner's reaction is simple and certain. The Holy Spirit, he reminds us, *is* a spirit; so is the soul; spirit meets spirit: what's the water for? We shall understand ourselves and the Faith better if we give our minds to the question. Given the bodiliness of Christ and the bodiliness of man, sacraments are essential.

We are not baptizing a soul; we are not even baptizing a body; we are baptizing a person. And the human person has a soul and has a body. In fact he is spirit *and* matter: so is baptism. So are all the sacraments. God, having made us a combination of spirit and matter, does not treat us as if we were spirit and nothing else. The existence of our body is not due to a slip of the creative hand, which God has ever since regretted and prefers to ignore!

With really spiritual men the feeling may be very strong that religion belongs to the soul, and that it is ridiculous to try to drag the body into it. There is a spiritual type, by no means confined to religion, which despises the body as much as an equally unbalanced sensual type despises the spirit. Some of the leading Catholic thinkers of the Middle Ages, so I read somewhere, thought of the body as "a negligible napkin." It was one of the peculiar glories of St. Thomas Aquinas—whose own napkin, so to speak, was far from negligible— that he saw the body's sacredness, built it into his philosophy, strengthened his theology with it, hymned it.

But it is hard to *see* it as sacred. Quite apart from what it necessarily lacks simply because it is material, the body seems to go out of its way to remind us of its ignominiousness—what with pus and mucus and all the things it expels from itself because it can find no use for them. A man of the Manichean sort may take a malign pleasure in the body's ignominies; a religious man of another sort may deplore them; either would feel that to see the body as sacred is to contradict the plain evidence of the senses. It is simpler to write the body off—they are afflicted with it at the moment, they hope some day to be free of it, meanwhile they resolutely turn their back on it. So to speak.

But for man there is only corruption in writing off the body. It is not just an academic question. The ignored body takes its revenge. Where that sort of spirituality reigns, the misery that comes to masses of men from the body—hunger and disease—goes unrelieved; the pleasures that come from the body either go uncontrolled and run away into lust and gluttony, or are met with a ferocity beyond all measure. There is only one formula for health—Augustine's—to see spirit as primary, but the body as having its own sacredness too.

Of this sacredness sacraments are a powerful and continuing reminder. They cannot be administered or received without recalling the mind to the decisive fact that Christ Our Lord had a body, a body whose ignominies did not diminish its sacredness. And for ourselves the truth stands clear that it is no "negligible napkin" to which the Holy Spirit comes with water and bread and wine and oil.

To those four things the bodily life of man at its simplest could be reduced. Their mere listing reminds us that God, we may say it with full reverence, is not as highbrow as some of his worshipers—he takes the body more seriously. And a glance at the seven sacraments shows us how close in his mind the life of grace is built into the natural life of man. Baptism balances birth, Confirmation growing-up, Extreme Unction death; for the two great choices of adult life come Matrimony and Holy Orders; Penance is for the healing of sickness, and Eucharist for daily bread.

Pause upon the Eucharist. All life must be nourished by food of its own kind. Our bodily life is fed by bodies—of animals or vegetables. It cannot be fed by ideas or ideals. But our mental life needs ideas and ideals: on a diet of steaks and such it would die away to a poor flicker. What then is the food for a life which *is* Christ? Only Christ, surely. We must "eat the flesh of the Son of Man and drink his blood," if we are to have life in us. That, as John tells us, is what Jesus said after the Feeding of the Five Thousand. At the Last Supper, as Matthew, Mark, Luke and Paul relate, Jesus told how this receiving of himself into our bodies was to be: he blessed bread and gave it to the Apostles to eat, saying, "This is my body"; blessed a cup of wine and gave it to them to drink, saying, "This is the chalice of my blood."

The plain meaning of the words is that what looks like bread is in fact his body, no longer bread therefore: what tastes like wine, is no longer wine but his blood. And so his Church has always seen it. Paul phrased it to the Corinthians with all clarity, "Is not the cup we bless a participation in Christ's blood? Is not the bread we break a participation in Christ's body?" And again, "Anyone who eats and drinks without discerning the body, eats and drinks judgment upon himself."

When Jesus first spoke of eating his flesh and drinking his blood, John says that many of his followers "found it a hard saying," and "walked no more with him." It is still a hard saying, and many of his followers have found another way of removing its "hardness." They accept the Real Presence, while finding meanings for "Presence" which would mean that we are not receiving Christ himself. But the phrase "Real Presence" is not in the Gospels. What Christ said was,

"This is my body." So they find meanings for "body" which make it mean anything but his body: but they find it hard to apply them to "This is the cup of my blood." They have removed the hardness by altering the saying! Do they walk no more with him? Only he can say.

That there is mystery here is obvious. The philosophical theory of Transubstantiation seems to me splendid, but it raises questions we cannot answer. Yet that deals only with the *how* of it. The *fact* of it is not affected, or the splendor of the fact. One is puzzled at the reluctance to give their plain meaning to words uttered by Jesus within hours of his death, on a matter which he had already declared to be a matter of life and death. Symbols do not nourish, one still needs food. That the use or non-use of symbols should mean eternal life or eternal death is unthinkable. That there should be a way of uniting Christ to ourselves bodily might seem too good to be true, but surely only one who despises the body would find the idea repellent.

Receiving Christ thus we are uniquely one with him: also we are one with all throughout the ages who by receiving him had become likewise one with him. "The one bread makes us one body though we be many in number" (1 Corinthians 10:17). The Eucharist is the life principle of the Church even more than of the individual Christian.

CHAPTER 25

THE ACID TESTS

Suffering and death test any religion acidly, as they test any system proposed for men to live by. How does the Church help you or me to meet suffering, to meet death? By sacrament and liturgy, wonderfully; intellectually, not very well.

I

Suffering tests men individually, but the test is at its fiercest when they feel that it tests God. I remember the first time that the pain of the world really broke on us of the street corner as an argument against the existence of a loving God. It was after the earthquake in Japan, nearly fifty years ago, when 30,000 people were killed in one day. Twenty years later we were to kill ten times as many Japanese in one day with our new bomb. I meet nobody who feels any guilt for himself or his country. The twenties were a simpler time. We felt we must do what we could to clear God's reputation!

Two of the answers given by our speakers have stuck in my head. One was, "I'll explain the earthquake, if you'll explain the universe." The other was, "All right: supposing there isn't a God, you've still got the earthquake." Neither was a mere debating point. Both were right for the particular questioner. Each was the beginning of a really useful discussion.

But in a general way there are no quick answers to the problem of human suffering. Answers like the above are just about possible when the calamity is an earthquake on the other side of the world; they are totally impossible when it is a question of a man's own sufferings or the suffering, agonizing and incurable, of someone very close to him. The feeling that someone else is being merely clever about what is agony to oneself would be quite intolerable. When the question of suffering is raised, we must show that it is a problem for us, too. We do not pretend to see the whole answer, but there are gleams of light that we can see and, with sufficient sympathy, help others to see. The one thing certain is that we should give our

whole mind to the problem before either our own suffering or someone else's forces us to face it. We certainly cannot hope to pull an
answer out of the air. The objection sounds so very unanswerable—
If God *cannot* prevent suffering, he is not all-powerful. If he *will*
not, he is not all-loving. That you may feel just about covers the possibilities.

I have never heard a sermon on it. For myself I found the same
need to clear my mind about the suffering of God's world as about
the violence of his Church. In the one instance as in the other, eyes
piously averted are an affront to God. In the following dialogue I
summarize years of my own thinking. The "you" is myself, of course.
So I say to myself: good.

O.K. If *you* were all-powerful and all-loving, what would you do?
It's a loaded question, of course. All-powerful includes all-knowing,
which you're not. But it is from your imperfect knowledge that you
are putting God on trial. So go ahead. What *would* you do about
suffering?

What indeed *is* suffering? My own definition is, "Any experience
you intensely dislike." The experience may be in body or mind. The
measure of the suffering is the intensity of the dislike and the intensity of the desire to be rid of it. If you hate it to screaming point
you call it agony. Not a perfect definition, you may feel, but at least
it makes clear what it is we are blaming God for not preventing.

You begin, of course, by examining what causes suffering, because
the causes are what you would have to remove. One way or another
suffering comes either from our own or someone else's collision with
the laws of reality or from the effect of what other men do wrong.
The laws of reality are there for the right running of the universe.
Without the law of gravity, for instance, we should be swept off the
earth's surface: without fire civilization could hardly have begun. A
man falling off a cliff will not appreciate the indispensability of the
law of gravity, a man who has picked up a red-hot poker will
not thank God for fire. A baby may be born with syphilis through
some earlier breach of nature's laws.

As I wrote in *Christ in the Classroom:* "The want of harmony may
be in the mind—e.g. craving for something one cannot have, a
woman perhaps. A man may be unable to have the woman because
she dies (physical law), or because she can't bear the sight of him
(psychological law), or because she already has a husband (moral
law). In face of the moral law one may have an illusion of freedom

—after all the man *could* have her if she were willing. But he would only have turned from one wrong relation with reality (*wanting* what he should not have) to another wrong relation (*taking* what he should not have). He may for the moment have eased his own craving (at least until it is replaced by boredom with her and a craving for some other lady). But has the mass of suffering been reduced, or only shifted—to the woman's husband perhaps, or to her children?"

So what are you going to do about suffering resulting from collision with the laws of reality? What do you blame God for not doing about it? Laws there must be—physical laws if the universe is not to be a chaos, psychological and moral laws if human life is not to be a chaos; not only in our ignorance, but in our willfulness, our clutching and evading, we are sure to collide with some of them. You might think, like the atheist heckler I have already mentioned, that you could make a better universe than God made, a universe with different rules: but as to the rules which best suit creatures, the creator is likeliest to know best: clearly God has no particular prejudice against polygamy, for instance—he thought it suitable for stags but definitely not for men.

Anyway, the laws are there, some of them we know, some we do not know yet. If they were never allowed to operate to our disadvantage, we could never learn what they are. It is hard to see how the race could reach maturity.

I find it hard to escape the conclusion that you could abolish all this vast area of suffering only by abolishing men, or at least by abolishing human responsibility and human will—which would come to the same thing. In a general way the same principles apply to the suffering caused by the wrongdoing of others. If every time the strong attacked the weak God intervened, then evildoers and victims alike would be no more than toy pieces on a chessboard. Maturity—for the individual and for the race—lies in learning to cope with the evil in others and in oneself.

The reader might well have felt that this was all too cozy and geometrical a treatment of suffering, given all the varieties of anguish and agony in it. To one actually suffering it can seem a mockery, and a callous one, first to put these points logically to him, and then urge him to trust in God. The line "Praise God from whom all blessings flow," is likely enough to set him raging over his own cancer, perhaps, or over his child who lived its brief life in agony and died in it. That, I think, was in the mind of the atheist who wrote the parody—

> Praise God from whom all cyclones blow
> Praise him when rivers overflow
> Praise him when lightning strikes the steeple
> Brings down the church and kills the people.

If it is not great poetry it is brilliant debating. But only debating. Get rid of God, and you still have the cyclones and the floods and the lightning: you have not reduced the world's suffering by a single tremor: all you have done is destroy hope. If there is no mind behind the universe then men are simply battered by blind forces which know nothing of them and care nothing for them and will have the last word of them, as they fall back forever into the bosom of dead matter. If there *is* a God, then even suffering may somehow be turned to our gain. Which view you hold makes the difference between hope and despair.

So the writer of Job knew and the writer of Ecclesiastes. They saw that if you can't trust God you can't trust, for there is none other beside with the knowledge and the love and the power. Yet compared with ours, theirs was a blind trust. They did not know God as Jesus was to reveal him and had no sufficiently clear idea of a next life for which life on earth was only a preparation.

The Christian may not understand why he suffers, but he knows that his sufferings can be used for his gain. We can trust our ultimate well-being to a God who became man and died in agony for us.

Yet to a person actually suffering all this may seem to be merely a stringing together of unrealities. Even we ourselves may find it hard to hold onto its reality when we see a baby dying in pain. The pain we gaze on is so unmistakably real, God and his heaven seem so remote, so much less certainly *there*. We can tell ourselves, a little shakily perhaps, that heaven will compensate the child everlastingly for its days of suffering on earth. But the unbeliever will resent this as sheer invention, thought up to clear the character of our dubiously existent God.

To a man in extreme suffering, promise of joy with God hereafter may have small effect, so vast a shuddering can pain cause, so mild a vibration comes from hope in God. You remember Kipling's lines:

> The toad beneath the harrow knows
> Exactly where each tooth-point goes.

> The butterfly upon the road
> Preaches contentment to that toad.

When the harrow is piercing ourselves we are in no condition to consider theological reasons. But before pain takes over we should have
given our whole mind to the certainty that in God's universe we shall
not be the losers by sufferings where we are not at fault.

The unbeliever is maddened by our bringing in of heaven and the
love of God. But we cannot be expected to leave God out merely
because someone else does not believe in him, and God cannot be
expected to run the universe without reference to what he himself
means to do here and hereafter. It is folly to expect an answer to all
the world's problems which would be equally valid if God did not
exist.

But at least let us show that we too see the mystery of pain. If we
are seen to shirk no fact, to write off no quiver of the world's pain,
others may be brought nearer to belief in the Christian answer.
There is no greater service we can render them. For it is life-giving.
With it men have shown that they can face suffering, not be broken
by it, grow stronger from it. If we reject this answer to suffering, we
are left with no answer. At best we can have an indignant sympathy
with the sufferer which does him no good—least of all if the sufferer
is ourself. Self-pity is one way to waste suffering—yet who can blame
us for it?

No man ever felt man's suffering more than Jesus or ever did more
for its relief, but he saw sin as incomparably the greater evil: Better
to lose eye or hand or foot, we have heard him say, than to be led by
them into sin: better to enter life everlasting with one of each than
be cast into hell with two (Matthew 18:8-9).

Measure this against the unbeliever's sarcastic translation of it,
"Work all day, feed on hay—You'll get pie in the sky when you die."
And now measure that against Paul's "As the sufferings of Christ
abound in us, so also by Christ does our comfort abound" (2
Corinthians 1:5). "Comfort" is a strange word to find there. Fundamentally it means strengthening. And whether a man believes in
God or not, all evidence shows that that belief does give strength.
In the eleventh chapter of the same Epistle we get some idea
of how much "comfort" Paul needed—five full scourgings of thirty-
nine lashes, three beatings with rods, shipwrecked three times, in
"danger from false brethren," so often sleepless, hungry, thirsty, cold,

naked. And a sting in the flesh all the time. No one will take him for a butterfly on the road.

It is John who gives us the phrase "God is love." He had been in Gethsemane when Jesus begged his Father to remove the chalice of suffering and had seen the suffering get worse. He was on Calvary, too, when Christ, dying, commended his spirit into his Father's hands.

What is ordinarily called the problem of suffering is how we can reconcile it with the love of God. Jesus never saw it so. The real problem of suffering, for him and for us, is how not to waste it. It would be a shame to waste what costs so much. Jesus did not waste his, and he shows how we need not waste ours.

There is an organic connection between suffering and the healing of sin. Sin is always the thrust of our own will against what is right and good. The reversal of that thrust, the turning of the will —from what itself has come to crave back to what God wills—*must* cause suffering. The acceptance of that suffering, as of all the suffering life forces on us, strengthens the will. In that sense suffering is not the demand of an angry judge, but the prescription of a physician bent upon our healing. And that surely is what Jesus meant when he said that all of us must take up our cross daily—which François Mauriac phrases in *God and Mammon* as, "What a time it takes for us to realise that we are born crucified."

But suffering is not only to be used for our own moral and spiritual healing. *In the Body the suffering of one may be applied for the healing of another.* Listen to Paul: "I rejoice in my sufferings for your sake, and in my flesh I complete what is lacking in Christ's affliction for the sake of his Body, that is, the Church" (Colossians 1:24). Provided we are not sunk in pious coma, this sentence gives us two shocks—that there is something lacking in Christ's sufferings, and that Paul (and therefore other Christians) can provide what is lacking.

Whatever the Godman could do, Christ of course did. If something was lacking it could only be something that could not be done by him, something that had to be done by men for themselves and for one another. Men are not merely to be spectators of their own redemption. Your love and mine are to have their place in the expiating of human sin. There is a co-redemptive suffering in which all are called upon to share. "The head cannot say to the feet, I have no need of you" (1 Corinthians 12:21).

This matter of suffering is only one example of the truth that Christ's redemptive activity was not finished, in the sense of being over. For the redemptive sacrifice on Calvary he needed only himself. But for the continuation of his work among men till the end of time—teaching, forgiving, suffering, praying, offering—he needed the Church. He continues to work in the world through a social body as he once worked in it through the body in which he was conceived and born and lived in Palestine, died and rose again and lives in heaven.

"He entered heaven on our behalf," says Hebrews (9:24). Note that "on our behalf." There was something he still had to do for men in his own self, and Paul told the Romans what it was—"Christ Jesus . . . at the right hand of God intercedes for us." Hebrews sets it out in slightly more detail. "He holds his priesthood permanently, as he is able for all time to save those who draw near to God through him, since he always lives to make intercession" (7:24-25). On Calvary, as mediator, in his own self he had healed the breach between the human race and his heavenly Father. That was done once for all, it needed no redoing. In heaven he presents himself, once slain, now forever living, to his Father as an "intercession." He is interceding, praying, for what? That what he won for all should not be refused by any. Christ, dying and rising, made our eternal salvation possible, but each for himself has to make it actual. Acceptance or refusal is ours. It is the whole point of our lives—and, as we have seen, men can accept (or refuse) by the whole direction of their will without having ever heard of Christ.

The Mass, then, is Calvary as Christ now offers it to his Father— that all men (ourselves included) may be given the light and the strength to find salvation in him. We do not simply go to Mass, we are not simply present while Mass is being offered. We are there to do something, to join with the priest, and so with Christ himself, in making the offering of himself to his Father for sinners everywhere. In this ultimate sense, as in teaching and in suffering, we are co-redeemers. It is the most important thing we ever do. And how difficult we find it to realize that.

II

How can anybody be happy in heaven, knowing that others are suffering eternal torment in hell? As it stands the question is grim. We can add elements to make it grimmer, applying it to a mother whose son is in hell (or a son whose mother is in hell, since we need not assume that mothers are invariably more virtuous than sons). The ultimate in grimness would concern one who had led another into sin, himself repented, and must contemplate the other's damnation—of which he was the immediate cause.

But at its very strongest the question is not as grim as some of the answers. One has heard and read such things as this: "Well, of course, those who go to hell will no longer have anything lovable in them." Surely that would be an even more sorrowful thought to have about someone dearly loved in this life! I have even heard the argument that the sufferings of the damned are needed to make the happiness of the saved quite perfect, since nothing adds a fine edge to one's own happiness so much as seeing the misery of those who have not got it.

About this sort of argument there is something quite revolting. Yet people who use it are not necessarily revolting people. They do it, I think, because they are so concentrated on the logical arrangement of ideas that they forget they are treating of real people with real feelings. It is very easy to fall into the habit of discussing human problems as though they were mathematics. We bisect triangles, for instance, and the triangles don't mind a bit. One has met books of apologetics which bisect human beings with as little compassion. Yet, when they have to meet human beings in real life, the writers may be wholly compassionate.

Actually our question belongs to one larger still: how can God himself be infinitely happy when men and angels are in ceaseless pain? After all, we have it on the word of St. John, who knew Our Lord better than most, that God is love. There is no gain in giving explanations which make his love unrecognizable, bearing no relation to anything that men, whom after all he made in his image, know as love. Great theologians, great philosophers, can see deeper and clearer than we, of course. But for most of us the true answer to our question is to say that we do not know.

Of hell itself how little we know. From Christ we learn that what

causes that ultimate failure is refusal of love, and the examples he
gives are almost all of failure in love of our fellow-men. The nightmare horrors are derived from a second- or third-century work of fic-
tion called the *Apocalypse of Paul*—the Church never accepted it,
Augustine dismisses it out of hand. What we know is that the iron
refusal of love means love of self grown monstrous, to the rejection
of God. The Church speaks of the pain of loss—all the needs unmet
that only God can meet. The individual has chosen self to the exclusion of God and man, and self is not sufficient. Futility, it seems,
must be the air of hell. Of other torment we are told nothing.

Neither Christ nor the Church says that Satan torments the lost.
We shall be unwise to write Satan off, since the Gospels clearly show
that Christ saw him as the Enemy. About Satan people find it hard
to keep their heads. There has always been a diabolist fringe who
prostrate themselves before a lordship he no longer has, making fools
of themselves and him with odd rituals from slaughtering pregnant
cats under a full moon to the desecration of consecrated hosts. All
of these rituals are in fact more of a tribute to Christ than to him,
and must bore him beyond the tears he cannot shed.

The admission that we know little of hell and its inhabitants is
not merely a way of sidestepping a difficulty, of evading an issue
that we dare not face. We know that there must be mystery in religion, because God is so immeasurably greater than we that our
minds cannot wholly contain him. But it is a psychological peculiar-
ity that many men who will assert the fact of mystery and its necessity, will twist themselves into incredibly complicated knots rather
than admit that any given truth about God, or any given element
in the relation of man to God, is beyond their vision.

God has given us glimpses and gleams of what awaits us when we
leave this familiar—yet, at that, only partly comprehended—world
of ours. He has not given us a diagram or blueprint of the world to
come. Indeed only the very unsophisticated would think such a diagram or blueprint possible. We examine God's revelation, not to take
the mystery out of it but to place the mystery where it belongs.

We know that heaven will be bliss—"He shall wipe away every tear
from their eyes, and there will be no more death, or mourning, or
cries of distress, no more sorrow" (Apocalypse 21:4). How can this
be, given that those in heaven will know the fact of hell? Again I say
that we do not know. God has not told us, and the whole experience
is beyond our own range. But the one thing certain is that all that

agony will not be a matter of indifference to the saved, any more than that it is a matter of indifference to God himself. The evil that sin had brought into the world mattered so much to God that, as St. Paul reminds us, "He did not even spare His own Son, but gave Him up for us all" (Romans 8:32).

How is God's infinite bliss to be reconciled with his caring so much for the sins of men and for the suffering of his Son? We cannot see the answer to that question either. If we could, then we could see how to reconcile the happiness of the saved with their caring about evil and the everlasting pain it causes. As a priest friend of mine once said in answer to someone troubled about a particular piece of human suffering—"Can't you trust, not only God's love, but his ingenuity?"

I have mentioned the question asked outdoors, "Are there toilets in heaven." The questioner was just having fun. Which is what most modern men do have about heaven—including, I fancy, Christians. And that really is even odder than the occasional eccentric question. No unbeliever playing the fool about life after death is as eccentric as the believer who makes no effort to find out what Christ actually told us about it. In fact the unbeliever's eccentricity arises often enough from the eccentric beliefs of believers.

You get the lines I have quoted more than once, written by a disciple of Marx, about heaven as invented by exploiters to keep the exploited from revolting—

> Work all day, feed on hay,
> There'll be pie in the sky when you die.

You get Marx's friend Engels flipping aside "the tediousness of personal immortality." Neither the disciple nor the friend, you observe, has attempted to prove heaven's non-existence: all the unbeliever can do is deride what he thinks believers believe. And all too often they do.

There were those early Christians who, hearing that if they gave up anything in this life they would get it back a hundredfold in the next, gave up their wives. Which links up with Islam's houris, and by a different route with Mark Twain's idea that the bliss of all heaven's inhabitants consists in sexual intercourse. The examples I have given (you may throw in for good measure Khrushchev's remark that the first astronauts hadn't met any angels in the stratosphere) illustrate the simple fact that Christians have not given any attention to what Christ said about heaven: all that has got through to the unbeliever has been a mixture of harps and hosannas and holy shouting, scriptural imagery without the reality imaged.

If I had to select our two or three worst failures to communicate, I should certainly include this—that I practically never meet a Christian who expects any joy in heaven to compensate for all the sins he must give up in order to get there: desire for heaven is little more than the feeling that hell would be even worse. To Engels' word "tedium" a nerve throbs responsively in many of us.

So consider what Christ actually says: "I go to prepare a place for you, so that where I am you may be" (John 14:2–3). It is to be a place of joy, joy that no man shall take from us. But in what does the joy consist, what in fact shall we be doing there? (I am assuming, on no strong evidence, that you and I *will* be there.)

The one verb we find—in Jesus, and John and Paul—is the verb to see! Jesus speaks of the angels seeing the face of his heavenly Father continually (Matthew 18:10). In his First Epistle John says, "We shall see him as he is." Paul has, "While we are at home in the body we are away from the Lord, for we walk by Faith, not by sight" (2 Corinthians 5:6–7). He put it more clearly in 1 Corinthians 13:12: "Now we see in a mirror, dimly [God reflected in the universe he has made], but then face to face. Now I know in part, then I shall understand fully, even as I have been fully understood."

The phrase we have come to use for life in heaven is Beatific Vision, "the seeing which makes happy." If we give no further thought to it, we shall find ourselves feeling that some lesser splendor might suit our commonplaceness better, toying perhaps with the notion that it might be nice if we could have an occasional weekend off from heaven's too great bliss. But we must look deeper into it.

The life of heaven will be life—not stagnation, whether pious or amorous. All our powers will be in full action in contact with Infinite Reality, in full relation with other men similarly in contact. Heaven is maturity for the individual and *therefore* for society.

What our activity will be we can no more imagine than a primitive man could imagine what a mathematical physicist is engrossed in: he cannot even be told: "What we are to be," says St. John, "does not yet appear." But it will not be tedium: and we shall surely smile if we remember that long-ago notion of an occasional weekend off.

CHAPTER 26

THE LUXURY OF THE FAITH

In membership of the Church I find a luxury. I do not mean some hyper-spiritual joy known to the mystic. I mean pleasure as the plainest and bluntest can experience it if they will give themselves the trouble, pleasure comparable to that of food, or color, or health. Comparable, I say, not identical. Senses and imagination have delights of their own sort—just as they have their own ways to certitude—which intellect and will need not strain to reproduce. But for mind as for body luxury consists in an awareness of needs richly met, of completion, of fulfillment. And mind's luxury, like mind's certainty, is not less than body's.

That anyone should associate pleasure with membership of the Church might surprise the outsider, who would imagine that the only pleasure available to us is whatever we can distill out of marching in step to the orders of the bishops, our drillmasters. The outsider's surprise is largely the result of our failure to grasp that that's what he thinks Catholic life is. He tells a Catholic friend, perhaps, that he doesn't want popes or priests coming between himself and God. It is possible for the Catholic friend to answer accurately, lucidly and lengthily—yet leave the objector convinced that he is not refuting the objection but admitting it! When this happens, there has been no meeting of minds because the Catholic does not know what is in the objector's mind and assumes that because he himself has known certain things all his life there is no need to say them.

Each Catholic has indeed his own personal communication with God—some have more, some have less, but none are without it and in quite ordinary Catholics it can be very considerable. Each has some amount of conversation with God, uttering (not necessarily in words) his own personal love, his gratitude for things received and his complaints about his own sufferings and his friends', his sorrow for his sins and his longing to do better. There is nothing we cannot tell God in the certainty that God wants us to. "Humani nil a me alienum puto"—Whatever concerns men concerns me. The Roman dramatist Terence says that. God had said it long before him and says it still. The Catholic knows from the Church that the Holy Spirit dwells in his own soul, increasingly active; he knows of the actual graces which give him, hiddenly but surely if he will respond, the guidance and the energies that he personally and particularly needs.

But to the objector he says nothing of this—it seems to him too obvious to need saying. He plunges straight to a defense—accurate, lucid, lengthy—of the Church's external organization. And the episode ends with the objector confirmed, by the very answer he has just heard, in his belief that the Catholic has no contact of his own with God: everything must pass through the Church, through the local depots it has everywhere, all managed from the vast Pentagon of the Vatican. He finds the whole idea repulsive. This fundamentally was what his objection was about.

We should begin by trying to make clear that for the needs—needs to receive, needs to give, needs to utter—special to each individual, the communication between the soul and God is immediate and personal. With that, half the objection is met. Only then should we remind him that individual needs are not the whole story: there are universal needs as well, needs each man shares with all; they are what the Church was founded by Christ to meet. Thus all men need certain *truths*—about God, and his purpose in creating them, and how they must act to fulfill his purpose. All men need sanctifying *grace*—to give them the power to live closer to God in this world and see him face to face in the next, which human nature does not of itself supply.

There is one word in the objection with which we began that must never be allowed to pass without comment—the word "between." It has two quite different values: a wall comes between two pieces of land to *separate* them; a road runs between two cities to *join* them. It is in the second sense that the Church comes between men and God. God, who made men, established this link as wholly suited to the kind of beings he made men to be.

God could, we suppose, have met each man's needs for truth and grace individually, as he gives each animal its own equipment of instinct to run its own life and cope with its own needs. But then animals' needs for one another are so very moderate, what they have to give one another is so very measurable. A Cat Church is as unthinkable as a Cat Parliament. What would even a National Council of Catholic Cats find to discuss? God, who made men and cats, made them different. For he made men in his own image and likeness. The God we image is not a solitary God: in his oneness is the community of Father and Son and Holy Spirit. And we too are meant for community—we have so many powers we could never exercise, so many needs that could never be supplied, save in our relations with other human beings.

The social element in man is not a convenient extra but of man's essence. And it is in terms of the community within the Blessed Trinity that Our Lord spoke of the oneness of his Church at the Last Supper: "I pray also for those who through their word shall come to believe in me—that they may be one as you Father in me and I in you, that they may be one in us, that the world may know that you have sent me" (John 17:20-21). The unity of his Church mattered so much that Our Lord counted on it as evidence of his own divinity.

In thus picturing life in the Church the Catholic can give the questioner a glimpse of why he can find luxury in it. Indeed he may be seeing this better himself. For the word "luxury" might faintly surprise even loyal Catholics, while to those of less certain loyalty it would sound like sheer humbug.

Priests who leave the Church, for instance, do not seem to feel that they are walking away from joy, even spiritual joy. They leave because they find the conduct of popes and bishops intolerable. Surely they "have not known of what spirit they are," to quote Christ's rebuke to James and John (Luke 9:55). One wonders what their Catholicism was, while they still had it. The Church is *Christ*, living in men and they in him. The well-doing of his servants is not our reason for belonging to it, their ill-doing no reason for leaving it. Their ill-doing may very well drive even the loyal to fury. More than once I have felt what a service to God or man this or that successor of the Apostles might render by dropping dead. Yet I was always aware that all the dislikables added together were a trifle compared with what the Church was giving me.

And I don't mean only the Mass and the Eucharist, immense as these are. I once surprised a Catholic audience by saying, "Expect of the Church nothing but sacraments and you will not be disappointed." I was in part warning them against the certainty of disappointment, but emphasizing the splendor of what is there all the same. Christ as food is indeed a luxury, but so is Christ as light. The difficulty is that we respond more easily to the Body of Christ than to his mind—somewhat as we find the appeal of goodness easier to feel than the appeal of truth. Alexander Pope could write of "The insupportable fatigue of thought": no one so far as I know has written of the insupportable fatigue of *food*.

There are minds to whom thought offers no pleasures, provides no rewards. So they reduce their Catholic life to Mass and sacraments and Commandments. They leave understanding to the theologians, themselves content to live in the half-dark. They may love God better than many a theologian. But in the half-dark they are cut off from the luxury that I write of here, the luxury of living mentally in the world unveiled by Our Lord.

Its high point is the vision to which Jesus admits us of the inner life of God. Within the oneness of God there are three Selves, enriching the oneness, not tripling it, not dividing it. The Father, knowing himself, produces the totally adequate idea of himself which is the Son; Father and Son fill the whole Godhead with their love, which is the Holy Spirit. And in grace this God indwells our souls, yours and mine, which means that the activity of Father eternally begetting Son, Father and Son eternally producing the Spirit, is taking place in our very selves.

To see this as luxury, to see any meaning in it at all, we must have done a vast amount of solid thinking. One not naturally addicted to thought may be impatient—why not cut out all this theologizing and come straight to God in repentance, gratitude, adoration? It is as though a man with a passion for music but bored with the theory decided to go straight to the piano. Whatever the richness of his musical intuition, he would never play like Paderewski or Horowitz, he would be more likely to play like me. So with the Trinity. It is music each one must work at for himself. Without the Trinity we shall know the God of Christ Jesus very sketchily indeed; and there will be less for the mind to luxuriate in.

It is the same with Christ: if we have only devotion in the will but no thinking on what Christ has given and the Church has developed, there will be less for our delight. Certainly in the mental living over again of his public life, in the mental and emotional living through of his Passion and Death and Resurrection there is plenty for love and gratitude. But if we leave it at that, we should not know what Paul meant by saying, "We have the mind of Christ" and "I live, now not I, but Christ lives in me"; we should not know the wonder of Christ's "I in my Father and you in me and I in you," which is the essence of our redemption. These and a score of like things go to make the luxury which awaits the exploring mind, luxury with that last fine edge of perfection which comes from the certainty that we shall never come to the end of either its light or its power to nourish.

But at the lower level of daily life there is luxury for us, of a quieter kind, in knowing the shape and purpose of life as a whole. As Jane Wyatt, star of *Lost Horizon*, the first Shangri-la movie, puts it in *Born Catholics*, "Living by conventions is a bore. Living by God is a challenge. I find that challenge in the Church." To be on a road and not know where the road is leading is to be lost. There is quite a luxury in not being lost. As the Irish ballad has it, "I know where I'm going, and I know who's going with me."

Who *is* with me on the road? Jesus himself, of course, living in me and I in him. And his mother and Joseph and the saints. Yes, the saints. Answering the Sadducees, who denied life after death, Our Lord said, "Have you not read what was said to you by God, 'I am the God of Abraham, the God of Isaac and the God of Jacob'? He is not God of the dead but of the living." Living too are Our Lady and her husband, and Peter and Paul and a host of saints since. The sanctity of all of them lay in their love of God and man: their love of man is not extinguished by seeing the face of God who created man, in the light of Christ who redeemed man. In a world where even Christian leaders have excommunicated the dead, we rejoice in our certainty of their continuing fellowship. One makes one's own choice among them. How they know of our prayers to them, I do not know. But they are still members of Christ's body as we are, and their strength can still help our weakness: until such time as we join them.

For, to return to our ballad, we do know where we're going. Consider that for a while. If one accepts survival at all, the next stage must be vastly important if only because we shall be such a long time dead. Our life here may seem to be endless in its slow crawl from year to year. But it is something less than a split second on the cosmic clock.

Even of our own individual existence, the bit between birth and death is so small a fraction. There is that comparatively recent "ancient man," the man of the Altamira cave drawings. He has been dead perhaps fifteen thousand years. The seventy years (give or take a few) that he may have spent on earth are a trifle in comparison—and must seem so to the man himself, wherever his spirit is.

For the Christian this postmortem endlessness is not wrapped in darkness impenetrable. It has in it the promise that we shall not continue to be the raw material out of which human beings are slowly hammered, but at last and definitively complete men and women. Nothing is more notable in our failure to make our own the mind, the *nous*, of Christ than the ignoring of his vast concern with what follows death. By the mercy of God we may be saved on a bare minimum of intellectual knowledge and moral virtue: we cost Jesus so much that it is hard to think of his lightly letting us go. But living in the reality of the goal as he reveals it affects the quality of our life here and now. It *is* a luxury to know where the road leads.

You will find people who will sneer back at you, "If that's what you mean by luxury, you're welcome to it." But what alternative have they? Contemporary man, we are told, is in search of his identity, who he is, what he is, why he matters. Leaving out divine revelation, begun in the Old Testament and completed by Christ, all he can know of himself is that he emerged from the bosom of matter (to the pleasure or horror of his parents, who had similarly emerged a while before); that he remains above the surface of matter for a while, only to be re-merged in it—all this in a universe which has emerged from nothingness, unmeant, unpurposed. To quote myself: "He must pursue his search for identity in the dark, until the dark swallows him as it has swallowed the myriads of men before him." The Christian knows that the human race, himself included, is here because a God of infinite knowledge and love and power willed it so, that man's goal is to attain the fullness of his manhood in a fullness of union with that same God, that whether he himself attains it or not depends on what he with God's aid makes of himself.

It is a luxury too to have been told by our Maker the rules for the right running of ourselves just as the similarly strict rules given by Ford or Chrysler for the running of our automobile are preferable to our having to work it all out for ourselves by trial and error. Only stupidity lies in ignoring Ford's instructions or Chrysler's, a more calamitous stupidity lies in ignoring God's. We do indeed break down and sin—which we have seen as grabbing immediate satisfaction and damning the consequences: even then, to quote myself again, there is a kind of gloomy luxury in knowing what the consequences are. It may sound strange but there is even a touch of luxury in the obligation to confess. After near seventy years of the confessional I still dislike it. But it is rather as one feels about a cold bath in winter—bleak to look forward to, not so bad when you're in it, you feel wonderful after it. By the time a man has decided to confess, of course, the worst is over. It is while the temptation is strong that he suffers. But even when the effort to stay on the road to our goal costs us agonizingly, we know what gain to set against the agony.

Every man is free to evaluate all this as he likes. To me there is luxury in it. Without it I should not know how to live my life intelligently, or to help others to live theirs. I could only play it by ear (and I have already spoken of the poverty of playing by ear). Knowing it, we still have the battle of life to fight. The practical problems of living are no easier to solve. Bodily pain, psychological pain, may make revealed truth as hard to delight in as they would make great music. The clutching, evading self has still to be coped with. But in any battle it makes a difference to know what the war is about. In the battle of life it makes a vast difference to know what we ourselves are.

I have quoted Matthew Arnold's description of himself and modern man:

> Wandering between two worlds, one dead,
> The other powerless to be born.

A first difficulty in the way of the new world trying to get itself born is the want of agreement about what man is—anything from a union of spirit and matter to a cog in the collective machine. The one clearly statable view is the Christian—that man is a union of matter and spirit; that he is made in the image of God and meant for everlasting union with him; and that Christ died for him. However he may have been damaged by his own sins or society's maltreatment, this is the reality of every man from time's beginning. It is the one definition which makes every man an object of reverence—and all history shows that what we do not reverence we will certainly desecrate.

I forget who said, "Give me the luxuries, I can dispense with the necessities." Thinking over the "luxuries" I have just listed—Trinity, Incarnation, Church, Mystical Body, Maker's Instructions, Life Everlasting and the rest, which would you dismiss as non-necessities? Anyhow, luxuries or necessities, I should be desolated to lose any of them. "I am easily satisfied with the best." I cannot think of a better quotation to end this book, indeed to summarize it.

What lies ahead of the Church? This book is about the Church as I have experienced it and I have not experienced the future.

Glance at today's questions. Will celibacy become optional for priests? A priest friend of mine has no desire to be married but is convinced that marriage is his priestly duty, indeed that in future only married men will be ordained. Will that happen? Will there be women priests, they too married? Will there be part-time priests, all working at another profession? Will there be less centralization and on what lines? Will the laity be given more to do? Will there be a return to unity between us and the Orthodox and what changes will that make necessary? How far will Ecumenism take us with Protestants?

All these may roughly be called structural questions. The Church will re-shape itself, more or less ideally. It always has. I do not know what the new shape will be. I don't even know what I want it to be.

As to changes which seem more directly to concern the Holy Spirit, the interpreting of revelation, for instance, I have even less reason to claim special insights. The tension between human minds and the Holy Spirit will produce who knows what? An Einstein might change our world view all over again, a Hitler might bring our world to destruction. An Augustine might renew the Church unforeseeably. I have no temptation to speculate on the unforeseeable.

When Pius XII died in 1958 no one had a notion of the things that have happened in the sixteen years since. Given that we did not guess what would happen in the last sixteen years, why should we think we can know what will happen in the next sixteen—to say nothing of the next sixty? Only the innocent would prophesy. The one thing I know is that those who expect Mass and the sacraments will not find the Church disappointing them.